THE GENIUS

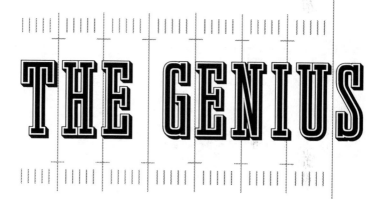

THE GENIUS

HOW **BILL WALSH** REINVENTED FOOTBALL
AND CREATED AN NFL DYNASTY

DAVID HARRIS

RANDOM HOUSE
TRADE PAPERBACKS
NEW YORK

2009 Random House Trade Paperback Edition

Published in the United States by
Random House Trade Paperbacks, an imprint of
The Random House Publishing Group,
a division of Random House, Inc., New York.

RANDOM HOUSE TRADE PAPERBACKS and colophon are
trademarks of Random House, Inc.

Originally published in hardcover in the United States
by Random House, an imprint of
The Random House Publishing Group,
a division of Random House, Inc., in 2008.

All photos are by Michael Zagaris,
except the photo on page 20, which is by Jeff Bayer,
and the photos on pages 27, 36, and 44,
which are courtesy of the Walsh family archives.

Grateful acknowledgement is made to Hal Leonard
Corporation and Alfred Publishing, Inc.,
for permission to reprint an excerpt from "This is It"
by Michael McDonald and Kenny Loggins, copyright
© 1979 by Tauripin Tunes and Milk Money Music.
All rights for Tauripin Tunes administered by
Wixen Music Publishing, Inc. Reprinted by permission
of Hal Leonard Corporation and Alfred Publishing, Inc.

LIBRARY OF CONGRESS CATALOGING-IN-
PUBLICATION DATA
Harris, David.
The genius : how Bill Walsh reinvented football and
created an NFL dynasty / David Harris.
    p.   cm.
ISBN 978-0-345-49912-7
1. Walsh, Bill, 1931–2007.   2. Football coaches—
United States—Biography.   3. San Francisco 49ers
(Football team).   I. Title.
GV939.W325H37   2008
796.332092—dc22   2008016566

www.atrandom.com

Book design by Simon M. Sullivan

146119709

CONTENTS

BILL AND EDDIE

Edward J. DeBartolo Sr., and Edward J. DeBartolo Jr.

"A LITTLE BIT OF DIGNITY AND CLASS"

t all began with "Mr. D.," though in the fall of 1978 few in the nine Bay Area counties used such terms of endearment when identifying Edward J. DeBartolo Jr., the hapless owner of their favorite football team. Nor was he yet referred to with the more hip "Eddie D.," or even the double-edged "Junior." Instead, it was "that rich kid whose daddy bought him a football team" or "that mafioso dipstick who destroyed the Niners" or, for short, "that asshole." Every fan within two hours' drive of San Francisco knew who you meant. DeBartolo had joined the NFL in the spring of 1977 as its youngest franchise owner, hoping to become a man of stature in the sports world, bringing honor on his family while realizing his own deeply held aspirations for belonging, triumph, and acclaim. So far, however, Eddie— barely thirty-two years old, short, pudgy, and in charge for the first time in his life—was a complete flop. And he finally figured out late that fall that he had to do something radical to reverse the situation before it was too late.

The most personally trying element in Eddie D.'s dilemma was his fear of disappointing his father, Edward J. DeBartolo Sr., the original "Mr. D.," who was described by his son as close enough to him to be "like my brother." DeBartolo Sr., now sixty-nine, was the architect of the family fortune. Born in the impoverished "Hollow" neighborhood in Youngstown, Ohio, in 1909, three months after the death of his natural father, Anthony Paonessa, "Senior" had taken the family name of his stepfather—an immigrant who neither read nor wrote English—and followed him into the concrete contracting business. Then, at the insistence of his mother, Senior worked his way through engineering school at the University of Notre Dame during the Depression by laboring all night at construction sites. He rejoined his stepfather's Youngstown contracting business until the Second World War, when he was drafted into the Army Corps of Engineers for the duration. Senior returned from the war with an officer's commission and a $1,500 nest egg reportedly won in military crap games, which he used to capitalize the Edward J. DeBartolo Corporation shortly after his first child and only son was born.

DeBartolo Sr. threw his new enterprise into the still-infant shopping center business and developed some of the first malls at a time when there were fewer than a dozen in the entire United States. Eventually his company built the largest enclosed shopping mall ever, as well as hundreds of similar properties in more than a dozen states, ranking as the nation's largest shopping center developer by the time the 1970s began. He also acquired several banks, numerous hotels, three horse racing tracks, the Pittsburgh franchise in the National Hockey League, and some seventy other subsidiary enterprises, all headquartered in Youngstown.

By the time Eddie fell on his face out in San Francisco, the privately held DeBartolo family business was worth at least $400 million and Edward Sr. would soon be listed in the Forbes 400 directory of the wealthiest Americans. He was also suspected of Mafia connections, largely because he was a rich Italian contractor from Youngstown. Eddie's father dismissed the innuendo with great annoyance. "This kind of talk is the curse of anyone successful whose name ends in an *i* or an *o*," he complained. "I got where I am by working my ass off every day of my life. I could have turned to certain characters in this town. I'm not saying I don't know them. But I solved my own problems."

Edward Sr. was the archetypal patriarch—almost as short as his son but thin, quiet, dignified, and always dressed in a dark suit. One friend who had known him for forty years said he had seen Eddie's father only twice without a tie, both times when he was wearing swimming trunks. In public he kept his tongue but in private was known to swear like a teamster. Such was the original Mr. D.'s stature around Youngstown that a thief who stole his briefcase returned it untouched as soon as he discovered who owned it. In more than forty years of working, Senior had never taken a vacation, and if he wasn't traveling he was always home for dinner at the end of his customary fourteen-hour shift. He started his day at five-thirty over a Styrofoam cup full of coffee, usually with Eddie. Senior's idea of a good time was to watch three televisions side by side, tuned to three different football games. His corporation's two-story brick headquarters in suburban Youngstown was just down the road from his enormous house and from his son's of similar size. When Senior traveled, he used one of the corporation's three Learjets—flying more than five hundred hours a year—and was surrounded by a small swarm of aides charged with executing the decisions he made on the spot. Upon his return, his son greeted him with a kiss.

Not surprisingly, Junior grew up wanting to be Senior more than he wanted to be anybody else. The expectations Eddie put on himself with that identification were "brutal," he would later admit. "It almost broke up my marriage before I realized I can't fill those big shoes. I can't be Edward DeBartolo Sr. and I don't have to be. I have to carry on a tradition, not an identity, and I'll do that in a different way. He's helped me by letting me handle things my own way, to be my own man." During the fall of 1978, however, that evolution was still very much in process.

According to Eddie, his greatest gift from his father was "the common man's touch," largely passed on during his childhood in Youngstown. Halfway between Pittsburgh and Cleveland, the DeBartolos' hometown had once hosted a legion of steel mills, fabricators, and blast furnaces, many of which were empty and rusting by the time Eddie got into the football business. And football was also part of his Youngstown inheritance. No region in America was more wedded to the game than the industrial Midwest and, rich or not, the DeBartolo scion was anything but an exception. He played on the junior varsity squad during his freshman year at Youngstown's Cardinal Mooney High School, but, still an inch and a half and several pounds short of his adult five feet seven and a half inches and 160 pounds, he was doomed as a player. Junior swallowed his disappointment and settled for making a lot of working-class buddies from the team who became regulars at the DeBartolo mansion for games of pool. Because he wanted to be just one of the guys, Eddie D.'s only distinguishing feature as a teenager was his sartorial flair. "Eddie came up the easy way," one of the Mooney High School faculty remembered, "but, other than his clothes, he never showed it." Even when he was an adult, one of Eddie's closest friends was a foundry worker from his JV days.

After Cardinal Mooney, Junior followed his father's footsteps to Notre Dame but Senior still kept track of him, using a contact in the football program to give him updates on how his son was doing. After graduating with a degree in business, Eddie was moved into the corporation and shuffled through assignments to learn all the company's functions. At each stop, other corporation executives were tasked with reporting to his father about the son. When on assignment in Dayton, Eddie reprised his Youngstown days and began hanging out with a group of players from the University of Dayton football team. He married his high school sweetheart along the way, fathered three daughters, and had just been named the family corporation's executive in charge of sports operations when the DeBartolos began pursuing the possibility of purchasing the Forty Niners early in 1977. The year before, they had made an unsuccessful $16 million bid in the auction to secure rights to the NFL expansion franchise in Tampa, Florida, a state where DeBartolo Corp. had numerous business interests.

By then, Eddie had begun the process of becoming his "own man," and, though often imitative of Senior down to the smallest details, Eddie's "own man" was also anything but a carbon copy. For starters, Junior was every inch the party animal that Senior was not. One acquaintance who enjoyed Eddie's typical restaurant hospitality recalled, "There was just bottle after bottle. I finally had to stop drinking because I couldn't function, but Eddie and his buddies just kept going." The younger DeBartolo also had a serious attachment to gambling, especially at the tables in Las Vegas, where he would soon establish a reputation as a high roller. Dressed to the nines in very expensive Italian suits, Edward DeBartolo Jr. "loved life," one Forty Niners employee explained, "and loved living it." When traveling for pleasure, he usually brought along an entourage of his Youngstown buddies and was rarely seen without his bodyguard, Leo, a very large man with a bump under his armpit where he kept his pistol.

"Eddie may not have been a gangster," one San Franciscan remembered, "but he sure looked like one when he rolled into town."

Eddie D.'s welcome also might have been far warmer had he bought some other team. Of all the region's professional sports enterprises, the San Francisco Forty Niners were closest to its collective heart. The team was conceived during World War II by Tony Morabito, owner of a local trucking company, and eventually became northern California's very first major league franchise, a historic recognition of the West Coast's status more than a decade before any other sport followed suit. Morabito had gone to the National Football League, asking the twenty-year-old association to expand and add San Francisco to its schedule. When the NFL declined, Morabito affiliated his franchise with the upstart All-America Football Conference organized in 1944 to compete with the NFL, and the Forty Niners began play in 1946, the year Eddie DeBartolo was born. When the two football leagues made peace in 1950, the Morabito franchise was one of three former AAFC teams to survive and merge into the more established league. By that time Tony's brother Vic had joined him as a partner. When the two Morabitos died, their NFL ownership passed to their widows, who were assisted in running the team through the sixties and into the seventies by a family friend. Along the way, the Niners won more than half of their games more often than not. "The operation always had elegance," one local columnist observed. "They weren't the meanest team . . . and they have never won a conference championship and never gone to the Super Bowl. But they had a special kind of style."

By 1975, however, it was common knowledge that the widows wanted to sell their 90 percent interest in the heretofore quaint local institution. The first potential buyer was Wayne Valley, an East Bay businessman who had been a limited partner in the Oakland Raiders NFL team until he had a falling out with the franchise's managing general partner, Al Davis. Davis now considered Valley an enemy and wanted no part of competing with him across the bay, so Al persuaded one of the Morabitos' minor partners to invoke his right of first refusal to derail Valley's bid. Davis was also worried that the Morabitos' asking price of $12 million was too low and would depress the value of all NFL franchises. By the end of 1976, Valley had been thwarted, the minor Forty Niners' partner had failed to come up with a legitimate offer, and the Tampa auction had set the asking price for NFL franchises at more than $16 million, so the Niners were back on the market. The Morabitos, recognizing the lay of the land, dispatched their attorney to Davis to ask his assistance in finding a bona fide buyer, a service for which he would eventually receive a finder's fee.

At the same time, the DeBartolos continued to pursue their interest in acquiring an NFL franchise and were approached by league insider Joe Thomas. Thomas had been fired as general manager of the Baltimore Colts shortly before he contacted Senior in Youngstown. He had been raised just a few miles away and the two Ohioans had met ten years earlier at a college all-star game and stayed in touch. By 1977, he was considered, in Eddie's words, a DeBartolo "family friend." Thomas told DeBartolo Sr. that the Forty Niners were on the block and offered to pursue them on Senior's behalf. Senior responded that he was interested, but only if Thomas would commit to actually running the club after he bought it. The DeBartolos signed Thomas to be their franchise's general manager before even beginning negotiations to purchase the Niners. Because of NFL rules prohibiting ownership by corporations or new owners who had financial interests in other professional sports, the DeBartolos quickly learned that NFL commissioner Pete Rozelle was going to insist the family insulate any NFL franchise it bought from the rest of its corporate holdings. The answer to that obstacle was to officially make Eddie the sole owner when the time came, rather than the corporation or his father. Senior also liked that approach because it would give his boy an exclusive niche, as well as a business to run on his own.

Nonetheless, Senior handled most of the negotiations, conducted through the intermediaries, Joe Thomas and Al Davis. By the last week of February 1977, after ten days of Learjet commuting between Youngstown and the Bay Area, the deal was almost done. The price was set at $17 million for a 90 percent controlling interest and Senior and Eddie flew to Oakland to sign the papers. The DeBartolos, however, arrived at Davis's office to find that the price had suddenly been raised by half a million dollars. At that point, Senior balked.

No, he told Davis, preparing to turn around and leave. "I don't do business that way." The price was supposed to have been set.

Davis urged him to stay, roll with the situation, and make the deal. It was a great opportunity, he argued. The extra half million meant nothing. In a year, they would double their money.

Eddie spoke up as well. He had looked into the NFL's projected growth and agreed with Davis wholeheartedly. "Do it, Dad," he implored. "Do it."

After only a little hesitation, Senior did.

In early April 1977, Edward DeBartolo Jr. was introduced as the new owner of the San Francisco Forty Niners at a press conference in the Venetian Room of the Fairmont Hotel on Nob Hill—arguably the city's swankest hostelry—for which the reporters had received three-color embossed invitations, complete with RSVP cards. Eddie and his father were staying in adjoining suites upstairs. Senior watched from the back of the supper club while his son held forth to all of the region's assembled media at the Venetian Room's podium, with Joe Thomas seated nearby.

It was not a pleasant experience for Eddie, then just thirty years old. Accustomed to deference, he felt insulted when he had to field harsh questions about his plans for the franchise, and he became noticeably pissed off. The hostile swarm of reporters was more than he could endure without complaint. Soon he was butting heads all over the room. "The more he talked," a witness later recalled, "the more people he alienated."

Finally, when asked what he thought he could bring to his new property that it didn't already have, Eddie snapped, "A little bit of dignity and class."

Afterward, one of the television reporters conducted an informal straw poll about the erstwhile Mr. D. among the attending media. Half were already convinced he was a full-fledged jerk and the other half were still undecided.

Joe Thomas

||||| ||||| |||||

YOU CAN ONLY KISS A GUY'S ASS SO FAR

t got worse.

And Joe Thomas was the biggest reason why.

The DeBartolos' "family friend" had made his name as a talented personnel chief under general manager Jim Finks at Minnesota, then in Miami under Don Shula, but by the time he left Miami for Baltimore, Thomas had already established a reputation for massive arrogance as well. "Even in a sport which runs to egomaniacs," one columnist observed, "Joe Thomas stands alone." He made more out of his own impact than anyone else did, routinely took credit for other people's successes, and was a legendary know-it-all. At Miami, his fellow staffers got so annoyed with the latter quality that they made him the butt of an office joke. On a signal as Joe approached, several began to loudly discuss the attributes of a fictional player. Thomas listened for thirty seconds, took the discussion at face value, then interrupted and pontificated with great seriousness and seeming erudition about this player, even giving a detailed evaluation of the player's strengths and weaknesses. Everyone else then laughed so hard they almost fell on the floor.

Thomas was first given a chance to become a general manager with ultimate football authority when air-conditioning multimillionaire Robert Irsay purchased the Baltimore Colts and hired him, largely on the basis of his press clippings. Joe Thomas then stripped the roster he inherited in a massive housecleaning of veteran players and rebuilt it with younger, untested talent. His first move was to get rid of the aging Johnny Unitas, thought to have once been the best quarterback ever and Baltimore's favorite player for more than a decade. Next, Thomas fired the team's head coach. The Colts' record immediately collapsed as Thomas continued to dump veterans, but rebounded enough to keep him on the job. Then he fired his second head coach and, when he had a difference with that coach's successor, tried to fire him as well. That third firing ignited a revolt by the players, who backed their coach and demanded that the owner intervene. Finally Irsay did so and fired Thomas, who quickly found work with his "family friends," the DeBartolos. "Thomas probably couldn't have found a general manager's job with any other NFL team," one sports columnist observed. "Only new owners, like the DeBartolos, who had not previously been involved in the league and weren't aware of the problems he had caused wherever he had been, would have hired him."

This widely shared conclusion was a large part of what generated Eddie's discomfort in the Venetian Room. The assembled reporters wanted to know just what Thomas's role was going to be and what DeBartolo intended to do about the man who currently had that job. In 1976, the Morabitos had signed a four-year contract for both head coach and general manager duties with Monte Clark, then the hottest assistant coach in the league. Clark had insisted on authority over all football operations, in part as insurance that a new owner wouldn't bring in a new general manager over his head and change the rules under which he worked. As it turned out, of course, that insurance provided no protection at all. Clark had taken a team with three straight losing seasons to an 8-6 record in his first year and the Niners were widely expected to make the Super Bowl playoffs in 1977. Monte Clark was consequently considered something of a savior. And he wanted nothing to do with Joe Thomas. "The only way I would stay is if I was over Thomas," Clark told friends, "and my first move would be to fire the son of a bitch."

Eddie spent much of his time at the Venetian Room podium explaining why the popular Monte Clark had to be relieved of his responsibilities. He had tried to keep Clark as the coach, he kept repeating, just without personnel powers, but Clark had refused, so Eddie had no choice. His loyalty was to the man his father had selected to run their team. "Mr. Clark's contract was in direct conflict with that of our general manager, Joe Thomas," he told the press. "Joe Thomas was a friend of ours long before we intended to get into football and some time ago we let him know that if we became involved, he would run the football part. . . . I ate my guts out trying to make it work but Monte would not redefine his duties. . . . This is a business, not a play toy. . . . We did not buy this team for a head coach. We're going to run this team the way we run any business. . . . We're not going to placate personalities."

DeBartolo Sr. was more succinct in a private side comment at the back of the room. "You can only kiss a guy's ass so far," he observed. "Then you've got to get rid of him."

With that, the Forty Niners' DeBartolo era began.

And Joe Thomas immediately set about ridding the organization of any evidence of its existence before Joe Thomas arrived. According to one reporter, "Thomas was a madman about it." All of the club's bound volumes of old game programs, all its thousands of accumulated photos, even its original charter from the AAFC were unceremoniously dumped. "I came into the team's headquarters down in Redwood City one day," a team employee remembered, "and there were all these boxes along the wall, stacks and stacks of them, all full of memorabilia and photos and stuff like that. I figured they were taking it up to storage at Candlestick Park but the secretary said no, they were taking all this stuff to the landfill. I couldn't believe it. I said, 'Really, where is it going?' I was told that Joe Thomas had said to get 'this shit' out of here. 'History starts today. We don't need any of this.' I took as much as I could." The franchise had long maintained an alumni organization for former players but Thomas quickly dismantled it. He even threw away the Niners' priceless library of old game films.

Joe Thomas was also considered at least a little "odd" by those with whom he had close contact. For no apparent reason, he had security doors installed throughout the team's headquarters so that it was hard to go more than fifty feet without having to be buzzed through a gate, like traversing the counting room of a casino or the front hallway of a medium-security penitentiary. It had previously been team policy to allow assistant coaches to keep the small honorariums provided by radio stations for on-air appearances, but Thomas notified the radio stations that while the assistants would continue to appear for interviews, the honorariums would be paid to Thomas himself. He bought a house down the Peninsula for his family, but owned almost no furniture. The few couches and chairs he did have had been scrounged for free out of the Forty Niners' offices. Thomas was also obsessed with his own image and how he was portrayed in the media. When several less than favorable mentions of him appeared in the local press, he fired the team's press officer.

One reporter, interviewing Thomas for the first time shortly after the Clark firing, was stunned. "I was in his office for at least four hours," he explained, "and I only said maybe a dozen words. He just talked and talked and talked. I eventually decided he was a total fraud. He gave me his whole life history, talked about his marriage, and talked about his life outside of football—which was practically nil. He went over virtually every player move he had ever made. I left his office in a daze."

The team's collapse began as soon as Thomas took the helm and then accelerated after his first season, in which the first head coach he hired managed a 5-9 record with the same players who had been 8-6 and seemingly headed for the playoffs the year before. Thomas fired that coach during the 1978 off-season and then took a shredder to the roster, releasing a horde of experienced players—including quarterback Jim Plunkett, for whom the Forty Niners had traded five draft picks only the year before. Plunkett would end up winning two Super Bowls across the bay with the Raiders. With few draft choices because of Clark's Plunkett deal, Thomas filled most of his squad's vacancies with castoffs from other franchises. His most visible move was a trade for running back O. J. Simpson, in which Thomas gave up five more future draft picks, including the next year's number one. Simpson had once been the league's best running back but was now a gimpy shadow of his former self. Thomas's apparent hope was that the legendary back, who grew up in San Francisco and was already recognized as a future Hall of Famer, would keep the team competitive during its rebuilding and also help sell the Niners' mountain of unwanted tickets. "You couldn't even give them away," one assistant coach remembered. Attendance had dropped to the lowest in the Forty Niners' history and was still sinking.

As the fall of 1978 approached with its expanded sixteen-game schedule, Thomas's handiwork was apparent everywhere. "The organization was a shambles," one assistant coach remembered. "The place was just in chaos. The right hand didn't know what the left hand was doing. There was upheaval everywhere you looked. The atmosphere was awful." As was the team the Forty Niners were about to field for the 1978 season. "We were so bad it was embarrassing," offensive lineman Randy Cross admitted. "We were about to go 2-14 and, I'll tell you, we weren't nearly that good. I was surprised we won any games at all. Other teams had no respect for us. They'd say, 'Wouldn't you rather play for a *professional* football team?' They never took us seriously and I can't say that I blame them. Joe Thomas was to football franchises what scorched earth is to landscaping."

While Joe had been ruining the team, Eddie had spent his first year getting a feel for being its owner. He flew into San Francisco in the company Learjet for games and for other franchise business more than two dozen times his first year, accompanied by his entourage or, if business was being done, by one or two executives Senior sent along from Youngstown to mind the corporate store. Eddie always stayed at the Fairmont. The setting was the perfect expression of his commitment to doing everything "first-class." His opening public task was a round of one-on-one interviews in his suite to try to clear the air after the Venetian Room disaster. Dressed "impeccably" in powder blue slacks and a matching silk shirt, Eddie paused during one of them—as he was discoursing on what regular folks the DeBartolos were—retrieved a carefully folded pair of tattered Levis from the other room, then held them up like a piece of evidence. "See?" he insisted. "We're normal."

Eddie D.'s offer of proof apparently carried little impact. As the losses began piling up that first season, DeBartolo was booed at Candlestick on game days. One week he was struck by an unopened beer can heaved out of the stands.

Another of Eddie's ownership duties was handling the franchise's business with the league. Most owners led their team's delegation to the National Football League's business meetings, convened three or four times a year. Eddie, however, almost always sent a corporate surrogate in his place. "Whenever I see him, I tell him to come to the meetings," Pittsburgh Steelers owner Dan Rooney explained. "He says he will but he never does." Agreeing to meetings and then backing out of them was a standard pattern for DeBartolo Jr., especially when it came to hanging out with his fellow franchise holders, most of whom were twice his age. He knew right away that he was not that kind of owner.

The part of being an owner that genuinely drew Eddie was his bond with those who played for him. He was that way from the very beginning, as though this were the Cardinal Mooney JVs redux. Throughout his life he referred to the Niners players as "my family" and meant it. "Eddie was a like a cheerleader with the team," one former Niner remembered. "He was young—younger than some of the guys whose salaries he paid. He wanted to be around players, to be one of the guys. He wanted to talk, to be your buddy. His heart was really in it. He got emotional when it came to the team. He wanted to win like he was one of us. And he was miserable and angry when we lost. He wasn't just the businessman sitting up in a luxury box. He had his heart at stake. He was down there with you and wanted to share your fate. If anybody said anything bad about the Niners, he wanted to coldcock them."

During games, it was impossible for Eddie to sit still in the owner's box, so he paced and fumed and sometimes hid his head to avoid watching the tense parts. Afterward, he was in the locker room drenched with sweat, just like his team. His togetherness with his players apparently also included socializing. After O. J. Simpson joined the club, reports of him and Eddie nightclubbing together soon got around, followed by stories that Senior had put a stop to taking ownership that far. In any case, Eddie's team was closest to his heart and he made a point of going around the locker room after games and thanking everyone personally "for playing so hard for me."

Nonetheless, even Eddie D.'s new "family" was insufficient compensation for the 1978 season, which was the worst ever in his football life. The fledgling owner, about to turn thirty-two, started off with a brave face, making preseason descriptions of his team as "young" or "growing," but he hadn't anticipated just how bad they really were. Thomas had told him the team would at least be competitive and interesting but they failed to show anything close to that in their winless preseason. After the Niners lost their first two regular season games as well, DeBartolo shooed the press out of the locker room for a closed-door session with his "guys." Down to his shirtsleeves with cuffs still buttoned and tie cinched tight, he told them not to get discouraged or lose heart. They were young and going to go through some rough water, but he still had faith in them.

The speech had no discernible impact. The Niners finally won one game three weeks later, making them 1-4, then lost nine more in a row. The first of those nine consecutive losses was on the road in Los Angeles, where the Rams, the Niners' traditional rival, dismantled them 27–10. The performance was bad enough that the announcers on the radio broadcast started making fun of the Forty Niners' ineptitude. That pissed off Eddie so much he stood outside their booth screaming at the broadcasters while they were on the air doing their postgame show.

By then, Eddie had begun skipping some of his Learjet trips to games and instead listened over a private radio hookup. When the *San Francisco Chronicle* questioned him about his absence, DeBartolo was apologetic. "I should spend more time out there and I will," he said. "I've been lax. But I'm a private person, a small town guy, and sometimes I feel uncomfortable in big crowds. But I owe it to the press and the fans to get out there more. We're struggling now, but we're moving in the right direction. We've got a great staff and good players. In a while it will show."

No one else in the Bay Area believed that. Fans began arriving at games with banners reading BLAME JOE THOMAS and, at Thomas's direction, security guards were dispatched to confiscate the complaints and remove them from public view. Halfway through the season, a quarter of the Niners' advance ticket sales were no-shows on game day. Thomas himself had taken to giving regular postgame speeches to his team, often when it was obvious the general manager had been drinking. He also began staying away from the press. When he did talk, one *San Francisco Examiner* reporter wrote during the last weekend of October, "Thomas [was] verbally fencing, keeping his answers to a minimum. . . . This from a man who . . . can go on for hours, apparently intoxicated by the sound of his own voice. . . . Thomas really doesn't have much to say because his team is quite literally stinking out the joint. Forty Niners fans have been staying away in impressive numbers each week [in] a resounding vote of no confidence in the new ownership and the hand picked general manager. . . . It's the G.M.'s style to elbow his way to the front when somebody's handing out praise but he's always ready to push somebody else out in the firing line if things aren't going well. [Still,] like it or not, the . . . 49ers are Joe Thomas' team and they stink."

Thomas received an advance copy of that *Examiner* story at the team hotel in Washington, D.C., the night before the Niners' game with the Washington Redskins. The general manager went apoplectic when he read it. Upon learning that the *Examiner* reporter was down in the hotel disco, dancing, Thomas stomped downstairs, charged into the club, and assaulted him right there on the dance floor. When bouncers dragged Thomas off, Joe screamed, "I'm going to get you," in the journalist's direction. Thomas was then removed from the disco and banned "for making a scene." When Eddie D. was asked for a comment about the ruckus, he only said that he was going to check with the company's lawyers to see if there wasn't some legal way to ban that reporter from covering his team.

The next day, the Niners lost again, 38–20, and afterward, Joe Thomas fired the head coach, the third such dismissal in Thomas's year and a half on the job.

The most common local response to the move was that Thomas should have fired himself instead. Eddie, however, was having none of it. One of the DeBartolos' cardinal rules was loyalty, and, in perhaps his greatest blunder yet, Eddie announced barely a week after Thomas's dance floor assault that he not only had faith in Joe, he was going to back that talk up by adding four more years onto Thomas's original six-year contract, meaning he would be general manager at least through 1986. Eddie no doubt thought this step was a way to show his mettle when the going was tough and thus project strength and certainty to stabilize the situation, but the news hit the local football world like a turd in a crowded swimming pool. At this point, those "that asshole" references to Eddie could be heard all over the nine counties.

Another of DeBartolo's goals had been to reassure Joe Thomas, but he didn't come close. More than a few people around the organization now spoke of Thomas's increasing "paranoia." In his state, Eddie's gesture of loyalty just bounced right off him. The next Sunday, his team lost 16–10. The Niners now had one win and ten losses and were still sinking like a rock. Thomas showed up in the locker room afterward, all lathered up and riding at least a couple belts of something alcoholic. The general manager stood on a bench and tore into his players, dutifully assembled around him in all stages of stripping off their gear. Thomas made it quite clear that he would not tolerate this level of play and revealed his own insecurities in doing so.

"If I go down the fucking tubes," he screamed at them, "I'm going to take all of you with me."

Back in Youngstown, Eddie D. had to have had at least some misgivings when he learned of Joe's locker-room rant. If so, they didn't become actionable until two weeks later, when the Forty Niners were matched against the Pittsburgh Steelers on *Monday Night Football*.

This was a very special game for Eddie D. It was *Monday Night Football* in that phenomenon's heyday and it was against the Steelers. For Eddie, who occupied a universe that centered on Youngstown, beating Pittsburgh was all about bragging rights for the rest of the year. On top of that, the Pittsburgh team would arrive in San Francisco 9-2 and on their way to their third Super Bowl title in the last five years. They were already widely recognized as the team of the 1970s and were thought to be the apex of the game's evolution, epitomizing brute force, built on defense and the running game, but also throwing deep every now and then when their opponents stacked in close. Playing the Steelers in front of a national audience was the definition of status in Eddie's view and made their game the critical encounter of this whole torturous season.

If those owner expectations didn't create enough weird crosscurrents for that Monday night, real life then multiplied the weirdness by a factor of ten on the morning of the game. Shortly before eleven on Monday, November 27, 1978, a former member of San Francisco's Board of Supervisors walked into the City Hall office of the mayor, shot him to death, then went down the hall and killed the board's one gay member as well. The murders instantly turned the Bay Area on its head. When Joe Thomas learned, he became convinced that the assassinations weren't yet over and that the next one would be aimed at him. He later claimed that his office had received a telephone threat to that effect, but most of the reporters down at Niners headquarters guessed he had made that story up. In any case, Joe Thomas spent the rest of the day in a frantic attempt to persuade NFL commissioner Pete Rozelle to reschedule that night's game, only to be refused in no uncertain terms.

The game went on to its predictable end. The Steelers were up 17–0 halfway through the second quarter and coasted to a 24–7 thrashing. The stands at Candlestick were as full as they had been all season, but many of those who did show up brought hand-lettered signs, such as XMAS WISHES FOR 49ER FAITHFUL: 1. A NEW OWNER. 2. A NEW GENERAL MANAGER. The highlight of the broadcast was a security guard, under instructions from "Forty Niners' management," ripping down a BLAME THOMAS banner pointed at television cameras across the stadium.

The Learjet ride back to Youngstown afterward was no doubt painful and well lubricated. And by the time Eddie landed he had crossed a threshold. Thomas was an embarrassment who had turned the DeBartolo name into a laughingstock, Eddie told his father. It was a complete reversal from his position at the beginning of the month and it would cost them money, but Eddie felt he had no choice if he wanted to save his franchise from complete disgrace. Like Senior had always said, "You can only kiss a guy's ass so far. Then you've got to get rid of him," family friend or not.

Senior agreed.

Edward DeBartolo Jr., the future "Mr. D.," eventual patriarch of one of the greatest dynasties in NFL history, had come to his senses in the nick of time.

It was at this point that Eddie sought out Bill Walsh.

Bill Walsh as Stanford head coach, 1978

THE RIGHT FIT

ddie D. didn't come up with the idea of hiring Bill on his own.

The initial suggestion came from Ron Barr, a sportscaster at Channel 4, then the San Francisco NBC affiliate. Barr had first met DeBartolo when the former had lived in Seattle during the early seventies and was active in a homeowners organization that opposed and eventually blocked a DeBartolo Corp. shopping center project in which Eddie had played a lead role. When Barr moved to San Francisco in 1977, his first assignment at Channel 4 was an interview with the Niners' new owner, during which Barr reintroduced himself. Barr was easygoing, Eddie had no hard feelings left from their Seattle encounter, and the two soon developed a friendship. They were roughly the same age and Eddie felt he could talk to Ron in confidence and be assured his comments wouldn't end up in the next day's news. Barr also knew Walsh well. At the time, Bill was in his second year as head football coach at Stanford University down the Peninsula in Palo Alto and Barr was producing the Stanford football team's weekly highlight show, on which he was paired with its coach. Barr thought Walsh was one of the smartest people he'd ever met and regularly used the adjective *amazing* to describe him.

Barr's suggestion was made the week after the Steelers game, when Eddie was back at the Fairmont. Eddie and Barr and one of Eddie's buddies from Youngstown met for dinner at an Italian restaurant down in the financial district. No public or private announcements had yet been made about the fate of Joe Thomas, but Eddie was grousing about what a mess Thomas had made and was openly mulling over whom to turn to next. At the time, his leading candidates were Chuck Knox of the Buffalo Bills and Don Shula of the Miami Dolphins.

When DeBartolo asked Barr what he thought of those two as possibilities, Barr told him to forget about them. Both were under contract so, by NFL rules, simply raising the issue with them would constitute tampering and be punished accordingly. Even if that wasn't the case, the Niners were in such disrepute that no one of Knox's or Shula's stature would consider jumping ship to coach in San Francisco. Then Barr brought up Walsh.

Eddie said no way. He wanted Knox or Shula.

Barr told Eddie he was missing the forest for the trees. Walsh was right here on his doorstep, fifteen minutes from the Niners' Redwood City headquarters, and was easily the best talent available.

DeBartolo seemed dubious but Ron pressed on.

If Eddie hired Walsh, Barr insisted, "I promise he'll win three Super Bowls for you."

Twenty years later, Ron Barr's clairvoyance would seem stunning. That evening, Eddie D. left dinner still thinking about it.

Barr's take on Bill Walsh certainly wasn't widespread around the NFL in December 1978. Though Bill was a visible figure of some repute, he was seen less as a sure thing in waiting than as a coach who had something mysterious wrong with him. Bill had made his name as an assistant coach under the legendary Paul Brown, head coach and owner of the Cincinnati Bengals. Even in Brown's considerable shadow, Bill had been lionized by the sports press as one of the coaching game's rising stars, an offensive mastermind with a track record of developing great quarterbacks. It had been widely assumed throughout the first half of the 1970s that whenever Brown retired to the owner's box he would designate Walsh as his successor on the Bengals' sideline. That, however, had not happened. Instead, Brown picked someone else to be his team's head coach, and Walsh left Cincinnati under something of a cloud. He landed with the San Diego Chargers, with whom he spent a season as offensive coordinator, and then moved on to Stanford about the same time Eddie bought the Niners.

Even after two years, the league's coaching scuttlebutt about Walsh was still dominated by his Cincinnati exit. Not having been good enough for Brown, who arguably knew him better than anyone else, made Bill suspect—especially since Brown not only refused to promote him but refused to recommend him to other teams and was bad-mouthing him as well. That Walsh was forty-five when he finally got his first head coaching job beyond high school level—a late age in his profession—and then only at a football backwater like Stanford, added to the sense that he was somehow flawed. On top of that, everyone agreed that he was an odd guy for a football coach, a kind of mad scientist rearranging x's and o's on a blackboard—too cerebral and too far outside the box. Differentness was not held in high regard around the NFL in 1978 and Walsh was consequently rated an intriguing possibility but not a safe choice for a head coach.

Walsh himself bridled at any talk of "flaws" but freely admitted to still being somewhat emotionally damaged that fall. "What happened in Cincinnati had been shattering to me," he remembered, "and it took me a long time to get over it. It was very difficult and for a while afterward I was very lost. The hurt and disappointment only receded by inches. It was an excruciating experience, the worst of my professional life."

The Stanford job had been balm to his wounds. First, it was a long-sought homecoming. Bill had graduated from Hayward High School in the East Bay, attended junior college at the north end of the Peninsula in San Mateo, and graduated from college in San Jose, epicenter of the South Bay. His wife, Geri, had grown up in Walnut Creek on the other side of the Caldecott Tunnel and they'd met at San Jose State. His first job had been at a high school in Fremont on the east end of the Dunbarton Bridge; his second was as an assistant at Cal across the Bay Bridge from San Francisco; his third was as a Stanford assistant at the foot of the Santa Cruz Mountains, which separate the lower half of the Bay from the Pacific Ocean. He often joked that he and Geri had spent a lot of time in Cincinnati singing "I Left

My Heart in San Francisco." Being back where he came from felt like a port in the storm. His children had been in three different schools in the last year and when he set them up in a house on campus, he felt like he had taken care of his family as best he could. He also found Stanford's academic prestige comforting. "Despite his confidence, Bill always had a kind of inferiority complex about his own intellectual roots," one of his best friends remembered. "The Stanford connection meant a lot to him that way." The affiliation also contributed mightily to his eventual christening as "The Genius."

For its part, Stanford had not been put off by the NFL's doubts and had pursued him with no small fervor. At the time, Bill was finishing his first year as San Diego's offensive coordinator, the highest paid assistant coach in the league, but was still burning to be a head coach somewhere. During his short tenure, he'd already been instrumental in San Diego's rise from 2-12 to 6-8 and the transformation of the Chargers' heretofore disappointing quarterback, Dan Fouts, into a future Hall of Famer. There was some loose talk that Bill might be in line to be the Chargers head coach at some point down the line, but he was in no mood to wait on that possibility. As soon as he learned of Stanford's interest he wanted the job. "I spent hours on the telephone," the head of the university's search committee recalled, "and I couldn't figure out why somebody hadn't picked him up as a coach. I tried to find out what was wrong with him. I couldn't understand why he wouldn't make a topflight coach, but here he was, forty-five, and passed over. Talking to him I became convinced that this man was either totally crazy or knew more about football than anyone else in the game. Ultimately, the committee unanimously recommended him."

And the results he generated had more than vindicated their choice. While the Stanford Cardinal had a long and proud athletic tradition and played in the Pac-10, one of the premier collegiate leagues, its high academic standards increasingly left it at a significant disadvantage on the football field. By the time Bill took the reins, its teams were outmanned, always short of depth and speed, and seemingly destined to be a league doormat, but he won with them anyway. "At Stanford," Guy Benjamin, his quarterback that first year, remembered, "the dilemma for players was always how do you respect a coach when you feel like you're smarter than he is. From the first day that was never an issue with Bill. He was above all that. There was no question he knew more than we ever would and we all bought in. He insisted on being called by his first name and treated us seriously, like we were all grown men with a job to do. I can't remember him ever raising his voice. He could have been a professor rather than the more typical football coaches we had been used to."

Seeking to take advantage of his team's intelligence, Walsh installed the most sophisticated passing offense anyone had seen outside of the NFL, and his team pulled it off. At the end of his first year, Stanford led the nation in passing and went to the postseason Sun Bowl, where it defeated LSU. In his second year, they led the nation in passing again, and at the time Eddie and Ron Barr were discussing the Forty Niners' coming vacancy, Stanford was scheduled to play Georgia in the Bluebonnet Bowl on New Year's Eve. It was a remarkable turnaround. "In many ways," a *Chronicle* columnist observed, "Walsh is the ideal coach for Stanford. . . . The man has done a remarkable job [making] the most of what he has. . . . Walsh has been able to utilize the talents of his best players to compensate for the weaknesses of the team and the Cards are playing better than anybody could have expected. . . . He is handsome and personable and he always seems to say the right thing. He looks and acts like a man who was bred for the role and he has made Stanford football the best show in town."

This performance was not lost on the NFL. Despite the persistent doubts about him, Bill's two years out of the league were dotted with nibbles about prospective NFL head coaching jobs. Before Walsh had even coached a game for Stanford, Joe Thomas had inquired through Al Davis if he might like the Niners job, but Bill, a friend of Monte Clark's, turned the offer down flat. Thomas's former boss Jim Finks, now the general manager of the Chicago Bears and an old friend of Bill's, met privately with Walsh when he was in Chicago on a recruiting trip and expressed the Bears' interest, even discussing a salary twice what Stanford was paying him. Walsh declined, citing his loyalty to Stanford and his wife, Geri's, desire to stay in California. The New York Giants brought him back east to give a talk about offensive football and sized him up, but the organizational structure there looked too top-heavy for Bill and he didn't pursue it. His most serious flirtation was with the Los Angeles Rams. The general manager there, Don Klosterman,

was another old friend. Bill made several trips to L.A. early in 1978 to negotiate with Klosterman and the Rams' owner, Carroll Rosenbloom, and at
times seemed on the verge of signing on as head coach. One Southern California radio station even announced that the deal was done. At the last
minute, however, Rosenbloom, who was in ill health, decided he needed
someone he thought would win right away and nixed Walsh in favor of
coaching retread George Allen, who had been to the Super Bowl before.

Throughout it all, Bill was ambivalent. "Despite the opportunities," he
remembered, "I didn't think much about the NFL when I was at Stanford.
I'd had to remind myself when I first took the job there that being a college
head coach had always been my aspiration when I started out in coaching
and now I had reached it. I became comfortable with that pretty quickly
and would have been comfortable staying at Stanford for the rest of my career. I was determined that I was going to work as hard as I could at my
Stanford job and not get into the business of campaigning for an NFL head
job and then being disappointed. I was still burned from my past experience
with the league and I was happy where I was. My wife was happy; my family was happy. I didn't feel some pressing need to move on. As far as satisfaction went, my time at Stanford was the greatest. I always remembered
that time there as our Camelot years."

That said, Walsh still knew he wouldn't prove himself until he returned
to the NFL and showed his detractors just how wrong they had been about
him. He also knew that Stanford was indeed a backwater and that his
achievements there would never be treated as more than an oddity. That
knowledge ate at him even as he kept declaring otherwise.

As much was obvious when Ron Barr consulted with Bill before Ron's
dinner with Eddie. Barr didn't want to raise Walsh's name if Bill had no interest in the job, so he told Bill that he was going to suggest him for the Niners head man when he and Eddie got together. Bill had responded that he
might be interested, but he didn't want anything to do with Joe Thomas and
he didn't want to end up competing for the spot with one of his coaching
friends either. Otherwise, he'd be willing to hear what Eddie had to say.

Several days after Barr and DeBartolo's dinner, Bill was in his office at the
Stanford Athletic Department, visiting with one of his oldest friends from a
group of San Jose State buddies from the fifties who still remained close.
This friend had gone on to become a corporate officer, and the two of them

often brainstormed with each other—this afternoon about how to adapt corporate planning techniques to running football programs. They were interrupted by the phone.

Eddie DeBartolo was on the line from Youngstown. He introduced himself and said he was coming out for the Niners' game against the Tampa Bay Buccaneers next weekend. He suggested the two of them meet for brunch at the Fairmont on Saturday.

Bill didn't know it yet, but his life had reached a pivot point.

*Bill Walsh with his parents
in Los Angeles, mid-1930s*

*Bill Walsh (#21) on the
sidelines as a teenager*

||||| ||||| |||||

4

GROWING INTO THE GAME

Edward DeBartolo Jr. may have been a "spoiled little rich kid," but no one would ever say that about the man he was thinking of hiring to coach his football team.

William Ernest Walsh had been born in Los Angeles on the last day of November 1931, during the nadir of the Great Depression. He marked the third successive generation of Walsh males named Bill, each distinguished from his predecessor by a different middle name. His father, William Archibald, was twenty-three years old at the time his son was born; his mother, Ruth, was nineteen. Bill was the first of their two children. Ruth had been born in L.A. and William Archibald had moved there at the age of six. Both their families—one with Irish roots, the other German—had emigrated to Southern California from Colorado, where the men had worked in the mines and brickyards around Denver. Bill's father had left school after the eighth grade to search for work wherever he could find it, enduring a long stretch of Depression unemployment during which he and Ruth had lived on little more than a daily meal of flapjacks. By November 1931, however, William Archibald had been hired on the automobile assembly line at Chrysler's Los Angeles manufacturing plant for thirty-three cents an hour and was supplementing his pay with freelance body and fender repair on the weekends. His boy, Bill, would have to work for everything he got.

The home of Walsh's childhood memories was a workingman's bungalow in South Central L.A., two miles from the Los Angeles Coliseum, in the residential corridor lining Vermont, Figueroa, and Normandie avenues. The house occupied a postage-stamp-size lot and had two bedrooms—one of which Bill shared with his sister, Maureen—a living room, dining room, bathroom, and kitchen, plus a garage and a tiny two-room cottage out back, which the Walshes rented out. In the evening, after dinner, the family often sat out on the front porch. Bill recalled the house as "quite nice" until he revisited it a few years before his death. "My God," he exclaimed, "it was a tiny little box just sitting there. The front porch was hardly as big as a sofa. And all the houses for blocks around were just the same." Most of the residents of South Central in those days were immigrants of one sort or another who spoke little or no English. The kids played in the streets after school or down at the playground for games of baseball or football, but there were no organized sports programs with coaches and uniforms. Virtually the only trips Bill took out of the neighborhood came every month or two, when the whole family would pile into their old car and take a Sunday drive to the beach at Santa Monica.

Bill's mother was the anchor of the Walshes' family life, keeping house until jobs opened up for women during World War II and she joined the workforce. His grandparents on both sides were also a regular presence, but by far the heaviest influence on his childhood was his father. "I don't think Bill ever had a great closeness with his dad," one of his best friends explained. "He was a tall man, kind of cold. He was like all the men of that time—my dad was similar—Depression men, closed-up guys with thick skins, the kind of fathers who left their children with a hole in their soul where that closeness should have been." William Archibald was, Bill remembered, "a hardworking guy who was typical of the men of his era. He worked and he drank and that was it. There were no other activities—no golf, no fishing, nothing. He couldn't afford them or he couldn't envision doing them. I guess he was a kind of sports fan from a distance, maybe listening to a game on the radio every now and then, but that was it." In his more candid moments, Bill would dismiss his father as "a lout" who had never been a father to him at all.

Bill would nonetheless credit William Archibald with instilling the "work ethic" that would later become a staple of Walsh's football career. Starting at age ten, young Bill was expected to spend his weekends helping his dad with his body and fender business. "While some kids were outside playing," he remembered, "I was out in the garage working with the men. My dad had things for me to do, sanding cars, getting them ready to paint. I didn't have a choice, but I was never mad about it. It was for the family and those were the days everybody did things for the family to survive. Other boys my age were doing the same thing for their dads. He'd give me a dollar every now and then when he thought I did a particularly good job. What stuck was the level of detail he demanded from me. His expectations were hard and stark. It wasn't like, 'Maybe you better try to.' It was, 'Get that goddamn thing over here and line it up right. That's not lined up right. Take it off and do it again.' He'd blow his stack if he thought you screwed up, even if you hadn't. It was tough love if you want to call it that. It had a real hard side to it." Sixty years later, when Bill's doctors were trying to identify the origins of the leukemia that was killing him, they would point to those teenage workdays with his dad, breathing without protection in a shop full of paint fumes and solvents.

There was still time for some sports in his Los Angeles childhood and of all those Bill played—including baseball, basketball, and gymnastics—football was always his favorite. When he was twelve, he and one of his buddies would visit the practice fields of the University of Southern California football team near the L.A. Coliseum after school and shag stray balls or anything else they could talk their way into doing. He saw his very first live football game at the coliseum one Saturday when USC hosted Notre Dame and his father and a bunch of his father's friends brought him along to cheer for the Fighting Irish. It was the only game Bill could remember his father ever watching. Notre Dame won, 13–0, thanks to the heroics of Heisman Trophy–winning running back Angelo Bertelli. The teenage Bill kept his eyes glued to the action, but Bill's dad and his pals were more intent on celebrating the outcome than following the game itself and were all drunk by the fourth quarter.

. . .

Bill finally got his own chance to play when he enrolled in Washington High School in nearby Inglewood. In those days, Washington might have been the best high school team in the country, led by its star halfback, Hugh McElhenny, an eventual All-Pro with the Forty Niners and member of the NFL Hall of Fame. While McElhenny was a senior, Bill was just a sophomore scrub, a skinny left-handed quarterback who hardly played, but he had had visions of doing great things when he got his chance.

Thanks to his father, however, Bill's dream of Washington High School stardom never had an opportunity to play itself out. As his son began his junior year, William Archibald Walsh decided to uproot the family and strike out in a new direction. The senior Walsh had friends up in Central Point, a tiny hamlet north of Medford, Oregon, and they convinced him there was a golden opportunity there in the body and fender business. World War II was over and the new civilian economy was starting to boom. So, right in the middle of football season, William Archibald quit his job at Chrysler, sold the South Central bungalow, loaded up the family car, and drove north to Central Point, where he sank his entire savings into the new enterprise. Bill was enrolled in the local high school and struggled to make the transition from his old school of 3,000 students to his new one of 120. He went out for football, but that far into the season there was no hope of playing quarterback, so the new kid was turned into a running back. By the end of the spring semester, before Bill had really settled in, his father's business had gone belly-up, they'd lost everything, including the family home, and the Walshes were moving back to California, this time the Bay Area. Chrysler was opening a new plant in the East Bay and wanted their old employee back as an assembly-line supervisor at the best wages William Archibald Walsh had ever made.

Soon the family was ensconced in Hayward, within commuting distance of his father's new job in San Leandro, living in a house out at 167th Street and Foothill Boulevard that was big enough for Bill to have his own room. He was enrolled at Hayward High School for his senior year. Thirty years later, the East Bay would be a continuous strip of low-rise urban life, connected by eight-lane freeways, but when Bill arrived in 1949, there were no freeways yet, urban density was confined to San Francisco and Oakland, and the rest was still a succession of separate towns and villages surrounded by agricultural land and country roads. His new high school's nickname was the Fighting Farmers. None of that bucolic character made Bill's transition any easier. "This was my third high school in three years," he remembered. "I had never had the same teacher twice in my whole academic career and all that adjusting had kept me from being much of a student. Having to be the new kid always destroyed me. I managed to make a lot of friends at Hayward, but without football I would have been lost."

Again, however, his late arrival squelched his dreams of being a quarterback. The Fighting Farmers already had two quarterbacks, so just like in Oregon, the new left-handed kid was relegated to playing halfback on both sides of the ball, though a special halfback pass was installed in the offense just to take advantage of his arm. Bill still wasn't fully grown, just five feet ten and 160 pounds, so perhaps his most remarkable asset was his capacity to play and understand every position on the field. "He had a feel for all of them," the Fighting Farmers' fullback recalled. "Football is a lot of instinct and he had those keen instincts even back then."

Off the field, Walsh was remembered as "an extremely jovial and carefree guy who seemed to laugh all the time. When I picture him I see him either walking around campus holding hands with his high school sweetheart, Muriel, or driving his car. He had a '35 Chevy, one of the few guys who did have a car back then. We did a lot of riding around in it and almost as much hitchhiking because it broke down all the time. He loved to party and looked on life as a good time. He wasn't a troublemaker by any standard, but he could get a pretty good blow on like the rest of us from a few beers. And Bill was not only a talented football player—he was very capable with his hands in terms of fisticuffs. He probably had one of the fastest left hooks I've ever seen. I always thought he'd have made a fine fighter. You knew if you hung around with Bill and the occasion presented itself that no one would have to carry him in a fight. He could hold his own and then some."

In 1950, Walsh became the first ever in his family to graduate from high school. At age eighteen, he was long on physical prowess, good humor, and spunk, but, by his own admission, still short on larger aspirations. His mother, Ruth, however, filled the vacuum. She had long dreamed that he would also become the first Walsh to graduate from college, so rather than follow his father's footsteps to the Chrysler plant in San Leandro, he followed her dream across the bay to San Mateo Community College, a two-year school where students without financial means could get a start at higher education. Bill found a cheap room and part-time work and played football both years there. In the second year, he finally got to start at quarterback, the opportunity he had hungered for since he took up the game. "I did okay," he remembered. "I made the All League team, but I never got very polished or accomplished as a quarterback. I never got the chance to practice at it enough. I certainly never lived up to my potential." His talent, however, drew some interest from four-year schools. The Naval Academy inquired and Oregon State recruited him to walk on, but Bill was ambivalent about where he wanted to go. Then he developed a crush on a girl who was headed for San Jose State College and followed her there in early 1952, hoping to win a scholarship at spring football practice.

San Jose State ended up having more impact on Bill than any other educational experience in his life. One major reason was Bob Bronzan, the head football coach. Bronzan, then thirty-three, was, by all accounts, ahead of his time. His teams pulled guards, blitzed safeties, ran the option, split the ends, and used three-receiver sets before anyone else on the West Coast. He was often credited with using a pro system for college kids. Playing as an independent against teams like Colorado, BYU, and Cal, Bronzan's 1952 team would go 8-2 and rank second in the nation in total offense. "He had a great football mind," Bill remembered. "He was a theorist and an excellent teacher who set a standard as to the detail of everything he coached and the organizational system he set up. He coached football like it was a science, a skilled sport instead of just head bashing." Almost a third of Bill's San Jose teammates would enter coaching and Bill himself would eventually credit Bronzan as the inspiration for his own decision to become a coach. That decision, however, was the furthest thing from Walsh's mind in the spring of 1952.

First the new kid had to succeed at spring practice and that was anything but easy. Bill had now reached his adult size—six feet two and 205 pounds—but a number of junior college transfers showed up that spring to compete for scholarships and there were only four such partial rides available. And Bronzan was a fierce taskmaster. "He treated us like shit," one of Bill's teammates remembered. Bronzan, a big man, regularly traded blows with his charges while making coaching points and, if he was displeased with how an afternoon practice went, wouldn't hesitate to bring the team back out under the lights at night to repeat it. Walsh's debut under Bronzan also began with his by now familiar disappointment. San Jose State already had three quarterbacks, so the coach shifted his incoming transfer student to the end position, where the team was thin. Swallowing his aspirations for a final time, Walsh won a scholarship and by his senior year was starting on both sides of the ball. "He wasn't all that impressive as far as physique was concerned," Bronzan remembered, "but he was an ideal person to coach. He was always alert. You never had to paint the whole picture for him. Just give him a few of the elements and he'd have it right away."

Like most in those days, Walsh's scholarship wasn't much—just fifty dollars a month—but for Bill it was the difference between going to college or not. He rented a garage for his car at four dollars a month and, for his first few weeks in San Jose, slept in its backseat. He eventually found a free room with an alumni family for a while and then made a habit of sleeping on couches in the apartments of friends for long stretches when his own housing money ran out. Bronzan also gave out points for good play that could be cashed in for meals at Archie's Restaurant, a local establishment run by one of the team's boosters, and Bill used his football performance to underwrite his board with Archie's burgers and pancakes. There was only a little money available from his family, but Ruth did his laundry and fed him whenever he came home to Hayward. The rest of his financial shortfall was covered by menial labor sorting papers at the school's journalism department. "He had a lot more dedication than you usually find in a college kid," one classmate remembered, "but he was also a lot more of a wild hair than you might have thought."

Bill was never a big man on campus, but perhaps his major splash at San Jose State was as a boxer rather than as a football player. Boxing was the only sport that ever seriously competed with football for his affections. He'd first taken it up in Hayward at a community gym that gave free pugilism training to young people after school. In those days he carried a picture of Irish Bob Murphy, a middleweight contender, in his wallet and fancied himself tough enough to follow in the fighter's footsteps. At San Jose State in the early fifties, one of his classmates remembered, "boxing was bigger than football or any other sport" and the annual intramural boxing tournament was one of the major social events of the year. It lasted three days and nights and all the school's organizations fielded teams. Bill, who couldn't afford to join a fraternity, fought under one frat's colors in the heavyweight division and at the end of three days won the championship to great acclaim. He was thought good enough to be offered a tryout for the school's prestigious intercollegiate squad but never pursued it. "I loved to fight," he remembered, "but I wasn't dedicated enough to really train the way I should have." Walsh nonetheless had a well-established reputation in student circles as a tough guy. A few classmates still recall the time a local hood was hassling people in a movie line and Bill stepped up and knocked the guy cold in the middle of the street.

Other than sports, the core of Walsh's life at San Jose was the group of a dozen or so pals he made there and kept close to his heart for the rest of his life. The friend who would be visiting Bill in his Stanford office when Eddie DeBartolo called remembered that "we hung out together almost all the time. We all had backgrounds as scrappers, fighters, and athletes. We all dressed like we were applying for a job at a warehouse. We had a lot of fun. We closed a lot of saloons together. We all had this kind of dependence on our manhood that stuck with us through the rest of our lives. We were devoted to being [a] certain kind of men and [a] certain kind of friends." None of them had enough money to join fraternities, but they cadged invitations to whatever parties they could find or shared jugs of cheap wine. Their favorite bar was the Tenth and Keys, where they'd drink beer and talk patrons with more money than they into playing the jukebox. Any country and western song would do, but Webb Pierce's "Back Street Affair" was considered the best. They weren't looking for trouble but every now and then it showed up and Bill was often in the middle of sorting it out. "We laughed like hell when we were together," one remembered, "and still do. Bill was just one of us, nothing special in those days, and as good a friend as God ever made."

The other character from Bill's San Jose days who stayed with him for the rest of his life was his wife, Geri. She was just a freshman when Walsh met her after his first season under Bronzan—and a young one at that. Geri Nardini had graduated from high school in Walnut Creek at age sixteen and was, by all accounts, drop-dead gorgeous. "All of us used to follow Geri across the campus lusting," one of Bill's friends remembered. "She was more than a knockout. She had that passionate energy, a kind of deep sensuality that comes not from the way she looks but the way she is." Another friend remembered her looking "just like Snow White in the movies." Bill fell for Geri like a ton of bricks. "I was registering for courses," she remembered, "and he was ogling me. He was ogling all the girls. Eventually he asked me to come to a boxing match with him. So I went to the arena to see him box. I remember how wonderful he looked." They made an impressive couple—she, beautiful, with dark Italian looks, and he, tall, blond, and Irish handsome. When she went out on a date with another guy, he gathered up two pairs of boxing gloves and went looking for her other suitor to settle their competing claims.

As Bill's graduation neared, his relationship with Geri got increasingly serious. The Korean War was just grinding to a stalemate and military conscription calls were still at wartime levels, so Bill knew he would be in the army almost as soon as he left school. Marriage at the end of college was also then the social norm. "It was kind of assumed in those days that if you didn't get a girl then," Bill remembered, "you never would. So there was a kind of desperation mixed with impetuousness to it all." Shortly before taking a BA in physical education with a minor in history, Bill, twenty-two, proposed marriage, and Geri, eighteen, accepted. After graduation, without notifying their parents, the couple sneaked off to Minden, Nevada, and tied the knot before a justice of the peace.

A month after that, Walsh began a two-year Army tour at Fort Ord down in Monterey, most of which he spent as a private in a physical training company. Among his assignments was teaching recruits how to jump off the deck of a troop ship, which required him to leap off a fifty-foot-high platform in full uniform into a deep pool every day. Geri soon rented an apartment off base and the two set up housekeeping on his army pay, which Bill supplemented by fishing for their dinner and boxing in army exhibitions—fifteen dollars a win, ten dollars a loss. During the last months of his army service, after his promotion to corporal, Geri gave birth to their first son, Steve, and between military duties and diaper changings Bill now spent a lot of time trying to figure out how he was going to support his new family after his rapidly approaching discharge. "I began to take life much more seriously," he explained. Walsh considered boxing professionally, having held his own with several professionals during his army exhibitions, but eventually dismissed the idea as a dangerous pipe dream.

That left coaching, the only other calling he felt he knew.

Bill Walsh coaching Washington Union High School, late 1950s

5

CLIMBING THE LADDER

A s was his way, Bill Walsh began his pursuit of coaching by trying to learn more about it.

He and Geri and the infant Steve moved back to San Jose in early 1956, where Bill enrolled at San Jose State as a graduate student seeking a master's degree from the Department of Physical Education. For the next year Walsh supported his family by pumping gas, handing out towels in the locker room, and umpiring high school baseball games. His faculty adviser at State was Bob Bronzan, for whom he coached the JV squad and the defensive line as a graduate assistant. Walsh's formal course work was made up of generalized education courses required for a California teaching certificate, but the heart of his master's program was a thesis, "Flank Formation Football, Stress: Defense." The thrust of this 192-page paper was an analysis of the pro set offense—then the cutting edge of football, utilizing split ends for the first time—and how defenses, heretofore used to packing six men on the line of scrimmage and utilizing only three defensive backs, had to adapt to defend against this new offense's enhanced ability to pass the ball. "My thesis was a very amateurish effort," Bill remembered. "The faculty committee critiqued it heavily, particularly since I had only one footnote in the whole thing, but Bronzan convinced them that no one had ever written on the subject before and they went ahead with my degree." It took Bill two tries to pass California's teacher certification exam, but after that, he was ready for the job market.

Thanks largely to a San Jose State alumni network among local school districts, Bill, twenty-five, was hired in 1957 at Washington Union High School in what is now the East Bay city of Fremont, then known as Centerville, the job having opened after the school's previous head football coach was discovered in a compromising position in the backseat of his car with a teenage cheerleader. Walsh was paid $4,650 a year, including a $250 bonus for having a master's degree. His responsibilities included teaching PE classes and driving the team bus. "This was the first work other than manual labor that I'd ever done," Bill remembered. "I'd always wanted to have a job with a desk and had always said to myself, 'If I ever have a desk,' as if it were my greatest aspiration. At Washington, I had one—a tin desk shoved up against a wall in the gym, but it was a desk." He set his family up in a rented house down the road in Newark, the cheapest housing available, and then threw himself into his new profession.

The team Walsh inherited, the Washington Union Huskies, had lost twenty-six of its last twenty-seven games and probably would have lost twenty-six more if Bill's timing had been any different. Fortunately for him, however, the East Bay's first freeway was being constructed to connect San Jose to Oakland and as it progressed north, housing developments followed. The year before Bill arrived, Washington Union had grown from 750 students to 3,000, generating a crop of much better athletes than the school had ever had. Bill immediately began plugging them into a new system of play, what he called "the Walsh offense," comprising all the ideas he'd been collecting all his football life. He switched offenses three times in his first year, but the drift was obvious. "In those days, almost all football coaches were afraid of the passing game," he remembered. "People thought it made you weak, that you couldn't have a tough team if you passed too much. It was a bizarre conclusion."

Which Bill rejected out of hand. "Everyone [else] was running three yards and a cloud of dust," one of his players explained. "Under him, we ran three wide receivers, a lot of motion and sprint-out pass patterns. Most teams we played only had two receivers in the pass patterns. We had three to five in every play. He'd say, 'This is your primary receiver, then I want you to look here, then here.' At that time everybody played a three-deep zone defense. He really attacked that area. He'd flood the zones with two or three receivers." Nobody among Bay Area high schools had seen anything quite like it before.

Nor had they seen anyone quite like Walsh. "At a time when most coaches intimidated and humiliated, he approached things differently," the school's basketball coach pointed out. "I noticed at the time that Bill's PE classes were having more fun than anybody else's. I couldn't figure it out so I watched him teach one day and what I saw was that he treated everybody in the class with tremendous dignity. Little fat guys who hated to dress out and hated to come to class all dressed for his class and were glad to be there because he treated them with great respect. It wasn't just the studly or the good athletes. He treated everybody the same way. They had more fun because of the way he treated them."

On the football field, the end result was success unlike anything Washington Union had seen in years. In 1957, Walsh's team won four, lost two, and tied two, the first time in ten years the school had won as many as four games. The next year, they won eight games and the league championship. The biggest game of Bill's high school coaching career was a 1958 matchup of Bay Area undefeateds, pitting his Huskies against the Lick High School Comets of San Francisco. The Huskies lost when their running back broke through and ran the length of the field for an apparent touchdown, only to fumble the ball on Lick's goal line and have a Lick defender pick it up and run it back almost a hundred yards the other way for the deciding score. It was the first loss in Bill's career that reduced him to tears in its aftermath, but far from the last. Even when he was just starting out, losses drove him into agony. And almost fifty years later, he would still wake up in the morning to memories of that lost high school fumble and painful questions about what he might have done to have made the game with Lick come out differently.

The year following Washington Union's championship turned into disaster when the school district was split, costing Walsh almost all of his returning lettermen, and the Huskies plunged to 1-8. Bill, however, was not planning to stay at Washington Union forever. This was no longer the reluctant adolescent his mother had to push into attending junior college. His previous lack of motivation had been replaced by a ravenous ambition, fueled by three fundamental conclusions he had already reached about his life. The first was his love for the game of football. He now had few doubts that coaching it was his true calling. The second was his disappointment with his own career as a player. Through a confluence of circumstances he had never managed to be the success he knew he could have been. That failure haunted him and he was determined never to allow himself to be sold short like that again. The third was his intention not to be his father, struggling in the throes of undistinguished mediocrity along the assembly line. Bill needed to accomplish big things and was prepared to do whatever that goal required.

During his off-seasons, he attended every coaching clinic he could get to, networking, learning the skills that led to bigger and better jobs. He practiced interviewing for potential positions and became known for his impressive skills at the blackboard, drawing *x*'s and *o*'s and teaching the game. After the 1959 season, he had an opportunity to put those to good use. Marv Levy, eventual coach of the NFL's Buffalo Bills, had been hired as the new head coach up at Cal and word soon got around he was looking for a local high school coach to join his staff. Bill's mentor, Bob Bronzan, arranged for Walsh to apply for the assistant's post. "We talked about the interview," Bronzan recalled, "and I told him, 'As soon as you can do it, get that conversation focused on defensing the pro spread, and make sure there's a blackboard in the room.' I knew if he got to the blackboard he had the job."

Bill apparently did just that and in 1960 moved Geri, Steve, and their new baby, Craig, from Newark up to Geri's old hometown of Walnut Creek, and commuted from there to Berkeley. Walsh stayed at Cal for three years, eventually rising to become defensive coordinator. "I wasn't ready for the job," Bill remembered, "and I floundered a bit. To be honest, I made a fool of myself trying desperately to succeed before I was really ready." Walsh described himself at the time as still "in many ways an immature young man." An example of that behavior was one weekend afternoon when he and Geri and another couple were driving in the Berkeley hills. A sports car came speeding past them, cut Walsh's car off, and when Bill honked, the driver flipped him the bird. Bill trailed the speeder until he entered a parking lot and then pulled in after him to settle accounts for the guy's one-finger salute. The sports car's driver was far larger than Bill and didn't hesitate to mouth off in response to Bill's challenge, so Bill knocked him on his ass with two punches, then drove off, leaving the offending driver dazed on the pavement.

At the same time he was continuing to grow up, Walsh was learning a lot about what kind of coach he wanted to be. "There was this religion of 'toughness' in coaching circles those days," he explained, "and all coaches were trying to be like marine drill sergeants and scare people into playing well. I got caught up in that for a while but I concluded it didn't come close to working. It was a kind of mass delusion. All the coaches thought the players loved them despite how badly they treated them, and all the players were doing was putting up with the coach so they could play football. Instead of loving and revering the coach, they couldn't stand him and were disgusted with him but they wanted to play football. They wanted the fellowship, they wanted the association, they wanted the excitement, and only put up with the bullying because they had to. Most played football in spite of the coach. By the time I left Cal I had decided that if you taught people to play the game better, that was real coaching—being a teacher rather than a thug." Sports psychologists would later describe Walsh's new approach as "non-aversive," and once he tried it out and found it worked, it would be one of his trademarks.

Bill's next stop after Cal was Stanford, where in 1963 John Ralston, future coach and general manager of the Denver Broncos, had been named head coach. Ralston had met Walsh at a coaching clinic and had coached against him when Bill was a graduate assistant running San Jose State's JV team. He already thought Bill "brilliant" and made him the first assistant he hired at Stanford, using him to recruit and coach the freshman team, and then run the defensive backfield. The staff Ralston assembled included not only Walsh, but also Mike White, future head coach at Cal and the University of Illinois; Jim Mora, future head coach of the NFL's New Orleans Saints and Indianapolis Colts; and Dick Vermeil, future head coach of UCLA and then the NFL's Philadelphia Eagles, St. Louis Rams, and Kansas City Chiefs. The interaction among them was seminal. The assistants were all living close to one another in Palo Alto, trying to get by on their $7,500 annual salaries and develop themselves for future opportunities. They and their families ate together regularly, with their wives taking turns with the cooking. Geri's Italian dinners were especially anticipated. All later remembered those days as Stanford assistants as "a special time."

Camaraderie aside, assistant coaching was a strenuous way to live. "The time demand was enormous," Mike White remembered. "There was always something to do or something we felt we had to do. You almost had to be obsessed to do it. It was just a 24/7 kind of job."

While the assistants bloomed under such demanding circumstances, it often had less favorable effects on their families, Bill's included. Certainly no one was more driven than he, in large part by his perspective on his own athletic career. Walsh felt he had gone unrealized as a player and was terrified that would happen as a coach as well. The result was an almost constant immersion in his craft. "Hour after hour and night after night," his son Steve would later recall, Bill "would be sitting in his den watching film. You'd want to say, 'Let's go do something.' But there was just no point in arguing because you couldn't win." And the better an assistant Bill became, the more frustrating his circumstance felt. "As a football thinker he was so bright," Dick Vermeil remembered, "that Bill was always ahead of the people he worked with. So he was always frustrated at being held back." At staff meetings, Bill would often be seen working his way across the blackboard, chalk dust flying as he laid out stratagems, and Ralston would be right behind him, frantically erasing his diagrams in hopes of keeping things more simple than Bill had imagined.

Walsh's next stop after Stanford was the pros. The offer that brought him there came from the Oakland Raiders in 1966. Over the next year of working with a team that played on Sundays he would learn more football than he had in all the previous decade and would also collide head-on with the first crisis of his coaching career. The job materialized after he met Al Davis, Oakland's managing general partner, at a banquet and the two spent an hour together in a parking lot conversation. Davis's head coach, John Rauch, then offered Bill a position as running backs coach, his first exclusive assignment to the offensive side of the ball.

Walsh would later describe the approach he learned in Oakland as "the foundation of my philosophy of offense." It had first been developed by the legendary Sid Gillman at the San Diego Chargers, then adopted by Al Davis during his previous tenure as Raiders head coach and handed on to Rauch. Sid Gillman was commonly referred to as "the father of the modern passing game," and Walsh found his first exposure to Gillman's system "an eye opener as to what was possible offensively. What everybody else was doing was primitive compared to Gillman's concepts." Gillman was the first to use the pass as the primary offensive weapon. "A football field is fifty-three and a third yards wide by a hundred long," Gillman explained. "We forced people to cover the [entire] width and the length." The result was a seemingly infinite array of passes, utilizing as many as five receivers on every play. "It was a fully dimensional approach," Bill observed, "utilizing the backs and tight ends much more extensively than other offenses. A typical NFL team might have three or four pass patterns for the halfback, but the Raiders' system had as many as twenty, and even they didn't use anything close to Gillman's whole playbook. To develop an understanding of it took time, but once learned, it was invaluable."

Other than the Gillman epiphany, however, Walsh's Raiders experience was the worst in his ten years as a coach. "The atmosphere there was not healthy, in terms of how they treated people and how they tried to get loyalty, trust, and respect out of their people. It was very formative in a very negative way. I learned a lot about how not to run a team."

The worst aspect of Bill's Oakland tenure in the immediate moment was simply the demands of the job itself. The hours expected of him were "impossible," far beyond anything he had experienced in his college jobs, and generated a personal crisis that almost ended his coaching career. Geri and the kids had continued to live in Palo Alto while he commuted and he was only back with them after they were asleep and before they woke. "You couldn't have a home or family under those conditions," Bill explained, "and it became clear to me I might very well lose mine if I kept on like that. Just to survive one year of it took a lot of growing up on my part. I was sometimes on the road for two weeks straight. It just wasn't a good life." And Geri eventually made it quite clear that she couldn't and wouldn't go on with it.

Forced to choose between the Raiders and his family, Bill Walsh resigned his job in Oakland and prepared to leave coaching. After a decade in the profession, he concluded, "there had been little financial reward or career developments to offset the sacrifices I had made," so he decided to look elsewhere. He thought he'd been wasting his life, and his disappointment at having reached that point sometimes felt like more than he could bear. In 1967, William Ernest Walsh filed an admissions application at the Stanford

Business School and waited for acceptance. His plan was to start his second career as soon as it arrived. In the meantime, Walsh supported his family by teaching a class at San Jose City College and overseeing the San Jose Apaches, a local franchise in the minor league Continental Football League, then being used by the NFL to develop talent.

As far as coaching football was concerned, Bill was convinced he had reached the end of his line more than a decade before he and Eddie D. ever crossed paths.

Bill Walsh (with hand on mouth) and
Paul Brown (in baseball cap) at Bengals practice

THE GREATEST DISAPPOINTMENT

A ll that changed with a completely unexpected phone call from Paul
Brown in early 1968. It turned Bill Walsh's life around and instantly re-
suscitated his career.

No one then in football had greater stature than Brown. *Sports Illustrated*
described his more than three decades on the sideline as "undoubtedly the
most successful coaching career, at all levels, in the history of football." Paul
Brown had started in Ohio in the 1930s as a high school coach whose teams
won 96 games, lost 9, and tied 3. He next coached Ohio State to three winning seasons during the first years of World War II and then went 15-5 over
two years with a military team from the Great Lakes Naval Training Station.
With the war over, he'd thrown his considerable talents into the insurgent
All-America Football Conference where the Cleveland franchise was named
after him and he served as its head coach, general manager, and chief executive officer. The Browns won four straight AAFC championships, then
merged into the NFL, where they won three more championships over the

next decade. Brown established a reputation along the way as "the greatest innovator in the history of the game." He was credited with, among other accomplishments, being the first head coach or general manager ever to employ year-round assistants, call plays from the sidelines, administer intelligence tests to prospective players, analyze films to prepare for games, and use times in the forty-yard dash to evaluate possible draftees. Brown had "implemented a highly organized and structured format that transformed the game into the modern era," Walsh pointed out. "His teams were noted for their almost mechanical, error-free precision."

Despite his legend, Paul Brown had been fired from his Browns fiefdom when a new owner acquired the franchise in 1963 amid complaints that the team's namesake was now over the hill. Quietly seething at the rebuke, Brown had been out of football for the last five years, refusing all job offers that didn't include an owner's share in the team he was being asked to coach. Now, however, he was mounting a comeback at the helm of an ownership group that had been awarded an NFL expansion franchise in Cincinnati, to be called the Bengals. This time, Brown, the new team's head coach, general manager, and lead owner, had "the last word on everything."

When he called Bill Walsh in the spring of 1968, Paul was piecing together a team and a coaching staff. Walsh was stunned at the overture. Apparently it was the result of several friends' recommendations but Bill had known nothing about it in advance. Right away, however, he realized that, whatever his plans for business school, he wouldn't be happy if he didn't pursue his calling as a coach at the game's highest level. Brown flew Walsh to Cincinnati for an interview. The Bengals' resident legend was looking for someone to help him develop a passing game; his first choice had already turned him down, and Walsh seemed a natural fit. He offered the Californian the job at twenty thousand dollars a year and Bill said yes.

Then Walsh returned to Palo Alto and had to convince Geri that this was the professional opportunity he'd been yearning for—one with enormous possibilities for the future—and that it would be a far more family-friendly venue than his stint in Oakland. He succeeded on both counts and in June the Walshes moved to the Midwest. "Before I went back there to meet with Paul Brown," Bill remembered, "I hardly knew where Cincinnati was. I knew it was in Ohio but I didn't know this was southern Ohio, on the north bank of the Ohio River, almost in Kentucky. The humidity in the summer was crushing coming from California, almost impossible to conceive of, but we adjusted. It was a good place to raise a family." Indeed, Cincinnati would become the closest thing his children had to a hometown and his third and final child, Elizabeth, was born there. Bill and Geri missed California but adapted. There was a large pine tree in the neighborhood where they settled and sometimes in the evening, after Bill came home from Bengals headquarters, they would walk down to it, inhaling its scent, and remember the Sierras and the state they'd left. The Walshes would stay in Cincinnati for almost eight years and when they finally moved, the uprooting would be traumatic.

For Bill, the work with the Bengals was everything he'd hoped for. His first year he was in charge of wide receivers and tight ends, quarterbacks were added during his second, and by the third year he was acting as what amounted to offensive coordinator, though without the official title. Perhaps the best part about the arrangement as far as Bill was concerned was that Brown, now in his sixties, gave his assistants enormous latitude in managing the team. The head coach didn't even stay in Cincinnati during the off-season. And when he was there, game planning and preparation was almost all left in the hands of his staff. One of the Bengals players in those years described Brown as "more of an administrator than a head coach," overseeing from a distance and tracking the team through the reports of his assistants. He had his own private locker room, kept a different schedule than his coaching staff, and was almost invisible to his team during the week.

That removed posture provided Bill an opportunity to expand his skills almost as if the team were his own. Brown even gave him unprecedented permission to stay home on Mondays to work out the offensive game plans and then come in and install them on Tuesday without even running them through Brown first. It was a seminal opportunity and Walsh took maximum advantage. Starting from nothing, the offense he developed combined the basics of Brown's old system with the Gillman approach he'd brought from the Raiders and the products of his own fertile imagination. Complex and multidimensional, it would be recognized as one of the best schemes in the NFL within four years of his tenure with the Bengals.

The offense's starting point was an attempt to compensate for the expansion franchise's lack of first-rate NFL talent, leading to an emphasis on getting the ball quickly to receivers running short routes before the defense could adjust to them. To facilitate that capacity to strike quickly in vacant territory, he trained his quarterbacks to throw timing patterns, predicated on the receiver reaching a designated spot after a designated number of seconds and often requiring the ball to be thrown before the intended receiver even made his final cut to reach his spot. Walsh enhanced the impact of that approach by flooding the defense with as many as five different potential receivers to cover, each timed to come clear in a prearranged progression that the quarterback followed. With each, Walsh used precision, positioning, and practice to overcome his players' deficiencies in speed and skill. Everything had to be exact. Walsh was "always very precise in everything he coached," one of the Bengals quarterbacks recalled. "He always told us over and over to 'be decisive.' He'd slap his left hand across his right palm when he said it. He was very diligent making sure we knew the progression of possible throws and he would drill it and drill it and drill it. He was a very detailed guy and it paid off." All three of the starting quarterbacks Bill coached at Cincinnati would eventually lead the league in completion percentage under his guidance. And as the team's talent improved, the system worked even better.

The trade-off for Walsh's having such a free hand at developing his offense was that for most of Walsh's stay with the Bengals, Brown received the credit for it. As much was apparent on game days: Walsh, unseen, was stationed up in the press box with a full view of the field, while Brown, wearing his trademark fedora, coat, and tie, prowled the sidelines in full view of the stadium and the television audience. When the Bengals had the ball, Walsh, unbeknownst to almost everyone watching, would select a play and tell it to the assistant sitting with him. That assistant would then call it down via closed circuit phone lines to an assistant on the sideline, who would relay it to Brown. Then Brown, with the thoughtful air of a grizzled offensive mastermind, would repeat the call to an offensive lineman he would then dispatch onto the field to carry the play to the quarterback waiting in the huddle as the cameras recorded the head coach's sideline ritual of apparent decision making. Brown would shuttle such messengers in and out all game long. "It was the most inefficient, cumbersome process imaginable," Bill explained, "but it preserved the fiction that Paul was pulling all the strings." Brown received credit for the offensive system when, as Bill remembered it, "he wasn't even sure what the system was." And as the once woeful Bengals became an offensive powerhouse, stories began appearing that marveled at how the seemingly ageless Ohio legend was once again on the NFL's cutting edge.

Bill accepted that arrangement because he was grateful for the opportunity and he had developed a genuine fondness for Brown, even though Paul was notoriously cold, standoffish, quick to take offense, and merciless when he did. For his part, Walsh was open about describing Brown as his "mentor." Brown in turn seemed to respond to Walsh with affection, even coming over to the Walshes' house for dinner on one occasion, a virtually unprecedented familiarity. Bill also assumed that the arrangement would not be permanent. In 1971, Brown gave him a $6,500 raise—an enormous sum in the pay scales of the day—and explained to his assistant that "I think you know what I had in mind." Walsh took that to be a declaration of Brown's intention to name Walsh head coach whenever he retired from the sideline—a sentiment Brown apparently repeated several more times over the next few seasons—and Bill coached his final four years at Cincinnati under that assumption.

In his daydreams, Walsh pictured himself commanding the Bengals on game day and was convinced the realization of his fondest professional dream was only a brief wait away.

By this point, Bill had passed forty years old and all of his previous callowness had disappeared. Still fit and handsome, his once sandy hair had turned prematurely silver in what would eventually become his signature stately, professional look, and his confidence had burgeoned. "After four or five years with Paul Brown," he remembered, "I realized I was ready to be a head coach. I looked around me and felt because of the experience I'd had, I could organize and orchestrate and plan and prepare and do all the things a head coach does as well as anybody. Some of it was learning from Paul's example and some of it was from my own independent thinking, but I was sure I was ready. I didn't make any secret of my feelings and, looking back on it, I wouldn't be surprised if that was somehow threatening to Paul. Paul was not someone who looked out for his assistants. He looked out for what he thought were his own and his club's interests and expected his assistants to adjust accordingly." In Walsh's case, that included Brown's repeated denials that any other teams had expressed an interest in him as a head coach, even though they had and he'd denied them permission to talk to Walsh, then concealed the approaches from Walsh himself.

By the 1975 season, however, the fiction surrounding the Bengals offense had worn through and the media began singling out Walsh as its architect, identifying him as a hot prospect for head coach, and creating, Bill noted, "a subtle difference in the way Paul treated me." At the same time, the media began to speculate about Brown stepping away from coaching. Brown himself refused to address his possible retirement from the sideline and, according to Bill, "near the end of the season, he became quite mysterious" about it. The Bengals won their division that year, then lost in the playoffs to the Raiders and two days later, New Year's Eve, the mystery of Brown's future was resolved. A local sports columnist called Bill at home with the news that the team was releasing an announcement the next day. Paul was resigning as head coach, the columnist explained, and he was naming Bill Johnson, the Bengals offensive line coach, to succeed him. Brown was out of town, as was Johnson, and neither could be reached for comment. What did Bill think about the move?

For several moments, Walsh couldn't find any words to respond.

Years later, when the hurt was scarred over, Bill had a ready analysis in response to the question, why? "When push came to shove," he speculated, "Paul just couldn't bring himself to turn it over to me. There was something like jealousy involved, mixed with a kind of resentment. I had my own ideas and thoughts about everything, including personnel and the rest. He just couldn't figure out how he was going to handle me if I became head coach. He must have been struggling emotionally to come to terms with his own retirement and the thought of losing control to me was just too much for him."

Walsh had no such analysis that New Year's Eve, however. This was "the greatest disappointment" of his life and he was overrun with pain and humiliation and almost panic. When he got off the phone with the columnist, Bill immediately told Geri they were going to have to leave, sounding very much like a man looking for a place to hide. But there was no such option in the immediate moment. "Paul was out of touch, purposely," Walsh remembered, "and he had Bill out of touch, purposely. He had put out a press release and he wanted people to digest the news; then he'd return to Cincinnati in a few days. Meanwhile, I was inundated by calls from the media because I was the only person available to speak for the Bengals."

Patiently, Walsh answered the calls and did all the interviews after the TV trucks showed up in his driveway. He told them that Bill Johnson was a good coach and a good friend and that it was a good move and the organization wouldn't skip a beat. His face revealed none of his feelings, but all the while he was dying inside. "Sometimes, I didn't think I could live through it," Bill explained. "At that moment, I was truly broken. It was crushing. I was very, very lost." He turned to his friends for consolation but he was almost inconsolable. "The rejection was devastating for him," one remembered. "We spent a lot of time together afterward and he was completely distraught. He was devastated to the point he had no idea where to turn. He didn't know if he could even continue in football."

Several days into the new year, Paul Brown returned to town and he and Bill had their first and last extended encounter on the subject. Bill was close to tears throughout. Brown, now as cold as Walsh had ever seen him, offered no explanation but did make it clear what he wanted to happen next. He expected Bill to remain loyal to him and the organization, which meant staying on to call the plays and run the offense just as he had been. He was willing to give him a raise, but Brown announced in no uncertain terms that he would not allow Walsh to leave.

Bill pointed out that his contract was up in another week and declared that he was leaving and there was nothing Brown could do to stop him. "I couldn't possibly have stayed," Bill remembered. "To have done so would have been tantamount to giving up my career. I would have been relegated to just being some journeyman offensive technician and nothing more for the rest of my professional life." By that point, he had already worked out a deal with the San Diego Chargers.

Brown was livid at the defiance, immediately interpreting it as a personal betrayal, and made it clear he intended to punish Walsh for his response. Paul Brown's last words to Bill amounted to a threat. He would never be an NFL head coach, the legend vowed. Never.

Bill Walsh left Cincinnati shortly thereafter, now driven by his need to prove his former mentor wrong.

For his part, Paul Brown did everything in his power to make sure his threat came true. "His vindictiveness was really something," Bill remembered. "He set about trying to destroy my career and discredit me any way he could." Within months, two NFL teams who had Bill on their short list for head coaching jobs backed off after talking to the Bengals' owner and being told that his former assistant was just "too soft" to lead an NFL team. Brown told another inquiring team that Walsh was "unfit" to be a head coach and advised yet another that they "shouldn't touch Walsh with a ten-foot pole."

A year later, shortly after Stanford University hired Walsh away from his assistant's job at the Chargers and finally gave him the opportunity to run a football program, he received an envelope in the mail, without a return address, but postmarked Cincinnati. Inside was a clipping from the *Cincinnati Enquirer* announcing Walsh's hiring at Stanford. Scribbled across it in a familiar-looking hand were the words "burnt bridges." There was no accompanying note or signature to identify the sender, but for the rest of his life Bill was convinced that it too had come from Paul Brown.

Eddie DeBartolo and Bill Walsh, January 1979

‖‖‖‖ ‖‖‖‖ ‖‖‖‖

7

OPPORTUNITY KNOCKS

No doubt Eddie D. knew of Paul Brown's opinion before his get-acquainted meeting with Bill at the Fairmont on the second Saturday in December. Brown was still too towering a figure in Youngstown to be overlooked and by the end of 1978 the Bengals' owner's attitude toward his former protégé was hardly a secret among the NFL circles in which the DeBartolos moved. On top of that, DeBartolo Sr. had been calling around about Walsh since Eddie first raised the Stanford coach's name, and even though Eddie's dad apparently didn't talk with Brown directly, he was certainly told what Brown thought. According to one source close to the situation, Senior was "not warm" to the possible hiring and told his son as much. That Eddie pursued Bill anyway is testimony to just how anxious he was about the state of his franchise and how intent he was on rescuing it himself. Eddie also knew that other teams were nibbling around Walsh despite Brown's negativity and was likely spurred by the worry that someone else might hire him before he had the chance. In any case, Paul Brown's criticism was soon moot.

Walsh was met by the broadcaster Ron Barr in the Fairmont's lobby late that Saturday morning and the two went up to DeBartolo's suite. Barr introduced Bill to Eddie and then left them alone with the sumptuous room service spread Eddie had ordered. Within ten minutes, Eddie D. was convinced he wanted Bill Walsh to be the Forty Niners' next head coach and Bill could see that he felt that way. "I just knew that he was the guy," Eddie remembered.

It was no surprise to those who had already experienced Bill that he made a great impression on Eddie D. For starters, he looked the role. Tall, tanned, and handsome, topped with silver hair that curled over his ears, Walsh exuded a kind of natural magnetism that was deeply attractive. He was also a great talker who believed in communication and was relentlessly articulate. And while obviously smart, his intelligence was usually leavened in social situations by a sense of humor that was more often than not self-deprecating, as well as playful, making him seem friendly and accessible. One on one, Walsh's attention was focused and immediately created a sense of connection. His pale blue eyes, one acquaintance remembered, "seemed to have hands in them that reached out and grabbed you when he focused them on you." Bill's confidence that Saturday at the Fairmont was palpable, as it almost always was whenever Bill felt he was on display. All in all, he was nothing if not impressive. One of the lawyers later involved in the hiring process recalled, "The moment he walked into the room, you got the feeling that he had presence, that he had style. He seemed to have a sense of awareness of what was expected of him."

For his part, Bill found Eddie "very young" and seemingly "a great guy." DeBartolo was always at his best as a host and bent over backward to make Walsh comfortable. Bill had already checked Eddie out with one of his friends on the current Forty Niners coaching staff and had been told "the jury was still out" on the kid. He was enthusiastic and obviously had more than enough money, but just how he would be to work for wasn't clear (nor was it exactly clear what role his father would play in the situation). Still, Bill's friend judged it "a hell of an opportunity." Nothing in the way Eddie came off that morning at the Fairmont set off any alarms. More than anything, Bill was impressed with Eddie D.'s "charm."

Eddie remembered the meeting's lasting a little less than an hour, during which "we talked about football [and] we talked about philosophy. We talked about family, about values." In the course of the conversation, Bill made two points about the possible Niners job that he considered non-negotiable. The first was that he would not work for or with Joe Thomas under any conditions. The second was that he would have to have complete authority over football operations. "The organization had to have a single figure with total control to have any chance of correcting the melee that existed under Thomas," Bill explained. He wanted a straight line between him and Eddie in the organizational chart, with no intermediaries. Less than two years earlier, when explaining why he was terminating Monte Clark, DeBartolo had described such a concentration of power, combining coaching and personnel functions, as irresponsible, unacceptable, and plain bad business, but with Bill he made no such objections.

Eddie offered Walsh the job before their first meeting was over. Bill tentatively accepted and the two agreed to an informal understanding to which neither was yet bound, subject to working out the details over the next few weeks while Walsh finished his Stanford obligations at the Bluebonnet Bowl. The plan was to meet again after that game and strike a formal deal. In the meantime, the fact of their discussion and all of its content were to remain a secret.

The Bluebonnet Bowl pitting Walsh's Stanford Cardinal against the University of Georgia Bulldogs was played on New Year's Eve. Eddie was back in Youngstown, hosting a party at his mansion and the televised game was one of the event's planned entertainments. A number of his guests gathered with him in front of the TV in his den. By then, he and Bill had talked several times briefly on the phone and their deal still seemed to be on track. Despite the ongoing secrecy of their contact, it was known to almost all of those watching in the den that the Stanford coach was "the offensive genius" DeBartolo was about to hire for his hapless Forty Niners. Eddie was anticipating a flood of congratulations on his choice as soon as his friends saw his new man coach.

From that standpoint, the game looked like it was going to be yet one more embarrassment for Eddie. Georgia came out and steamrolled Stanford in the first half. Walsh's team could barely even get a pass off and had hardly moved the ball at all by the time it went into the locker room at half-time, trailing 16–0. Bill then gathered his team and gave what he remembered as "one of the best halftime talks I had ever given. I talked about my team as people and about their pride in their university and how millions would be watching and all that kind of stuff. We just roared out of the locker room." Then they kicked off and Georgia took the ball right down the field and made it 22–0. Georgia players were now making mocking gestures across at the Stanford sidelines, dismissing the Californians as hopelessly effeminate.

Back in Youngstown, the guests had cleared out of the den and several of them ribbed Eddie about this new stiff he was about to hire to go with all those he'd already fired. Walsh himself looked up at the scoreboard, visualized Eddie watching with all his friends, and thought, "There goes that Forty Niners job."

But the game has four quarters and Georgia had started celebrating too soon. Bill adjusted his beleaguered offense to account for the ferocious blitz being thrown at it and the Cardinal began moving the ball with short passes to the backs and wideouts. Walsh's defense produced two key turnovers and suddenly the game wasn't over at all. Instead, Stanford scored once and then again and again and again. Eddie was celebrating in front of his TV when Stanford took the lead 25–22. The game ended with the Cardinal driving for yet another score. Eddie D. emerged from his den feeling redeemed by his faith in Bill and was quick to chortle in the faces of the previous doubters.

Emotionally, that victorious Stanford comeback stood out as Bill and Eddie's first mutual experience. "It sort of connected the both of us," Walsh remembered, "even though we were halfway across the country from each other when it happened."

Stanford's team landed back in the Bay Area on January 1, and Channel 4 dispatched Ron Barr down to Bill's house on campus to do a live feed from his front lawn for the evening news. By then, the San Francisco papers were full of speculation about Walsh's future and whether or not he might be the Niners' next coach. "Bill gave a kind of vanilla response indicating that nothing was happening but that he was open to all possibilities," Barr recalled. When that live spot was done, the two of them went inside Bill's

Bill Walsh meets the press as the Forty Niners' new coach, January 1979

house and taped a second interview about how excited Bill was to have been given the Niners job. Barr planned to use the tape after the hiring had been announced.

As close as that eventuality was, however, no one had yet told Joe Thomas. With speculation of Walsh's hiring now all over the media, reporters found Thomas in Hawaii scouting a college all-star game. Asked if he'd been fired, Thomas responded, "I don't know anything about it. I'm still the general manager as far as I'm concerned. Before I left [for Hawaii] I had a long talk with our owner. He said I'd be back."

Eddie let Thomas in on the secret with a phone call the day that story ran.

That same day, Sunday, January 7, 1979, Eddie and Bill met again at the Fairmont to seal their deal. This time DeBartolo was accompanied by his lawyer and the DeBartolo Corp. executive who was his father's right-hand man. The last detail to be worked out was what Bill would be paid. Before they left Youngstown, DeBartolo Senior had taken the lawyer aside and instructed him to make sure Eddie didn't offer anything more than $120,000 a year, but Bill had another figure in mind. When Eddie cut to the chase and asked Walsh how much he wanted, Bill thought for a moment. The previous year the Rams had agreed to $150,000 as part of their aborted approach and Bill intended to ask for the same. But as he started to say the figure, he added $10,000 to it in an impulsive reaction that surprised him. When the lawyer heard $160,000, he got ready to haggle, but Eddie preempted him.

Junior, caught up in the excitement of the moment, was in no mood to bargain. "You've got it," he snapped.

Both Eddie D. and his lawyer would refrain from mentioning the number to his father for weeks to come.

And with that, Bill Walsh was hired. The last obstacle had been cleared and the opportunity he'd been seeking his entire professional life was now his.

Bill left the Fairmont with a smile on his face that would eventually become familiar to the fans of his new team, late in games when the Niners had just finished off their opponent and the outcome was no longer at issue. The grin showed no teeth—just a line of lips across his face with both ends turned up only slightly—but joy filled his cheeks and eyes to bursting. In that moment, forty-seven years old and standing on the front porch of football history, Bill Walsh was positively radiant.

THE MIRACLE

John McVay and Bill Walsh

‖‖‖‖   ‖‖‖‖   ‖‖‖‖

MARCHING ORDERS

t the time the Forty Niners introduced their new head coach to the assembled press in the Hyatt House hotel on San Francisco's Union Square, the possibility of his new team winning a Super Bowl within three years was not even discussed. Indeed, had Bill Walsh so much as hinted at such a prospect, he would have been laughed out of the room. Bill was only secretly hoping to get the team up to respectability during that span. Everyone there would have agreed with him that more than that would require nothing short of a miracle.

Certainly the headquarters Walsh inherited down in Redwood City showed few signs of incipient dynasty. There were high schools with better facilities. "It was a dump," one assistant coach remembered, "easily the worst in the NFL." Located at 711 Nevada Street, in the heart of a suburban neighborhood forty-five minutes south of San Francisco, the Niners' offices and practice fields occupied a corner of a community park operated by Redwood City's recreation department. The NFL franchise had been on a lease there since the late 1950s, when it had moved south from an even smaller space at San Francisco's old Kezar Stadium after Candlestick Park had been built. There wasn't enough acreage allotted to the Niners for a full hundred-yard football field, so the team made do with two fifty-yard fields side by side, one natural grass, the other synthetic turf, both surrounded by cyclone fencing. During heavy rains, the fields flooded so deeply that the team had to move to the higher ground where the community's youth soccer teams played.

The headquarters building itself—a gutted tract home onto which a second story and additional single story wing had been added, then painted red—was typical of the league's mom-and-pop era with its smaller rosters and coaching staffs, but that era was long since past. At a distance, the structure could have been mistaken for an abandoned grammar school or a run-down motel. Inside, the headquarters seemed even smaller. There was a locker room downstairs the size of a large studio apartment, next to a meeting room not quite big enough to hold the entire squad, so team meetings always involved several players standing out in the hall. The trainers facility amounted to several benches and two old whirlpool baths. The shower room included only six shower heads and the water turned scalding if anyone flushed a toilet. "The weight room was a joke," one player remembered. "Hundreds of colleges had better ones." Rehab equipment for the injured was shoehorned into a corner near the lockers. Position meetings took place either in several rooms the size of residential bedrooms or in the larger meeting room divided into cubicles by temporary partitions. The floors were plywood. The coaching and administrative offices were upstairs, with Bill having one of the private offices and Eddie the other, usually padlocked in his absence. The assistant coaches shared a larger room whose walls were covered with blackboards. If Bill wanted to contact one of his staff, all he had to do was speak up to be heard, even at the other end of the building. If the locker room downstairs was quiet, the players could listen to the coaches talking on the floor above.

One of Bill's first visitors to his upstairs office was Edward DeBartolo Sr. Senior arrived with a phalanx of bodyguards—"right out of *The Godfather*," according to one observer—prompting one assistant coach to joke to another about not making any sudden moves for fear of being shot. It was Senior and Bill's first encounter and they hit it off right away. Eddie's father thought Bill was an intellectual and liked that. For his part, Bill was impressed with Senior's combination of patience and tough-mindedness. "He was a very special man," Bill explained, "a total pragmatist. Whatever the circumstance, he always made the most out of it. Over the years, he became a source of counsel and we often talked privately about how things were going."

That first day, Senior's advice was succinct. Despite the limitations of their headquarters, he wanted everything the franchise did to be "first-class," no exceptions.

And those marching orders never changed.

Bill's initial concentration, once he'd signed up his assistant coaches, was on finding a general manager. His original understanding with Eddie had been that all decisions about football, including personnel, would be his and that he would find a general manager to run the larger organization's business and that GM would report to Eddie directly. The arrangement was at variance with the predominant NFL model in which the GM controlled personnel and hired the coach, not vice versa, and that immediately created difficulties for Bill's search. He approached executives in Miami, Los Angeles, Seattle, and Baltimore and they all wanted more authority and a far more traditional arrangement. Plus they were extremely leery of tying their fates to the Niners. One said quite frankly, "There's a smell to this organization I don't like." Others were more circumspect, but it didn't take long for Bill to conclude that "good people didn't want to take on such an overwhelming task" and that he might have to rethink his approach.

The one volunteer for the job came out of his own organization and generated the first minor crisis of Walsh's tenure. Upon learning of the GM search, the team's incumbent head of scouting confronted Bill at the Nevada Street offices. The scout was so upset he was shaking and began insisting that he be hired, vehemently listing all his qualifications. The general manager's job was, he thought, his due. And if Walsh did not agree, he was going to lead the entire scouting staff in a mass resignation. A half dozen of the team's scouts were in town in preparation for that spring's NFL draft, staying at a nearby motel. The head scout claimed that they all wanted him to become general manager and if he returned to them empty-handed, they would all quit in sympathy. He offered Bill a day to give him a response.

It was a critical moment in the draft process to lose his scouts, but Walsh didn't hesitate. "I'll tell you what," he told the head scout. "I can give you an answer right now. You're not going to be general manager and you can take your fucking scouts anywhere you want them."

The head scout turned on his heel and left to make good on his threat, but an hour later the other scouts called Bill from their motel. They told him they had no intention of quitting and wanted to keep their jobs. Bill said that was fine and told them to come over to headquarters and go back to work. The head scout was quickly replaced and, after that, wasn't heard from again.

Shortly thereafter, Bill flew east to meet with Eddie D. in Miami, where the owner was staying in the Doral Hotel. Bill reported to him about his abortive search for a general manager and expressed pessimism about their original plan. Instead, Walsh had a new suggestion. Why didn't he just enlarge his own responsibilities and take the general manager title as well as director of football operations? He'd find someone to help with administrative detail, but with this consolidation, the entire organization would be under a single operational authority, which just might be the only way to accomplish the reorganization that success would require.

Eddie D. jumped at the offer without further discussion. "Great," he said. "Let's do that."

Eddie seemed relieved to have the issue dealt with and not the least bit concerned that he had just awarded total control of his NFL franchise to a man who barely two years earlier had seemed destined to be an assistant coach for the rest of his life, had yet to log a down from scrimmage as an NFL head coach, and had virtually no history as an administrator.

In retrospect, it would be hard to overestimate just how important that move was to Bill Walsh. "If I had a word for Bill," one of his former players remembered years later, "it would be *control*. It's almost impossible to think of him without it." He was by character an orchestrator, a man with an artist's sensibility who needed to arrange all of the little pieces of any activity into a functioning whole of his own design. Decades later, on his deathbed, as Walsh took the final sacraments and discussed his approaching end with his priest, the cleric felt he should caution Bill that this was not a process he would be able to choreograph, and he urged him to relax and leave this last chapter to God. It wasn't easy. Control was at the man's core.

Having control now as he prepared for his professional ascent not only meant that he could do whatever he deemed necessary to build the organization but also cleared the psychological space in which his genius could flourish. Without it, he might have been just a very good football coach and nothing more.

This control, however, would not be without its flip side. Every detail of the franchise was now Bill Walsh's responsibility and, driven and obsessive as he was, he could never quite free himself of the demands, even when he would desperately need to.

Walsh's ultimate reputation as The Genius would rest on three pillars of accomplishment. The first was his performance as architect and administrator of a football dynasty. In effect, Walsh was now a CEO, though the business of football in those days was still secondary to the game and the skills involved in franchise administration were less the financial management and marketing of the future NFL than the logistical support and community relations that had characterized the league for the previous decade. For guidance in this new role during those first few months, Bill relied mostly on what he had learned under Paul Brown and, to a lesser degree, what he'd picked up from Al Davis, but much of what he did was simply his homegrown vision of how things ought to be.

Walsh began constructing his organization that January, relying on one premise and two operational principles. The premise was that all the components of the Forty Niners' structure had to be a single unitary construction, all pointed toward the same direction, all generating the same energy, interdependent in the goal of creating a great football team, from the janitors on up. Everything it did would be funneled toward advancing the Niners to the Super Bowl, the team a seamless extension of the organization that supported it. Walsh's first operational principle was that everyone in the organization had a role to play and needed to devote themselves to playing that role as well as they could. And while the organization had multiple roles, it had no strata. Everyone, big or small, was of import, equally deserving of respect and equally responsible for succeeding. His second principle was that everyone who had any kind of contact with the organization must be afforded "credibility, respect, and dignity." He wanted no one making enemies unnecessarily and put all employees on notice that they must "demonstrate this Forty Niners approach toward anyone they deal with," no matter how trying that might be. There was a Forty Niners Way and it had to be embodied by the entire organization in all its dealings.

That said, he next laid out all the organization's job titles in "the Red Book," a catalog he kept in a red binder, including a written description of everyone's role and responsibilities so no one would be confused about what was expected of them. Many of those slots were vacant in the aftermath of the housecleaning that accompanied Joe Thomas's departure, and Bill began filling them. At the executive level he was looking for people he felt comfortable with and felt he could count on under pressure; people who had "functional intelligence," noting that "one person who is not very bright but very aggressive can destroy an organization"; people who knew how the NFL operated; and "people who would be enthusiastic and inquisitive and thrive on work." Once he hired them, one employee remembered, "Bill wasn't a micromanager. He left them alone to do what needed to be done however they chose to do it, but he expected them to deliver and let them know in no uncertain terms if they didn't."

Perhaps no one Bill Walsh hired in those early days demonstrated all the qualities Bill was looking for more than John McVay, the man who became Bill's principal administrative helpmate for the next decade and perhaps, after Bill himself, the primary reason he was so successful at rebuilding the franchise.

Like Walsh, McVay had begun as a coach. An Ohioan by birth, he'd played college football there at Miami University (of Ohio) for the legendary Woody Hayes and then for the legendary Ara Parseghian before coaching high school ball around the state. After three years as an assistant at Michigan State under Duffy Daugherty, he returned to Ohio as the head coach at the University of Dayton. There he met Eddie DeBartolo, who was in town working at his family's Dayton Mall and had started hanging around with some of the players on McVay's squad. McVay eventually left Dayton for the World Football League, a short-lived effort to compete with the NFL that went belly-up in 1975. From there, the New York Giants had hired him to work in their front office, then dragooned him into the interim head coaching job after their head coach was fired in the middle of the season. By 1979, his contract with the Giants had run out and he was looking around for work. He'd first met Bill the year before, when the Giants had brought the then Stanford coach out for a seminar with their staff about offensive football.

Both Walsh and DeBartolo wanted to add McVay to their team, but Eddie was the one who made the first call. "I'd known Eddie," McVay remembered, "and I was talking to him on the phone and congratulated him on hiring Bill. He wanted to know what I was going to do now and I said I didn't know. He said, 'Why don't you come to work for us?' That's how it started. After I talked to Bill I came out and began work immediately." Among the official titles McVay would work under during his Forty Niners career were director of player personnel, director of football operations, vice president for football administration, administrative vice president, and assistant to the president.

"John was the person who assured stability for the organization," Walsh remembered. "He was so solid. Whatever role he had he carried it out beautifully. He had a lot of input about personnel or any other category of things to do with the football team. He had an administrative role with other employees and provided marvelous counsel for me all the way through. I don't know what I'd have done without John McVay. He was nonconfrontational and nonabrasive to the extreme, never upstaging anyone, but if he didn't agree with me, he'd tell me straight out. His desk was right next to my office, so our relationship was constant and always close. He was the glue that held the organization together from the time he first arrived."

Asked to describe his own role, McVay explained that he "did all the things Bill needed done but didn't want to do or didn't have time to do himself. I watched the organization so he could concentrate on coaching, and I gave him someone to talk to when he needed [it]."

Asked to describe Bill's role, McVay chuckled. "Bill was King," he explained, "simple as that. All the bucks stopped on his desk."

Though never imperious, King Bill did bring a touch of the imperial to his presence around 711 Nevada Street from the very beginning. He left no doubt this ragamuffin castle was now his domain. No detail was beyond his purview and he exercised an almost rigid adherence to his own vision. Bill wanted what he wanted, wouldn't settle for less, and could be, in the words of one of his coworkers, "a real prick about it." He expected the headquarters to be neat and staged regular inspections to make sure all the desks upstairs and down were free of piled papers or accumulated junk. He could not walk past a crooked picture hung on the wall, compulsively straightening every one he encountered. Eventually assistant coaches started secretly tilting them just to watch him stop and put them right. Once in those first months, when Bill was headed out of town for a few days, he left a custodian with instructions about some other pictures he wanted hung while he was gone. When he returned and found the task still undone, he fired the custodian the next day.

The Bill Walsh era had begun: everybody was now going to be held accountable.

Dwight Clark and Joe Montana

9

AN EYE FOR TALENT

mportant as the front office organization was, talented players were the franchise's bottom line and, even though they'd had limited opportunities to assess their roster up close, both Bill Walsh and John McVay were in complete agreement about how deficient their team was almost as soon as they moved into 711 Nevada Street.

"We were acknowledged as the least talented, least experienced team in the NFL," Walsh remembered, "and with less chance to improve than an expansion franchise. I had never been with an organization with such poor talent. Even the Chargers, who had been considered one of the NFL's weakest teams when I got there, possessed superior talent, in quality and quantity, to the Forty Niners. The Bengals in their first year had been better as well. The list of what we didn't have just went on and on."

McVay's analysis was more succinct. "We were pitiful," he explained. "Simply improving was a monumental task."

And there weren't a lot of sources for acquiring the talent with which to do so. Free agency in its modern sense did not yet exist. NFL policy in 1979 bound players to their teams in perpetuity or until the teams relinquished their rights to them, so it wasn't possible to bring in talented veterans whose contracts had expired elsewhere. Such players weren't free to negotiate with anyone but their previous employer. The only free agents on the market were either college players who weren't drafted or veterans who had been cut by their previous teams. Trades were another possibility, but the Niners had few if any players other teams wanted. That left the draft as the team's most significant hope for betterment.

First implemented in 1936, the draft—described by Walsh as "the very foundation of the National Football League"—established an orderly process by which the NFL's teams could allocate among themselves the players hoping to enter the league each year from the amateur collegiate ranks, without having to bid against one another for their services. Each spring, the teams went through this talent pool, choosing players one at a time in the reverse order of the teams' finish in the previous year's standings, worst team first and so on. Once selected, a prospective player could negotiate only with the franchise that chose him. The number of rounds the teams cycled through varied over history, but the 1979 draft would include twelve rounds, divvying up 336 players twenty-eight ways. The average player chosen would last less than five years in the league. Teams that had successful drafts would manage to get at least two years of significant contributions from 80 percent of their choices and most teams weren't that successful. Despite the draft's dominant role, it was by all statistical analyses a crapshoot. Thanks to their 2-14 record in 1978, the Forty Niners would have had 1979's first choice, theoretically giving them a chance at the very best player available, but Joe Thomas had traded that choice for the rights to O. J. Simpson, so the Niners, starved for talent, would have to begin with the second round, the twenty-ninth choice overall.

Though no one yet knew it—including Walsh himself—the Forty Niners' most significant advantage in that process would be their "king." Bill Walsh would become a draft day legend over the coming decade—perhaps, according to Dick Vermeil, then head coach of the Philadelphia Eagles, "the best ever at manipulating the draft to his ends." Walsh had, according to John McVay, "a keen eye for talent. He was just uncanny. I've never seen anyone with an eye to match his." Bill would build and rebuild his team three times over the next decade, using the draft as his principal implement.

And along the way, he would select three players who would eventually be recognized as perhaps the best ever to play their respective positions in the history of the NFL. In the end, his work identifying and accumulating talent would be the second pillar supporting his enormous reputation.

Walsh's unparalleled draft day accomplishments would be all the more remarkable for just how complex the process of determining NFL talent was. Unlike sports such as baseball or basketball, where skills are far more obvious and generalized, professional football is a specialized game in which each of twenty-four positions and the skills required to play it differ depending on circumstances that vary from team to team. "You can take a baseball player," one NFL veteran pointed out, "give him a different hat, the same bat, and he's going to hit the ball. Same with basketball. But football is a game of systems and different situation-type players." A star in the NFL, if on a different team with different roles and expectations, might not be a star at all, or even stay in the league very long. Predicting success in football, as Walsh did, was a three-dimensional process, requiring not only an assessment of athletic talent but also the ability to project a player into the situations in which he would be used. And, at this, no one was better than Bill, aided immeasurably by the fact that he wasn't picking players for someone else to coach but players he would put to use himself.

Walsh began making his legend right out of the chute, in 1979.

First, he established a process. The starting point was the individual reports on hundreds of prospects amassed by the team's scouts over the course of the college football season, then filtered through Bill's own requirements. "I instructed everyone scouting that I wanted to know what the redeeming quality is that this person has that will help us win," Walsh explained. "Don't just tell me what he can't do. Tell me what he can do. Can he cover kickoffs? Will he be alert and ready if ever called upon? That quality alone might be a value and is worth treating as a skill in itself. Don't just say he can't do this and can't do that. Find every player's possible contribution and identify the reason to take him rather than just the reasons not to."

The scouts' reports would then be amplified by the investigations of the team's assistant coaches, operating under the same instructions. Many franchises didn't involve assistants in the evaluation process—following the oft-repeated dictum "Coaches coach and scouts scout"—but Bill belonged to the opposite school. When he was at Cincinnati, Paul Brown had always dispatched his assistants to watch college games on Saturdays to assess prospects, and Walsh maintained that approach at the Niners. Among the assistant coaches' assignments was sorting through all of the videotapes of potential picks and collecting the ten best and ten worst plays of each for Bill's perusal. Then Bill met separately with the scouts, having them rate each prospect, and repeated the process with only the coaches. After that, he gathered both groups together and did it all again. "We created an atmosphere in meetings in which a scout or coach was able to express himself completely," Bill explained. "If he overstated or understated in any category, he could change his opinion later without being criticized. We were interested only in results. They could change their mind without being ridiculed. Everyone was expected to participate."

The end product of these sessions was "the board," a complete listing of every player the scouts and assistants rated worthy of consideration, including a projection of the round in which they expected each of the players to be chosen. There was also a breakdown by position, with particular emphasis on the areas Bill identified as having immediate needs.

The two areas at the top of Walsh's list for 1979 were offensive speed and quarterback. The first category would eventually yield James Owens, a running back from UCLA whom Bill projected turning into a wide receiver, picked with the first draft choice Walsh ever made, at the top of the second round. Owens was a high hurdles champion in college as well as a football player, but would prove so injury-prone that he was gone from the Forty Niners in two years, from the league in six, and survives in NFL memory only as a trivia question.

Bill Walsh's search for a quarterback, however, would yield the cornerstone of the Niners' approaching dynasty.

At the time, the Niners had only one quarterback on their roster, Steve DeBerg, who'd played college ball at San Jose State and been with the Niners since 1977. "We thought Steve DeBerg just might be our quarterback for the future," Walsh remembered. "I had not had time to evaluate Steve, but all reports were very positive. He could throw the ball with accuracy and feel. We were looking for somebody in the draft who would at least have the potential to be his backup. If the new quarterback was good enough to outperform Steve and replace him at some point, so much the better." Bill insisted on personally eyeballing the leading quarterback possibilities that spring and his principal helper in checking them out was his new quarterbacks coach, Sam Wyche.

Sam and Bill had first met when Walsh joined the Cincinnati Bengals. Wyche had shown up as a free agent at the team's first training camp, having played quarterback for Furman University and spent the previous year with the minor league Wheeling Ironmen. "I remember walking down the hall during training camp in the dormitory where the coaches occupied the first floor and the players the second and third," Wyche recounted, "and I walked by Bill's room where the door was open and he was lying on his bed between practices. He yelled for me to come in and we talked. It was the first time a coach had ever spent his free time with me. From that moment on I had loyalty to him." Despite Wyche's weak arm, Walsh kept Wyche on the Bengals as a backup through three seasons. "I developed him to the upper reaches of mediocrity," Bill would later joke. Sam went on to backup status at four other NFL teams, eventually winning a Super Bowl ring with the Washington Redskins. By then Bill had targeted him as a potential coach. "He was bright, had a great sense of humor, and had a real organizational command," Bill explained, "everything you'd want in a coach." Walsh tried to recruit Wyche for his staff at Stanford, but Sam was tied up in a sporting goods business he'd started in South Carolina and declined. When Bill tried again for the Niners two years later, Wyche signed on. This was his first full-time coaching job.

For the quarterback search, the Niners draft apparatus had identified fourteen prospects deserving further examination. Sam would usually make the first visit, working the prospect out, and if he considered the player worthy of a look from Bill, Bill would follow. Walsh's initial favorite was Phil Simms from tiny Morehead State in rural Kentucky. Just getting to Morehead for a personal inspection required a jostling ride in a chartered plane through rain squalls to an airport whose terminal was an aging house trailer. Bill interviewed Simms, spent the day watching films of his college games, then had dinner with him before repeating his arduous plane ride out. "I left feeling Phil was our man," he remembered, "but it would soon become evident that other teams were looking at Phil and he would likely be drafted before us." Indeed, Simms would be taken by the New York Giants with the seventh pick in the first round.

Steve Fuller from Clemson University was also close to the top of the Niners' quarterback list. Walsh arrived at the Clemson campus in South

Carolina to find with great irritation that Wyche had booked him into a raunchy hotel used for frat parties. Bill stashed his suitcase there anyway and then called Fuller to work him out. The phone at Fuller's apartment was answered by his roommate, a wide receiver named Dwight Clark, and Bill invited Clark to come along to catch Fuller's passes. Walsh was not impressed with Fuller—who would go to the Kansas City Chiefs with the twenty-third pick in the first round—but Clark captured Bill's attention despite not even being listed on the Niners' scouting charts. Clark had only caught twelve passes his senior year, but at six feet four, 215 pounds, he reminded Bill of Chip Myers, a receiver of similar size he'd used to great effect at Cincinnati.

"I took an immediate liking to him," Walsh remembered. "He was a delightful human being, outgoing with a great sense of humor and very natural with me. He was not supposed to have good speed but he had a loose stride that would be excellent in the open field and in the film I eventually saw on him he ran away from defensive backs for a fifty-yard touchdown. I was looking for a big receiver who could go against linebackers and catch the short and medium-range passes underneath coverage and I thought he would be an excellent candidate."

Clark was equally impressed with Walsh. "He didn't seem like a typical coach," Dwight recalled. "He was polished and smart, real sophisticated. He just seemed like a cool guy—easy to talk to and very intelligent, especially about football. We started talking about pass routes and all their variations. The stuff he was talking about was a little bit over my head but he made me feel at ease about the whole thing. I learned a lot on the move that day."

Walsh eventually used a tenth-round choice to get Clark—despite his scouts' advice not to waste a draft pick on him since they were sure he wouldn't be drafted by anybody else—and the receiver would become a Niners legend, the second-most-celebrated acquisition of the team's 1979 draft.

By mid-April, however, two weeks before draft day, the Forty Niners' quarterback question was still unresolved. The leading candidate seemed to be Steve Dils, who had led the nation in passing for Bill at Stanford, had the advantage of knowing the Walsh offense already, and would likely still be available during the third round, but Bill was convinced that Dils would never amount to more than an NFL backup and was reluctant to settle for that. There was, however, another prospect whom no one with the Niners had yet worked out, a quarterback from Notre Dame named Joe Montana. The Niners' new scouting director, Tony Razzano, had Montana ranked as the best quarterback in the entire draft but none of his scouts agreed. Montana's career at Notre Dame had been inconsistent, fluctuating from starting to third string and back again, but Razzano sensed intangibles that were very special. "Joe has a feel," he explained, "a second sense. He knows where everybody is around him. It's an uncanny ability. There were question marks, but somehow I just knew."

The more standard take on Montana was that he was a risky pick, at least as high as the third round. He did not fit the standard model for quarterbacks at the time—big, rugged, with a bazooka for a throwing arm. Joe was six feet two, 185 pounds, and frail-looking, with skinny legs. There were also a lot of doubts about his arm and his ability to deliver the ball deep downfield. Every franchise Bill talked to about him thought Montana would go no higher than the fifth round at best. Walsh, however, was no particular fan of the standard model for quarterbacks. He thought most scouts had little idea of what made a quarterback successful and placed far too much value on arm strength and physical stature. He remembered the 1971 draft, when all three quarterbacks taken in the first round—Jim Plunkett, Dan Pastorini, and Archie Manning—had met the standard model and the Bengals had picked Kenny Anderson in the third round who, though deficient in all the scouting categories, ended up outperforming them all. Walsh had seen Montana play only once, for a brief interval on television in the airport during the hours after his Stanford team had won the Bluebonnet Bowl over Georgia, when Montana was in the final stages of leading Notre Dame to an incredible win—coming back from a three-touchdown deficit with a quarter to go in the freezing rain against Houston in the Cotton Bowl. That alone made him an intriguing possibility.

During the third week of April, with draft day just over the horizon, Sam Wyche was dispatched to check Montana out at the same time he gave the once-over to James Owens. Joe was staying with his girlfriend down in Manhattan Beach in Southern California and Owens was at UCLA. Walsh wanted to know if Owens could catch the ball, so Sam called Joe and asked him to come over and throw passes to him. Owens turned out to be a decent receiver to go along with his burning speed but Montana really caught Wyche's eye. "He was nifty and quick," Sam remembered, "and he had a kind of charisma in his presence that was special, even though he was otherwise a quiet kind of guy when he wasn't on the field, something of a hip-pyish kid." When Wyche returned to the Bay Area he told Bill that he'd better take a look at this guy Montana. He just might be the one.

A week before draft day, Bill and Sam flew back to Los Angeles and repeated the workout of the week before. Owens again got passing grades as a receiver but Montana was the star of the afternoon. "You could see his ability right away," Walsh later explained. "It's so important that a quarterback be able to get back quickly and set up, and then be able to improvise if the play breaks down. I sensed just watching Joe in that workout that he'd be able to do that in time. He had such quick feet, Joe Namath kind of feet, just super quick. People said he didn't have a strong arm but he threw the ball fine. He was quick, agile, and fluid in his movements, almost like a ballet dancer. I was really excited by his potential." On their flight back to San Francisco, Walsh told Wyche that his mind was made up. He'd pick Owens in the second round and Montana in the third.

On May 3, the NFL convened its 1979 draft in a ballroom in New York City. Each team had a representative there, connected by phone to the franchises' headquarters. The Forty Niners draft operation was centered on the second floor at 711 Nevada Street, which was full of scouts and coaches. There, as picks were made, names were taken off the board. Anyone with something to say about which player the Niners should choose next could do so, but no one was allowed to talk when Bill was speaking. "Bill would listen to what everybody had to say," John McVay remembered, "then he'd make up his mind and pull the trigger." That decision was then called to the representative in New York and submitted to the league. Even though he'd never done this before, Walsh carried his first draft off seemingly without doubts. Bill could be deeply insecure in his private thoughts, but this was rarely ever in play while he worked. Instead, both his absolute confidence in his own judgment and his decisiveness were apparent to everyone.

In what would eventually be recognized as his typical fashion, Bill also attempted to play the process for all it was worth and did so with no small amount of nerve. Owens was there to start the second round, just as Walsh had planned, and after surveying a number of other clubs, he was still convinced no one would be looking for Montana in the third round. Consequently, he agreed to switch positions. After the Dallas Cowboys had traded their third-round pick—the eighty-second overall—plus a veteran defensive lineman to the Seattle Seahawks for the Seahawks' seventy-sixth pick, Walsh agreed to trade the Niners' pick—the fifty-sixth—to Seattle for the eighty-second and a veteran linebacker. Then the second floor at Niners headquarters waited for the chance to take Montana. Eddie D., a Notre Dame alumnus, was there, and Bill, seemingly oblivious to the tension, joked with him in the hall. "You ready for another Golden Domer?" he asked. Others, including Razzano, the scouting director, were more nervous, convinced someone would step up and take Montana before they had the chance.

That didn't happen. With the eighty-second choice, via Dallas and Seattle, the San Francisco Forty Niners chose quarterback Joe Montana from Notre Dame.

Looking back, this moment of enormous portent occurred with an odd air of anticlimax. Joe Montana learned what had happened sitting with his agent in The Kettle, a Manhattan Beach coffee shop. "A few things struck me as positive," he later recounted. First, "Bill picked me over Steve Dils, a quarterback he'd coached at Stanford. I thought most people would have selected Dils before me because he had a more consistent record in college. Also, San Francisco was a team in transition, a team searching for an identity. This meant I would get a good shot at the quarterback job."

For his part, Bill Walsh predicted at his May 4 press conference that James Owens would be a great player and that Joe Montana stood a chance of being "pretty good."

The understatement of both the coach and the draft choice would seem laughable in the light eventually cast by their mutual future. Under Bill Walsh's direction, Joe Montana would become arguably the best quarterback to ever play the game, and by selecting him despite the almost universal doubts about his future, Bill Walsh had just initiated the most significant professional collaboration of his career, adding the stuff of miracles to the Forty Niners' arsenal with the best third-round draft pick in NFL history.

Bill Walsh at his first 49er training camp

10

HOW TO COACH

en years later, when Bill's string had run almost to its end and he was starting to come apart under the pressure, it would be hard to recapture the unbridled enthusiasm he brought to preparations for that first season, but in 1979, he was like a teenager with the keys to the family car for the first time. His sense of urgency was constant. By the beginning of summer, he'd moved his family off the Stanford campus to a house in Menlo Park, ten minutes from Forty Niners headquarters, and arranged to spend some time with them at Lake Tahoe before his team's first training camp began, though Geri and the kids saw relatively little of Bill during that Sierra vacation. He spent most of his days designing the approaching camp and by the time the Walshes returned to the Bay Area, he had produced a schedule for the camp's entire five weeks down to the minute, including what was to be taught, when, and how.

Bill showed his schedule to his assistant coaches upon his return and they were incredulous, having never seen anyone plan out a camp like that before, despite having together spent dozens of years in the NFL. Teaching players how to play the game and organizing them into a successful team, the third pillar of Bill Walsh's reputation, was the craft closest to his soul. His definitive coaching decade began late that July at Santa Clara University, a half hour south of 711 Nevada Street, where he, his assistants, and all the players he'd been able to accumulate isolated themselves from everything but football and, under his leadership, took the first halting steps into the team's extraordinary future.

Walsh's approach started with coaching his coaches and then letting them do their jobs. He knew that his assistants would have to do the bulk of the necessary teaching and had chosen them because he knew they were good at it. His concentration was on making sure they did so in the way that would make his system work. Before he left for Tahoe, he required all of them to take the responsibilities of the positions they coached and break those down into all the particular skills that would be required to carry those responsibilities out. His offensive line coach, Bobb McKittrick, for example, isolated thirty-eight techniques that were necessary for his linemen's role in the offense. Bill believed that "teaching skills is the foundation of all coaching" and once those skills had been identified, the coaches were required to design and develop drills that could be used to improve and perfect them. "Each drill must have a direct relationship to a specific action the player would experience in a game," Walsh explained. Those drills then formed the backbone of the Forty Niners' training system and were integrated into training camp in whatever sequence their designers determined was most effective.

One of Walsh's central concerns in his camp regimen was to avoid overtraining. Almost all coaches at the time used preseason camps to stress conditioning and toughness—scrimmages with full contact twice a day, exercise to the point of exhaustion, often using military boot camp as their model—but Walsh believed that this approach led to "excessive physical and emotional fatigue" that in turn led to decreased concentration, resilience, and ultimately, performance, not to mention higher rates of injury. He often cited studies that showed football players trained that way were more exhausted going into a season than they were coming out of it, exactly the wrong equation. So in the interest of breaking camp fresh rather than spent, he always limited the most strenuous parts of practice and always scheduled recovery time, even though that approach was commonly dismissed as "soft."

Daily routines were divided into three types, depending on the level of contact—full pads, just shoulder pads and helmets, or just shorts and T-shirts—and the types of practice were scheduled with the dangers of overtraining in mind: usually the most strenuous was followed by something lighter and off time was always scheduled after two strenuous practices in a row. Typically, days began with a wake-up at seven-fifteen, with a two-and-a-half-hour practice between nine and eleven-thirty, breaks for lunch and rest before afternoon meetings, followed by either an afternoon practice for an hour or free time. After dinner, the team separated into offense and defense to be taught the plays and formations that would be worked on the next day. Curfew began at eleven. At his first meeting with his staff after coming back from Tahoe, Bill presented the entire script and they helped him finalize it with all the particulars of how those practices would be spent. Afterward, Bill remembered, "Everybody now knew exactly what we were going to do and how we would allot every minute of our time."

While much of *what* was to be taught was left to the technical insights of his assistants, the *how* of their teaching was to follow Walsh's model. "The entire Forty Niners' approach was based on self-respect and self-esteem," Bill later explained. "The point was to help a player be better and to reinforce him in the process. Performance enhancement was the theme of everything we did." A sports psychologist who later studied Walsh's methods described them as "creating a positive learning environment." Their assumption was that "playing 'correctly' because of fear of reprisal does not describe an ideal performance state. [So the Forty Niners] created . . . behavior change and behavior maintenance through their use of positive reinforcement. The process works like this: first, appropriate behavior is described. For example, each player's responsibility [in a particular play] is described. The behavior (skill) is then performed under the coach's watchful eye. The behavior is critiqued by the coach in very specific terms. All appropriate behavior is reinforced. If the skill was not performed correctly, the appropriate movements were described again by the coach to the player. . . . The coaching staff consistently described appropriate behaviors and gave specific feedback [in a way that was] orderly, planned, and positive." Offensive tackle Keith Fahnhorst, who was with the Niners for more than a decade, would later say he could not recall one of Bill's coaches ever screaming at him, although that was standard practice on every other team in the league.

Walsh also had very different ideas about how to practice. The common approach was a lot of walking through assignments as part of group memorization, then scrimmaging with full contact—a routine that involved too much standing around followed by a lot of beating one another up. Bill abhorred wasted time on the practice field and thought it stupid to make his players prove how tough they were every day in practice. He wanted his players constantly busy improving themselves instead. He kept his practices short, but every minute was scripted and performed on a strict timetable, with players sprinting from one segment to the next. He emphasized practicing techniques with precision and attention to detail, over and over. He felt that skills often broke down late in games and that the only insurance against this was endless repetition, creating a muscle memory that freed players from thinking about what they were supposed to do and let them react automatically. Most important, all of that was to be done at game speed. Players tended to practice in slow motion and with approximate parameters if left to their own devices, but Walsh would have none of it. He insisted his team drill with the same tempo, precision, pace, and intensity as on game day, believing games were only as good as the preparation that preceded them.

All of this was relatively unheard-of in 1979's NFL—"Bill revolutionized how people practiced," one former NFL head coach observed—but that was only part of what made that first training camp different for most of the players there.

For starters, he didn't want them to call him Coach, as was customary among other teams. He insisted on being called Bill. It was an almost revolutionary gesture. "No coach did that kind of thing then," wide receiver Mike Shumann remembered. "I mean it was unheard-of. Coaches were like your parents and nobody in those days called their parents by their first name."

When Bill greeted his squad on the first day with a half-hour lecture, he didn't talk much about winning and losing, and not at all about being tough, as almost every other coach in that era did, but rather about improving themselves as players. That's what this training camp was about: how to be better football players. And if they didn't get better, he warned them, there would be consequences. He knew they were skeptical of his new approach and were likely thinking that they would give it a shot here and if it didn't work out, give it a shot somewhere else. He advised them not to kid themselves. The Niners had been 2-14 last year. This was the bottom of the barrel. If they couldn't play here, they couldn't play anywhere. Bill never raised his voice while making that threat, but no one doubted he meant it, even if they were on a first-name basis. "It was like he'd read our minds," Randy Cross recalled.

On that first day, like the thousands to follow, Bill Walsh came across to his players as comforting and accessible on one hand and distant and threatening on the other, inviting them to relax but never allowing them to feel completely comfortable. Finding the right balance between those seeming contradictions would always be an open issue for Bill and would shift during his time at the Niners' helm. It would also cause him much inner turmoil. Sensitive enough to know and agonize over the pain he caused, he knew he needed to cause it nonetheless.

In 1979, he still had to work at reinforcing his hard side. He was spurred on in part by his memory of Paul Brown's claim that he would never become a head coach because he was too "soft." The need to disprove his former mentor was still fresh in those days. Bill was also convinced that "the last thing I wanted to be known as was 'a players' coach.'" To him, the description evoked desperately currying friendship with the men who worked for him rather than calmly earning their respect, whether they liked him or not. So he made a point of keeping his distance—"you could see him working to keep us at arm's length sometimes," Dwight Clark remembered—and exercising his authority with a very cold edge when he felt he needed to send a message.

Early in training camp, Bill chanced upon a rookie free agent sticking his head out of one of the dormitory windows and shouting at a passing coed. Bill cut the guy on the spot. Such childishness had no place among professionals working in the football business.

Another day, on the practice field, he instituted an example that would be duplicated in almost every Niners training camp to come. A player of dubious talent had just made yet another mistake and Walsh, with great theatricality, intervened. "Get this guy out of here," he instructed the nearest assistant coach, loud enough so everyone could hear but sounding less angry than simply fed up and disgusted. "Get him a plane ticket back to where he came from. No, scratch that. He's not worth it. Get him a ticket on the goddamn Greyhound bus. I don't want to see him again." Sometimes Bill would vary the routine to include instructions to pack up the guy's belongings in a cardboard box. After several years of repetition, simply mentioning bus tickets or cardboard boxes would be enough to evoke the same message: Bill held the lever to the trapdoor and he had no qualms about pulling it.

Nonetheless, Walsh was having fun at that first camp and often made a point of sharing that fun with his team. "He still had some of that assistant coach mentality in those days," Mike Shumann remembered, "getting close to his players. He set the tone with his sense of humor. He clowned around a lot in those early years."

It seemed like every day at camp brought a fresh influx of new prospects as Walsh culled through other teams' rejects looking for someone better than he already had. More than three dozen cornerbacks alone would come through, staying a day or two or three and then being given their walking papers. Sometimes they were gone before any of their teammates even learned their names. One day Bill made a joke out of the migration by showing up at a team meeting late, dressed as a taxi driver, complete with scuffed leather jacket and Yellow Cab hat. "Anyone need a ride out of town?" he inquired as he walked through the door.

Perhaps the apex of his clowning at that camp came at a meeting before one of the Niners' first preseason games, scheduled to discuss the team's dress code for road trips. After the team assembled, Bill led a parade of coaches into the room, all of them in costume. Walsh himself was dressed as General George Patton, including uniform, helmet, and swagger stick. He instructed his team to take a good look at these guys. "Strange, aren't they?" he observed with a twinkle and a playful grin. "You wouldn't want to look like them, would you?" One coach was wearing bib overalls, no shirt, and no socks. Another was dressed in plaid shirt, plaid pants, plaid socks. Bobb McKittrick, who normally sported a shaved head, was wearing all white, including a long smock, strings of beads, and a long blond wig. Bill's final model was a coach dressed in pressed pants, a subdued shirt, and shined shoes. His only oddity was a huge salami stuffed into his pants so a bump protruded in front of his crotch as he walked. "We all got the meaning," Joe Montana remembered. And everybody broke into guffaws.

"Bill is a complex fellow," Joe later observed, but "when he's on and in a good mood, he always leaves us laughing."

Those seemingly opposite postures were only two of the dozens of staples in Walsh's motivational arsenal. Most of the others were fitted to particular individuals. "He was a great manager of people," one of his tight ends remembered. "Most coaches just use a kind of one-size-fits-all approach but Bill understood that different guys have different buttons. Fifty guys weren't all motivated the same way. Bill put in the extra work to figure out each of their personalities and what drove each. He had an uncanny knack for finding everybody's button and understanding when to push it. He knew who to tweak and who to stroke. Most coaches gave the same canned speech to everybody but he just zeroed right in on who you were."

Dwight Clark experienced that knack after just a couple of weeks of camp. "I always prided myself on working harder than anybody else," Dwight explained, "and it didn't take Bill long to figure that out. At that first training camp I was feeling exhausted by the time we got to the third week—from the workouts and all the mental energy required to learn a new system. And by then I was completely taken with Bill. He was such a cool guy, unlike anybody I'd ever had contact with before, and I just wanted to play my ass off for him. Then one day we ran into each other in the hallway after some meeting late in the day. Bill asked how I was doing and, of course, I told him I was doing fine, but he kind of shook his head in a friendly way and said it looked like I was fading on him a little bit out there. That's all it took. The next morning's practice I found another gear."

Sometimes Bill's communication was nonverbal, just a facial expression or a glance. Most players first experienced it during preseason games and it left a mark. "Bill could kill you with a look," one remembered. "He'd be on the sidelines and he wouldn't snatch off his headset or do anything obvious to the stands, but you couldn't miss the message. If you screwed up and came out of the game, he would give you a look that made you feel about two inches tall. He wouldn't say a thing—just look. He didn't believe in embarrassing players but he did believe in getting his point across. That look was the worst. Once you got it, you'd do whatever it took not to get it again."

When Walsh felt like being more demonstrative, he often did so by indirection. One of his favorite techniques involved using one of his assistant coaches as a foil. While he refused to yell at his players, he felt free to do so with his coaches and often indulged in it by prearrangement with the assistant, if he felt he needed to make a point. Typically, if Bill was watching a drill and saw things he didn't like, rather than jump on the players, he would intervene and chew out the assistant coach for not getting them to do it right. He knew players identified with their position coaches and hated putting them in a position to catch hell, which felt worse than catching hell themselves. He thought the technique saved embarrassing the players yet provided motivation. "He feels if an assistant has to take it," Sam Wyche explained, "the players will ally with the assistants. Sometimes for a second or two, I really disagree with that. When he yells, 'Sam, can't you get him to move his feet?' I know he is speaking to the player at times like that and I'll always be loyal and roll with the punch, but right when it's happening you tend to grit your teeth."

Throughout his career, Bill, in the words of one of his assistants, "worked every possible angle to get the most he could out of the people who played for him" and when they were done, all of them would describe him as a "manipulator" of the first order. Otherwise, they were often unsure what to think of him. "He's not a simply described man," Joe Montana observed after several years of being coached by Walsh. "I've never felt I've figured him out."

There were, however, at least a couple of Bill's traits that were apparent from those first days in Santa Clara and never changed.

The first was that he knew what he was doing. Walsh always believed that coaches led by demonstrating competency rather than giving rousing locker-room speeches. Knowing what to do and when to do it was all the players needed from a coach. The rest was window dressing for the coach's own benefit. Mike Shumann, who had come to the Niners after starting his career with the Miami Dolphins, noticed Bill's mastery right away. "We hopped from drill to drill in our practices," he remembered, "and it was quickly obvious that every drill had a meaning, had something to do with a larger picture. Shula at Miami had been real organized too, but the practices didn't seem to lead anywhere. With Bill, everything had a reason behind it and he made sure you knew what it was." By the end of that first camp, players had begun calling Walsh "the Silver Fox" behind his back.

The second was simply his presence itself. "He brought life with him wherever he went," Joe Montana recalled, "he filled every room he entered." And so it was at that first camp. Walsh didn't hide behind his head coach status, remaining virtually absent from daily routines the way Paul Brown had. Rather, he was a hands-on presence at practices, popping up everywhere, with a comment here, a critique there, and was infectious in all circumstances. "Bill brought this sense of doing things whenever you saw him," Dwight Clark recalled. "There was just an attitude. He walked with a strut almost. He was very confident in what he could do—not cocky, just very confident. When you were around him you started feeling it too. He would tell us things that were going to happen and they actually did and we started believing his attitude was true. He made us confident despite ourselves. He made us believe just by being that way."

Bill Walsh at the chalkboard, holding forth

11

FORTY NINERS FOOTBALL

Every evening, when the Niners training camp convened its final team meeting of the day before breaking into offense and defense to introduce the plays for the following morning's practice, Bill Walsh talked to his players for fifteen minutes or so about "some facet of the game." He would do the same in team meetings at 711 Nevada Street prior to installing game plans during the regular season. And he would continue doing so year after year after year, revisiting all the most important lessons regularly. There were no accompanying diagrams of *x*'s and *o*'s to these lectures, just his thoughts on "things that matter"—how to hold a lead, how to come from behind, how to cope with injuries, and how to play away from home—practical guides to situations they were bound to face. He also spoke about how to deal with the media and even gave his players advice on how to manage their money so they didn't end up out of the game and broke.

Mixed in with those lesser topics was an assortment of larger strategic principles that, when taken together, formed the backbone of what Bill called "Forty Niners football" and what he expected would be the essential building blocks of his team's character:

Beat the opposition to the punch. Always hit the other guy first, before he can land his blow on you. "This is a game of inches," he explained to one training camp audience. "The key is to hit him before he does the same. Get there an inch before he does." To illustrate how this worked, Bill fell back on the example of boxing. Early in a fight, often both boxers would throw punches almost simultaneously, with one's arriving perhaps a quarter of an inch ahead of the other's. At first that barely quicker punch seems to make little difference, but as the fight wears on and that pattern of advantage continues, the quarter inch becomes an inch and then two. By the middle rounds, the earlier puncher assumes dominance and can strike at will, beating his opponent into submission. The Forty Niners always looked to strike the first blow. They always moved quicker to assume the attack. During games under Walsh, the players on the sidelines would often shout, "Beat 'em to the punch," "Beat 'em to the punch." This principle was also why Walsh never talked much about toughness. "Toughness sounds like a guy in a bar fight," he explained, "standing still trying to hit someone. Football doesn't stand still. We wanted explosion and decisiveness, not macho bragging rights." Like the boxer, the Niners would use quickness to wear down opponents early and then dispatch them late. It was the way they played the game.

Set a standard of performance and meet it. "You have to develop an ethic so that on every down you play as well as you can play," Bill argued. "From week to week, it is your personal, internalized standard of play that makes the difference." The issue in NFL competition was not trying to play as well as your opponents; the issue was playing as well as you could play, regardless of how the other team was playing. "The object is to play so well so consistently that your opponent caves in." And the process begins in practice. If they didn't expect much of themselves there, the same would be true in a game. The Forty Niners had to maximize their individual skills and by doing so, they would become a piece of the larger puzzle that allowed the team to win. They didn't wait for a coach to tell them to deliver their best. They established that standard themselves and were always dissatisfied if they didn't meet it. "What matters most," he insisted, "is what you expect from yourself. The players who do the best are those who expect the most.

They play every down matched against their own expectations. That's how you win games and sustain a season." The Forty Niners didn't play down or up to the level of their opposition. They played to meet their own standards and they expected nothing less from all of their teammates.

Be precise in all things and always pay close attention to detail. Contrary to the typical approach, Walsh's Forty Niners were expected to think of football as an exact sport, with each play constructed out of a myriad of details, all of which were essential to success. In a game of inches, performance was measured in inches as well. Rounding off or settling for approximate versions was a sure way to lose. "The foundation of a standard of performance," Bill explained, "is attention to detail." Pass patterns designed to go eleven yards with a forty-five-degree cut toward the goalpost after a shoulder dip toward the sideline weren't supposed to be run ten and a half yards and fifty-five degrees standing straight up. It was part of every player's job description to carry out his assignment exactly as it had been drawn up on paper. "We practice not just to be good," Bill insisted, "but to be perfect. That is always the goal." "Almost" was never sufficient. Walsh held the same standards for coaches as well. Once during camp, when a coach issued the generalized praise "Nice play," Bill took him aside and chewed him out. Say what exactly was nice about it, he told him, or keep your mouth shut. That kind of boilerplate comment was worthless. Be precise about everything. Walsh intended the Forty Niners to be a precise machine that settled for nothing less than exactly what he had in mind—and a team that accounted for everything from the location of the out pass to the way their jerseys were tucked in.

Everyone has a role and every role is essential. Walsh understood that stars were indispensable to his team's success and he would try to accumulate as many as he could, but he was still convinced that "championships are won with the bottom half of the roster." He told his players that they were all important and that they all had to be ready to make their contribution at all times. Their role might not be as visible as a lot of others but they had to concentrate on being as good at it as they could be. And "if you did your role well," one of his players remembered, "he would recognize you for it. He would design plays for your skills. He always knew which guys plugged in best in which situation. By valuing everybody's role, he made sure nobody checked out and that everybody kept their head in the game." Walsh told his players over and over that "you have to fit in a role and think, 'what can I do to help find something that contributes?' " Everyone who put on the uniform, even if only for a week during training camp, was a Forty Niner and every Forty Niner was as important to the team's success as any of his teammates.

Preparation breeds execution and execution breeds success. The NFL was full of coaches lionizing emotional "intensity" as the underpinning of victory—"you have to want it more than the other team"—but Walsh didn't buy in. "Players must execute," he argued. "They can't depend on emotion to win. It doesn't matter how much you want to win the game. Everyone in the NFL is intense. It's foolish to think we can out intensity them. The bottom line is: Can we execute a series of plays almost flawlessly? Only through repetition and experience with those plays can each player complete the necessary assignments. If you want something too badly, you can throw yourself out of sync trying to make a play that isn't really achievable. It's not the attitude or the personnel that does it. It's how well you do things. Don't count on heroics. Count on execution, on the things we have practiced and are good at." That was the reason for repeating drills and plays endlessly in practice. It was the reason the Forty Niners prepared for every contingency ahead of time, on the practice field, so responses would be automatic when the game called for them. "Everybody in the NFL is intense," Bill warned. "The difference is who's prepared and who isn't."

Keep your wits at all times. The football player's ultimate opponent was the pressure that came with attempting to perform in front of sixty thousand people in the face of great adversity, fatigue, and often discouragement, not to mention the skills of their opponents. "Nobody has the forces working on them that we do when trying to do a job," Bill pointed out. Maintaining concentration and focus was essential. "An individual who wants to be successful as a football player must have the ability to bring all his capacities to bear on what he is doing," Walsh continued. "A wandering mind can create mental lapses and cause his performance to be affected negatively. You can't ever allow yourself to get frustrated, confused, disoriented, or hysterical during a goddamn game. The confused, disoriented guy gets knocked all over. You have to find a way to think under pressure." Again, Walsh's leading antidote to such mental collapse was the fruits of preparation. The constant repetition of fundamentals would mold players' skills into their makeup and free them to simply act without having to think about what they were doing, an essential for defeating pressure. The more a player's skills were honed, the more consistent his fundamentals, the more immune he would be to stress. The same was true to the degree he had anticipated situations and practiced them ahead of time.

Communication is vital. Players had to talk to one another and to the staff about everything in order for the Niners' system to work, so Walsh cultivated communication. One player who'd come over from Dallas was amazed at the contrast. The Dallas head coach "told the assistant coaches what to do and the assistant coaches told the players. And none of the information went the other way. [When] I got to the Forty Niners, we'd have these meetings and Coach Walsh would let the other coaches do things. The coaches would say in the meeting, 'Hey, we could do it this way or could do it that way. What would be the best way to do it?' " At Dallas, he remembered, "nobody said a thing." Walsh considered communication the only sure way to correct internal stumbles. "The minute there is a difficulty," he insisted, "you have to be ready to attack the problem and find a way to communicate about it without being difficult. It's part of building leadership throughout the team. The critical factor is that when you make a mistake or a miscalculation, admit it. We openly talk when things go poorly and initiate a process to reverse and change the miscalculation. [The] Forty Niners are always talking to each other and always listening."

Football requires endless adaptation. "You have to be adaptable to different circumstances and situations," Bill pointed out. "As soon as you set your mind hard and fast you limit your value. You have to account for the ebb and flow. Every football game is full of it and you have to account for it. You can't overreact by becoming sky high when things are going well and become arrogant and self-satisfied, then when things are low, get hopeless. If you adapt to each shift and continue to concentrate, continue to work at it, the momentum will flow back to you. You're going to be lucky and unlucky and you never know the way that's going to run. You have to account for that as well and adapt to the circumstances that fall your way. You have to find a way to live with misfortune and play your way through it." Nothing ever goes quite the way it's planned, despite all the preparations you make. If you refuse to recognize new realities, you work against yourself. And when things go wrong, you don't point fingers—you fix them. While maintaining their core standards and consistency, Bill wanted the Niners to be resilient and always change their approach as the situation required.

Count on one another. The interrelationship of players is what would make this a genuine team or not. "The critical factor whenever people work together," according to Walsh, "is that they expect something of each other. It's not just that the coach expects a lot of the players—it's the fact that the players expect a lot of each other. We establish a standard of performance here where each man is an extension of his teammates. We prepare for every contingency and through all of this there is a single thrust—sacrifice for your team because you infinitely care. You are truly a Forty Niner when you aid and assist each other, when you believe in each other." At practices, he expected everyone to help the others get better. Ultimately all players were accountable to their teammates. The team didn't belong just to the coaches—it belonged to everyone who put on the uniform. And, though Walsh didn't use the word much in those early days, the bond that would carry them through adversity to the best of times was the *love* they brought to one another. Football was a mutual proposition and the more mutual the Niners were, the better they would be.

When Bill introduced these notions at that first training camp, he knew full well that most of the players listening to him would likely not be around to carry his vision to fruition, but he didn't hold back in anticipation of finding new players. He put his credo in circulation as soon as he could. He was convinced that his team would never get better until it knew who it was, and that providing such an identity was the head coach's central function.

Bill Walsh being carried off the field by his players, including Keith Fahnhorst (#71) and Steve DeBerg (#17), after victory over Tampa Bay, 1979

||||| ||||| | |||||

12

THAT KIND OF SEASON

ill Walsh's debut in the NFL drew little notice outside the nine Bay Area counties, and even there the response was mostly wishful thinking. No one said anything at all about the arrival of a genius. In truth, Walsh's first team had all the earmarks of repeating as the worst in the league. One NFL coach whose team defeated those Niners would be fired for not winning by enough of a margin, being told at his termination that if he couldn't beat San Francisco by twenty points, he couldn't coach.

"The worst area was the defensive secondary, which was outmanned and inadequate," Bill remembered. The linebackers were "especially weak." Before he took the Niners job, Bill had heard that the team's returning defensive line was a strength, but when he finally saw them play he realized they were "well past their prime." The offensive line had four players who would form the nucleus of future success—Randy Cross, Keith Fahnhorst, Fred Quillan, and John Ayers—but for the 1979 season, they were "too small and inexperienced to be considered much more than barely adequate." Quarterback Steve DeBerg "wasn't mobile but he gave us a way to move the ball," even though he was prone to throwing interceptions at critical moments. His understudy, Joe Montana, "showed promise" but was not ready to run any NFL offense, much less one as complicated as Walsh's. At wide receiver, Mike Shumann was "sure handed" but "lacked breakaway speed," Freddie Solomon "had remarkable quickness" but was "totally inconsistent," and Dwight Clark was just a rookie playing mostly special teams and trying to keep his head above water. At running back, Paul Hofer was "a good back" but injuries would end his career within two years; O. J. Simpson had a great history but "his knee was so bad there were times he couldn't even trot" and he would retire as soon as the season ended.

When the team broke its 1979 training camp, there were fewer than a dozen players on Walsh's almost fifty-man roster who would still be there two years later when the miracle showed up. In the meantime, Walsh and John McVay continued to look for upgrades at every position. They searched through other teams' culls, working them out between practices, signing the ones who seemed to have talent, though many would then be cut within a week to make room for another aspirant who hinted at more promise. The team even held a tryout camp near Eddie D.'s home in Youngstown, at which more than two hundred hopefuls showed up, many on their lunch breaks from blue-collar jobs. The Niners held a similar camp at Redwood City, where more than five hundred were given a chance to audition for the NFL. Some showed up at the tryout in work boots, others in souvenir jerseys. At one point, Bill gave a look to a twenty-nine-year-old bouncer whom Eddie had recruited at a place called the Big Shot Saloon.

That process would continue during the season. "They brought in new guys all the time," linebacker Dan Bunz remembered. "We had the 'defensive back of the week.' They'd bring a guy in on Wednesday, work him out in a couple of practices and he'd be starting on Sunday." When one of those itinerant defenders made a good play on game day, Bunz would have to consult the back of his jersey before congratulating him because he had no idea what his teammate's name was. Such mystery players would continue appearing in the Niners' huddle right up to the last game. "It was like *The Gong Show* back there," one running back remembered. "If a guy made one mistake he was gone. They never gave a guy a [second] chance—and most of the guys they had didn't deserve one."

Nonetheless, there was relative optimism as the Forty Niners commenced Walsh's first season. The *San Francisco Examiner* forecast five wins out of sixteen games, largely because it considered Walsh "a great coach." Bill himself thought they might win as many as six. "I felt pretty good about how fast the players were learning and assimilating the system," Bill explained. "We were pretty proficient in what we were doing. But until you play somebody, you don't know." His hopefulness was also a function of his enthusiasm for his job, but, enthusiastic or not, Bill was never one to harbor illusions for very long and these vanished almost immediately.

The season opened on the road in Minnesota, where the Vikings were in a down phase and Bill thought the Niners might sneak out with a victory. Even so, Bill didn't talk about winning in his pregame speech, only about playing well. They came close, but when Minnesota was awarded a disputed touchdown in the last ten seconds of the game, the Niners lost 28–22.

The following week, the Dallas Cowboys came out to Candlestick and the contest promised to be a massacre. The Cowboys, referred to as "America's team," were at the apex of the league's talent pool, famed for their fearsome "flex" defensive scheme that dominated most teams. The Niners, however, moved the ball, picking up a touchdown on one drive and a succession of first downs before punting on several others, and consistently forced the Cowboys to start their possessions deep in their own territory. The home team actually led 10–6 at halftime, but the lead didn't survive into the fourth quarter. With the Niners down 12–10 with ten minutes left in the game, Freddie Solomon dropped a pass that would have turned into an eighty-yard touchdown and put them back in front. Then DeBerg threw an interception on the next play that the Cowboys took in for their own touchdown. When the Niners got the ball back, DeBerg was sacked for a safety, making the score 21–13. Finally the Niners gamely drove to the Cowboys' five-yard line but fumbled the ball away and had to watch Dallas run the clock out. "We at least left the field with some kind of respect," Bill remembered.

It would be that kind of season.

The Forty Niners would go 2-14 for the second straight year, losing five games by a touchdown or less and another seven by less than two touchdowns. While admitting that a loss was a loss, Bill would point out that there were better and worse ways to lose and most of their losses were in the better category. Randy Cross, who had described the previous year's Niners as "the worst two and fourteen team ever," described this year's version as "the best two and fourteen team ever."

And he was right.

Despite their awful record, the Niners' 1979 season—thanks to the franchise's newly anointed "king"—would live on as a football landmark, an elbow in the game's development that would be visible for years to come. Bill Walsh had arrived and, three decades later, his advent would be ranked among the more significant events in NFL history. Two and fourteen or not, the game would never be played quite the same way again.

The foremost reason was his offense.

The game as commonly practiced in the 1979 NFL was without much subtlety and was infinitely predictable. Ball control was the prime offensive object and that domination was considered a by-product of the running game and only the running game. Despite the pioneering work of coaches like Sid Gillman and Paul Brown, the pass was largely an afterthought, utilized only when the running game came up short. The adage was that when you passed the ball, three things could happen and two of them were bad. Teams ran on first down, ran on second down, and only then, faced with a third down and long yardage, would they pass. The other use of the pass was always late in the game, when trailing. And the passing game itself was conceived of almost exclusively in vertical terms. The object was to go downfield, often as far as possible. The pass patterns run by receivers involved a minimum of deception and the strategy directing them was largely devoid of complexity. Many teams just sent their receivers out and told the quarterback to throw the ball to whichever one he thought was open. A 50 percent completion rate was the established standard of quarterback excellence. *Smash mouth* was the game's favorite expression and the frontal assault was not just a strategy but almost a matter of honor. "Men were men," one NFL veteran of the time observed, "and if you didn't run over people, you weren't playing football."

The transformation Walsh was about to bring to the game was aided enormously by two rule changes recently instituted by the NFL. The first limited the amount of contact a defensive back could make with an offensive pass receiver. Heretofore, the defense could shove and jostle the men they were guarding all the way down the field until the ball was actually in the air, making precise disciplined routes extremely difficult to run. Limiting that kind of activity to within five yards of the line of scrimmage opened up enormous possibilities, of which Walsh would take great advantage. The second rule change concerned the way the offensive line was allowed to block. Previously, any use of the hands was considered holding and drew a ten-yard penalty. In theory, blocking was to be done with the shoulders alone and the hands were to be kept against the offensive lineman's body. Now, the hands could be used, even extended to the front and pressed against the opponent, as long as they stayed inside the blocker's shoulders and didn't actually grasp the man being blocked. This made pass protection blocking far easier than it had been, again opening up increased opportunities for the passing game.

And the passing game Walsh brought was unlike anything else in use. First developed in Cincinnati, then enlarged and installed in San Diego, further enlarged and reinstalled at Stanford, and now enlarged even further and installed again at his Santa Clara training camp, it was sophisticated and imaginative—favoring maneuver and deception over confrontation, choreography over blunt force. His playbook—two and a half inches thick, ten plays to the page, with names like "Double Wing Left Near, F Short, Roll Right H.B. Sail" or "Brown Right Tight Zoom, A Left 76 X Shallow Cross"— was three times the size of any his players had ever seen, and grew almost daily. To multiply the offense's deception, all plays could be run out of as many as a half-dozen different formations so they looked completely different to the defense trying to thwart them. Rather than simplify his approach until his team caught on, Bill had introduced the full system that summer, knowing full well it would take far more than one season for them to come close to mastering it.

The offense's essential premise was that the passing game could be used for ball control even more effectively than running had been. Walsh never had fewer than three receivers in patterns on any given play, often as many as five, utilizing not only the two wide receivers and the tight end but both running backs as well. All the patterns were coordinated so that covering one or two would always leave another one open. Much of the passing was for less than ten yards and all of it designed to create mismatches or overload zones, or to find and exploit the holes in coverage. Rather than just vertical, he added a horizontal dimension as well, spreading the field with crossing patterns underneath the linebackers and forcing the defense to defend its entire width. Passes were thrown on timing, as the quarterback read through a progression of options, each designed to come open in succession, and often the ball was released before the intended recipient even looked back at the quarterback. The patterns were designed to get the ball to a receiver quicker than the defense could respond and cover him. All routes were adjusted to the defensive coverage, then run to precise spots to which the quarterback threw. And passes were thrown on first down or second down as well as third, early in the game even more than late.

Walsh conceived of his short passing game as just long handoffs over the line of scrimmage and counted on 50 percent of his yardage coming after the receiver had made the catch. The result was a drumbeat of incessant completions—four yards, six yards, ten yards—accumulating first downs, keeping the pressure on the defense that, never able to quite catch up, often became more and more frustrated as the game progressed. The approach was derided as "dink and dunk" but it worked, even in the hands of Walsh's 2-14 acolytes. After one game that year, the opposing coach, having just survived a close call in which the Niners had, as usual, collected more than three hundred yards of total offense, mostly through the air, scratched his head with a perplexed look as he accepted Walsh's postgame congratulations. "God," he exhaled with noticeable relief, "you can really throw the football."

That was an understatement. Proof of as much could be found in the play of Steve DeBerg. Walsh's starting quarterback would stay in the league for almost two decades as a journeyman starter and backup with another three teams after Walsh's, but Bill was extremely aware of his limitations and had already decided he was not a long-term answer to the quarterback position. DeBerg's slow-footedness was a handicap and his penchant for critical mistakes drove Walsh up a tree. Nothing was worse for his offense than interceptions, and his quarterback threw a lot of them, even under Walsh's tutelage. That said, the system Walsh brought nonetheless transformed DeBerg. In 1978, he had completed 137 of 302 passes, a completion rate of 45 percent. Under Walsh in 1979, Steve DeBerg threw 578 passes, more than any quarterback in the history of the NFL, and completed 60 percent of them, also more than any other quarterback in NFL history. At the end of the season, the Forty Niners, whose offense had ranked twenty-eighth—last—in the league the previous season, would rank sixth.

That didn't, however, necessarily translate into wins. The Niners blew a lead against the Rams and lost by three. Against New Orleans, DeBerg threw three interceptions, the defense gave up more than five hundred yards, and they lost by nine. Playing Seattle, the Niners were driving to go ahead late in the game, then threw a pass in the flat that was intercepted and run back the length of the field for a touchdown, securing another defeat. Through it all, Bill worked at bolstering his squad. One of his favorite lectures to them was about how to hold themselves in the face of adversity. He pointed out that when zebras were under attack by lions, in the final moments their posture changed, they bowed their heads, and submitted to their fate. Walsh told his players never to bow their heads, to keep standing straight, never adopt the posture of defeat, and refuse to give in. When the Niners arrived in New York at 0-6 for a game with the Giants, several of the Giants' locker room staff remarked to the Niners trainer that "they had been expecting to see a team that looked dispirited and like it was just going through the motions. Instead the Niners looked confident as though they were expecting to win. The Giants hadn't expected that attitude at all." Nonetheless, the Niners left New York 0-7.

Their first win came in week eight, when they returned home and beat the visiting Atlanta Falcons 20–15. Appropriately, the team gave the credit to their coach. By then, most of them were convinced that the Silver Fox could find a way to move the ball against anybody.

That search for a way to win began each week on the weekend before Sunday's game, when Walsh would talk with the Niners advance scout and take several hours to look at the next week's opponent on tape, just to get a feel for how they played. Then on Monday, he would hole up in his office and watch several of the opponent's games, pausing at places to run the film back and forth to watch particular players and how they responded to particular situations. He took notes on a yellow legal pad in his left-handed scrawl, dividing his notations into categories by situation and circumstance, numbering each thought. By the time he was through with the tapes, he would typically have fifty or sixty ideas on his list. In the meantime, all of his assistant coaches had been going through a similar process, each assigned to concentrate on particular offensive categories. On Monday evening, they would all assemble with Bill in the upstairs coaching room at 711 Nevada Street and begin to construct the game plan.

The plan was divided into categories by situation, with each category given a space on the room's blackboard, where plays they thought would work were listed and then discussed by the room at large. There were plays for first and ten; plays for short yardage on third and two or less, subdivided by how far they had to go and usually including four runs and two passes; plays for third and three, for third and six, for when they needed to pick up ten yards on second and twenty, for use against the blitz, for use against a goal-line defense, for use against the nickel defense, and for use inside the opponent's twenty-yard line. There were also "special plays" that utilized some trickery, such as reverses and plays that could succeed when they were backed up against their own goal line. There were audibles to be called by the quarterback at the line of scrimmage when he recognized a particular situation and needed to change the play call in response. Two other categories were plays for "the four-minute offense," designed to run out the clock when the Niners had the ball and a lead, and for "the two-minute offense," when the Niners had the ball with time running out and needed to score. More categories were added or subtracted from week to week.

Typically, the meeting would agree with little dispute about three plays and then twenty minutes would be spent arguing about a fourth, and on like that into the night. At times in these discussions, Bill's face would light up, he would excuse himself from the room, then return after several minutes with a new play he had just designed. The discussion would also focus on what formations to run particular plays from, how to avoid being predictable and just repeating what they had done before, what personnel to use in given situations, and whom among the opponent's personnel to target for attention. The process would last through Tuesday and the end result would be a list of categories and plays, usually totaling between eighty and ninety, all of which could be reduced to fit on both sides of a legal-size sheet Bill would carry with him on the sideline during the game. Bill would install the game plan on Wednesday morning at the meeting of offensive players, standing by an overhead projector and using transparencies to review each play he intended to use. At the same time, the defense was in another room, installing its own game plan. Practices for the rest of the week would be devoted to working on particular categories, but Walsh would continue tinkering with the plan sometimes right up until the morning of the game.

One corner of the sheet of plays Bill carried on the sideline was "the script," which listed the first twenty plays he intended to run. He had started this kind of scripting when he was in Cincinnati and Paul Brown always wanted to know ahead of time what "the openers" were going to be, meaning the first four plays. Walsh next started developing longer scripts just for his own use and when he got to San Diego, started distributing them to the team before the game. "Scripting the plays reduced some of their anxieties," he explained, "and gave them something to focus on." His list started with ten, then grew to fifteen, and eventually to twenty-five. The system was flexible enough to adapt to situations, sometimes went out of order or was interspersed with other plays by force of circumstance, but usually 80 percent of the list was eventually run. This allowed Bill to use early plays to set up later ones, see specifically how the other team would respond to formations, force the defense into a reactive mode in which their pre-snap maneuvering had no effect on what his offense did, establish the mix he wanted of runs and passes, and let him make "decisions much more thoroughly and with more definition on Thursday or Friday than during a game, when all the tension, stress, and emotion can make it extremely difficult to think clearly." The script was posted at a meeting the night before the game and became part of his team's psychological preparation. One of the Niners' signatures in the dynasty to come would be their remarkable success rate in the first quarter of games, for which Walsh's scripts were given a large share of the credit.

Eventually, these innovations by Walsh would be scrutinized and exclaimed over, but not in 1979. The Niners' losses insured that. A last-minute interception produced a loss in Chicago by a single point. Oakland, New Orleans, and Denver beat them by less than two touchdowns; the Rams topped them again, this time by six points; and then they lost by three to St. Louis on another last-minute interception. By the time the Niners returned to Candlestick for their final home game against the Tampa Bay Buccaneers, they were 1-13 and in serious danger of finishing even worse than the year before.

More than forty-four thousand fans showed up for the game—the largest crowd of the year, though still far short of Candlestick's capacity—largely because the retiring O. J. Simpson was honored in a ceremony before his last home game. The Niners responded by playing inspired football. Even though the Bucs were 9-5, on the verge of clinching the NFL Central Division title, and obviously no pushover, the Niners offense moved the ball at will and even the defense stepped up, intercepting five Tampa passes. The final score was 23-7 and the margin could have been larger. It was a dominant performance, the first ever of the Bill Walsh era. "To finally win a game like that the way we did was something of an inspiration," Bill remembered. When it was over, his players mobbed him, lifted him on their shoulders, and carried him across the field. Thousands of delirious fans then stormed onto the playing surface and tore the goal posts down. Even a final loss on the road in Atlanta the next week wasn't enough to entirely ruin the sweet taste of that win.

When the team returned to the Bay Area to clean out their lockers at 711 Nevada Street, Bill would describe himself as "more relieved than disappointed" to have the season over. Fourteen losses had been far more of a trial than he had ever let on while it was happening.

"I've had to ask myself whether I'm the kind of person who can take this kind of situation," he admitted to the *San Francisco Chronicle*. "I know I'm the right person for the job. I don't doubt myself. It's simply been a question of whether I could take the continuing frustration."

Nine years later, after the miracle had long since arrived and the legend of The Genius was well established, the ultimate crisis of Bill Walsh's professional life would still be framed by that 1979 quote in the morning paper.

Charle Young greets Eddie DeBartolo in the locker room

13

BUILDING A TEAM

In those early days, as the franchise struggled to reach mediocrity, Bill got nothing but support and enthusiasm from his boss, Eddie D. "Eddie was still new to football," Bill remembered, "and wasn't yet in a mind-set to demand much. His team had been a mess since he bought it so he still had modest expectations. He was just loyal and enthusiastic and happy to see his team even playing as well as it was." As 1980 began, the young Mr. D. was reveling in the Niners' improvement and thanking his lucky stars that he had fired Joe Thomas when he did. The team might have been 2-14, just like the year before, but they were now fun to watch, obviously better, and getting more so. And Eddie was no longer at risk when he ventured out in Candlestick during home games. From his seats in the press box, the only urinal available to the Niners owner was the public one out in the stadium, where he could now stand and pee in perfect safety next to the fans who had been throwing beer cans at him only the year before.

If anything, Eddie D. was now even more enamored of his "guys" than he had been. He flew out to San Francisco some forty times during Bill's first year, never missing a game or a significant event. He also flew to road games to cheer his team on. "He was seated just behind the press and agonized his way through the entire game," the *Chronicle* reported after the Niners' trip to New York to play the Giants, "yelling encouragement when the team did something well and muttering some choice expletives when the Forty Niners were fouling up. By game's end his cheeks were flushed to a color that almost matched his burgundy sports jacket and the bags under his eyes were pronounced." As soon as each game was over, Eddie was down in the locker room, hugging the players as they came in, fouling his clothes with dirt and sweat without restraint. Sometimes he would be perspiring so much the trainers would give him towels to wipe his face off. "I remember him in the locker room after games," Dwight Clark recalled. "I was young and trying my damnedest to stay on the team that first season, so I played real physical when I got the chance and I ended up getting in a lot of scuffles with defensive backs. I sort of got a rep for that kind of behavior. When I came back to the locker room, Eddie would be there and grab my face mask and say, 'Thank you for fighting for me today.' And he meant it with all his heart. He was so into it he was just one of us."

Eddie and Bill would talk at least once a week on the phone, sometimes several times, as Bill kept him up to date on what was going on with the franchise. Even when it later became difficult between them, Walsh would still describe DeBartolo as "the best owner in the NFL." Partly that was because Eddie never impinged on Bill's autonomy in anything concerning the operation of the franchise, but even more so, it was because Eddie put his money where his mouth was. The younger DeBartolo took the family dictum to go first-class with religious fervor. He never denied a financial request from Bill, even though it sometimes meant hiding expenditures from his father for fear of being upbraided for his spendthrift ways. Most teams traveled in smaller airliners like Boeing 727s, but the Niners chartered larger DC-10s or L-1011s so the players could be more comfortable; most teams arrived at road dates the day before the game, the Niners got there two days early to better acclimate; most teams found cheaper places to stay, but the Niners were lodged in the best hotels—all thanks to Eddie D.

And Eddie was saying all the right things. "I provided the team with, in my opinion, the best football coach in the country," he told one reporter that year. "It's just a matter of patience, just sitting back and waiting for the good times to come. And I think they will. I really do."

To make Eddie D.'s prediction come true, Bill turned back to the search for players as soon as the season ended, again culling through those the other teams didn't want, examining them with a fresh eye. Walsh's efforts in that arena had already yielded several successes and would yield more: Dwaine "Peewee" Board, a light but fast defensive end, cut by the Pittsburgh Steelers and picked up on waivers, would start for almost a decade and eventually become an assistant coach; Dwight Hicks, who had been cut by the Philadelphia Eagles and was out of football working in an Ann Arbor health food store when the Niners signed him, would become an All-Pro free safety and anchor the defensive backfield for a half-dozen years; and Mike Wilson, a wide receiver cut by the Dallas Cowboys, would play significant minutes for the rest of Bill Walsh's tenure. Walsh even found a player at the big Redwood City tryout day, further burnishing his reputation as a talent sleuth. He and John McVay were surveying the hundreds of would-be players from the second-floor fire escape on the back of the Niners headquarters while the assistant coaches were putting them through their paces fifty yards away. After watching for several minutes, Walsh drew McVay's attention to "that tow-headed kid down at the end with the backs." He can play, Bill said. "Sign him." That "kid," Bill Ring, would stay with the Niners for five years as a special teams player and a situational halfback, and one of those years he would be voted the team's most inspirational member by his teammates.

Walsh's primary source for new talent was still, of course, the draft. In 1980, the Forty Niners had a first-round choice that might have given them the rights to the very first player chosen, since their 2-14 record tied them with the Detroit Lions for worst in the league. Unfortunately, the tie was decided by a coin flip, which the Lions won, leaving the Niners to pick second. Bill knew the Lions were going to pick the only player he thought stood head and shoulders above all the rest, halfback Billy Sims from the University of Oklahoma, so he eventually traded that second pick to the New York Jets for the Jets' two picks later in the first round. These he used to select Jim Stuckey, a defensive end from Clemson, and Earl Cooper, a running back from Rice, both of whom would provide journeyman service for several years. Part of Walsh's rebuilding strategy was to focus on a particular position each draft, and this year his concentration was on linebackers, picking four, three of whom played significant roles, at least briefly. The best pick among them was Keena Turner, a light but very fast outside linebacker from Purdue, who, after an injury-marred rookie year, became a fixture in the Niners defense for the next decade and one of the team's acknowledged leaders.

But Bill was not content to construct a team just with successive crops of rookies and reclamation projects. He was convinced his squad had to have a mixture of youth and experience in order to be successful, and the 1980 off-season marked his first of many forays into the trading market in search of established veterans who had enough gas left in their tanks to provide mature role models for his squad as well as skills that had already stood the test of NFL play.

His first such acquisition proved to be both critical to the Niners' future success and illustrative of how much value he placed on character when filling his roster. Tight end Charle Young had once been one of the league's stars. Drafted out of USC by the Philadelphia Eagles in 1973, he had quickly established himself as perhaps the best receiver in the NFL at his position and was voted Rookie of the Year. Two All-Pro seasons followed that, but his productivity fell off during his fourth year at the Eagles and when the following off-season was dominated by a contract dispute during which he refused to re-sign at the terms the Eagles offered, he was traded to the Los Angeles Rams. The Rams, however, were a team that concentrated on running the ball and had little idea how to use Young's skills, so for the next three years he had sat on the Rams' bench, making cameo appearances on occasional passing downs. By now accustomed to retooling players other teams couldn't appreciate or utilize, Walsh gave the Rams a call.

They were a little surprised to hear from him. It was widely assumed around the league that Young had lost at least a step, but that gossip wasn't enough to discourage Walsh. He remembered how good Charle had been in Philadelphia and thought that even if Young was no longer at that level, he would still be an upgrade over his current tight ends. "Ordinarily, the Rams wouldn't have made a trade like that inside their division," Walsh pointed out, "but they didn't consider us a serious competitive threat." He acquired Young on the day before the draft for a fourth-round pick. "He may not have been the super performer he had been," Bill later remembered, but "I was confident he would work well in our offensive scheme. He was physically tough and he could still make the crucial third-down catch. He was still capable of playing well, and most important to us, he was a great leader."

Walsh's projection of Young's impact would prove on the mark, particularly on that last count. An ordained Baptist preacher, Charle brought character in abundance, leading the team in pregame prayers and offering inspirational sermons to anyone in his vicinity. "Without struggle, you never grow as a person," went one of Charle's off-the-cuff soliloquies. "Take the oyster and the eagle. The oyster has everything given to him but he must go with the tide. The eagle is born in a nest so uncomfortable that he does not want to stay. He must learn to hunt on his own. I like the symbol of the eagle. I want to fly, to swoop, to soar." Irrepressible as well as articulate, Young approached everyone in the locker room, asking them questions, and challenging them to demonstrate what they were doing to help the club. The effect of his presence was immediate and lasting. He "was the most inspirational man I ever played with," one of his teammates later wrote. "His words rang with truth, wisdom and strength. I was fascinated by the manner in which he talked to our team. He transformed players who had accepted losing into men who believed they could work miracles."

The other trade Walsh made that offseason wasn't nearly so successful. In this case Bill was blinded by his own appetite for pure talent. Thomas "Hollywood" Henderson, an All-Pro linebacker with the Dallas Cowboys for the last five years, was notorious for his ego and sideline antics, but he was only twenty-seven years old, still in his physical prime, and, when right, one of the best football players Walsh had ever seen. In the last weeks of the 1979 season, Dallas's coach, Tom Landry, had become fed up with Henderson's behavior and thrown him off the team. The Cowboys still owned Henderson's rights and Walsh and McVay had begun discussions with them before the season was over. Bill was intrigued by Henderson's skills and impressed by what they could do for the Niners' anemic defense. He was fast, strong, and incredibly agile, and Walsh would later say Hollywood knew more about his position than anyone he had ever seen play it. There were, however, rumors of substance abuse connected to Henderson which McVay checked out with the Dallas hierarchy. The Cowboys front office denied any truth to the rumors and described their oddball linebacker as "clean as a whistle." Walsh ended up trading a fourth-round draft pick for Hollywood.

And, at first, Bill was thrilled to have him. When he ran Henderson through drills, he was stunned at the man's physical ability. Bill had also spent several hours in phone conversations with the linebacker before the trade and found him intelligent and likable. After Henderson joined the Niners, Bill even took the unusual step of inviting him over to his house in Menlo Park for dinner. It was a pleasant evening, though Bill wondered about Henderson's bladder because he kept leaving the table to use the bathroom throughout the visit. Bill Walsh knew nothing about cocaine addiction at that point in his career, but Thomas Henderson would be his first hands-on lesson in the subject.

Walsh's disappointment with his acquisition began at training camp and quickly snowballed. The linebacker would play impressively for one day and then be sidelined for the next week with various ailments, ranging from impacted wisdom teeth to a sore neck to twinges in his hamstrings. Good as he was, Henderson was never on the field, and Bill began to lose his patience. As Walsh later learned, Henderson was spending a good deal of his time while recovering from his injuries snorting coke back in his dorm room or in the restroom between team meetings or out in his Mercedes Benz in the parking lot. "He'd come in every day like he was sick," one teammate remembered, "looking like he'd rubbed a powdered doughnut on his nose." Soon all the other players "knew he was over the edge," another recalled. "It was obvious and unfortunate." Eventually even Bill caught on that something was seriously wrong and his great trade was going to have to be aborted.

Walsh's problem was that the terms of the collective bargaining agreement between the NFL and the NFL Players Association forbade cutting a player when he was too injured to practice and Henderson was covered under the rules because of his various ailments. To get around it, Bill eventually resorted to subterfuge. After a practice one day, Walsh found Henderson, who had missed the workout, asleep on the locker-room floor, with guys stepping around him. When Bill woke Hollywood, asked if he was all right, and received an affirmative answer, the coach convinced him to get his pads on and come out on the field to help him with a defense he was considering for the next game. Henderson bought the story and Bill recruited several players to go out and practice with him. Then he had the team cameraman film Hollywood going through his drills in case he ever needed to prove his point with the union. The next day, Henderson was cut and Walsh was glad to wash his hands of him.

Bill had acquired some essential elements to add to his roster during that second off-season, but the biggest addition to the Niners that year came through development of who was already there.

Joe Montana had arrived at his first training camp following a prolonged contract negotiation that had only been resolved by Walsh's last-minute intervention in the process to settle terms with Joe's agent. Joe was worried that the coaches and players would think that "because I'd played hardball with my first contract, I was some prima donna," but he found no signs of such resentment. "I was relieved," he remembered, "but I was scared as hell."

In his trepidation, Montana found common ground with his fellow rookie Dwight Clark, who was himself convinced he wouldn't survive the first cut and never unpacked his bags for the whole camp. The connection between him and Joe was deep and instant. "We first met in a coffee shop at Howard Johnson's," Clark recalled. "Joe walked in and I didn't know who he was. I thought he was a kicker. He seemed to be too small and scrawny to be anything else. When I introduced myself I almost fell off my stool when I found out it was Joe Montana. He had led Notre Dame in a comeback win against us at Clemson but I never would have guessed. We became friends real quick, both of us in a strange world and in a little bit over our heads. The receivers and quarterbacks were in the same meetings all the time and the two of us would stay after practice to work on stuff together." Dwight, Joe remembered, "took some of the pressure off. He was comforting; we could talk openly about football and about our fears and this made the whole situation a lot easier for me."

When Walsh kept bringing quarterbacks in for tryouts that first summer, Joe worried and wondered if his days were numbered, but nothing could have been further from reality. Bill had plans for him. "Walsh made no secret that he was grooming him," Randy Cross remembered. "He was clearly the quarterback of the future."

Quarterback was the position Bill Walsh knew best and he had already established a reputation as the master at developing people to play it. It was no accident that the offensive system he had developed depended on the quarterback to be successful. Having been frustrated in his own playing career at the position, he brought to his coaching a natural affinity for how quarterbacks needed to play and had already produced quarterbacking standouts at Cincinnati, San Diego, and Stanford. Joe Montana, however, would be his ultimate accomplishment and cement his legend.

For Bill, playing the position right began with footwork. The way a quarterback retreated from the line of scrimmage, set himself, and stepped to throw determined what then followed. Sometimes he would even have quarterbacks filmed from the waist down to better teach them the correct form. He insisted he could always tell the outcome of the play just by watching the quarterback's feet. In the Niners' system there were three different drops the quarterback made, each one setting the timing for the action of the receivers and the ensuing play. The three-step drop was the quickest, designed to get the ball out almost immediately. After pivoting from center, protecting the ball as he did so, the quarterback took three large steps—or shorter ones depending on the play—planted his back foot, stepped, and threw. The five-step drop featured three large steps and two smaller ones, the seven-step drop, three large steps followed by four shorter. At the back of the drop, the quarterback had to reverse his momentum and turn it toward the line of scrimmage, using a short hitch step to do so, adjusting his posture for the throw or buying time if he needed it. The proper throwing position was with knees bent. If the quarterback threw off stiff legs, inevitably the ball ended up flying into the ground. Montana and the other Niners quarterbacks practiced these drops endlessly, sometimes under Walsh's gaze or, more often, with quarterbacks coach Sam Wyche watching. Even then, however, Walsh was tuned in. The shout "keep your knees bent, Joe" was often heard from a distant part of the field where the head coach was seemingly occupied with something else.

The second essential quarterbacking skill in Walsh's system was reading the progression. Each play had as many as five pass routes being run and three designated receivers the quarterback would look to in succession: the primary, the secondary, and the alternate or outlet, all within a time frame of little more than three seconds. If the first wasn't open, the quarterback would immediately shift to the second and, if he was covered, find the third, to whom he would dump the ball off quickly, usually working from deepest to most shallow in order. By the time the quarterback reached his third option, it was assumed the pass rush would be on top of him. All the Niners pass plays were designed so that if two of the options were covered, the third was sure to be open. At practice, Wyche would shout "one, two, three, guarantee" over and over to invoke the system.

To develop facility at making the necessary decisions, Walsh had designed a simple drill. Bill would station receivers in three different positions downfield simulating where they would be in game conditions, while he stood back behind the quarterback. He would then signal one of the receivers to hold his hands up in a catching position while the other two kept their hands to their sides as the quarterback dropped to throw. The quarterback then had to look at each in their proper order, recognize the one with hands up, and deliver the ball, all at game speed. After each repetition, Walsh would offer advice or corrections about the player's motion or timing or technique. And the drill was repeated over and over and over again. As usual, Bill wanted to establish a muscle memory of the proper movement even before having it tested against defenders.

Throughout the instructional process, Walsh continued to be impressed with Montana's "natural athletic rhythm" and at how quickly he learned and responded to coaching instructions, but Joe was hardly dominant. "My first pro camp," he later wrote, was "an uncomfortable and strange environment [and] qualified as something that was downright frightening. I couldn't shake the feeling that people were expecting a lot of me. If I made one mistake, it was one mistake too many." At first, he tried to make each effort perfect and, as he remembered, "when you start pressing this hard it usually leads to screw ups." Of which Joe had plenty. "We didn't think he was going to make it," wide receiver Mike Shumann remembered. "Some days he couldn't throw a spiral to save his life. We called it a tight wobble. He was raw. But he got a lot better working with Sam Wyche and it was obvious Bill saw something in him. And when he finally got in a game, you could see he saw the whole field and had something special even though he didn't quite know what he was doing yet."

That first season, Joe saw very limited action after the preseason. Walsh's plan was to "spoon feed" Montana. "It was a matter of developing his readiness by using him in situations where he had a good chance to be successful," Bill explained. Walsh had seen a lot of players at the position demoralized by too much early exposure to the NFL pass rush and wanted to avoid that at all costs. Usually, he would insert Joe into games in the second quarter for a series. "In practice," Bill remembered, "we worked repeatedly on specific plays with Joe. When he was placed in a game, we called only those plays, because he could be confident that he could execute them." He was also used in situations where his mobility was called for. Often Steve DeBerg would guide the team down the field and when they got close to the goal line, Joe would come in to run a roll out or keeper that utilized his feet. This plan insured that Joe could function inside of carefully arranged protective limits each week and spend most of his time watching DeBerg and learning the system as an observer.

At the end of the season, Bill felt his plan was working and was excited at Montana's prospects, even though he'd thrown only a total of twenty-three passes in game action. "Joe was wonderful to coach," he explained. "He could do everything you asked. You weren't trying to overcome a weakness. He was such a smooth, graceful athlete. Whatever you taught him he could do. When it came to selecting receivers, reading through a sequence, he just learned everything. It was just a question of adjusting him to the way the game was played in the NFL, building his confidence, and getting his feet under him."

In those days in the National Football League, it was widely assumed that it took four or five years to groom a rookie into a starting quarterback, but by the time Walsh's second training camp opened, Bill was sure Joe would be ready a lot quicker than that.

Bill Walsh addressing his team at halftime before the great New Orleans comeback

14

THE LEAST LIKELY MOMENT TO SAY THINGS LOOK GOOD

Years later, when trying to describe the torment inherent in coaching, Bill Walsh would reference the continual whipsawing between aspiration and disappointment—often picturing himself as ricocheting around a vast wasteland bounded on the one hand by the need to affirm his teams' possibilities, without which success was impossible, and, on the other, by the need to protect himself from the pain accompanying almost inevitable shortfall and failure. In his memory, the vulnerability inherent in his situation was without respite. Every one of his more than thirty seasons on the sidelines fit inside that emotional equation to greater or lesser degrees, but the Niners' 1980 season would prove exemplary.

Walsh's public projections as that year's training camp opened were intentionally modest and hedging. At his first weekly press conference Bill refused to make any predictions of wins and losses. Instead he listed a series of statistical goals: ten more touchdowns, 350 yards a game of offense, giving up 40 fewer yards per game on defense. "If we do these things," he cautioned, "then you can say the team is making progress, aside from the won-lost record." Public anticipation of success around the nine counties was nonetheless up from the year before. The Niners' marketing slogan for the season was "Roaring Back" and it was widely believed that, as the *Chronicle* had headlined one of its sports columns during the off-season, THE 49ERS ARE TURNING IT AROUND. Bill publicly tiptoed past these rampant expectations as though they were hibernating predators, but was privately hopeful. "I knew we were better," Bill remembered, "but I wasn't sure just what that would look like."

Foremost among Walsh's unstated goals for 1980 was securing his first Forty Niners victory in a road game. Bill felt nothing was more important in the development of the franchise than learning to win away from home. "A squad doesn't become a quality team until it can win on the road against strong opposition before a hostile crowd," he pointed out. And the Niners, far from "quality," went into the 1980 season having lost an NFL-record eighteen road games in a row. As a consequence, Bill addressed his squad regularly on the subject. Playing in other cities was not tourism, he reminded them. It was business. The only thing they should pay attention to out there was football. It was always fifty against fifty thousand when on the road, he emphasized, Us against Them in the starkest terms. When the Niners took the opponent's field, everyone in the stands would be screaming their lungs out, looking to dominate and humiliate them. They had to band together in the face of that or be overwhelmed. But when they reached the fourth quarter and could hear the vendors up in the stands, they would know they had succeeded. Nothing felt better, he declared, than to hear the silence fall on the other team's stadium.

Bill, who liked to read military histories, would often cite historical episodes to reinforce his theme of thriving against seemingly impossible odds in hostile territory. He would speak with great passion about how the British army in Burma endured defeat after defeat at the hands of the Japanese before finally standing with their backs against the wall and bringing the Japanese advance to a halt. Other favorites were Stonewall Jackson's forced march and flank attack in the Civil War that turned a seeming Confederate defeat into victory, the stand of the Jewish partisans in the Warsaw ghetto against extermination by the Nazis, and the thirteen dive bombers that turned the Battle of Midway into one of the greatest American victories of the Pacific theater of World War II. From sports history, he told the story of how Harrison Dillard survived disappointment and failure to eventually win the hundred-yard dash at the 1948 Olympics and how boxer Lauro Salas, a seemingly hopeless underdog, survived being beat bloody over fifteen rounds by the great Jimmy Carter to win the Lightweight Championship in 1952. Bill used any example he could find to get his team's attitude right, often embellishing it for greater effect. "We conditioned our minds to be fierce and almost hateful when we went somewhere to play," he explained.

His first chance to break his team's road losing streak was the 1980 season's opening game against the New Orleans Saints, down in Louisiana at the Superdome. The Saints, coming off an 8-8 record in the 1979 season, were favored. To prepare for the noise level of an indoor stadium, Bill had his team practice with rock 'n' roll at full blast over the stadium loudspeakers on the day before the game. On game day, he gathered everyone in the locker room one last time before taking them onto the field. The Forty Niners had been humiliated for years, he told them, and now it was time to stand and fight.

And they did. Steve DeBerg—still the starter at quarterback, with Joe Montana rotating in for select plays or series—produced one of his best games ever as a Forty Niner, completing twenty-one of twenty-nine passes and throwing only one interception. The offensive line dominated and the Niners accumulated more than 150 yards running the ball. When they scored their third touchdown in a row late in the third quarter on a twenty-seven yard pass and made the score 20–7 after a botched extra point, they seemed to be in control. The defense, however, was still suspect and became even more so when injuries over the course of the game forced it to use a makeshift lineup. The Saints responded and soon tied the game 23–23. Then, in what the *Chronicle* described as a display of "character and its ability to overcome both its own mistakes and injuries," the Niners team drove down for a field goal and the lead, 26–23. The Saints, with their fans screaming loud enough to shake the stadium, had one more chance and began a drive at their own ten that lasted until they reached the Forty Niners' sixteen-yard line with time running out. There, on the last play of the game, with the Niners desperately trying to get the right number of men on the field and only managing to line up ten, the New Orleans kicker missed a chip shot field goal and, for the first time in more than two years, the Niners had won in someone else's hometown.

Years later, Bill still considered that victory a landmark in Forty Niners' history. He was full of emotion as he walked out of the Superdome by himself, headed for the locker room to join his celebrating players. "I remember looking around at the Dome," he recalled with an almost wistful expression, "and thinking, Finally, there's some result to all the things we'd gone through. I took great pride in that win for a long time."

It also seemed to inspire his team. At home the next week, the Niners matched their win total from the previous season with a 24–21 victory over the St. Louis Cardinals in overtime. Then the Niners flew to New York to play the Jets. In the locker room before that game, Bill explained the facts of NFL life to his team. They would never gain respect until they won in New York, he told them. It was like how it used to be with boxers, where they didn't count until they'd fought in Madison Square Garden. This was the media capital of the country and a win here was a requirement to even make a blip on the national radar screen.

His team responded with the best half they'd yet played for Bill Walsh, and perhaps the most encouraging part of it was the performance of Joe Montana. When inserted for his regular series, Joe, who had already scored a touchdown on a bootleg after being substituted for DeBerg near the goal line, drove the team down the field and finished the drive with a touchdown pass to Dwight Clark, Dwight's first ever as a Forty Niner. Before the game was over, Montana had thrown another touchdown to Clark as well. All told he was four for six passing and looked smooth. After the game, relaxing before the ride home, Bill and Sam Wyche agreed that "we've got a quarterback"—and they weren't talking about DeBerg. The whole team had been dominant in that first half, gaining seventeen first downs to the Jets' six, 257 yards to the Jets' 115, and started the third quarter ahead 24–0. Once again, however, the defense collapsed. After Peewee Board sustained a season-ending knee injury, the Niners had only three defensive linemen with whom to finish the game and the Jets stormed back. The Niners offense had to hang on but managed to score enough to keep the lead and secure their first New York victory, 37–27.

In the locker room afterward, Walsh's team was jubilant. Walsh himself was worried about the defensive injuries when he spoke to reporters and called that moment "the least likely time to say that things look good" since he had no idea how they could manage next week or the week after with such a decimated defense. His mood wasn't yet shared by the team, however. The previously sad-sack Forty Niners were now 3-0, victors in the Big Apple, with a two-game lead over the rest of their division and off to the best start by this franchise in twenty-eight years.

"I'll say it right now," a celebratory Steve DeBerg told the *Chronicle*. "We're going to challenge for the divisional title. We believe that we've got the best team in our division."

He had, of course, spoken far too soon.

A week later, the losing began. First there was a three-point defeat at home to the Atlanta Falcons, followed by a 48–26 thumping by the Rams down in Los Angeles. And after that the losses cascaded, turning the once promising season to wreckage.

For Bill, each of the losses was a private torture. He took every defeat as a humiliating personal failure, with his own mistakes always arrayed in the foreground, leaving him mortified and deeply insecure. "After a loss," he explained, "there is an enormous doubt that sets in about whether you'll ever win again. Two losses in a row and it seems like the future is just a void, a kind of black hole in which none of the things you once had confidence in even exist. It's an emotion near panic. But I couldn't let that on to anybody. I had to make sure everybody else had their heads on straight and was turning around and getting ready for the next game. It's an incredibly lonely existence in which I had no support system to speak of and had to swallow my feelings. I could never wax philosophical about losing. I was too sensitive for my own good. There was just this sick feeling afterward that only got worse with each new loss." He usually had at least one drink, sometimes several on the flight home after a loss. The night of a defeat, after staring morosely into space for several hours, Bill often took a sleeping pill to prevent himself from waking in the middle of the night in a deluge of second-guessing and self-criticism. The next day, while barricaded in his office putting together a game plan for the next Sunday, he stopped for long stretches to listen to Willie Nelson or Waylon Jennings on the stereo, trying to regenerate his confidence and get out from under the cloud that never quite went away.

Bill always found a way to go on, but it was never easy.

The game Walsh later described as the season's "low point" came in week six, against the Cowboys down in Texas Stadium. The Niners were still 3-2, and he thought they could play with Dallas, given their performance of the year before, but, he recalled, "they showed us just how far we were from the upper strata of the league." The final score was 59–14 and it wasn't that close. Steve DeBerg had his worst day as a Forty Niner, completing twelve of thirty-five passes and throwing five interceptions. Paul Hofer, the Niners' best running back, had his knee torn up and was effectively lost for the season. "They were beating the crap out of us," Joe Montana remembered. "Bill kept looking back at the bench for people to put in the game. Occasionally, he looked at me and, I must admit, I was scared. I didn't want to go in, so every time he looked around, I turned my back on him." And Dallas poured it on, using trick plays and throwing deep even after the game was long since decided. "The Cowboys were like that in those days," Bill remembered, "very contemptuous, and with fans who were just as cocky, taunting the visiting team when the Cowboys were on a roll."

The performance in Dallas forced Bill's hand on Steve DeBerg. The quarterback had thrown thirteen interceptions in the team's three losses and the coach had finally had enough. At his press conference on Monday morning, Walsh announced that the time had come for Joe Montana to take the reins of the offense. Henceforth, he would be the team's "number one" quarterback and DeBerg would be the backup. And, Walsh promised, it would not be a momentary change. He didn't believe in switching back and forth between quarterbacks, so Montana would be given a loose leash. Joe had looked good in his preseason appearances and his brief moments earlier in the season, and Walsh expected he would do even better as the starter. When asked, quarterback coach Sam Wyche described Montana as "one of the most dramatically improved players on the ball club" and Joe himself expressed confidence. "I didn't feel real comfortable with the offense last year," he told reporters later in the day, "and this year I do. I feel real confident."

Against the Rams the following Sunday, Joe did reasonably well, completing twenty-one of thirty-seven for 230 yards, but they lost again—though by a smaller margin than in their first game with L.A. Then the Niners hosted Tampa and lost by a point, bringing their losing streak to five. At Detroit the next week, Montana played so poorly Walsh pulled him after the first half and inserted DeBerg, but it still didn't help. The Niners lost by four, despite forcing several second-half turnovers in Detroit territory. And the streak was now up to six.

Uncharacteristically, Bill now made a desperate move. The Monday after the Detroit loss, Walsh announced to the press he was retracting his quarterback change and returning DeBerg to the starter's job, despite his previous failings. Bill said he thought it would help Joe to watch the opening of games from the sidelines and then be used in a relief role. Bill admitted that he was contradicting what he'd always said about a two-quarterback system and allowed that he was "doing this reluctantly." He explained that he had canvassed some of his players about what to do about the team's quarterbacking and that a number had suggested putting DeBerg back in the starting role because he had "more command" of the offense. He also thought "this experience might be best for Joe." One of the reporters asked if this meant he'd lost confidence in both his quarterback options and might use a high draft choice next spring to get yet another one. Bill replied that he hadn't thought about it much, but it might be a possibility.

In the meantime, the *Chronicle* noted the next morning, "The 49ers now have a full blown quarterback controversy. When [Walsh] made Montana the starter, his indication was that it would be Joe's job for the season. After Montana's first start, he made a point of saying that 'Joe is the quarterback. It's that simple.' Yesterday, Montana was the quarterback no longer and it was not that simple."

DeBerg was, however, no obvious help. The next game against Green Bay raised the string of losses to seven when the Niners came up a touchdown short, after DeBerg ended their last offensive possession by throwing an interception. Montana didn't play at all. During the week that followed, the *Chronicle,* under the headline THE PROBLEM THAT'S RUINING THE 49ERS, took Walsh to task for his handling of the quarterbacks: "The debate over who should play quarterback, which at first was merely confusing, may now be threatening the development of the team." Bill didn't say so when asked for comment, but he took that criticism personally as well, which only magnified his agonies.

Then the team flew to Miami and, if the Dallas game was 1980's "low point," as Bill later claimed, the Dolphins game was a close second. This time the Niners lost 17–13, again ending their last possession with a DeBerg interception that allowed Miami to run out the clock. On the drive prior to that, the Niners had kicked a field goal, had it called back on a penalty, re-kicked another one, had *it* called back as well, then thrown a pass for what appeared to be a first down, only to have the referees spot the ball inches short. "What I remember most about the game," Bill later wrote, "is that every time the officials made a call, Miami coach Don Shula would be on the sideline, yelling at the referee, and the officials would come over to explain the call to him. I couldn't get an audience [with them] before, after, or during the game. . . . I could see that the officials figured the Dolphins were a power in the league and that the Forty Niners were just another team on the schedule." In any case, the losing streak was now eight, just one short of the record set by the Joe Thomas regime in 1978.

On the plane ride back to San Francisco, Bill Walsh was inconsolable. Sitting at the front of the plane by himself, looking out the window, he broke into tears and spent most of the trip wallowing in despair. "It was a heartbreaker to have lost like that," he remembered. "And by that time I was really distraught and worn out. I just basically broke down. No one was sitting with me. I had made sure I sat by myself and the others were gravitating to the back of the plane by then, staying away from me. Maybe the flight attendant saw me lose it, but no one else did. Sitting there in tears, I decided that I couldn't get the job done. It could be done possibly but it might take two or three more coaches to do it. It was such an overwhelming job. I wasn't embarrassed by my efforts but it just wasn't happening. I mean, eight straight losses in your second year. There was no reason to think I could make it happen. So I decided to step away at the end of the season. I was convinced I was done and planned to tell Eddie that he had to find someone else."

Bill did not, however, tell Eddie he was through. Instead, after a stiff dose of Willie Nelson, the skies cleared and he began to prepare for a home game with the New York Giants. As was often the case when Walsh found his way out of an emotional paroxysm, he emerged almost refreshed, with a new mental clarity. One of his first moves was to reinstall Joe Montana as the number one quarterback, where he would now stay for the next decade. The "quarterback controversy" was over. Then, on Sunday, the Niners defense, one of the NFL's worst, found itself, sacked the Giants quarterbacks ten times, and held the visitors to just fifty-one net yards passing. The final score was 12–0 Niners. Afterward, Eddie D was down in the locker room, his shirt soaked through, celebrating as though they'd just won a championship.

The next week, the New England Patriots, a playoff team that was projected by many to make it all the way to the Super Bowl, came to town, and the Niners played even better than the week before. This time, the defense intercepted six Patriots passes. On offense, Montana had his best game yet, completing fourteen of twenty-three for three touchdowns, and the home team won by four. "I thought Montana played superbly," Bill told the press afterward. "He certainly is a quarterback with a future. There isn't any doubt about it." The press reports the next day claimed it had been more than three seasons since the team had had a better win against a better team.

Then, once again, the roof fell in. New Orleans, their next opponent, had not won a single game since the Niners had opened the season by beating them and they figured to be a pushover. Instead, Walsh's team came out in the first half and delivered what the *Chronicle* described as their "most pathetic performance in the last few years." The offense could do nothing and neither could the defense. The score at halftime was 35–7. The Saints had accumulated twenty first downs to the Niners' two, run forty-five plays to the Niners' nineteen, and outgained the home team 324 yards to 21. As the visitors returned to their locker room in jubilation, they were pounding on the runway walls and shouting that they were going to make it 70–7 before the game was over. Fans were already leaving the stadium in droves and for the second half there would be more empty seats in the stands than full ones.

By his own account, Bill returned to his team's locker room as "depressed" as he'd ever been at that stage in a game. But he passed none of that on to his squad. "It's critical under stress to maintain your normal procedures," he explained, "and not disrupt the players further." He and his staff concentrated on analyzing what the Saints were doing and how they could counter it, being as specific as possible. The only speech he gave made little attempt to berate or to inspire. He told them he wasn't going to embarrass them. They were doing a good enough job of that by themselves. Chances were they were going to lose but the question still to be answered was how. They could either roll over or fight back. "In the next thirty minutes," he said, "you're going to learn a lot about yourselves. You'll have a better understanding about how you stand up to absolute adversity. You may like yourselves, or you may not." There was a chance they could win, he finished. They would have to execute flawlessly and count on the Saints to make mistakes. They couldn't allow any more scores from the Saints and they would have to score every time they got the ball back.

And, to the amazement of everyone left in the stands, the Niners came out and did exactly that. Their comeback that day was the greatest in NFL history. No team had ever overcome a larger halftime margin.

The third quarter started poorly, when James Owens mishandled the kickoff and could only get the ball out to the Niners' twelve-yard line. But on the first play from scrimmage, Montana hit Dwight Clark for a forty-eighty-yard gain and the Niners' charge was on. They quickly drove to the end zone and made the score 35–14. The defense forced a punt and then Joe hit Dwight again, this time for seventy-one yards and a touchdown, and the score was 35–21. On their next three possessions, the Saints fumbled twice and punted once. The Niners converted both fumbles into touchdowns with scoring drives of eighty-three and seventy-eight yards. Throughout the comeback, Montana was magical, directing the offense and leading his team. "Joe was simply outstanding," Bill remembered. "This was the game where his teammates learned to believe in him." All told, the Niners gained 409 yards in the second half, finally tying the score, 35–35, with little more than a minute left in regulation and forcing overtime. Dwight Hicks then intercepted a Saints pass in the extra period and the Niners drove from their own seven to the New Orleans twenty and kicked the winning field goal. Sheer ecstasy swept through the locker room unchecked afterward, and Eddie came out of it looking like he'd played the second half himself.

This extraordinary victory would be a team landmark for decades to come. "Modern Forty Niners history started there," Bill explained. "That second half against New Orleans was where we first learned who we could be."

It didn't matter that the season's final two games were losses. The future had been foreshadowed and the unlikeliest of miracles was now waiting in the wings.

Hacksaw Reynolds (#64) and Ronnie Lott (#42) on the sideline

15

"OUR TIME WILL COME"

To realize that future, however, Bill Walsh had to spend the off-season engineering the Niners' biggest infusion of talent yet. Training camp for the 1981 season was moved to Sierra College in Rocklin, California, just outside of Sacramento, and by the time his team left Rocklin, five rookies, ten free agents, and four veterans accrued through trades had been added to the roster.

There were also two significant additions by subtraction.

The first was another example of just how far Walsh was willing to go in order to bolster his team's internal chemistry. Ron Singleton was a massive six-foot-seven, 300-pound left tackle who had become a starter during the 1980 season. No position on the line was more critical to Bill's offense than the left tackle because the man playing it was charged with protecting the right-handed quarterback's blind side, usually against the other team's most accomplished pass rusher. No passing offense could function without that block being made. Ron Singleton had begun in the NFL as a 220-pound tight end from Grambling State University whom Walsh had given a tryout at San Diego during his year there as offensive coordinator. Singleton had then been cut by the Chargers and picked up by Joe Thomas for San Francisco, where Ron added eighty pounds and was converted to tackle. Bobb McKittrick, the offensive line coach, had been developing the neophyte lineman since Bill took over the franchise. Singleton was an enormous specimen by the standards of the time—when 300-pounders were virtually unheard-of—and by the end of the 1980 season, Walsh was convinced "he was going to become a really good tackle."

Singleton was not, however, much of a favorite with his teammates. He had a reputation for taking cheap shots at practices, and during the previous season his fellow offensive linemen became convinced that he had feigned being too ill to play when the Niners were up against the New York Giants and he would have had to block Gary Jeter, one of the best defensive ends in the game. "He had Jeteritis," right tackle Keith Fahnhorst observed. Walsh noted Singleton's unpopularity, but that didn't warrant putting his quarterback's blind side at enhanced risk until Singleton overstepped himself during off-season workouts at 711 Nevada Street. The lineman had become convinced that he was now one of the best in the league at his position—"that wasn't yet even close to being true," Walsh pointed out—and hired an agent to renegotiate his contract. The agent then met with John McVay and Bill and insisted that his client's salary be almost doubled. When they refused and word reached Singleton, the player became upset and began acting out down in the locker room, throwing objects, slamming lockers, and screaming. When the team's equipment manager tried to calm him down, Singleton, who was black, reportedly called the equipment man, who was white, several racial epithets. At the same time, Singleton's agent accused Walsh of refusing the tackle's demands because he was black and claimed his client was a victim of racial prejudice.

At that point, Walsh lost his temper. He wasn't about to put up with that kind of shit from anybody and Singleton wasn't worth the trouble he promised to cause. He had to be excised from the squad as quickly as possible before his grousing infected the locker room. "Our organization stood for honesty and fairness," Bill explained after his anger cleared, "and we would not tolerate being insulted." In the immediate moment, still furious, he instructed one of the Niners' front-office staff to clean out Singleton's locker, put the contents in a cardboard box, take it to the tackle's house, and leave the box in front of his door. Ron Singleton learned he'd been cut when he found it sitting there. No other team picked him up and he was out of football by the time the season began.

Cutting Singleton left Walsh with a giant hole at left tackle that he ultimately filled by moving Dan Audick, a 245-pound guard, into the spot and playing the whole 1981 season undersized on the blind side as a consequence. Even so, Bill never regretted the move. "If you have rotting apples," Charle Young pointed out, "you have to do something about it. The message couldn't have been clearer: I run this ship and we all row in the same direction. If you can't do that, I'll replace you, no matter who you are and where you play."

The second key subtraction was made after training camp had begun. Walsh now had no doubts that Joe Montana was his number one quarterback. Joe had finished the previous season with a 64.5 percent completion rate—a franchise record—and had obviously captured his teammates' loyalty with the second half he played in the great New Orleans comeback. "The guy does not respond to a pressure situation with a panic response," Sam Wyche noted. "He responds with more poise and it has a ripple effect throughout the whole offense—throughout the whole team, actually." Indeed, before the next season was over, it would become an article of faith among the Niners that when the offense needed to make a play, Joe could be counted on to find some way to do it. As training camp began, however, Steve DeBerg was still on the roster as Montana's backup, creating an uneasiness that all Bill's pledges of primacy couldn't dissipate. "Bill told me I was going to be the number one," Joe remembered, "but I had my doubts. . . . With Steve around I figured it would be another season of us going back and forth."

That discomfort wasn't personal. Montana and DeBerg were training-camp roommates who in many ways were almost identical. Both were often described by those who knew them as the most competitive person they had ever encountered. The pair competed at everything from throwing rocks to video games, relentlessly and without quarter—and got along well while doing so, though Joe often felt guilty about his roommate being used as a placeholder while Bill got Joe ready to assume the job. DeBerg was also close to Walsh and had earned the coach's respect by being nothing but professional about the situation, helping Montana and never complaining, even though he thought he should have been the starter instead. For Bill, however, sentiment had no role in his decision. A week into camp, he traded DeBerg to the Denver Broncos for a future fourth-round draft choice and then traded with the Miami Dolphins to acquire Guy Benjamin, who had played for Bill at Stanford, to back Joe up. The change "helped me psychologically," Montana later acknowledged. "When Bill traded Steve, I knew the job was mine."

It was not a move without risk. Montana had yet to prove that he could be a consistent topflight starter and a number of teams would not have acted so boldly, particularly with a player most still had great doubts about, but Bill was comfortable taking chances and was convinced that Joe "would not only do well but that he would become one of the best in football."

The Niners' most dramatic infusion of talent that off-season came through the collegiate draft. While getting Montana in 1979's third round would prove a coup, this 1981 effort by Walsh would become legendary for both the depth and volume of its yield. Bill had said upon taking the Niners job that it would take at least three drafts to make the team respectable, this was his third, and going into it he felt the Niners still had a lot of ground to cover just to reach the upper edges of mediocrity.

His defense was worst off by far, and as a consequence he would end up spending six of his first seven picks on that side of the ball, all six of whom would prove to be anywhere from productive to outright great. This concentration on defense also reflected Bill's theory that his system of offense could cover for talent shortages but not so with defense, where talent was essential and could not be compensated for. In 1981 it was also obvious to him what part of his defense needed the most help. The previous season, like the season before it, had involved a seemingly endless search for defensive backs. Thirty-two had been through the roster from the start of training camp to season's end, and the Niners had still ended up last in the league in pass defense, crippling the franchise's progress. "Nothing is quite so discouraging to a team," Bill pointed out, "as knowing no lead is safe because the other team can score so quickly through the air." And as he prepared for the 1981 draft, all Walsh had to show for his endless effort to shore up the squad's defensive coverage was Dwight Hicks, the free agent McVay had signed away from his job in a health food store, now the starting free safety and, by Bill's standards, his club's only legitimate NFL defensive back. Bill meant to change that in a big way come draft day.

Thanks to their 6-10 record, the Forty Niners were selecting eighth in the first round, when the best players would be available. Among them were two defensive backs who stood out above the rest—Ronnie Lott, a safety from USC, and Kenny Easley, a safety from UCLA—and Bill thought one of them might slip far enough for him to snatch. He was convinced that Lott would go with one of the first four picks, so he concentrated most of his predraft attention on Easley. He interviewed the UCLA player and watched more film by far on Easley than on anyone else in the draft. Easley was also excited by the Niners' interest and the possibility of staying in California, so much so that he had his agent send letters to all the teams drafting ahead of the Niners stating that his client would not play for them if picked.

But predicting other teams' behavior on draft day was an iffy process at best. Two running backs and a linebacker were taken before Seattle's pick in the number four slot and Seattle was one of the teams Bill expected to pick a defensive back. He was surprised Lott had dropped even this far and was even more shocked when Seattle, ignoring his agent's threat, picked Easley. Two more linebackers and a quarterback led up to the Niners' pick and Walsh, without hesitation, pounced on Lott.

It was a fateful selection. Ronnie Lott would be the second pick by Walsh who would eventually gain recognition as perhaps the best ever to play his position and a future first-ballot selection for the NFL Hall of Fame. He would also become everything to the Niners' defense over the next decade that Joe Montana was to its offense. What was more, he would be the team's emotional heart, making everyone around him better players. "We'll be playing along at one level," George Seifert, then coach of the team's defensive backs, observed, "when Ronnie will just level a guy with a tackle, and all of a sudden, our whole effort will step up." Lott's intensity and professional devotion would be unmatched for as long as he played and he would be voted into the Pro Bowl almost every year he wore a San Francisco uniform—first as a cornerback and then later as a safety—starting with his rookie year when he would set a record for interceptions returned for touchdowns, finish second to future Hall of Famer Lawrence Taylor in Rookie of the Year voting, and third behind Montana in balloting for the season's MVP.

When Bill called Ronnie after his selection, he promised no miracles. "We've got a young team," the coach explained. "We are going to build and get better and better. Our time will come."

Picking Lott would have been enough by itself to make the 1981 draft a distinguished year, but Walsh had only just begun. In the second round, the Niners had two picks. Bill used the first one on defensive tackle John Harty from Iowa and the second on Eric Wright, a safety from the University of Missouri. Bill and his staff had coached Wright during the collegiate Senior Bowl at the end of the 1980 season and projected turning him into a cornerback. Six feet one and 180 pounds when drafted, Wright would be considered big for the position, causing some teams to doubt he could be converted, but he quickly proved all of them wrong, becoming a "shutdown corner" capable of stifling the opposition's best receiver week after week. After three years, Walsh would describe him as "the best cornerback in football." Eric Wright would eventually make the Pro Bowl as well and might have contended for the Hall of Fame had his career not been cut short by injuries.

In the third round, Walsh went for yet another defensive back, Carlton Williamson, a safety from the University of Pittsburgh. "Carlton had a reputation as a really physical player," Bill remembered, "and we sorely needed somebody who could come up with the big hit. We had him listed behind Easley as the best strong safety in college football." Williamson too would end up in the Pro Bowl. The Forty Niners had no pick in the fourth round, having traded it to Dallas the year before for Hollywood Henderson, but in the fifth round Bill picked yet another defensive back, Lynn Thomas, Williamson's teammate at Pitt. Thomas would play well in his rookie season, usually as the first defensive back off the bench for use in nickel defenses when an extra back was called for.

Walsh's decision to use four of his first five draft picks on defensive backs was well off the NFL's beaten path and by itself would have secured his reputation as "different." Most teams would have picked one or two and gone on to other positions. But the move that proved truly remarkable was what Walsh then did with his draft picks when they got to training camp. Lott, Wright, and Williamson were almost immediately installed as starters alongside Dwight Hicks. "All these players had been in successful college programs," he later explained. "They were accustomed to playing pressure games before huge crowds, so they would have a better chance of adapting to NFL football." Still, the move was nothing if not audacious. The San Francisco Forty Niners would start the season with a defensive backfield composed of one two-year veteran and three rookies, two of whom were playing positions they had never played in college. It was an arrangement that conventional football wisdom considered a recipe for short-term disaster at the very least.

And pulling off a miracle under those circumstances would make the miracle even more so.

Walsh's most significant free-agent signing that off-season happened after the draft in June. Jack "Hacksaw" Reynolds was an eleven-year-veteran middle linebacker who'd become involved in a contract dispute with his previous team, the Los Angeles Rams, and had been released by them in May. The Rams described him as over-the-hill but he had led the team in tackles during 1980 and been selected for the Pro Bowl. Not particularly big—six feet, 235 pounds—he was legendary for his study of the game and his intensity. He'd earned the nickname Hacksaw while playing at the University of Tennessee, when in a fit of frustration after a loss, he had sawed a car in half all by himself. Once Hacksaw had become a free agent in the spring of 1981, he hired an agent to shop him around to several franchises, asking for $1 million over five years, a large salary in those days and an awfully long-term contract for a player at that stage in his career. After serious inquiries from four different teams, the last remaining bidders for Reynolds were San Francisco and the Buffalo Bills. John McVay spearheaded the Niners' negotiating effort while Bill was on a brief vacation in Aspen, Colorado. Walsh, however, joined in by phone as the negotiations reached their endgame.

"Hacksaw had played against us," Bill remembered. "He was such a fiery player. I made the deal with him from a friend's house in Aspen. He wanted a lot of money but Eddie never blinked an eye when I told him how much. Hacksaw's agent also insisted that we include in the contract that Hacksaw could coach with us after he was done playing. I made the agreement figuring I could take on a coach if I could just get a player for a few years. I talked with Hacksaw on the phone and he had all kinds of hard questions for me. He wanted to know what his role was going to be and this and that, all with attention to the smallest details. He also considered himself an expert at evaluating a team and its athletes, so he told me everything that was wrong with us. He was a pretty opinionated guy but I went right along with him. I agreed and agreed and agreed. But it was well worth it. He was such a godsend for our squad. He had such a work ethic and was still a very good football player in a small area. He wasn't very good at chasing down pass receivers, but in the internal area behind the line, he was still very good. In those days, we didn't have anyone on the squad with such a work ethic who could set such a standard for our younger players."

Bill was hoping to get the equivalent inspiration out of Reynolds on the defensive side as he had out of Charle Young with the offense and he got even more than he'd hoped. Hacksaw showed up at Rocklin lugging his personal projector for watching game film and a battered briefcase full of spiral notebooks and pencils, all sharpened, many down to the nub. "At meetings," George Seifert remembered, "he'd sit down at a desk and he had this big old box crammed full of his pencils and a pencil sharpener, and he'd just go through them. He would sit there and write down everything. From the standpoint of study habits, coaches naturally try to advise and encourage players to look at a lot of film, study, and take good notes just like any teacher would. But here was a person that was basically doing what coaches always said and that had a profound effect upon the players." Early in training camp, Ronnie Lott asked to borrow a pencil from Hacksaw and was refused. Reynolds told the rookie that he wouldn't be a success in this league until he brought his own pencil to every meeting so he'd better start now.

When the squad moved down to Redwood City, Hacksaw Reynolds became the only player the coaches trusted with a key to 711 Nevada Street. He was often the last to leave, usually carrying reels of film to watch overnight, and the first to arrive, brewing coffee for the defense to drink when they showed up. If a coach changed something he'd said at an earlier session, Reynolds would call him on it, pull out one of his spiral notebooks, and quote chapter and verse from his notes of the previous meeting. For the first several weeks in Redwood City, he lived out of his locker and sometimes spent the night there on the couch. On game days Hacksaw was so amped up that he reported for breakfast at the team hotel already dressed in full uniform and pads, with his eye black on. He drove himself to Candlestick in full uniform—including helmet—behind the wheel of a battered 1970 Lincoln Continental that spewed smoke, looking to other motorists like some crazy fan on the way to the game. When asked, he explained that he didn't want to waste his energy at the stadium getting dressed when there were more important things to think about.

Hacksaw Reynolds was, Ronnie Lott observed, "a crazy old turkey." But his approach worked. His obsessive film watching gave him a knack for calling out the opposition's plays before they ran them and his concentration started infecting others almost as soon as he arrived. At the first curfew check in Rocklin, the linebackers coach looked into Hacksaw's room and found him with his projector running, watching game films on the dorm room's walls. His only comment to the coach was to ask him to bring some more film.

"Hacksaw did a lot for this team," Lott remembered. "He created a lot of good habits for this organization. He taught a lot of people how to win. He even taught some of the coaches how to win." Walsh agreed and would later describe Reynolds's acquisition as the most telling personnel move he ever made. "Jack gave us leadership and maturity and toughness and set an example for everybody," he explained. "As strange a guy as he was, he really put us on the map. I think that single addition was the key to our success."

The effect of all of Walsh's off-season activity was not immediately obvious, however. The Niners started the 1981 season losing to Detroit by a touchdown, turned around and beat Chicago at home, then went to Atlanta and were blown out by seventeen points. With his club at 1-2 and unimpressive, Bill remembered, the "questions at the weekly press conference were getting more and more pointed, with reporters demanding to know when they could expect a competitive team," and when the coach pled with them to give his squad a chance to find its way, "they looked at my plea as just another excuse."

And they weren't the only ones with doubts. Right offensive tackle Keith Fahnhorst, who'd been a Niner through the two previous regimes and was one of the current team's locker-room leaders, was so discouraged after the Atlanta loss that he asked to be traded. Fahnhorst too was told to wait. The next game was with New Orleans and preparations for it were accompanied by a tangible sense of desperation among the coaches. Sam Wyche rode to work at Nevada Street every morning with defensive coordinator Chuck

Studley and the two were frank with each other about just how dicey the season was starting to look. Studley even said that if they didn't beat New Orleans they just might not win another game all year.

On the last Sunday in September, however, the Niners managed to handle the Saints by a touchdown in an ugly game that inspired little in the way of confidence, and the nine counties entered October full of grumbling about once again having to wait until next year.

Bill Walsh talks to Fred Dean after Dean's debut against Dallas, 1981

┊┊┊┊┊ ┊┊┊┊┊ ┊┊┊┊┊

16

WHO'S NEXT?

n his later years, Bill Walsh's face lit up whenever he spoke of the 1981 season. He described it as "the most satisfying" of his career. By all accounts, he enjoyed himself more and more as it progressed and was at his most engaged and least distant. He was not without worries, but there was little dark angst or private agonizing. Several of his players would later say this was the last year he seemed to be having fun at his work. "Walsh loved coaching that season," Ronnie Lott offered. "He was warm, open, and genuine." And he never coached better.

What made the year so transcendent was the magic of his team realizing itself. Seemingly against all odds, the elements he had so carefully collected catalyzed into a seamless whole—just as he had imagined in his most optimistic moments—generating a momentum that eventually became an almost spiritual force as the season progressed, empowering everyone it included. There were more than a dozen teams in the league who had more talent and by all rights should have been better than they, but were not.

"There weren't many number one picks among us," Guy Benjamin observed. "We weren't the guys you would pick if you were picking a team. But when we started winning, this magic synergy cut in. Guys started making plays they had never made before—different guys in different games—and everyone's play went up as a consequence. Nobody was untouched by it. The effect was like a vacuum that just sucked you along to play at that level. That synergy just started to happen and then everything fed on itself. We came together and never stopped." In the end, theirs would be a triumph of collective play and mutual reinforcement. "Everybody's pulling on the same end of the rope at the same time," Hacksaw Reynolds explained, "with nobody having a real big head and everybody having confidence in each other."

Soon, the results spoke for themselves. After their stumbling 2-2 start, the Forty Niners would win eleven of their twelve remaining regular season games. Four of those wins would stand out as landmarks.

The first was the victory on the road over the Washington Redskins during week five that started them on their way. Bill later described the Washington contest as "the first game that showed what kind of team we could be." After taking the opening kickoff, Joe Montana led the offense on a thirteen-play, eighty-yard drive that made the score 7–0. The Redskins then answered with their own drive down to the Niners' twenty-two, where they ran a sweep to Ronnie Lott's side. Just as Lott came up to make the tackle, the Washington runner leaped into the air so the top of Lott's helmet hit squarely on the ball and sent it tumbling into the air. Dwight Hicks grabbed it on the fly and ran eighty yards for another touchdown. Two more ball-control drives generaled by Montana led to a touchdown and a field goal and the Niners went into the locker room at halftime leading 24–3. In the second half, Hicks intercepted a pass and ran it back more than seventy yards to the Washington twenty-two. The offense took over but Montana threw an interception on their second play, so the defense was right back on the field. Then on Washington's first play, Hicks grabbed another interception and ran it into the end zone to make the score 30-3. Two late Washington touchdowns made no difference and the Niners were 3-2.

Walsh later described the formula of quick-striking defense and ball-control offense that first evidenced itself in Washington and would become his team's signature: "The role of the defense was to go in and hit them so hard and so quick that we'd shatter them, we'd shock them," he told *Sports*

Illustrated. "We don't have massive people; we don't have gigantic linemen or linebackers. But we're quick strikers, hard, punishing tacklers. We did that and we held the ball on offense. When you can do that, you . . . attack [their] game plan itself. It's not like completing a ninety-yard pass. That will get a defense fired up. They'll say, 'Damnit, you won't do that again!' I want them saying over and over again, 'Damnit, we've got to stop them from making first downs. Damnit, they just completed that five-yard pass again.'"

Playing that way in Washington, his team proved they were better than everyone thought. They still had no idea just how good they could be, but they were learning.

The following week Dallas came to Candlestick for the Niners' most significant test thus far. First, however, Walsh added one final ingredient to his squad that would prove critical.

Fred Dean was among the league's elite pass rushers, though hardly the typical physical specimen usually found on the defensive line. Only six feet two and 227 pounds, with skinny legs and hips and broad shoulders, he nonetheless generated enormous force to go with extraordinary quickness, often throwing far larger offensive linemen out of his way on one play, then running around them on the next. He did all this without ever lifting weights and despite being a chain smoker of menthol cigarettes. One of his teammates found him in the weight room one day, smoking a Kool, and asked what was going on. Fred responded that he was thinking about lifting but had decided to sit down and wait for the feeling to pass. Weights or not, Fred generated force and acceleration the likes of which Bill Walsh had never seen in another player. Dean was farm-boy strong from stacking hay bales growing up in Ruston, Louisiana, and had been drafted by the San Diego Chargers in the second round out of Louisiana Tech, where he'd played linebacker. The Chargers had turned him into a defensive end, where he averaged almost ten sacks a season over six years and was named the NFL's 1979 defensive player of the year.

Dean had signed a long-term contract as a rookie and now felt himself considerably underpaid. San Diego had refused his demands to renegotiate his deal, so Dean had been refusing to play for the first four weeks of the season. Finally, San Diego's owner had lost his patience and decided to trade him. The market was limited because Dean—shy and something of a loner who loved quoting Shakespeare—had acquired an undeserved reputation as a malcontent and many teams considered his salary demands exorbitant. That did not deter the Niners. John McVay finalized a deal with the Chargers GM the week of the Washington game, giving up a second-round draft pick in 1982 and the right for San Diego to switch that year's first-round picks should the Niners' be earlier than their own, but Dean wasn't available to play in Washington because he was still waiting for his new contract. McVay finished that contract negotiation by the start of the next week, almost tripling Dean's salary. Bill checked ahead of time with Eddie, laying out how much it was going to cost; as usual, Eddie didn't drag his feet. "If you think he can help us win," he said, "get him." Dean helped and then some. For the rest of the year, Walsh remembered, Fred Dean was "unstoppable."

During the practices leading up to the Dallas game, Bill reminded his team on several occasions of last year's drubbing and just how humiliated they had been as Dallas ran up the score. He left no doubt that the Cowboys—arrogant bullies that they were—had held them in complete contempt then and felt the same way now. The effect was tangible. Come game day, Bill recalled, "we were sky high. We couldn't wait to play these guys." Which made the outcome simultaneously shocking and predictable. "One team was overconfident and self-satisfied, the other intense and inspired," Walsh explained. "We exploded and they were flat."

The Niners took the opening kickoff and drove for a touchdown. Then they held the Cowboys for three downs, took a punt, and launched another touchdown drive. Next, Dallas fumbled and Montana turned that into another touchdown, followed by another Cowboys three and out, and a Niners drive for a field goal. The score was 24–0 before Dallas even had a first down. Fred Dean announced his presence in that first quarter by knocking a Cowboys offensive tackle over backward and then throwing their quarterback to the ground before he'd even had a chance to look downfield. Dean sacked the Cowboy quarterback three times in the first half, once again in the second, and was also credited with forcing Dallas to throw before they were ready another seven times. In the meantime, Joe Montana passed for almost three hundred yards, hitting Freddy Solomon for a first-half score and his buddy Dwight Clark for a seventy-eighty-yard touchdown after intermission. Ronnie Lott intercepted a pass and ran it in for another. The final count was Forty Niners 45, Cowboys 14, and it wasn't that close. Afterward, the *Chronicle* described the game as "the most important win since Bill Walsh took over as coach and general manager."

Whipping the Cowboys handily was a benchmark inside the locker room as well. After that, Randy Cross pointed out, "we knew we could win and went into the 'Next Mode.' Our mindset from then on was just 'Who's next?' It didn't matter who they were. We were ready for them, just tell us who's next."

Walsh used the victory's aftermath to reinforce his team's hunger to overcome its doubters. At the time, *Monday Night Football* on ABC was the hottest property in sports television and one of its features each week at halftime was to show highlights from the previous weekend's games. The Cowboys were regulars on those highlights, but the Forty Niners had never appeared on them and didn't that Monday either. ABC was featuring a game between Dallas and the Rams the following week and apparently chose not to deflate the anticipated audience by recounting Dallas's embarrassment at the hands of the upstarts from San Francisco. Walsh seized on that slight at his Tuesday morning press conference and used it to hone his team's edge through the press.

The Forty Niners were still not being accorded the proper respect, Walsh railed. "We're not accepted nationally, obviously. The football elitists, jockstrap elitists don't consider us in the comfort zone. There are power sources, influence sources in the National Football League, forty-five-year-old men who are football groupies who prefer that we do not exist. . . . It's obvious, it's blatant. In my opinion, it's a disservice to the public."

Years later he would ascribe the outburst to his being "impetuous and foolish," but at the time Bill wanted to make sure his team felt they still had a lot to prove and that there were lots of people trying to prevent them from doing so.

Dallas had been a yardstick game, allowing Walsh's team to measure itself against one of the acknowledged best. And the Niners faced another, perhaps even more daunting yardstick three weeks later, when they went into Pittsburgh to take on a football legend. By then San Francisco was 6-2 and Pittsburgh, winners of their fourth Super Bowl just two years earlier, were 5-3. The Steelers, an AFC team, had not lost a game at home to the Niners'

NFC in a decade and, in the words of one sports columnist, "try to scare the wits out of you . . . with the attitude that they are big and bad, and they're going to shove the ball down your throat." Where the Dallas matchup had been between two "thinking man's" teams, this would be a game all about hitting one another. Most pundits labeled it a mismatch. Pittsburgh was the NFL's reigning symbol of brute force and, despite its reborn defense, San Francisco's success thus far had been largely attributed to luck and its offensive finesse. But the Niners were not about to concede the issue. Before their first game, Bill had posted a sign that would stay by the locker-room door for the duration of the season. It declared, WE WILL NOT BE OUTHIT, and had been signed by every one of his players. This was the day the team would make good on that pledge. In the end, Bill would call it "one of the biggest games in the Forty Niners' history."

It was also a bragging rights game for Eddie D. He was there in Three Rivers Stadium with his father and a whole section full of DeBartolo Corp. employees bused in from Youngstown, all decked out in Forty Niners red, sitting together surrounded by a sea of Steelers black and gold. Eddie'd never beaten the Steelers since he'd owned his team and he wanted to so badly he ached. It was also a big game for Joe Montana, who'd grown up not far away in western Pennsylvania. "To say I was in awe of the Pittsburgh Steelers was, and still is, an understatement," he remembered. "They still had a lot of the players from their [last] Super Bowl team. As far as I was concerned, if we could go into Pittsburgh and beat them, we were good enough to win it all. They were our litmus test." Unfortunately, Joe also went into the contest with badly bruised ribs that would limit him throughout.

To motivate his squad before taking the field, Bill delivered his Burma speech. The Japanese army at that point in World War II had seemed unbeatable, he pointed out, and as the British army retreated, the Japanese captured and executed British stragglers at every opportunity, taking no prisoners. When the Brits were down to a force of barely a thousand, they found themselves backed up against the foot of a mountain with no place to run and they had to stand their ground, having no choice but fight or be massacred. And in a legendary stand, they fought the Japanese to a standstill and saved Burma from invasion. Today, a long way from home, Walsh argued, the Niners were in the same position. It was fifty against fifty thousand and they would have to beat the Steelers their own way or be thrown back into the years of humiliation they were trying to escape. "We have to fight back," he implored. There was no other option.

The game was "rock 'em, sock 'em" from the first whistle, with fights breaking out on the field early and often. "We had to be physical to survive," Bill pointed out afterward. "The fights were not ragged, cheap shots. They were hard-hitting plays where we would not back off, and neither would they. The fights showed up early and I interpret that as positive. It means we played head-to-head from the start and didn't resort to fighting when we were behind." The hitting throughout the game was vicious, epitomized by the play of rookie safety Carlton Williamson. Twice in a row the Steelers sent wide receivers on crossing patterns into his zone, and he knocked both of those receivers out, leaving them to hobble off the field after several minutes lying on the turf with trainers huddling over them. No one, home or visitors, was giving any quarter.

The two teams were stalemated in the first quarter, neither able to muster a score, but in the second quarter the Forty Niners offense, which had trouble moving the ball all day, managed to convert an interception by Eric Wright into a forty-six-yard drive, capped by a touchdown throw from Montana to Charle Young. Then Williamson fell on a Steelers fumble and, unable to move the ball for a first down, Montana managed an eight-yard run that got the ball into field goal range and added another three points. They led 10–0 at halftime, but the game began coming apart for the Niners in the third quarter. Montana threw an interception at the fifty-yard line that was run in for a touchdown, then threw another that was run back thirty-one yards and turned into another Pittsburgh touchdown one play later. At that point, almost everyone in the stadium, even some of those in red, expected the San Francisco upstarts to fold.

Instead, Walsh's team fought back. First they drove sixty-eight yards, only to have a field goal attempt blocked. After stopping the Steelers again, this time by virtue of Ronnie Lott's fumble recovery, another Niners drive came up short. Then the defense made yet another stop when Carlton Williamson intercepted a pass and ran it back twenty-eight yards. The Niners' ensuing final drive covered forty-three yards in nine plays and left them in the lead, 17–14, with five and a half minutes left to play. The rest of the game was the Niners' defense fighting tooth and nail to keep the Steelers from scoring. Finally, with time running out, the defensive line collapsed Pittsburgh's pass protection on a fourth down with three yards to go, and the game was over. There were plenty of heroes: Montana had played one of his worst games of the season but had come through when they needed him; Dwight Clark had caught seven passes; the offensive line had dominated the line of scrimmage; and the young defensive backs, now dubbed "Dwight Hicks and His Hot Licks," had been spectacular. Terry Bradshaw, the Pittsburgh quarterback, described them as the best he'd seen all year, bar none.

Afterwards, the Forty Niners' locker room was bedlam. Everyone was screaming and jumping up and down, Walsh included. Eddie D. and his dad were there, celebrating with all the rest, thousand-dollar suits be damned. "I don't want to get too excited," Eddie told the press. "It's going to take another draft, another year to have a real contending club, but these kids we have are amazing." No one else in the celebration was so cautious. Dwight Clark later called the game "the turning point of the whole season. When we got into the locker room after the game and even Bill Walsh was jumping up and down like we were, you knew we were a good team."

And when the Niners' charter flight reached San Francisco International in the middle of the night, several thousand fans were out there to greet them.

This season would bestow visibility and even stardom on a number of the Niners, but none of them more than their coach. For much of the year, Bill Walsh was singled out as the symbol and prime mover of their unlikely run, usually pictured on the sideline overseeing his troops.

His presence there was iconic and, to the larger football world, seemed as different as his team. Unlike the rest of the league's head coaches, he wore a headset that connected him to his coaches up in the press box who had an overview of the field, and with several coaches on the sideline as well. All were feeding him information, starting with the down and distance, and all were under orders to keep it short and shut up if he talked, which was rare and usually only to request specifics about what defenses the other team was using in given situations or how the others thought a particular play might work. Mostly, he listened and consulted the one-page game plan he kept under a transparent plastic cover in his hand, sending in a play and then immediately turning to the next, never yelling or expressing panic or even hurry. The headset made him look like a NASA space-flight controller and contributed mightily to his burgeoning reputation for genius.

Silver-headed and invariably dressed in a white sweater and tan pants, Walsh also seemed elegant, an island of refinement in what was otherwise a sea of physical brutality. No one else in the game looked anything like him. His face never betrayed emotion, almost always assuming a professorial expression that seemed evidence of thoughtful detachment and intellectual meditation, always pondering, seemingly never perturbed or even ruffled. One author described it as "the pose of a man before a fire with a glass of port in one hand and a volume of Matthew Arnold's essays in the other." An admiring sports columnist noted that "you half expect his headset to be playing Mozart." Precise, determined, and confident without ever being cocky, his team played like he looked.

The fourth of the season's landmark wins was full of personal vindication for Bill, though he never said as much publicly. After the Niners' record reached 10-3 and they had clinched their division title, their next opponent was the Cincinnati Bengals, also 10-3 and considered by Walsh to be "the best team in the league by light years." This would be Walsh's first trip back to his old haunts since Paul Brown had denied him the head coaching job five years earlier and Bill had fled, "embarrassed and in despair, wondering how I could ever return and face these people." The Bengals were on their third head coach since Walsh's departure, having gone 6-10 the year before, and were loaded with high draft picks. Their offense was ranked second in the NFL, their defense in the top five, and they were on a five-game winning streak in which they'd won every game by at least two touchdowns. At his weekly press conference, Bill praised them profusely and indicated he might very well rest his starters and just use reserves, since his team's place in the playoffs was now guaranteed and their chances against the Bengals would obviously be slim at best. He also said that there was no revenge factor involved in playing Paul Brown's team, none at all.

Both statements were less than the truth. The former was an attempt to lull Cincinnati into thinking his team wouldn't be at its best and perhaps rob his opponents of a little emotional edge. In truth, he was planning to play his starters, and all week long he drilled into them that they would have to hit as hard as or harder than they had in Pittsburgh to have a chance. The second statement was a kind of standardized denial, hoping to defuse his homecoming, but his team, at least, saw right through it. "The players knew that he wanted this game bad," Joe Montana explained. "I don't think it needed to be said." Bill himself would later admit that "this truly was going to be a once in a lifetime experience for me." And so it was.

The game itself was one-sided. The Niners forced six turnovers—including four by the young secondary—out of a team that had only given up fifteen in the preceding thirteen weeks; Montana threw for two touchdowns and ran for a third; Dwight Clark caught enough passes to become the team's first thousand-yard receiver in a decade; and Fred Dean, returning from an injury to his sternum, manhandled the Bengals offensive line all game long, getting one sack and countless hurries. All the vaunted Cincinnati offense could muster was a single field goal. Halfway through the fourth quarter, with the victory in hand, Walsh put in his backups to finish the game, just like he'd intimated earlier in the week. And up in his owner's booth in the press box, Paul Brown watched it all with noticeable discomfort. Bill never saw him, but his wife, Geri—along for the team's return to her old home—did and greeted her husband's former mentor, but Brown seemed ill at ease throughout the encounter. Afterward, according to the *Chronicle,* Bill was flashing a smile "that could be seen all the way across the Ohio River."

Looking down at his old town as the Niners' charter flight lifted off on the way home—the lights below so familiar to him for so many years— Walsh, still beaming, experienced an enormous sense of relief. The shame and despair of his five-year-old rejection had finally been dissipated. "It was a very satisfying feeling," he remembered, "very, very satisfying."

At that point, Bill also allowed himself to think that if this roll carried his Niners all the way to the Super Bowl, he might very well get a rematch.

Bill greets his team outside the team hotel before Super Bowl XVI

17

WORST TO FIRST

s an old man, remembering the success he had crafted after just three years at the Niners' helm, Bill Walsh was most proud of its impact on the Bay Area. He had always wanted to matter in the world outside of football and the 1981 season would gain him that stature throughout the nine counties and beyond, enshrining him as a civic savior as well as a championship football coach. "I thought it would be so important to have a team in which everybody could take pride," he remembered. "A successful sports team would cut across all social, ethnic, and cultural levels and give everyone something to share. San Francisco was a city in conflict with itself at the time and we helped heal it, far more, I think, than most sports franchises did for their cities."

At the time, one University of California sociologist observed, "The Bay Area's sense of itself, its internal image of what it was about, had been devastated. The Bay area had always been 'the left coast,' like a section of western Europe set down in America. It thought of itself as cosmopolitan, advanced, intellectual—with an overriding belief that its differentness was its strength. Then three things happened in the late seventies that literally shattered all that. The first was the mass suicide in Jonestown, where a previously respected religious congregation moved from the city down to Guyana and went over the edge. The second was the assassination of the mayor and the board of supervisors' one gay member by another board member. And the third was the AIDS epidemic, which had just begun to decimate the area's huge gay community. Those things literally sent shock waves that shattered the social and cultural confidence at a very fundamental level, from the lowest strata to the highest strata. Then Bill Walsh came along and the Niners made their magical run to the Super Bowl and all of a sudden there was something the people in the Bay Area could wrap their minds around again and believe in."

What the Niners provided in that historical moment was a team that not only won, but that won by playing the game in a manner that complimented the way most of the people within two hours' drive of San Francisco wanted to think of themselves. Walsh's team was the champion of the thoughtful, besting the short-sighted and doctrinaire, winning battles with their mindset, both efficient and daring at the same time, and carrying it off with seeming aplomb. They were dominant by virtue of acting outside the accepted box, and in so doing became the vanguard of a reborn communal identity, living proof on Sunday afternoons that the Bay Area's ethos could not only survive but prosper no matter what it was up against. And the Niners were worshipped accordingly. There were no more empty seats at Candlestick and, by December, it seemed as though everyone in the nine counties was talking about "our team." Come January, the road to the Super Bowl ran through San Francisco, which had the best record in the NFC, and now, for the first time in a long time, home field advantage meant something there.

The first to test it were the New York Giants, winners of the wild card game the previous week. The Niners had won the matchup between them in the regular season, 17–10, also at Candlestick, but this time the Niners' home field was even more daunting. Rain had dominated the San Francisco weather for several weeks—so much so that the Niners had to abandon their inundated practice fields at 711 Nevada Street and move their workouts down the road to Stanford, where the fields had better drainage—and as a result, the sod at Candlestick was an oozing, gooey mess. To make things even worse, Candlestick's water table rose with the tides in the nearby bay, forcing even more water up out of the ground. The city attempted to resod the surface of the field but once cleats touched the new grass, hunks of it were sent flying around like cheap toupees in a wind storm. Between plays, a special crew would rush out to try to tamp down as many divots as possible. The Niners were at least familiar with the effects, giving them a leg up in the slop, and the poor footing would be instrumental in surmounting their biggest tactical challenge.

The Giants' strong suit was a ferocious defense led by Lawrence Taylor, a rookie outside linebacker who was revolutionizing his position. The *San Francisco Examiner* described him as "a bigger, faster Fred Dean" who was already considered the best linebacker in the entire league and was a phenomenal pass rusher. In the wild card game against the Philadelphia Eagles, he had been unblockable and single-handedly dismantled the Eagles offense. The issue facing Walsh was how to get Taylor blocked. In most schemes, including the Niners', blocking a rushing outside linebacker was a task for either the running back or the tight end, but neither stood much of a chance against Taylor. He was simply too much for them to handle. The Eagles had tried to use their left tackle on him with no success and Bill knew his own left tackle was even less suited to the task than the Eagles' had been. After much consultation with offensive line coach Bobb McKittrick, the Niners settled on pulling left guard John Ayers in passing situations, counting on the center's block to cover the resulting hole, and using Ayers, six feet five and 270 pounds, to protect Montana's blind side.

The maneuver was essential—Walsh's game plan called for passing on seventeen of the first twenty-two plays—and worked better than even Walsh had imagined. Ayers, a Texan who trained in the off-season by hitching himself to a six-foot-high tractor tire and dragging it through a ploughed field, shut Taylor out. "I couldn't figure out what to do with him," Taylor later admitted. In the end, the rookie, slowed by the sloppy field, tried to run over Ayers and failed miserably. And once Walsh saw that Montana would have time to pass, he knew the game was won. By halftime, Joe had completed fifteen of twenty-two passes for almost 300 yards and the Niners led 24–10. The final score was 38–24.

And the Super Bowl was now just one game away.

. . .

The contest for the conference championship was held at Candlestick a week later against "America's Team," the Dallas Cowboys. Bill Walsh would later call the game "the greatest in the Forty Niners' history."

For the Niners' fans, the matchup was full of ghosts. San Francisco had last appeared in the playoffs during three straight years between 1970 and 1972 and all three times the Forty Niners had been eliminated by the Cowboys, in games that were decided in the fourth quarter by Cowboys comebacks. On top of that historic grudge, the two current teams simply didn't like each other very much—and Dallas was quick to say so. Too Tall Jones, Dallas's Pro Bowl defensive end, told the press early in the week that he didn't know who any of the "no name" Niners were but made it clear he thought their season was a fluke and declared he had no respect for them under any circumstances. Jones and his teammates also announced that their regular season blowout at the Niners' hands was meaningless and for this game, "the real Dallas Cowboys" were going to show up and teach them a lesson they'd never forget.

Bill made sure his team heard about that attitude all week long. While the rains had eased and game day would be sunny, the Niners were still unable to use the fields at Nevada Street, so Eddie flew the whole team to Los Angeles, where they used the Rams' facilities to prepare for the game. Throughout, Walsh kept talking about the Cowboys. "This goddamn Dallas team," he railed. "They can't keep their mouths shut. They're doing the same thing again this week. They say, 'This time the Forty Niners will be meeting the real Cowboys.' Their press releases are all about how they're going to kick ass. They're so arrogant. . . . Nobody ever beats the 'real' Dallas Cowboys. If they lose, there's always somebody missing, the airplane food isn't just right, or their accommodations are wrong. Well, I'm fed up with this bullshit. . . . So let's be ready for them. . . . We're going to knock them all over the field."

Having played Dallas three times in the last three years, Bill knew what the Cowboys did and why they did it. Their "Doomsday Defense" had a history of crushing its opponents, but it was predictable, always adjusting the same way against specific formations. He thought he could confuse their front four with fakes designed to give them false reads and could force automatic adjustments in their defensive backs' pass coverage by using two tight end formations and sending a man in motion, creating mismatches against his wide receivers. He was convinced he could get someone open for a pass whenever he wanted. On top of that, Bill knew his team was quicker than the Cowboys at every position—an advantage Dallas failed to account for—and that speed difference would allow the Niners to move the ball on offense and attack the Cowboys on defense. And he was right. Using that game plan, his team would outgain Dallas 393 yards to 250. Nonetheless, the game would be far closer than the statistics.

For home games, Bill's ritual was to ride to Candlestick with Billy Wilson, a former Pro Bowl wide receiver for the Niners during the fifties and now an administrative assistant, and Bill maintained this for the biggest game in his career thus far. After some aimless chitchat about the weather and their families as they drove up Highway 101, he and Wilson talked about Dallas. Billy shared his memories of those previous playoff defeats and offered that this current squad was the best Cowboys team he'd ever seen. Then the two friends went through Dallas's strengths and how the Niners would counter them, with Bill coming back again and again to his team's quickness. As usual, Bill could not have seemed calmer. Once in the locker room after his team had finished its warm-ups, he gave no speeches, taking a short nap, "to pull myself out of the stress and tension and sort of meditate," and then went through the room, shaking hands with everyone on the roster and offering each some personalized encouragement.

The game began at 2:01 PM PST, on a field whose footing was considerably better than it had been the week before. The Cowboys received the kickoff but could do nothing with the ball and had to punt. The Niners then drove for their first touchdown. The most notable play of the drive came on a rollout by Montana that was sniffed out by Too Tall Jones, who looked like he was about to throw Montana for a loss until Joe gave him a fake that sent the defensive end sprawling. Montana stepped up, completed a pass, then turned to the prostrate Jones and shouted, "Respect that, motherfucker!" From that point the first half was back and forth, with Dallas finally going ahead 17–14 on the strength of a drive made possible by two penalty calls that gave the Cowboys almost fifty yards and which Walsh would later list among the worst officiating he had experienced in more than a quarter century as a coach. Nonetheless, the Niners might well have been in the lead were it not for their turnovers. Before the game was over they would fumble the ball three times and throw three interceptions, nullifying their offensive advantage. Given those mistakes, Joe Montana remembered, "we were lucky to only be down by three points."

Bill made no speeches at halftime either, only going through plays and assignments in his usual calm and businesslike fashion before the team returned to the field. The back and forth continued in the third quarter, as did the Niners turnovers, but as the fourth quarter began, the home team was clinging to a 21–20 lead. Then the Niners fumbled again close to the fifty-yard line and the Cowboys drove the short field for a touchdown that put them in the lead, 27–21. "A big hush came over the crowd" at that point, Charle Young remembered, making a sound "as if a coffin had closed on our season." Still, the Forty Niners fought back, driving deep into Dallas territory when they got the ball, only to have their effort aborted by Joe's third interception of the day. Dallas, however, could do nothing with the ball and after nine plays punted deep into the Niners' territory, giving the home team one more chance. As Montana and the offense took the field, the ball was spotted on their own eleven-yard line with 4:54 left in the game.

What followed would become the stuff of legends.

Bill understood that the situation could not have been more dire. Backed up as the Niners were, the Cowboys defense was going to turn its pass rushers loose and use five defensive backs to throttle the passing attack. No one expected the Forty Niners to run the ball, especially since the running back they had on the field was Lenvil Elliott, who was thirty years old, had been out with knee surgery through the entire regular season, and had only been added to the roster for this game. But Walsh, who'd first coached Elliott at Cincinnati, knew the back was "reliable" and savvy. He also knew the all-out pass rush would give his offensive line good blocking angles for running wide. So Bill confounded everyone, giving Elliott the ball up the middle for a six-yard gain, then, after completing a pass in the flat to Solomon for six, he sent Elliott around right end for another eleven, followed by the same play to the left for seven more. A penalty against Dallas and another short pass and the Niners were at their own forty-six-yard line with the clock stopped at 2:00 to play.

Walsh now had the Dallas defense on its heels, unsure what he would do. "Bill was ahead of everybody," Dwight Clark remembered. And he maintained his advantage. After a five-yard pass, he called Freddy Solomon's number and sent him around end on a flanker reverse that picked up fourteen. Next Joe hit Dwight for ten, then threw to Freddy over the middle for twelve more. At 1:15 with the ball on Dallas's thirteen-yard line, Bill called a time-out to talk things over with Joe. The first play afterward was a pass for Freddy Solomon, who was open in the end zone, but Montana threw the ball wide and out of his reach. Breaking his usual professorial calm, Walsh bellowed in frustration at the miscue. Then, regaining his composure, he called Elliott's number again on a sweep to the left, getting the ball down to Dallas's six, where the Cowboys called a time-out to give their defense a chance to regroup. There was now less than a minute to play.

Bill and Joe huddled again at the sideline. They had two downs to play with here, Walsh reminded his quarterback, so if a receiver wasn't open, throw the ball away and they'd try again on fourth down. The play Bill called for third down was "Brown Left Slot Sprint Right Option." As designed, Dwight Clark would run a short hook and Freddy Solomon would run past him, hopefully wiping his defender off on Dwight in the process, and complete a short out in the end zone. At the same time, Montana would run to his right, parallel to Freddy's path, and throw to him on the move. Solomon was the designated target but if the play broke down, Clark was supposed to wheel around and run along the back line of the end zone so Joe would have another target. It was a play they had been practicing since training camp, but had been so rarely used that the wide receivers had been complaining about having to go through it every week as part of Bill's "just in case" drill. Today, however, they had already used it once to score their first touchdown when Freddy found himself open in the end zone. The last thing Walsh told Joe as he returned to the field was to throw it away if there was trouble but don't under any circumstances try to force the ball in and risk another interception.

Almost nothing about the play went as planned. Dwight ran his initial route just as it was drawn up but was unable to pick the defender off of Freddy, who, besides being covered, slipped on the turf and was nowhere to be seen. In the meantime, Too Tall Jones hadn't rushed straight in as anticipated but had instead floated to the outside. Keith Fahnhorst, the Niners right tackle, was supposed to block Jones, but before he could get to him, Fahnhorst was cut down by the fullback's block on the linebacker, leaving Too Tall free to chase Joe. Meanwhile, Montana was retreating toward the sideline looking for someone to throw to. Fortunately, Dwight had wheeled for the back line as he was supposed to. With Too Tall and a couple of other Cowboys in his face, Joe made a couple of pump fakes to slow them down, then spotted Clark running across the end zone. "I was off balance and falling back," Joe remembered. "There was only one kind of pass to throw:

Put the sucker up high and hard." The ball managed to clear Too Tall and at first looked to be a throwaway. The defensive back closest to Dwight was sure it was over the Niners wide receiver's head and uncatchable. But Clark caught it anyway. Soaring as high as he could, with arms outstretched, Clark recalled, "it hit my hands and I juggled it, but I caught it on the way down." Immortalized as "The Catch," that play would become one of the most famous in NFL history.

The game's last fifty-one seconds produced some anxiety as the Cowboys tried desperately to get into field goal range, but a game-saving tackle by Eric Wright and a sack and fumble recovery by the defensive line preserved the victory: Niners 28, Cowboys 27.

Afterward, Eddie D. rushed around the locker room, hugging every one of his "guys" in a state of hysterical ecstasy. Montana, the picture of cool under pressure all day long, hyperventilated on his way off the field, passed out, and had to be revived by the equipment manager. Bill Walsh—elated, spent, and already thinking about the next game—changed out of his sideline clothes and put in an appearance at the party being held in Eddie's owner's box before driving down the Peninsula to decompress in the hot tub out back of his home in Menlo Park. When Bill left Candlestick, the stadium was deserted, but Eddie and his buddies were still going strong.

Super Bowl XVI was the rematch Walsh had been anticipating since his return trip to Cincinnati a month and a half earlier. In the classic Hollywood ending to this miracle story, Bill would have to best the man who both gave him his start and then tried his hardest to make it impossible for Bill to get this far.

The game itself would be the highest-rated sporting event in television history, drawing more than 110 million viewers. During the week of practices in Redwood City before Super Bowl week began, the facilities at Nevada Street couldn't hold the number of reporters and camera crews now attending Bill's press conferences, so a temporary trailer was brought in and set up near the headquarters for use by the media. Walsh convened his press conferences with his usual aplomb and seeming equanimity, "a man with milk white skin who always looks as if he's just stepped out of a steam box," one reporter hyperbolized. "He has a faraway, slightly spiritual look, like a martyr in a medieval painting." When questioned about playing

Paul Brown's team, Bill once again denied that the history between him and his former mentor had any bearing on the football game that would be played on January 24. Once again, however, his team was unconvinced. "Make no mistake, Walsh would have done anything to beat the Bengals," Ronnie Lott asserted. "Although he didn't verbalize his feelings to us, it was obvious that Walsh was obsessed with showing up Brown."

And Bill was far more worried than he had been the first time the two teams had met. The Cincinnati talent advantage seemed far more daunting now and most pundits had installed the Bengals as favorites, despite the regular season outcome between the two. In game planning, Walsh wracked his brain for plays that were far enough off the wall to catch Cincinnati unawares. The Niners' doubters had long claimed that Walsh was "doing it all with mirrors," using trickery to hide an inferior squad, and Bill had always disputed the claim. For this game, however, he later admitted it was true. "I was looking for anything to gain an advantage," he remembered. "I wasn't desperate but I went deep into the playbook for stuff we never would have used in a regular season game." Usually about 80 plays, Walsh's game plan grew to more than 120 before he was done. Joe Montana described it as the most detailed and complex he'd ever encountered.

Otherwise, however, Walsh's worry was nowhere to be seen. Indeed, Dwight Clark observed, he'd "never seen Bill so loose." Everything that came up was fodder for his humor, using, in Ronnie Lott's words, "every opportunity to turn problems and distractions into jokes and jabs to keep us from worrying too much about the game."

This year the Super Bowl was being staged in Detroit's indoor arena, the first Super Bowl ever held in a cold weather city, and after the week of practice at home, the team flew there for the final week of pregame hype. For the first time ever, Bill did not fly with them. He left early to stop in Washington, D.C., where he received the Coach of the Year award at a banquet of the Touchdown Club, in front of an audience that included President Ronald Reagan and most of the town's leading politicians. This recognition was one of a host of such honors Walsh was selected for that year, winning all the various Coach of the Year votes hands down. He then flew to Detroit, where the temperature was minus seven degrees, arriving a couple of hours before the Niners' charter flight. Looking for one more way to keep his team loose, he paid a bellhop twenty dollars to borrow his uniform and when the Niners' buses arrived at their hotel from the airport, he was out front in disguise, attempting to carry their bags. At first, no one recognized him, but when they finally did, his masquerade gave the whole team something to laugh about for the rest of the week.

Bill kept the same approach on game day. As usual, the Niners went over to the stadium on two buses. The early bus left around nine in the morning, carrying all the players who wanted a lot of time to get ready—including Hacksaw Reynolds, already dressed in full uniform from the time he ate breakfast—and all the support personnel, like the trainer and equipment manager. The other bus left around eleven, carrying everybody else, including Bill and Eddie. The first bus reached the stadium without incident, but the second bus got to within half a mile and was then stalled in an intractable traffic jam, caused by a police roadblock clearing the way for a motorcade carrying Vice President George H.W. Bush. When the backup showed no signs of abating, Eddie D. couldn't take it anymore and, accompanied by his guest, O. J. Simpson, headed off cross-country through the snow drifts. Bill then got on the bus's public address system and told his team that they were missing the game but that the equipment manager was calling plays, his assistant was at quarterback, and they'd just scored to take the lead, 7–0. The ensuing laughter broke the tension.

When the second bus finally reached its destination less than two hours before kickoff, Bill still seemed as loose as ever. He had always had a rule against anyone playing music out loud in the locker room, but this time he waived it. Joe Montana had a song from a Kenny Loggins cassette cued up on his boom box and Walsh insisted he play it over and over again, out loud, at top volume.

> *This is it!*
> *Make no mistake where you are.*
> *This is it!*
> *Your back's to the corner.*
> *This is it!*
> *Don't be a fool anymore.*
> *This is it!*
> *The waiting is over . . .*
> *For once in your life, here's your miracle*
> *Stand up and fight!*
> *This is it!*

Walsh didn't have much to say in the way of a pregame speech. He reminded his team that they had beaten these guys before and that football was like boxing, where you carry a loss for life. The Bengals would know they'd been beaten the last time they saw us, he predicted, and they'd be gun shy.

Bill's prediction at first seemed right on the mark, once his team had weathered an opening-moment hiccup. The Niners received the kickoff and promptly fumbled the ball away on the return, giving the Bengals the ball on San Francisco's twenty-six-yard line, and Cincinnati then drove down to the five. But a sack pushed them back to the eleven and then Dwight Hicks turned the situation around with an interception and runback that set the Niners up on their own thirty-two. That was followed by an eleven-play, sixty-eighty-yard drive for a touchdown. The biggest gain came from a trick play in which Montana handed the ball to the halfback, Ricky Patton, on a seeming sweep, who handed the ball to Freddy Solomon going the other way on a seeming reverse, who flipped the ball back to Joe, who threw a fourteen-yard pass to Charle Young. For those in the know, that call was Bill Walsh thumbing his nose at Paul Brown. When Walsh worked for him, Brown had always insisted that such "special" plays be in the game plan and that his team always run them first before the other team had a chance to try theirs. Now Walsh—knowing the Cincinnati owner was somewhere up in the Silverdome's luxury boxes—beat him to the punch and smiled inside.

The first half continued in that vein. Bill had installed an unbalanced line for that game, a ploy he had never used before, and the Cincinnati defense seemed confused by it. Their offense was unable to do much either. After the game-opening fumble, San Francisco played mistake free and led at the half 20–0, the biggest halftime margin in the history of the Super Bowl. The game, however, was far from over.

In the third quarter, the *Chronicle* later observed, "the 49ers strangely lost their will and got pushed around like a woozy fighter." The Bengals drove the length of the field for their first touchdown, and when the Niners were unable to do anything on their next possession, the Bengals drove down the field again. Momentum had now shifted completely and a note of desperation began to seep through the Niners' sideline. The Cincinnati advance was relentless and, now late in the third quarter, they found themselves with a first and goal on the Niners' three. What followed next was the most critical series of the game, long remembered by Niners' fans as "the Stand."

On first down, Cincinnati sent its 250-pound fullback into the middle of the line, where he was swarmed over by Hacksaw Reynolds and four others and stopped at the one. During his tape study leading up to the game, Hacksaw discovered that the Cincinnati backfield unintentionally signaled the run by the way they lined up, so when they tried to repeat the fullback's run on second down, linebacker Dan Bunz was able to stuff the lead blocker and Hacksaw led a charge to finish the ball carrier off for no gain. On third down, the Bengals tried to fool the Niners defense and threw a pass to their halfback, who caught the ball slightly behind the line of scrimmage and was immediately drilled by Bunz, again for no gain. Now it was fourth and goal and everybody on the Niners' side of the ball knew the Bengals were going to send their massive fullback into the line one last time and when they did, he was met by a half dozen defenders and only got halfway to the end zone before being buried. The score was still 20–7.

The sideline was jubilant but the Niners offense had to start its next possession backed up against the goal line and only succeeded in gaining enough room to make their ensuing punt easier. Cincinnati took possession and began another drive and this time the Niners had no answer. Early in the fourth quarter, the score was 20–14 and San Francisco had yet to make a first down in the second half. Looking back on this game, a number of Forty Niners players attributed their lackluster offense to Bill's uncharacteristic loss of nerve. "It was the first time I ever saw Bill trying not to lose rather than trying to win," wide receiver Mike Shumann remembered. "His play calling had just tightened up and he got really conservative for the first time since he came here. I think he just wanted to beat Cincinnati so bad. Whatever the reason, there was a little rumbling on the sidelines at that point. We were all saying we had to get more aggressive." Bill would later point out that the Bengals had switched to an attacking style of defense during their comeback and that he hadn't wanted "to take a chance on an interception or a quarterback sack that could turn the game around."

The situation, however, was now critical. Facing a second and fifteen on their own twenty-two, Bill called a "drift" pass for Joe, in which he dropped back and then drifted away from pressure while his receivers got open. Joe then found Mike Wilson for a twenty-two-yard completion along the sideline and a Niners first down at last. Walsh followed that with seven straight running plays to move the ball and use up some clock, then kicked a field goal to extend the San Francisco lead to 23–14. Then on Cincinnati's next

Eric Wright (left) greets fans at the Forty Niners' victory parade

possession, Eric Wright intercepted a pass and carried it deep into the Bengals' territory. Another spate of runs ate up more clock, followed by another field goal, and the score was 26-14. Cincinnati was able to drive one more time to make it 26-21, but a desperation onside kick failed and the San Francisco Forty Niners, 2-14 two seasons earlier, were Super Bowl champions.

And the miracle was now complete.

"This is the highlight of my life," Bill exclaimed afterward. "Anything can happen now."

The Niners were up much of Sunday night celebrating their Super Bowl triumph at their Detroit hotel, then flew west in their chartered airliner and landed at San Francisco International early on Monday afternoon. The players' bags were hauled down to Redwood City, but the players and staff were loaded on buses to go into San Francisco. They were told there was a parade along Market Street planned, to be followed by a victory celebration in front of City Hall. Most responded with grumbles. A number of them were hung over and almost everyone just wanted to go home. That was not possible, however, so they dutifully loaded up. The buses took them to a pier along the Embarcadero where they were switched to motorized cable cars for the parade, to be led by Bill and Eddie. The police expected some twenty-five thousand people to watch the motorcade but Bill doubted it would even be that many. "We started down the Embarcadero," he remembered, "and there were just a handful of people on a corner and a handful on the next corner. And I thought, 'God, is this going to be embarrassing, going down Market Street stalling traffic. No one's gonna be there!' Then we turned the corner onto Market Street and it was unbelievable."

San Francisco's signature boulevard was swarmed over as far as the eye could see. Official estimates later judged the crowd at five hundred thousand minimum. No one could find a precedent in the history of the nine counties for such a turnout for any reason, let alone a football team. With the exception of a lane just wide enough for the procession to squeeze through, the street was solid humanity all the way back to the storefronts. "Everybody was delirious," Ronnie Lott later wrote of that day. "Cheering loudly, waving wildly, 49er fans were hanging from lampposts and windows. They piled on top of cars and phone booths. . . . The whole experience choked me up. I had tears in my eyes for most of the afternoon. It was my real life fairy tale." Bill was no less moved. "I saw young people, tall people, short people, people of color, Asian people, much older people," he explained. "I saw every cross section of people, all standing in unison, from the executives who came out of the office buildings to the people who clean the streets, right next to each other, screaming. It was just the most electrifying moment I've ever had." When the procession finally reached City Hall, the mayor presented Bill with the keys to the city, while he received perhaps the biggest cheers of the afternoon.

One of the signs waving among the sea of a half million people pressing up to the stage said it all.

WHAT, it asked, HATH WALSH WROUGHT?

LOST, THEN FOUND

III

*Bill Walsh, Joe Montana, and Eddie DeBartolo
with their Super Bowl trophy*

||||| ||||| |||||

18

LIFE IN A FISHBOWL

The immediate aftermath of the Forty Niners' miracle season was long on euphoria but short on reflection, so it took a while for Bill Walsh to come to grips with what he had just accomplished. He would later say the enormity of it first touched him in an epiphany not long after returning from Detroit, while he and Geri were driving to the Napa Valley, where Eddie D. was hosting a celebration for the entire coaching staff and their wives at the Silverado Country Club. The Walshes were headed north on two-lane Highway 29, through scattered hamlets under a damp gray sky. Neither was talking. The soundtrack from *Chariots of Fire,* an inspirational story set around the 1924 Olympics and one of Bill's favorite films, was playing at high volume on the car's tape deck. What happened next came without warning.

First, Bill was inundated by the emotional anguish he had felt leaving Cincinnati six years ago, then that despair dispersed almost as quickly as it had appeared and, with startling immediacy, he suddenly saw himself just days earlier, being carried off the field on his players' shoulders and lifting the gleaming Super Bowl trophy in the clamor of the Silverdome locker room, having arrived at the top of the football world, where he had wanted to be since his first job at Washington Union High School. In that moment of sudden ecstatic clarity, he later explained, "at first I couldn't believe that had actually happened. It was so surreal I couldn't believe it. But then I knew deep inside myself that it had, it really had. My dream had come true." The joy that recognition unleashed started Bill crying. Tears ran out from under his sunglasses and down his cheeks. Geri, looking out the passenger window, lost in her own thoughts, was oblivious and he made no effort to draw her attention.

Euphoria was an almost constant companion during Bill's first few months of 1982. His new stature was obvious almost everywhere he turned. When he and Geri went to Hawaii for the NFL's annual meetings, he was the guest of honor at the coaches' reception—an old boys network that had heretofore kept him at arm's length—and everyone wanted to shake his hand. Out on the streets of Honolulu, the Silver Fox who looked like he listened to Mozart on his sideline headset was stopped everywhere he went. People congratulated him or offered thanks—they all knew who he was and what he'd done and wanted to tell him so. And he got the same treatment wherever he went. "I feel like I've been living in a fishbowl," he noted later in the year. "I can't get any privacy. Even driving down the freeway, people honk and wave."

Awards also continued to pile up well into the spring. The San Francisco Chamber of Commerce and the California State Legislature passed resolutions in his honor and seven different bodies selected him 1981's Coach of the Year. In late February, he and Geri flew to Kansas City, where one of those, a civic group known as the Committee of 101, had been polling the nation's football writers every year for decades and recognizing the press's selections as the season's best. During the awards ceremony in a ballroom at the Westin Crown Center Hotel, the applause that greeted Bill from the crowd of eight hundred when he was called to the podium to accept his prize was far more thunderous than for anyone else. "The response was overwhelming," one reporter noted, "almost as if he were in the Bay Area, not the nation's heartland." Bill recognized the statuette for the award, having seen one sitting behind Paul Brown's desk in Cincinnati. In those days,

Walsh had admired Brown's award and fantasized about what it would be like to win something like that. Now the fantasy had come true, and for an instant it felt like almost more than Bill could bear.

He shifted behind the podium and looked out in the audience for his wife. "I'd like to introduce my companion for the last twenty-seven years," Walsh began, but he could go no further. The words locked in his throat and a sob welled up instead, followed by tears he couldn't squelch. It took Bill a moment to recover and finish introducing Geri, followed by a brief acceptance speech. Then he left the podium to more applause, forgetting to take his statuette along.

Even after the honors and euphoria were done and he was back at the grindstone, Bill Walsh's life and career would never be the same. From here on, like it or not, he was The Genius.

Even as an old man, with his death approaching at a gallop, Bill Walsh felt obliged to distance himself from that nickname when it came up—as though it were a trick question on cross-examination, framed to make him seem presumptuous or self-absorbed. His eyes, however, gave him away. At the mention of "The Genius," they warmed and glistened around their edges even as the rest of his still handsome expression deadpanned. And with that fleeting expression, he quietly but not quite secretly embraced his nickname despite himself. Bill Walsh was pleased to be thought of that way, even if he still couldn't admit out loud how much pleasure it gave him.

"Genius?" Bill answered instead. "Genius? Beethoven was a genius. Einstein was a genius. I just taught a bunch of grown men how to play a game."

The moniker stuck nonetheless. It was first called to his attention at one of the Super Bowl press conferences when a writer approached him and asked how he felt about it. Bill answered that if some people chose to say that and considered it appropriate, Bill himself had no control over it and the reporter ought to direct his questions to them. He tried not to let on how thrilled he was to have such a reputation, but the truth was, Bill's son Craig later pointed out, "he loved being called The Genius and reveled in the glory of it." In a game in which, as one columnist put it, "anyone who subscribes to *National Geographic* is considered an intellectual," Bill was from Stanford, looked like a professor, worked from a long script of plays he invented, was indeed smarter than almost all of his contemporaries, and spoke in complete sentences that were often about something other than the sports page. From that perspective, his new nickname was unavoidable.

Bill quickly came to see it as a mixed blessing, however. Despite the compliment "The Genius" bestowed, it gave other teams another reason to want to beat him and inspired no small amount of resentment. Humiliating Walsh was now an honor for all those other coaches consigned by his reputation to status as lesser intellects, effectively putting a bounty on his head. For their part, his staff made the nickname an object of good-natured kidding—when "the Genius" misplaced his car keys and the like—and his players accepted it as what Keith Fahnhorst called "part of Bill's ego trip that was okay with us." But many not as close to him took it as an indication that he was full of himself, thought he was better than everyone else, and had far more ego than he was prepared to admit. Walsh was nothing if not protective of his image and it never stopped bothering him to be thought of that way.

Perhaps worst of all, the label created a host of expectations that he would have to meet or exceed simply to avoid being considered less than himself. Henceforth, it was taken for granted in many circles that Walsh, acclaimed brain that he was, could win games simply by focusing his attention on them, creating the daunting prospect of almost automatic failure for someone in whom the terror of coming up short was rarely more than a half step removed.

One of the effects would be to push Bill even deeper into the well of anxiety lurking behind his professorial public persona. "From that point on," Randy Cross observed, "he was still called Bill but he was never just Bill anymore. He had something more to live up to." The way Ronnie Lott later described it, "The Genius" would be an albatross around Bill's neck. "The more recognition Walsh received," Lott wrote, "the more he was under the microscope . . . and [the more he] grew distant and unapproachable. At times, he turned into a basket case. . . . I think that was because he was afraid people would find out that he wasn't a genius. . . . Walsh had to work hard at it. He was painfully methodical. He wasn't Einstein or Mozart. And he knew that."

In any case, the rest of Bill's career would be conducted in the shadow of a standard of mastery that was often impossible to meet, no matter how smart he was or how hard he tried.

. . .

No one's expectations would end up having more impact on Bill than those of Eddie D. The younger DeBartolo loved being Super Bowl champion. And Eddie's sense of vindication—at having risen from the ashes of the Joe Thomas disaster to top dog in the NFL—was only slightly less than Walsh's. "Those of us observing Eddie thought the experience had humbled and matured him," one of the *Chronicle*'s columnists later admitted, but "we were dead wrong." The Niners' accomplishment gave DeBartolo bragging rights on everyone, and he played his newfound stature to the hilt, feeding his sense of his own importance and his sense of entitlement.

One of the venues where Eddie D.'s new standing was immediately obvious was in Las Vegas, where he had become a regular high roller. That spring, Bally's casino held an Eddie DeBartolo Night: at a ceremony out on the gaming floor, in front of a crowd enlarged by casino employees in disguise, the Forty Niners' owner was presented with the replica of a football stadium in recognition of his team's accomplishments under his leadership. Eddie flew in from San Francisco for the occasion and brought along Bill and John McVay and several other Niners executives and their wives, as well as his buddy O. J. Simpson, and picked up the tab for everyone. Eddie also gave each of his guests five hundred dollars when they checked in and insisted that everyone join him at the tables. There, he often kept shoving money in front of them when their pile of chips grew short. Eddie himself celebrated his evening by losing tens of thousands of dollars over several hours, staying at it until long after Bill and most of his other guests had gone off to bed. When one of Eddie's remaining entourage finally suggested to his boss that Bally's was playing him for a sucker, Eddie left in a huff and took his DeBartolo Corp. jet back to Youngstown in the middle of the night, chartering another Learjet to haul Bill and the others home the next morning. Several months later, however, Eddie was back in Vegas to accept similar honors from the Hilton.

Being a champion also generated a new assertiveness for Eddie in his owner's role, particularly when it came to playing daddy to his "Forty Niners family." The rings he had crafted for everyone in honor of their Super Bowl victory were large and very expensive and it was already DeBartolo's practice to help his players with house financing or reward his favorites with trips back to Youngstown, where he routinely gave them presents like trips to Hawaii or Rolex watches. But now he also inserted himself into the salary process, which had heretofore been Walsh's responsibility, and did so without consulting Bill first.

Joe Montana and Dwight Clark were the Niners' new icons, as well as Eddie's favorites, and both were about to enter the last year of their respective contracts and wanted to renegotiate. Bill, however, had established a uniform salary process and was unreceptive to such renegotiation. There was also a deadline on new contracts approaching because the league's labor agreement with the NFL Players Association was about to expire and once it did, no new individual contracts could be negotiated until another pact with the union was worked out—in all likelihood a long and acrimonious process. When Eddie learned of the situation, he called Joe and Dwight directly and suggested they come back to Youngstown and talk it over, face-to-face and without their agents.

Once Montana and Clark got to Ohio, the process went smoothly. They and Eddie D. spent a lot of time laughing and eating and drinking and shooting pool until Eddie dispatched them one at a time into another room to meet with his lawyer, Carmen Policy, and hammer out contract terms while the other passed the time at the pool table with DeBartolo. Those negotiations with Policy took about an hour each and when they were over, Joe and Dwight had new deals exceeding a half million dollars a year, roughly triple what each had been paid before—and in time to beat the NFLPA deadline. Together the two were now scheduled to make about 20 percent of what the entire fifty-two-man team had been paid in 1981.

When Bill learned what had transpired, he was "livid," according to one of the Niners beat writers. Seemingly without a thought to the team's larger salary structure or even so much as a heads-up in Walsh's direction, Eddie had turned Bill's salary process on its ear. "It changed the whole system," Walsh explained. "We were trying to pay enough to keep players around but not go overboard, and that went right out the window. It wasn't so much Joe as Dwight. Joe was a quarterback and players expected that position to make more than everybody else, but Dwight was now the highest-paid wide receiver in the game and that put everyone else on alert. As soon as word got out, Ronnie Lott was in my office demanding the same kind of deal. I mean if Dwight could be paid that much, certainly Ronnie deserved it as well. And when the time came, I would have to tell Ronnie we would match it. And it wouldn't stop there. Everybody else on the team felt the same way."

Within two years, thanks in part to Eddie's peremptory decision to play "Mr. D." and take Joe and Dwight under his wing, the Forty Niners, who'd ranked twenty-seventh in total salary during their Super Bowl run, would have a payroll ranked in the top three in the league.

Shortly after Montana and Clark returned from Youngstown, training camp for the 1982 season opened and the ranks were already full of grumblings about how Eddie's favorites had been able to go around Walsh and make special deals for themselves, an option not available to everyone else. Bill was pissed about it too, but the Niners were Eddie's team and, as much as Walsh was in control of it, the owner was the one element to whom that control did not apply. When it came to Eddie D., The Genius would have little choice but to grin and bear it as best he could.

Bill Walsh with Russ Francis (left) and Bubba Paris

BACK-TO-BACK?

Bill Walsh's immediate challenge was how to repeat the Niners' success now that it would be anticipated rather than unimaginable. In some ways repeating was as daunting as building the team had been when he first took over. Back-to-back championships were exceedingly rare in the NFL. "You lose that sense of urgency," one Super Bowl–winning coach explained. "The glamour of being champions distorts what it will take to do it again and obscures the fact that you'll have to do some things better than you did before. On top of that you lose some players and everyone else is inspired to play the world champs, so you get their best game and they're not the team you see on film playing someone else. You can't sneak up on anybody. It's just real hard to climb that mountain all over again." As a consequence, since the advent of the Super Bowl only two teams—Green Bay in the sixties and Pittsburgh, twice in the seventies—had repeated, and both those franchises had been the dominant dynasties of their decade. Walsh spent much of his off-season—once the award ceremonies were over—trying to find a formula that would let his Niners join them.

"We can be a very good team next season," he offered that March. "I question whether you'll see many 13-3 seasons from anybody, but we'll be up there. We got the absolute most out of everybody last season. [On paper,] the pieces aren't there for a dynasty, but I know one thing: as long as Joe Montana quarterbacks this team, we have a chance at a dynasty. I'm hopeful we'll still get inspiration from older players like Charle Young and Jack Reynolds. And we're hopeful the rest of our players are still young enough that they'll play with the same enthusiasm they did [in 1981]."

To renew the spirit that had carried them to the championship, Bill recognized he would have to alter his approach a bit. "You have to constantly make changes," he pointed out. "You don't want routine practices. You don't want players to get in a comfort zone and become complacent, because that's when you start losing. [To accomplish that] we'll probably have a shorter camp this year. We won't bring in as many players as we have in the past. We'll change our practices. Because we'll have a much more established team than last year, we'll do more individual coaching."

By the opening of training camp at Rocklin in August, Bill had also made alterations to his personal coaching demeanor. "Walsh himself seems more relaxed," the *Chronicle* observed, "more at ease on the practice field. Sideline observers still wonder what he scribbles on those 3x5 cards in his hand, but his manner has changed. He can still throw a mean glare occasionally [but] the occasions when he yells at a player or an assistant coach for screwing up are much less frequent this summer." Nonetheless, Walsh managed to repeat some of his usual training camp rituals—this time cutting a defensive tackle who had taken his pads off during a practice without permission with the declaration, "Get him out of here. Don't even let him shower." And the need to "defend our championship" was never far from Bill's lips. "Defend, defend, defend," Joe Montana recalled. "That's all we heard."

Walsh's "relaxed" demeanor was, in truth, only a façade covering his usual deep-seated worry. He would later say that "only the experienced or most intuitive mind" could actually anticipate the fallout from previous success of this magnitude and, at that moment, he was neither. He recognized he was still groping, despite his public displays of confidence, and it made him nervous.

And his nervousness was appropriate. Bill didn't realize it yet, but he was on the verge of what he would later describe as by far the "greatest humiliation" of his career with the Forty Niners.

The one thing Walsh was sure of in advance of the 1982 season was that repeating would not happen by standing pat. The Packers and Steelers both had returned a large core of extremely talented players to bring to the task when they went back-to-back, but the Niners did not. Bill's team had played over its head on the way to the Super Bowl and he knew he could not count on their doing that again. He had to keep adding talent and, to that end, made three significant acquisitions in the off-season, expecting that they could inject into his roster the fresh energy that repeating would require.

The first was tight end Russ Francis. Already something of an NFL legend for his iconoclasm, Francis was also the physical archetype of his position. Six feet six inches tall and 242 pounds, he blocked like a tackle and caught passes like a wide receiver. Russ, the son of a professional wrestler, had once held the national high school record in the javelin throw and had been offered a professional baseball contract when still a schoolboy. He took up football at the University of Oregon only because he was looking for scholarship money to pay for lab books. Nonetheless, he had shown such obvious talent that he'd been drafted into the NFL by the New England Patriots. By early 1982, Francis was a six-year veteran who had been named an All-Pro for three years running before suddenly quitting after the 1980 season, when the Patriots refused to trade him to a team on the Pacific coast so he could be closer to his home in Hawaii. He had then retired to the islands to spend his time riding motorcycles, flying airplanes, and skydiving—explaining that he had "never really liked football" and wanted to do something else for a while. The Patriots still owned his rights but he had made it abundantly clear that he never intended to play for them again.

Among the retired Francis's new activities was a stint of television reporting during the Pro Bowl in Hawaii and it was in that role that he first met Walsh, right after the Detroit Super Bowl. Off camera, the two talked about Francis's future. "Russ Francis had the reputation of being the best tight end in football," Walsh pointed out, "a real All-Pro. He was a maverick kind of guy, no question about it, but he was sort of a fun guy too. We visited and talked—which was tampering, of course, but I was intrigued and did it anyway. We didn't get specific in that first conversation, but he said he was out of football and said he wasn't going back."

When Bill returned to the mainland, he nonetheless told John McVay he wanted to make a run at acquiring Francis from the Patriots. "Bill had something for Francis," McVay remembered. "He liked him and had a feeling that he would really be an asset if we could get him and then get him to agree to come back." Part of Bill's attraction to Francis was the importance Walsh placed on the tight end position. For the rest of the decade, a lot of football would be enthralled with a new generation of "spread" offenses in which four and five wide receivers were used and the tight end virtually eliminated, but Bill was the complete opposite. He believed that in any offense, the more options the better, and that the tight end, a kind of universal joint between the running and passing games, was key to making sure the defense remained in the dark about his team's offensive intentions. And he drooled at the thought of what he might be able to do with Francis in that position.

Walsh and McVay spent the spring in talks with New England over Russ's rights, culminating on draft day, when, in exchange for the Niners' first- and fourth-round picks, plus switching places in the second round, Francis was shipped to the Niners. Just a week earlier the deal had seemed dead, but the Patriots revived it with a call from their owner, Billy Sullivan, to Eddie D. That led to intense talks that included Walsh, Sullivan, McVay, and Francis's agent and lasted right through the opening round of draft day until the Niners had only fifteen seconds left on the clock to exercise their pick, the final one in the first round. Shortly afterward, a new contract flush with DeBartolo cash helped persuade the tight end to come out of retirement, saying he was motivated to return by "a feeling that something was still undone." Walsh had suggested including a clause in the agreement prohibiting skydiving and motorcycle or airplane racing but dropped that idea early in the negotiations. When finally on the roster, Francis would end up being the wildest hare Bill ever coached, as well as perhaps his best tight end.

Bill's second acquisition in the 1982 off-season was another tribute to his desire to add speed to the wide receiver position and his penchant for converting track-and-field athletes to football players. Renaldo Nehemiah was world champion at the 110-meter hurdles and would be perhaps the fastest man ever to suit up for Walsh. Nehemiah hadn't played any football since high school and, Bill admitted, "was sort of a challenge for me. Despite his lack of experience, he seemed to have a lot of the makings of a good receiver." Since Nehemiah was still in his prime and used to making excellent money on the track circuit, it took another relatively lucrative contract to lure him, but he signed as a free agent and became a Niner in time for training camp, giving Bill what he imagined would be the most potent deep threat he'd ever had.

The third acquisition was through the collegiate draft. During March, as the Niners were assembling their board in preparation for draft day, Walsh told the *Chronicle* that one of his priorities was to find a left offensive tackle to replace the undersized Dan Audick, "the kind like the Raiders have, one of those 300-pounders." That wish was gratified by using the second-round pick he'd switched with the Patriots to select William "Bubba" Paris from the University of Michigan, six feet six and 305 pounds at the time he was drafted. Walsh considered getting Bubba in the second round a considerable coup. He'd expected the tackle to go in the first five or six picks, and had the Patriots trade not happened, Bill would have used that first-round pick on him. Indeed, the Niners had already written Paris's name on the card the team's representative was about to submit to the commissioner back in New York before the Francis trade finally came through. Bill described Bubba to the press as "a ten-year offensive tackle who has Pro Bowl capabilities. He's just the man we've been looking for to play left tackle for us. You spend your entire career looking for a Bubba Paris."

The reason Bubba had lasted into the second round was that, despite the Niners' glowing evaluations, a lot of draft prognosticators had serious doubts about his motivation. There were also questions about his weight. Paris's coach at Michigan had required him to play at 270 pounds but Bubba had only passed that standard by jimmying the team's scale so it would register no higher than that. The Niners expected him to play at 285, but when he first reported to 711 Nevada Street, Paris was up to 315 and climbing. The contract Bubba signed included a weight clause that called for significant financial penalties should he exceed his required weight and, on signing day, Bill was optimistic that that would be sufficient to keep him in line. Once down to 285, Bubba was expected to be dominant—massive enough to blow opponents off the line on running plays but quick enough to pass block with the best. As for the critique that his new pick didn't play as hard as he should have and lacked motivation, Bill was openly dismissive.

"We feel we can motivate anyone," he declared. Just to emphasize his point, Walsh installed Paris as a starter as soon as he was signed, as he had done with Lott, Wright, and Williamson the year before. Bill made it clear he thought Bubba would anchor his offensive line for the next decade.

This time, however, none of Walsh's off-season moves had the impact he'd expected.

Russ Francis, talented or not, wasn't welcomed by his teammates when training camp opened. Not even close. He was there to take Charle Young's job and Young was a favorite of almost everyone on the roster—enough reason for a lot of players to keep the newcomer at arm's length. Francis, though being paid more than most of the team's 1981 stalwarts, was also not much of a practice player and insisted on being irreverently light-hearted, even when only he found the situation funny. This, at least initially, rubbed more than a few players the wrong way and caused them to doubt his commitment. His knack for offending his new teammates was increased by recurrent back spasms that kept him rehabbing in the pool by himself rather than working on the field with the team. The other players nicknamed him "Flipper," and he won the team's "High Diver" award, presented every training camp to the player who takes the "biggest dive" by spending the most time out of practice and in the training room. By late August, the *San Francisco Examiner* was running headlines such as HINTS OF DISSENSION IN 49ERS CAMP and Francis was half of the controversy.

Renaldo Nehemiah was the other half. He too was making better money than most, even though he hadn't played a down since high school. He'd also been given a "no cut" clause, so he didn't even have to fight for a job like everyone else, and several defensive backs reported that coaches had instructed them to take it easy on him so he wouldn't get hurt. Even so, the converted track star managed to pull a hamstring and spend almost as much time as Francis with the trainers. Nehemiah couldn't avoid the obvious resentment of his teammates. "They gave me constant nonverbal cues," he remembered. "The air was tense around me." Before training camp was over, several of the team's veterans presented him with a baby pacifier, supposedly a humorous tribute to his baby face, but actually a derisive statement that they didn't think he had the heart required to be a football player.

Bubba Paris, the other new addition, was accepted more readily—by everyone except the displaced Dan Audick, who left camp for three weeks with "emotional problems" and then threw a locker-room fit when he returned. Bubba had a difficult time nonetheless. He hadn't done much pass blocking in college and while Bobb McKittrick was teaching him the necessary techniques, Bubba's learning curve put all the team's quarterbacks in danger during the exhibition games. Paris was soon given the nickname "Highway 77," after his uniform number, because opposing defensive ends ran right through him. Backup quarterback Guy Benjamin received two concussions at the hands of the men Bubba was supposed to block, but Walsh stuck with his rookie tackle. Despite the fines levied under the terms of his contract, Paris still hadn't reached 285 pounds, and McKittrick thought the extra weight was causing him to miss blocks. Even so, the line coach predicted, Bubba "will be the best left tackle Bill Walsh has ever had" by the time camp was over. Instead, Paris tore up his right knee in the final exhibition game and was out for the season. Walsh would have to find a left tackle on some other team's scrap heap to cover for the loss.

Bubba's was only one of the team's myriad injuries. Most notably, Randy Cross, the team's best offensive lineman, had broken an ankle in an off-season accident, and Peewee Board, a mainstay on the defensive line, would be lost for the season with a knee operation, but there were more. At one point fourteen of Walsh's twenty-two projected starters were unfit to suit up. By the time the season began, the Niners were, in his words, "a different team" that already appeared to be in the early stages of disarray.

And they played like it.

The opening game against the Raiders was sloppy, full of mistakes, and ended with a 23–17 loss. Against the Denver Broncos the following week, the Niners blew a halftime lead and lost the game when Joe threw a pass behind a receiver that was tipped and intercepted as they were driving to finish the Broncos off. Then the defense drew a suspect pass interference penalty that enabled the Broncos to kick a field goal as time ran out—Denver 24, San Francisco 21.

Afterward, Bill, despite his fury at the last-minute penalty call, was publicly upbeat. "We outplayed our opponent," he insisted. "No one should count us out."

He was, however, whistling in the dark.

. . .

As his 0-2 team entered week three, Bill was still convinced they would turn things around in time to make a run at back-to-back championships, but he had to put his scheme for effecting that reversal on hold. Time had run out in the NFL's labor negotiations and for the first time in league history, the regular season was about to be suspended while the players went on strike. "That shot all our plans to hell," Walsh explained.

The Forty Niners were among the more reluctant of the league's strikers. Partly that was because of their feelings for Eddie D., who made it clear he would take any walkout personally and whom no one wished to offend. But mostly it was because of strong misgivings about the union's approach. Rather than fighting for genuine free agency, the Players Association was demanding a leaguewide salary scale with a guaranteed 60 percent of the franchises' revenue allotted to player salaries. The Niners' union rep, tackle Keith Fahnhorst, had been part of an unsuccessful effort inside the union to derail this approach, and everyone on the squad was reluctant to go to the mat over it. Perhaps the stiffest critic of the NFLPA strategy was Joe Montana, who had publicly resigned from the union back in July. "Everyone was saying we should pull together and support a walkout," he later explained, but "why should I have supported something I didn't believe in?"

Most of his teammates were divided over what to do and when they met to discuss their options, those divisions became heated. "There was a lot of bad-mouthing going on," Montana explained. "When I tried to make my point my own teammates put me down . . . saying, 'we know why Montana doesn't want to strike: he's making a million dollars a year, he doesn't want to lose that money.' [The strike was] something that half the players wanted and half didn't. Neither side could see the other's point. . . . It was a nasty situation." Unable to resolve the conflict, the Niners simply kept postponing a strike vote as the deadline approached. Finally, when the walkout began, they agreed to go along without ever endorsing the strike itself. "It was obvious we have to support the rest of the players in the league," Fahnhorst explained.

Official word that play was being shut down reached the team before their first practice after the Denver game, but they held a last workout anyway. Afterward, Bill convened an unusually long team meeting. He had been through an abortive strike while with the Bengals in 1974, when the union staged a brief walkout from training camp, and his principal concern was that the team be unified, whatever they decided to do. He identified internal acrimony as the biggest danger and implored his players to maintain their cohesion as a team at all costs. By league rule, only people with injuries would be allowed to use the facilities on Nevada Street and then only for treatment. Everyone else would have to work out on their own and the players had already organized their own workout sessions for nearby Menlo College. Bill spent a long time at the meeting talking about how every player had to make sure they maintained their physical and mental preparedness to play football. No one knew when this shutdown would end, he pointed out, but when it did, they had to be ready to "defend our championship."

After the meeting, the team began its walkout. "The players left their Redwood City training camp looking like they were going on a road trip," the *Chronicle* reported. "Players packed T-shirts, shorts, shoes and other equipment—even footballs—in their equipment bags before heading home. . . . None of them knew when they'd be coming back [and] judging from [their] attitude, it was obvious they never before had been involved in a serious labor-management dispute. There seemed almost a party atmosphere among them, and no one appeared concerned about what they'd do for money." As they gathered their stuff, Walsh visited the downstairs locker room—an unusual occurrence—and circulated among his team, saying goodbyes and notifying everyone that they had to be weighed by the trainer before leaving. They would be expected to return at the same weight as when they left, he warned. "We just hope we come out of this thing in better shape than our opposition," he told one of the reporters covering the scene.

An hour later, 711 Nevada Street's downstairs locker room was deserted.

At first Walsh thought the walkout might be over after a week, but that estimate wasn't even close. Each week thereafter Bill hoped for the best and each week he was disappointed. Over and over again, he meticulously prepared plans for the next game on the schedule, all to no avail. He also went out on the road scouting college games and spent no small amount of time worrying about his team, wherever he was. "They were supposed to be working out on their own," he acknowledged, "but those kind of workouts never amount to much." And everything Bill did while the strike went on was pervaded by a bittersweet longing for what wasn't happening. "I miss the adventure of my profession," he told a reporter who came by Nevada Street to check on him. "I miss the range of emotions from utter dejection to exhilaration. They're stressful as you go through them, yet your body is conditioned to deal with them. On the upside, fall is a beautiful time of year. I just realized that. [But] this is our time of year. I feel almost in exile."

The 1982 players strike would last almost eight weeks and during that time, Bill made two attempts to impact its course. At one point, fueled by momentary desperation, he contacted Charle Young and asked Charle if he thought everyone would join in if Charle came back to work. Young said they wouldn't—the team was still split—and that it was a bad idea that would make things worse, so Bill dropped it. His other attempt was a series of recommendations about disputed issues, which he sent to the owners' negotiating team, but his ideas went nowhere. Otherwise, he just waited with everyone else, hoping the strike would end sooner rather than later and reflexively straightening picture frames and inspecting desks around the headquarters. Eventually, he started worrying that the strike would last so long the whole season would be cancelled.

That didn't happen, but by the time the union finally caved in, having accomplished virtually none of what it had set out to do, and the season resumed, the damage to his team's inner workings had already been done.

"We simply were divided on the issue and could never regroup," Joe Montana later wrote, and "when the strike was over, no one forgot what happened. . . . There were grudges and we weren't playing as a team. We weren't working together and people weren't talking to each other. How can you win under those conditions? I never believed it would end up that way. I figured when the strike ended, everyone would forgive and forget. I was wrong. A lot of players' heads weren't into the game [after we came back]. We definitely couldn't regain the feeling we had had the year before. . . . The season was ruined for us."

Bill Walsh headed out the tunnel to the field at Candlestick

20

THE COLLAPSE

The strike, however, wasn't the only culprit. After the 1982 season was over, Walsh would identify three other circumstances behind his team's collapse.

He would label the first "complacency," though he felt that word insufficient to capture the extent of the shortfall in his players' attitudes. "There was a loss of will," Bill complained, "a loss of need and personal sacrifice." It was generated by the team's inability to put their previous success behind them. "We were so pleased with what we had done, because it was unprecedented that we had accomplished so much so quickly, that we were overconfident and self-satisfied." Such complacency, quarterbacks coach Sam Wyche noted, "happens to you without you knowing it. It's just human nature, especially for a team that hasn't been winning before and didn't yet have a legacy or tradition. Suddenly you're invited to every golf tournament in the off-season. It's hard to rekindle the same hunger. You lose that sense of your backs against the wall." Charle Young agreed. "Pride goes before the fall," the locker-room preacher pointed out. "Everyone got caught up in the hullabaloo of success. They got fat, sluggish in the head, heart, and body. Little things that you used to fight through, people wouldn't do anymore."

Bill summarized the second reason behind the 1982 collapse as "distractions" and their impact was apparent to many others in contact with the team as well. "We had too many guys writing books," John McVay observed, "or on speaking engagements, or otherwise enjoying the fruits of the Super Bowl. We just got so distracted our edge disappeared." In Walsh's mind, Joe Montana was the poster boy for this issue. No one had been catapulted higher in the public eye by the 1981 miracle, and it seemed as if everyone wanted a piece of him in the aftermath. One town in the state of Montana even changed its name to "Joe" in his honor. After a spring spent on the rubber chicken circuit collecting honorariums and appearance fees, Montana committed himself to taping a weekly television show during football season for one of the local channels and also commuted around the country on his off days, pursuing commercial opportunities arranged by his agent. Joe would vehemently deny all the extra activity had a negative impact, but the *Examiner,* like a number of observers, would describe his physical condition at season's end as "a mere shadow of the man who won MVP honors at Super Bowl XVI," claiming, "he literally wore himself out making extracurricular appearances."

The third additional factor was drugs. Cocaine, described by one San Francisco gossip columnist as "God's way of telling you you're making too much money," cut a swath through professional sports in the early 1980s and hit the Forty Niners and the rest of the NFL hard. Niners players were snorting lines of the white powder at team parties and even using it in the team hotel on the night before games. "Half the team was doing it recreationally," one of the squad's heaviest users later admitted. "I'm not saying they were as bad as I had gotten with my habit, but they were doing it." Walsh was receiving regular reports of player drug abuse from the NFL's security arm and from local law enforcement throughout the 1982 season. He would later identify a dozen of the regulars from his championship team whose play had been impacted by their cocaine use during that post–Super Bowl year. "I sensed there were team members who were so involved in drugs that their performance was affected," he explained, "but I was obligated by my personal code not to go public with it, and in fact, I denied over and over that we had a drug problem." Once the season was over, however,

Walsh would drop that pretense. "Drugs were a primary culprit," he declared years later. "Some of our key players didn't show up to play and cocaine was the reason why."

All of those explanations were, of course, after the fact. In the meantime, the strike was finally over, and starting in the third week of November, Walsh had a season to finish.

The restructured 1982 NFL schedule would last a total of nine games—two of which had already been played—to be followed by playoffs in which the top eight finishers in each conference would have berths. With his team already 0-2 in their pursuit of a second straight title, there was growing talk around the league about how the 1981 Forty Niners had been a "fluke" and for the remaining seven games, Bill struggled desperately to stave off collapse and the humiliation he knew would accompany it.

The Niners started the second installment of the season successfully, handling the St. Louis Cardinals 31–20 and producing what the *Chronicle* would later describe as their "best football of the season," but then they stumbled through their next contest, with New Orleans, losing 23–20. The following game was against the Rams, the only team they would play twice in the abbreviated schedule. The Rams also had only one win and for the first time this season, Bill thought his team looked "like champs" against them. On their way to a 30–24 victory, the Niners "executed well," despite being short on running backs, moving the ball down the field whenever they had to on the arm of Joe Montana, who compiled more than three hundred yards passing for the fourth game in a row. The defending champions went into San Diego the next week just a game south of .500, with a real chance to get into the playoff hunt.

Their encounter with the Chargers, however, was the most vexing yet. It would later be described as "a shoot-out" between San Diego quarterback Dan Fouts, whose career Walsh had rescued in his year there as offensive coordinator, and Joe Montana, leader of his 1981 miracle. The Forty Niners defense was having a down year—both its young backfield, Dwight Hicks and the Hot Licks, and its star pass rusher, Fred Dean, were playing badly week in and week out—but this game was the defense's worst ever. Before the shoot-out was over, they had given up 538 yards, the most allowed by any team Bill Walsh coached—444 of them through the air. For his part,

Montana threw for more than 300 yards for the fifth week in a row, an NFL record. But with the defense as lame as it was, the Niners had to score just about every time they had the ball, challenging all Walsh's offensive ingenuity simply to keep his team in the game. Down 31–17, the Niners mounted a ferocious comeback and took the lead, 37–34, with just six minutes left in the final quarter. Then Fouts took his team and cut through the Niners like a knife through soft butter. With just seven plays, the Chargers drove seventy-two yards to victory, 41–37, and the Niners were helpless to even slow them down.

Afterward, Walsh was distraught. He asked his assistants to give him a little privacy before he had to face the postgame press conference and then he retreated into the coaches' room and broke down. "I let it all go," sobbing and moaning through clenched jaws, he remembered. "It all hit at once. The world champions, all of the recognition—and now, once again, we were losing week after week by close scores, as we had in my first two years. Now, the reality set in. We were champions of the National Football League but we still 'weren't there yet.'" When he'd regained his composure, Walsh went out to face the reporters, all of whom wanted to know what the Niners, down to 2-4, were going to do now.

At the following Monday's practice back on Nevada Street, Bill told his team that the way things were going, any 5-4 team would make the playoffs and so would a couple of teams that had losing records. At this point, he offered, "it's up to you."

The challenge seemed to have little if any immediate impact. The next Sunday they lost to Atlanta 17–7, then rebounded the following week and won at Kansas City. Headed into the year's final regular season game, again with the Rams, they had a shoddy 3-5 record, but thanks to the lousy play throughout the league, all they had to do was beat Los Angeles, still stuck at one win, in order to make the postseason. That game, Bill would later explain, was one "I will remember as long as I live."

Walsh's tension was apparent during the week of practice leading up to this showdown. He was even more worried than usual about preparing for every possibility and nagged his assistants accordingly. He also fretted about Montana's physical condition. His quarterback had suffered considerable defensive abuse thanks to the team's left tackle woes, was nursing a bruised tailbone, an inflamed elbow, and a very sore knee, and looked positively "gaunt" and fragile. Joe was coming off two straight subpar performances as well and Bill knew his team could not afford a third. His anxiety left Walsh in no mood to be trifled with and toward the end of the week he got into it with Russ Francis. Francis had been steadily complaining about being used as a backup over the preceding weeks and Walsh was tired of hearing it and tired of Russ's practice habits—so much so that Bill, who rarely ever lost his temper in front of his players, lost it big-time and gave Francis what his teammates deemed the worst public ass-chewing the coach had handed out since he'd been at the Niners. The outburst cleared the air between the two of them but gave Bill little relief from his nightmares about everything that could possibly go wrong on Sunday. Nonetheless, his team, playing at home, entered the game nine-and-a-half-point favorites.

Walsh's worries did not dissipate after the action began. He later admitted to feeling "terribly distressed" all game long, even though his team jumped out to an early lead thanks to a ninety-three-yard punt return in the first quarter. Otherwise, bad omens began popping up all over. Montana, on his way to perhaps his worst performance of the season, tried one swing pass and missed his wide-open receiver by five yards, then tried another and threw it right to a Rams defender, his first of two interceptions on the day. John Ayers, the Niners' best offensive lineman all year long, left the game with a sprained knee and didn't return. The Forty Niners' pass rush was virtually nonexistent. Nonetheless, after the Rams tied the score in the second quarter, Walsh's team seemed to seize control of the contest. They drove eighty-nine yards, featuring a key fifteen-yard reception by Dwight Clark—who was putting the cap on his second straight Pro Bowl season— and two fifteen-yard personal foul penalties on the Rams, making the score 14–7. After stopping the Los Angeles offense, the Niners then went the length of the field in five plays, including a twenty-one-yard completion to Clark, a twenty-three-yard completion to Francis, and then a twenty-nine-yard touchdown throw to Nehemiah, his first touchdown as a professional football player. The usually automatic place kicker, Ray Wersching, missed the last extra point, but the Niners led at the half, 20–7.

The second half, however, was Bill's nightmare come true. Despite facing the NFL's worst defense, his offense could only generate two first downs in its first four possessions and was so inept, he considered pulling Montana and going the rest of the way with Guy Benjamin. In the meantime, his defense kept giving up big plays. The first was a forty-one-yard pass when Ronnie Lott, who Walsh felt had been a step slow ever since returning from the strike, stumbled and lost track of his man. That led to a Rams touchdown. The second big play was a forty-two-yard catch for a second touchdown, made possible by Lott and Carlton Williamson both blowing their coverage and leaving a Rams receiver wide open. Now deep in the fourth quarter, the Niners were down 21–20 with time left for only one more drive.

And for a few minutes, they suddenly seemed like the miracle team of the year before. Knowing the Rams would be looking for him to pass, Walsh started the drive with two straight runs by Bill Ring, netting almost twenty yards. Two passes followed for twenty-five more. Then Dwight Clark dove between two Rams defenders, reached out with one hand, and snagged another that brought the Niners down to the Rams' thirteen-yard line. San Francisco was facing third and three at the Rams' six with only two minutes left, then Montana rushed a pass to the halfback swinging out of the backfield that might have been a touchdown but sailed wide instead.

With that, Walsh sent Wersching out to win the game with a chip shot field goal. This had been one of the situations Bill had agonized about during the week, causing him to grill his special teams coach about whether there was anything in the Rams' arsenal that they needed to prepare the kicking team for, only to be told to relax, there was nothing to worry about. Instead, the Rams surprised the Niners when play resumed, running a defensive stunt for which the field goal unit was completely unready. The maneuver freed a rusher who came through the line untouched and swatted Wersching's kick to the ground. The Rams then ran the clock out and the Forty Niners' 1982 season was over.

At the press conference afterward, Walsh confessed to his own "embarrassment and humiliation" and looked like it.

"Bill Walsh was a study in agony," the *Chronicle* noted. "There was a wan smile on his face. It was the kind of smile someone flashes when everything is lost. You smile because the only other thing to do is cry—and you do that later, in private."

The next day, the Forty Niners players returned to Nevada Street to pick up their belongings and complete the team's end-of-the-season process—weighing out, supplying off-season contact information, and assembling for a last team meeting with Bill. The big room was full to overflowing as they waited for their coach and then waited some more, buzzing with side conversations as the wait extended, wondering what was going on and where the hell Walsh was. Finally, John McVay came in and told them that Bill wasn't coming. McVay said they should just finish their business and Bill would see them in the spring when they returned for next season's initial team workouts. McVay tried to reassure the players that Bill's absence was no big deal, but a significant number of them were upset that their coach had stood them up without so much as a goodbye.

Walsh would later explain that he had stayed away because he was worried he might say something foolish, as by that point he was already deep into emotional free fall and unremitting internal torment. He resented his players and felt they'd deceived and betrayed him. He thought he had cared far more about defending their title than they had, and like a jilted lover he found that imbalance mortifying. On top of that, Walsh was listening to an incessant chorus of imagined critics in his head calling his accomplishments a "fluke" or a "flash in the pan" or a "one-shot wonder." He heard them call him "The Genius" now as an act of derision, chuckling among themselves as they did so, and he was so ashamed he wanted to flee and hide. Bill would later admit that he "wasn't thinking very clearly," but he had fallen deep into his personal black hole and it would take a while for him to pull himself out. In the meantime, he was becoming convinced that the time had come for him to give up and get out of the game.

Bill had stayed up late on Sunday night, talking with Eddie D., and then after his no-show at the Monday team meeting, he flew back to Youngstown with McVay for further meetings. He told Eddie that he wasn't sure he had what it would take for him to continue. He felt crushed and completely spent and didn't know if he would ever recover. Maybe the best thing would be for him to find a replacement. As he saw it, he had three options: either resign as coach and stay on as general manager, resign both jobs, or resign neither and continue as before. He told his boss that he didn't yet know which one to choose.

Apparently Eddie was at least a little shocked by the hysteria Bill brought to the situation. Walsh certainly sounded like he meant it when he talked about hanging up his headset. For his part, Eddie had been extremely put out at the disaster that had overtaken what should have been their back-to-back championship, but Bill's state brought him up short. The Niners' owner had been complaining to Bill throughout the season, always, according to a Walsh confidant, "after he'd been drinking heavily," usually in the form of rhetorical questions like "What the fuck is going on?" or "What the hell are you going to do about this?" Now, however, faced with the real possibility of losing his coach and the risk of his franchise sliding back into the mediocrity from which Walsh had rescued it, Eddie chose not to push the issue. He even resisted pressure from his father, who thought Walsh was a "quitter" to behave like this and ought to be fired forthwith. Instead, Eddie told Bill to take some time and figure it out.

After returning from Youngstown, it was clear that the first of the options Walsh had laid out to DeBartolo was the one Bill was seriously considering and he began to explore the possibilities for replacing himself as coach while continuing to act as general manager. He even went so far as to approach two coaches to explore their interest in the job, both of whom were old friends. Mike White, then the head coach at the University of Illinois, was the first one he called. White found Bill the most upset he had ever seen him, even more than he had been after his rejection by Paul Brown. Mike listened to Bill's tale of woe and commiserated, but didn't believe he was serious about giving up coaching. He told his old buddy from their days as Stanford assistants that he was just exhausted; these feelings would pass and then he'd get back on the job and go at it again. White didn't say as much, but he also thought trying to work under Bill in these circumstances might very well prove impossible. Walsh next approached John Robinson, former head coach of USC who was then an administrator at the university. He too doubted that this was anything but a momentary emotional fit Bill was going through and was wary of working under him even if it was a serious opportunity.

Bill was still unsure about what to do, but his mind was nonetheless clear enough to use his dilemma to improve his situation should he decide to return as head coach. Always loath to engage in face-to-face conflict, especially with people with whom he was close, Bill wanted to get rid of two of his assistants but was having trouble bringing himself to do it directly. This was particularly true in the case of defensive coordinator Chuck Studley. He and Chuck had been longtime friends from their days as assistants in Cincinnati and Bill had persuaded Studley to uproot his family and move west when he took over the Niners, but they had knocked sparks off each other during the last year, when Walsh felt his coordinator had "started to take me on personally and fight me on things." He also felt Studley's defensive approach lacked sophistication. Unwilling to break with his old friend by dismissing him, Walsh instead told his coaches that he didn't know if he was coming back and gave them all permission to go out and find replacement jobs for themselves while other teams were hiring. Both Studley and the special teams assistant who had told Walsh not to worry about the Rams blocking a field goal availed themselves of the opportunity to leave, allowing Bill to successfully clean house with a minimum of personal ugliness.

In the meantime, Walsh continued to pursue his general manager duties, traveling to the Senior Bowl in Mobile, Alabama, to get a firsthand look at some of the best talent available in the upcoming draft. While there, he also finally came to terms with his future. The event that galvanized him was a dinner with two old friends, Jim Finks, GM at the Chicago Bears, and Jim Hanifan, head coach of the St. Louis Cardinals. Finks remembered Walsh as "very depressed" that night and, dressed in a dark blue suit, "looking more like a banker than a coach." Bill, swarmed by self-pity, immediately started pissing and moaning about how sick he was of watching football players, trying to decide who was good and who wasn't. He just didn't have it anymore, he complained. He just didn't have it. Finks and Hanifan listened for a while and then lost their patience.

Finks told Walsh he was full of shit. He hadn't even begun to scratch the surface of his abilities and he ought to knock this crap off and go back to work. Hanifan added that Bill should just stop all this feeling sorry for himself. He sounded like a goddamn girl. He needed to pull himself together. Coaching was what he was meant to do.

His friends' blunt and unsympathetic response stunned Walsh, but by the time he got back to his hotel room, the dark cloud that had been hanging over him since the Rams game had begun to dissipate.

The next day, Bill called Eddie D. in Youngstown. By that point Eddie was losing patience with Bill's crisis as well. It had been almost three weeks and while Eddie insisted that he wanted Bill to return as coach, he now had to know one way or another what Bill was going to do.

Walsh didn't hesitate. He was coming back just like before, he told Eddie. And he was going to win another Super Bowl.

Bill and Geri Walsh

21

PAIN AROUND THE EDGES

E ven after he'd put his crisis behind him, the Niners' 1982 collapse marked Bill Walsh indelibly and, in retrospect, stands out as a watershed moment. Among other things, the shape of Bill's relationship with his players was never quite the same afterward.

"Bill was very personable early on—in 1979, '80, '81," Randy Cross explained, but "I think that whole experience in '82, between the strike and losing like we did, affected his relationship with us. That was a turning point for Bill. We had all built up so much trust between us in 1981 and then we totally abused it and misused it. He never made that mistake again. From that point on he was different: further away, more protected." Many of Cross's teammates agreed with his assessment. Walsh was still accessible, still made jokes and played the occasional prank, and still kept his dealings on a first-name basis, but he no longer invested himself in his players in the same way and stopped blurring the separation between personal and professional as he had in his early days. Henceforth, he kept things on a business footing and set his priorities accordingly. "When we had to rise out of the depths, I was right there with the players all the time," Bill explained, "but it got more difficult. I had a lot of duties and there were some tough decisions I had to make about people's careers and the like. If I was more distant, I was probably still closer than most coaches." Nonetheless, he was now almost exclusively the boss—interested, engaged, and often benign—but several steps further removed than he'd once been and intent on keeping it that way.

As a consequence, relationships that once seemed simple were now inevitably more "complicated." And nowhere was that more true than in his dealings with his two best players, Ronnie Lott and Joe Montana, both of whom would eventually write memoirs that presented their relations with Bill in a less than enthralled light.

By 1983, Ronnie was already looked upon as the team's leader in the locker room, the guy who regularly stood up as the coaches were dismissing the team meetings to say one more thing to call people's performance into account or demand more from his teammates. He had also adopted the role of speaking up for his fellow players with Bill and the rest of the staff whenever he thought it appropriate. And Lott was extremely upset when Walsh didn't show up when the team met after the loss to the Rams. He described that moment as "the turning point in my relationship with Walsh."

His first response at that Monday no-show was concern that something might have happened to his coach, but when Ronnie learned the next morning that Bill had failed to appear not because he was injured or ill but because he was too angry and emotionally attenuated to deal with his players, the defensive back was immediately disillusioned and offended. "From that moment on," he explained, "I wondered whose side Walsh was on. Who was the real Bill Walsh? And most of my teammates wanted to know the same thing. I have always believed that when you're the captain of the ship, you go down with the ship when it sinks. You do not fluctuate. In 1981, everything had been wonderful. We had reached the top of the mountain and he was a coaching genius. Then we lost to the Rams, and he didn't want to be around us. . . . All Walsh had to do was show up and say 'I'll see you guys next year.' Period. Because he hadn't done that, I doubted him as a leader—my leader and the leader of the 49ers—for the rest of my career."

Lott was also uncomfortable with Bill's new, more distant stance. "He did a fantastic job of building and coaching the 49ers," Ronnie allowed. "He controlled every aspect of the organization. . . . He had a remarkable eye for talent and a keen understanding of the defensive side of the game. [But] when it came to personal, one-on-one relationships, Walsh had a difficult time communicating from the heart. He was calculating and controlled with his emotions. I wanted him to exude . . . warmth and compassion . . . but that wasn't in his make up. With his multiple roles as the coach and the man in charge of personnel and contract negotiations, he elected not to form close bonds with the players. That was hard for me to accept. . . . The two of us never had a heart-to-heart talk. . . . We only had surface conversations about the mood of the players or business matters. . . . I regret that we never sat down and talked about life. We never laughed together."

None of Lott's feelings affected his play or his respect for Walsh's football skills, but they did form an emotional subtext that would continue to figure in the team's dynamics and cause him to butt heads with Bill on more than one occasion.

Joe Montana was never the vocal leader that Ronnie was—his off-field personality being more reserved and less assertive—but he too had been upset by Walsh's no-show and postseason emotional collapse.

"Why didn't he come to the meeting?" Joe complained. "I can't answer that question because I still don't know. But I'll tell you this: When I think of him pulling a no-show it still bothers me. Not only didn't Bill come to the meeting, he gave everyone the impression that the 49ers were gutless wonders, a team who didn't care about winning it all again. 'They didn't want to win as much as I did,' Bill told the press. No one wanted to win that Los Angeles game more than I did, and Bill knew it. He talked a lot during that season about how I was doing too much off-the-field work and how I wasn't concentrating on playing quarterback. That was pure bunk. Football always comes first for me. [By talking that way] he mistreated his players—people who played to the max, played in pain because, win or lose, we all believed in Bill. [Then] he compounded his actions during the off-season by keeping the team on the edge of our collective seats, not knowing if he would return as coach. Bill never talked to his players during that off-season. This upset me. . . . We realized he was going through troubled times. . . . I felt for him, but he should have confided in his players."

In Montana's case, the aftermath of the 1982 collapse only complicated a relationship that was already complex and highly charged. That much was inevitable between Bill and his quarterbacks, particularly Joe: Walsh already demanded more from that position than from any other, but his expectations were even higher for Montana, with whom he never seemed satisfied. "Creative tension" would eventually be identified as a hallmark of the internal workings of Walsh's teams, and his dealings with Joe were the leading case in point. Bill was "a demanding guy to work for," Keith Fahnhorst pointed out. "He didn't treat any two players the same on the whole team. He'd baby a guy who needed to be pampered, but screw with the guys who probably should have been appreciated most, because he wanted to keep them motivated. I'm talking about guys like Joe Montana. In a lot of cases, it seems Bill has been messing with him since the first Super Bowl." The result was what Joe's buddy Dwight Clark described as a "love/hate" relationship. "I respect Bill as a coach," Joe complained, "but as a person on and off the field, he confuses me. . . . I never gave anything short of 1,000 percent for Bill, and I never received a compliment from him, never a touch of humanity."

On the sidelines, the friction between them could be glimpsed when Joe would come off the field after a failed third down and Bill would demand to know why Joe hadn't done this or that. Montana would mumble a reply and then walk past until he was out of earshot. Then he'd growl, "Fuck you, you white-haired cocksucker," and throw his helmet on the bench. Joe's teammates became familiar with his attitude. "We talked about Bill all the time," Guy Benjamin recalled, "and Joe was adamant, the way he would put Bill down. In meetings, when Bill would go off on one of his tirades, Joe would turn to me and say, 'Your boy's flipped out again.' He called him a 'dumb, stupid motherfucker,' which was his catchall phrase for anybody he didn't like. He told me one time that Bill didn't want him to have the TV show because Bill didn't want competition, as if there was competition on that level. There was ego, of course, but it went beyond that. Joe felt a real resentment."

Again, however, the friction never got in the way of playing football. "Each of them was in fact perfect for the other," one of the reporters covering the team noted. "Bill's system made Joe and Joe made Bill's system. On the field, their communication was perfect, but off the field, it was nonexistent. They didn't talk except to discuss plays and game plans."

For his part, Walsh considered such frictions inevitable in the coaching process. "As much as I might have cared about what they thought at some level," he offered, "I couldn't indulge that. My job was to coach."

. . .

There were two other sets of relationships that dogged Bill's tracks as he regrouped for the 1983 season, one professional and one personal.

The professional one was with the press corps. In the beginning, of course, that had been a small group that was mostly thrilled to have someone smart, articulate, and free of coaching clichés to write about, giving him something of a free pass, but that treatment waned as expectations rose and attention expanded. Now there were often as many as seventy-five reporters who showed up in the press room after games or at the Niners' Nevada Street press trailer for the weekly Tuesday briefing, swarming in search of an angle or a lead or some dustup with which to juice their stories. The process made Bill feel "very vulnerable" and by 1983, he had become, according to one of the Niners' beat writers, "much more calculated and cautious in what he said." And, while still maintaining what he thought was an open and friendly approach in which "I tried to be reasonable and give my honest opinion about things," Walsh's discomfort was more obvious.

"Dealing with the press was a major challenge for me," he later explained. "On an individual basis, I had grown to appreciate and thoroughly enjoy the company of most sportswriters. But collectively, there was a lemming mentality that develops, almost a herd instinct. I'd convinced myself that they were doing their job and I was doing mine, but there really wasn't a connection between us. It was almost like oil and water. They had no loyalty to the team. In fact, some of them considered it a better story if we lost. There were some who were out to get me, so to speak, to embarrass me. It was a game of cat and mouse in press conferences. Being smart and articulate—the fact that I could come up with answers and didn't get too ruffled—probably egged them on. It was a contest of matching wits. You walk into the room and you're staring at twenty good people and one criminal, a guy with a need to rip. You know he's in the room. You know he's plotting. You know he's gunning for you and working at trying to get you, but if I show it, then it seems that I'm paranoid."

In truth, there was an element of paranoia in Bill's attitude. He would, for example, go to his grave insisting that the San Francisco press corps was equaled in ferocity only by the one in Philadelphia—a description that made most reporters laugh if they'd had any experience with the far more rabid sports pages up and down the Atlantic coast. Walsh also insisted on telling a story about his history with the press that displayed a similar projection. According to Bill, when the team was 1-2 in the 1981 season, an unnamed reporter had written a four-part series about how the Niners were doomed to failure and Walsh had to go. Bill insisted that the first installment had been printed, but then the rest was never published because the team started to win and win. For Walsh, the episode was a classic example of how the press was always ready to undercut him and his team on the slightest pretext. But when pressured to identify the writer of this alleged series, he came up with different names and different newspapers on different occasions and could produce no clippings or citations or any other evidence such a series ever existed. In retrospect, Bill's story illustrates his attitude but otherwise seems to have been a figment of his imagination.

Some of Walsh's feeling of vulnerability around the press was a result of his need to feel in control colliding with the media's inherent uncontrollability. The rest was a function of his hypersensitivity about how he was perceived. While steadfastly claiming he never read the stories written about him, Walsh in fact read them all, and took the commentary very personally, seemingly with the same part of his brain that processed losses. As a result, his approach to the press was often founded on the anticipation of personal trauma. "The first time I interviewed him," one reporter remembered, "I went in thinking he was bigger than life, The Genius and all that. But it was shocking talking to him, seeing how thin-skinned and brittle he was. It was bizarre. It made me really uncomfortable. I literally thought he would crack at some point. It made me want to soothe him. Of course another part of me couldn't stand him. He was so condescending to the press and clearly treated us as so beneath him. He could be positively chatty when you went off the record, but otherwise he acted like a man walking through a minefield. I ended up liking him, but he wasn't at all what I had expected."

Walsh's sense of grievance toward those who covered him and his team found direct expression in some of his talks at team meetings. "You know the newspapers in San Francisco delight in it when we lose," he told his players in advance of one game. "That's what they'd like." Similar statements were made before a number of other games as well. Those sentiments also found less direct expression following games the Niners won, after the press had raised doubts about their prospects the week before. In those instances, Bill would almost gloat, making snide references to the fact that they'd pulled out a victory despite what "some people" thought or even though "some people" expected them to fail. As far as the press was concerned, those moments were Bill at his worst. He was usually far more gracious toward them after a loss.

In any case, Bill would spend much more of his remaining career than he liked to admit watching the media over his shoulder, worried they might be gaining on him.

The other set of relationships that consumed even more of Bill's energy was with his family. During his crisis, when media speculation about what he would do and why he would do it was legion, one columnist suggested that "domestic problems" were a key factor in his dilemma. Walsh and his wife, Geri, now in their twenty-ninth year of marriage, demanded a retraction for the reference and received it, but there was no denying that family remained an unsettling issue for him. In that sense, little had changed since his stint with the Raiders some seventeen years earlier. He still placed the highest importance on nurturing and maintaining his family—at least in theory and rhetoric—but he still had little choice about giving his work the highest priority. And when he did have such a choice, he made it in favor of his work anyway. Like it or not, his family lived a rung or two down the ladder from his professional obsession and they paid more than their share of the wages of his Genius.

Geri had grown accustomed to his long hours away and his incessant distraction but was still not comfortable with them. When he was home, he was useless around the house, even in the traditional male fix-it roles. In the kitchen, he was barely able to boil water. Geri handled all the family bill paying and oversaw the children's schooling and the like. During football season, Bill was so preoccupied and out of contact with normal life that, once, for two weeks in a row, he ran out of gas at exactly the same spot on his drive home from Redwood City to Menlo Park on exactly the same day of the week. He lacked even a rudimentary sense of direction on the road and was barely able to follow directions. Bill liked to take Geri out to dinner, seeing it as a treat to lift her cooking responsibilities off her shoulders, but even there the long reach of the game was never far away. Sometimes she would see him zone out at the restaurant table and could tell he was revisiting last week's contest or sorting through the one to come. While standing together with his arm around her on one occasion while they waited for a table, she noticed that the hand he laid on her arm was unconsciously tracing the diagram of a play on her shoulder. When he paused, she asked, "Did it work?"

Her good humor, however, had its limits and she was not averse to telling him so. "Bill was so immersed in his job," one family friend noted, "that Geri felt pushed into the background. And she made that tough on him." She had taken a degree in design and home decoration while they were in Cincinnati and worked occasional freelance jobs, but the advent of "The Genius" and Bill's notoriety after the 1981 miracle kept the subject of unequal burdens and rewards a raw spot in their marriage. "He made a lot of comments to me about his wife demanding this and his wife demanding that," one of his Forty Niners confidants remembered. Certainly by this point, their marriage was feeling the strain of its ongoing contradictions. On the one hand, according to a friend, "Bill needed Geri to balance his life and was deeply attached from all the years they'd been together. And he thrived on having a predictable home life, which she provided. She took care of him and he needed that. But he also needed a confidante and an intimacy that he couldn't find in their marriage anymore. She was such a strong personality. The result was a tempestuous relationship in which they were both pulled together and pushed apart."

Among other things, Geri was always close to having had enough of the coaching life and, described by friends as "feisty" or "fiery," she often stayed on his case about it. When a reporter from *Sports Illustrated* asked her before the 1982 season how she thought about her husband's eventual retirement, she answered with a smile and a decidedly pointed inflection, "Well, *I'm* ready." Retraction or not, there can be little doubt that she made that feeling well known to Bill as he stewed about his future.

Bill's daughter, Elizabeth, was still too young to weigh in on the subject, but his two sons, Steve, twenty-seven, and Craig, twenty-three, made it clear that the issue was now water under the bridge for them and that the damage his coaching did had already been done. In truth, Bill had hardly a clue how to parent. "He never knew quite what to say to his sons," one friend noted. When asked for a public comment, Steve answered that his father was "an average father" who had done "an adequate job" and that the demands of Bill's job had been "inconvenient," but another observer close to the family described Bill and Steve's relationship by 1983 as "almost complete alienation." Walsh's firstborn had abjured all athletics, left home as soon as he finished high school, and made a life for himself as a radio and television reporter, as independent of his father's aura as possible.

His brother, Craig, about to graduate from UC Davis, made it clear he thought his father had not been there when he needed him. "He was more absent than present," Craig remembered. "It's similar to having a dad in the military except the military doesn't fight a war every Sunday. You have to struggle for attention. I could count on one hand the number of times I played catch with my dad. He'd always come home tired of throwing and that was the end of the subject. He never came to my Little League baseball games. He saw maybe five of the football games I played in from junior high through college. I just played football because I liked it. Other kids always assumed that he gave me special coaching but nothing could be further from the truth. I never got any instruction from him. And I certainly didn't look to him for gratification. Essentially, I kind of grew up without a dad."

The distance between his family's reality and Bill's idealized notion of "family" was an unavoidable fact of his life as he turned his attention to the 1983 season, and it would be a source of turmoil, discomfort, and unease for years to come. But as yet, it wasn't even close to compelling enough to make Bill Walsh decide to do something else.

Bill Walsh sends Joe Montana in with a new play in the NFC championship game against Washington at the end of the 1983 season

22

IIIII IIIII | IIIII

SERIOUS BUSINESS

Whenever Bill Walsh reflected on his crisis after the 1982 season, he always expressed gratitude for the way Eddie DeBartolo stuck with him through it. By now, they had developed a strong bond, in touch week in and week out and, other than their disconnect around the Montana and Clark contracts, functioned smoothly together. Out of Bill's presence, Eddie D. sometimes dismissed his coach as "not as smart as he thinks he is," revealing a thread of resentment, but otherwise, Eddie, now thirty-six, was still respectful and supportive. He made that support obvious to all concerned in May 1983, when he extended Bill's contract and officially bestowed the title of president on him, a post previously held by Eddie himself. This new title didn't involve any change in Bill's duties, which continued to be the same as always, and DeBartolo Jr. was henceforth designated chairman of the board.

Besides reinforcing Bill's morale and publicly reaffirming his standing at the Niners, another likely impetus behind Eddie D.'s decision to give his head coach a titular promotion was Eddie's current difficulties with the National Football League's twenty-seven other franchise holders. Appearing to enlarge the popular and respected Walsh's organizational profile was a way of deflecting some of the unwelcome NFL attention then being focused on Eddie's Forty Niners and their connection to the DeBartolos' other sports businesses.

The root of the NFL's dispute with DeBartolo was the inception of the United States Football League, an upstart organization that cast itself as a potential competitor to the NFL's professional football monopoly. The USFL's business plan was to play in the spring and it began its first season that March with franchises in Los Angeles, Oakland, Tampa, Denver, Detroit, Philadelphia, Boston, Birmingham, Phoenix, Memphis, Chicago, and New Jersey. While not competing head-to-head over spectators or television audience, the two leagues were competing over players, and the USFL was very aggressive about recruiting established NFL veterans and incoming college players with salary offers well above the NFL's going rates. In effect, the competition created a limited version of free agency, and the impact was felt on rosters around the National Football League over the next two years. The Forty Niners would lose three of their veterans to the USFL and ended up in bidding wars over several more. Other franchises' experiences were the same or worse. The process reframed the league's salary scale almost instantly, in a way the previous year's strike hadn't come close to doing.

That financial impact aggravated the NFL's owners, as did the disruption of their rosters, but the National Football League's ability to respond was severely limited. The league was already engaged in a debilitating antitrust lawsuit with the Raiders' Al Davis over his attempt to move his franchise from Oakland to Los Angeles without NFL permission, and any league attempt to suppress the USFL's competition was guaranteed to land them back in court, once again facing triple damages for violating the Sherman Antitrust Act. The NFL's frustration focused on DeBartolo after the insurgent league announced that it was going to expand even further the following year. One of the new USFL franchises would be the Pittsburgh Maulers and press reports soon revealed that the new league had already given an option to purchase the Maulers to wealthy shopping center magnate Edward DeBartolo Sr. He was interested because his corporation already owned Pittsburgh's sports arena, its National Hockey League franchise, its Indoor Soccer League franchise, and the region's cable television network.

Adding spring football to that collection of programming had a natural synergy that was, in Senior's view, "good business."

Eddie D.'s fellow NFL owners, however, considered any such DeBartolo participation in the rival league a blatant "conflict of interest" and were up in arms at the traitor in their midst. Their upset was such that Eddie, who rarely attended league meetings, made a personal appearance at one in March and another in May to address the other owners about his family's situation. Along with one of the DeBartolo Corp.'s attorneys, the Niners' chairman of the board insisted that his franchise—under the guidance of Bill Walsh—and the Maulers would be completely separate organizations, sharing no information or functions and effectively walled off from each other, making any conflict of interest impossible. The rest of the NFL, however, wasn't buying and ended the meeting as pissed off as when they began. One owner described Eddie afterward as "a spoiled rich kid" who "doesn't know his ass from second base." The outcome of the discussions was an instruction to commissioner Pete Rozelle to name a committee of several owners and general managers to investigate the situation and come up with possible league responses. That committee would spend until October at its assignment and the results would be reported at the league's fall meeting.

For his part, Eddie D. agreed to talk to his father and see if Senior wouldn't change his mind about exercising his USFL option, but the Forty Niners' chairman of the board made it clear he didn't expect anything to change. "What can I do?" Eddie asked reporters afterward. "My father has been a business success all his life. Do you think I'm going to tell him what to do? The man has made me—in more ways than one."

In the meantime, the Niners' new president was back at work on the second floor of 711 Nevada Street, having emerged from his emotional nosedive reenergized and refreshed. Bill had also found new motivation and focus: now, much as proving Paul Brown wrong had carried him to Super Bowl XVI, redeeming the 1982 collapse had become the driving force of his professional life. And, eventually, he would do so in spades.

That process began with rebuilding his team, and the first place he focused was the vacancies among his coaching staff. Altogether, three of his assistants had found other work when Bill's future still seemed up in the air, plus he had lost a fourth when Sam Wyche, whom Bill would have liked to keep, accepted an offer to become head coach at Indiana University with his mentor's blessing. Sam was the first of what would become a legion of head coaches to spring from Walsh's lineage. To replace Wyche as quarterbacks coach, Bill hired Paul Hackett, previously an assistant at Cleveland. Bill had met him through his friend Mike White, for whom Hackett had coached at Cal. Ironically, Hackett had been Walsh's chief competition for the Stanford head coaching job back in 1976. "Paul Hackett was similar in many ways to Sam," Bill explained. "He was impetuous and aggressive and very ambitious. He was also bright, knowledgeable, and totally dedicated. I've never met a man who thrived more on the game."

The most significant of Walsh's off-season coaching changes was his decision to promote George Seifert from defensive backfield coach to defensive coordinator. The previous season's debacle against San Diego in which Dan Fouts had shredded the Niners defense at will had convinced Bill that his team needed to become far more sophisticated in its pass defense schemes and, even though Seifert had only two years of NFL coaching experience, Walsh thought he was the man to make that transformation. "He was an excellent technician and taskmaster," Bill pointed out. "He had a gifted mind and was extremely well organized" with "a unique aptitude for the technical aspects of the game. He was not a light, quick-witted, amusing type of coach but a very demanding, no-nonsense, business-oriented man who quickly got the respect of players because of his expertise and concentration, and his willingness to work long hours. He put together a style of defense that was fully dimensional with a flexibility that enabled it to deal effectively with new and varied offenses. George's defenses were often a step ahead of everybody."

With his staff reformulated, Bill turned to adding more talent to his roster. His principal concentration this off-season was on running backs. He felt he hadn't had a credible back in his offense since Paul Hofer retired, and his team's inability to run the ball had been one of the glaring weaknesses exposed during the 1982 collapse. Teams were loading up against the pass and he had nothing to back them off with. He also considered the ability to rely on the ground game when leading in the fourth quarter essential, matched only by the need to be able to rush the passer on defense in the same circumstance. To find players who could give him that running option, Walsh turned once again to manipulation of that year's collegiate draft. He knew that the first-round pick he held—San Diego's originally, exchanged for the Niners' as part of the Fred Dean trade—was too late to get the runner he coveted, so several weeks before the draft he traded it back to San Diego for the two picks the Chargers had in the second round. Then he used one of those second-round picks to swing a trade with the rival Los Angeles Rams.

The Rams had the second pick in the first round and were intent on using it to draft Eric Dickerson of Southern Methodist University, thought by most to be the best back coming out of college that year. They already had another runner on their roster, Wendell Tyler, who had twice gained more than a thousand yards in a season, the definition of a quality back. Tyler had done so after an extraordinary recovery from horrendous injuries suffered in a car crash four years earlier and was a fan favorite. To avoid any controversy over his fate, the Rams wanted to move Tyler before bringing in Dickerson. At the same time, the Rams had a new general manager who, Bill remembered, "was somewhat naïve about the implications for the Rams if Wendell Tyler made a big difference for the Forty Niners." There were other teams interested in Tyler as well, but the Niners were the most aggressive. John McVay did the bulk of the negotiating and Bill, who was traveling, checked in with him over the phone when they got close to a deal. As finally executed on draft day, the trade involved one of the Niners' second-round picks and its fourth-rounder in exchange for a package of Tyler, a journey-man defensive end who didn't make the Niners roster, and the Rams' third-round pick.

In retrospect, Walsh considered the exchange a steal. "Wendell some-times hurt our offense with his fumbles," Bill later pointed out, "but he gave us a quickness and explosion in our running game that we'd never had. He was one of the quickest backs into the hole the game has ever seen. He was also a great blocker for a running back, one of the best in the NFL, and though not a naturally gifted receiver, he made a number of critical recep-tions." Within two years, Tyler would set a new Forty Niners single-season rushing record.

Having secured one back to revitalize his offense, Walsh used his other second-round pick to draft another. In Bill's system—again against the popular current of "spread" formations with no tight end and one-back or no-back sets—he wanted two backs, with almost interchangeable skills, and used that arrangement on every down. He felt the two-back set kept his of-fense ambidextrous and, again, multiplied his available options. His choice for the second slot, Roger Craig, out of the University of Nebraska, was somewhat under most teams' radar. He had gained more than a thousand yards rushing his junior year, playing at tailback, but then he had been moved to fullback as a senior to make room for Mike Rozier, an eventual All-American. Craig was big enough at 228 pounds to do the blocking required but was also fast enough to run the high hurdles during track season. All of that excited Walsh, but what he didn't know was whether Craig could catch the ball, an essential skill for any back in Bill's system. Craig had only caught a total of sixteen passes in his four years at Nebraska, eight as a senior, in a system that only had two pass patterns for running backs.

Paul Hackett was assigned the task of figuring out if Craig could catch, so the new assistant reviewed film of his eight senior catches over and over, but still couldn't be sure. Nonetheless, Hackett gave him an enthusiastic endorsement, as did the team's scouts. Walsh drafted Craig with the draft's forty-ninth pick—the sixth running back taken—and Craig responded by practicing the passing game all spring, catching at least a hundred passes a day and quickly making himself into the archetype of a Walsh running back. Within three years Roger Craig would become the first back in NFL history to gain a thousand yards as a rusher and a thousand yards as a pass receiver in the same season. "Craig was the best all around back since Hugh McElhenny," Bill remembered. "He could do everything. He was a great receiver, a great runner, could block, and was a tremendous competitor. He would end up being the best running back I ever coached." His presence also added another dimension to Bill's offense that it had not had before.

Having reformulated his offensive backfield, Walsh went into that year's training camp with only a couple of items of old business to attend to.

The first was at tight end. Bill had used Russ Francis and Charle Young in rotation during the previous season, sometimes starting one and sometimes the other, but that created a touchy situation and couldn't possibly last. "It was like having two vying bathing beauties," Bill remembered. "One had to go." So, recognizing that Francis was the better talent, Walsh asked Charle to accept a backup role. Young, whose contract had expired and who was looking to negotiate another, balked at the idea. He felt he had beaten Francis out in practice and deserved the starter's role. "Bill wanted me to lie down and give Russ Francis the job," Charle explained, "and I didn't think that was the Forty Niners way. He wanted me to just make room and everything was for me to give and for me not to receive."

Instead, Young reminded Walsh that when he'd first come to the Niners, Bill had promised him that if they ever got in a disagreement they couldn't resolve, he'd give him his release. Charle asked for that release now and Bill obliged, allowing him to go out and find another team and receiving nothing in return.

That left Walsh with just Francis—the same guy who at one training camp buzzed the practice field flying a P-51 Mustang. "Russ pushed Bill's buttons more than anybody else," one Walsh confidant remembered. "He never practiced the way he played. He would stand and look at airplanes flying over during practice. You couldn't control him and Bill always had trouble with things he couldn't control. If he hadn't been so productive, Bill would have cut him in a hot minute." On the other hand, Walsh often treated Francis like a kind of mascot. "I had somebody in Russ I could really tease in front of the rest of the team," Bill explained. "I'd get a lot of laughs and he'd laugh. I could tease him and he could take it. He was a source of humor for all of us. Even if he got a little bit mad, an hour later he'd be laughing about it."

The most memorable of those "little bit mad" incidents occurred after they had been talking in the coach's office and Bill told Francis that if the tight end's mother had had better control over her son he wouldn't have ended up so unmanageable. The remark hit Francis the wrong way. Bill was sitting behind a desk covered with various papers and, in a burst of anger, Francis stood up and lifted the desk by one edge, intending just to slide all the papers off into the coach's lap, but the desk was extremely heavy and he lost control of it. The desk then flipped onto its side, knocking Walsh out of his chair and pinning him to the floor. Bill began yelling at Francis to get the goddamn thing off him, but Francis walked out, stopping at Bill's secretary's desk as he left. He told her the boss was in his office and needed her help.

Having "solved" his tight end dilemma, the other piece of old business facing Bill was at left tackle. Bubba Paris had recovered from his knee injury and been reinstalled as the starter, but the issue of Bubba's weight remained unresolved. On a couple of occasions, he weighed in the 290s, but otherwise the quest for 285 quickly became a quest to stay close to 300. Bubba would dutifully show his meal trays to the coaches so they could make sure he wasn't eating too much, but then between the last evening meeting and curfew he would sneak down to the local pizza parlor and buy a family size with extra cheese and a quart of Pepsi to go. When the Niners broke camp, the maid cleaning Bubba's room discovered an enormous cache of chicken bones left over from other takeout expeditions stashed in the dresser. Once, when Bubba's weigh-ins kept getting lower and lower until he was a few pounds under 300, it finally seemed like Bubba had it under control. Then Bill discovered that the scale was next to a coke machine and a pile of wooden soda crates. Bubba had been secretly resting his elbow on the crates whenever he weighed. When Bill moved them, Bubba tipped the scales at 325.

Nonetheless, the coach still considered Paris his best option at left tackle and, overweight or not, he would play reasonably well for the next few years before finally eating himself out of a job.

All in all, Bill felt good about the team he'd put together on the eve of the 1983 season. There were four new starters on offense and three on defense, as well as almost a dozen new reserves. At the time, he called it the best group he'd yet assembled, the miracle year included.

When Ronnie Lott was later asked to characterize the 1983 Niners, he likened the 1981 team to an infant that Walsh had to nurture and support, and portrayed the 1983 team as more grown-up, kind of an adolescent that didn't need Walsh as much and was far more capable of standing on its own. At the same time, the 1983 team was subject to the flaws of adolescence and was both erratic and inconsistent. They were world beaters one week and manure eaters the next, and you never knew ahead of time which would show up.

They started off losing to Philadelphia—a mediocre team that would win only four more games all season—after the Niners' potential winning touchdown was called back on a holding penalty. Then they entered a seven-game stretch in which they lost only once—to the Rams at Candlestick when their tying field goal was blocked. The last victory of that run was a rematch with the Rams down in Southern California and amounted to their best game of the season to that point. At the time, both teams were 5-2 and tied for the division lead. The Niners started the contest slowly and never did get their entire arsenal of weapons into play. Their revived running game fell flat, gaining fewer yards than any of their previous efforts, so they had to rely on Montana's arm to stay in contention. Joe would throw for more than 350 yards, the second largest total of his career. Down 21–14 early in the third quarter, he hit Freddie Solomon, who made a spectacular catch deep in the Rams' territory but injured himself in the process. Solomon was then replaced by Renaldo Nehemiah, who proceeded to have his best game ever. He immediately caught a twelve-yard pass across the middle on which he got hammered by the defensive back but held on. The Niners bogged down there, but a Wersching field goal made the score 21–17.

The Rams offense responded with a touchdown, upping their lead to eleven points, but Montana took the Niners down the field again, using Nehemiah at opportune moments, first for nine yards, then for twenty-seven down to the Rams' eleven-yard line. After two incompletions aimed for the tight ends, Walsh called Nehemiah's number again, a successful eleven-yard slant for a touchdown, and it was 28–24. The defense, however, was struggling, and the Rams passed their way down the field for another touchdown, again stretching the lead to eleven and setting off a huge celebration on the Los Angeles sideline. At that point, the *Chronicle* reported, "the 49ers looked like a beaten team," and the Rams players, according to Randy Cross, "were over there high-fiving and celebrating, real excited like they were trying to decide where they were going to go after the game." Montana, however, answered right back yet again. After another short completion to Nehemiah, Walsh sent the speedster running flat out straight down the field, drawing two Rams defensive backs and opening up the middle of the field, and Dwight Clark ran into the vacated space and Joe hit him for a forty-seven-yard touchdown, 35–31.

And then the defense came to life. After they pinned the Rams at their own eight-yard line on the kickoff, the Los Angeles quarterback tried to pass his way out of the tight spot, but Peewee Board tackled him in the end zone, stripped the ball away, and recovered it for another touchdown, and the Niners took the lead for the first time with 6:40 left to play, 38–35. On their next possession the Rams went back to their passing game and Niners linebacker Willie Harper intercepted a pass and ran it back to the Rams' four. Another touchdown followed and San Francisco won the game 45–35, taking over first place in the division. Inside the Niners' locker room, according to the *Chronicle,* the "celebration appeared to match the emotional level of some of the big games during the Super Bowl season."

Eddie D. was in the thick of it, hugging everyone. The league's report on his "conflict of interest" was in by now and his fellow owners were suggesting that if his father didn't get rid of his USFL franchise, Eddie might be forced to sell the Niners, but Eddie had long since made it clear he would never do that. "Nobody's going to take this team, including the league," he asserted. "The league can't afford the lawsuit and I can. Enough of this BS about a conflict of interest. That's ridiculous." And after this victory over the Rams, the chairman of the board was expecting to rub his defiance in the league's chest by sending his team back to the Super Bowl.

And "his guys" seemed like they might well be up to it. "I almost underestimated the character of our team," Walsh told the press afterward. "It's just a pleasure to be associated with them. I feel like I'm along for the ride. They have an incredible will to win, to compete and not let down. This victory leaves me speechless."

That said, Bill's team promptly went into a nosedive during which they lost four of the next five. Two of those defeats were particularly galling.

The first was against the Miami Dolphins at home. Ronnie Lott had perhaps the worst day of his career and was beaten twice for touchdowns and then was called for a forty-four-yard pass interference penalty that led to a Miami field goal, which put the visitors ahead 20–17 halfway through the final quarter. The Niners, however, fought back and drove deep into the Dolphins' territory largely on the legs of rookie Roger Craig, who was having his best day yet as a professional. Then, on Miami's twenty-one-yard line, with 1:12 left in the game, Craig fumbled, Miami recovered, and the game was over. In the locker room afterward, no one said a thing and Eddie gave out no hugs. Instead, he grabbed a wall phone and slung its receiver so hard its innards fell out.

Bill then emerged to face the press with, one reporter wrote, "a smile on his pale face [but] it was the kind of smile you put on after the roof blows off the summer cabin for which you forgot to purchase the homeowner's insurance. You smile because it looks better than grinding your teeth. . . . He said his team's effort was excellent and he wasn't worried. When someone asked about certain 'failures' in the Niners' play, the smile fled Walsh's face like a burglar running down a dark street. [He then] said, 'Folks, you're being immature about this. . . .' He said a tough loss is not a failure."

An even tougher loss came two weeks later on the road against the Atlanta Falcons—a team on the decline and headed for a seven-win season. The tone was set right before halftime, with the Niners up 14–7 and driving.

Bill called a pass to Nehemiah across the middle; the speedster caught it, took two steps, and then was knocked unconscious when the defensive safety arrived and planted his helmet on Nehemiah's chin. The ball bounced loose and Russ Francis was in a position to recover it, but instead he ran to assist Renaldo, who looked to be very seriously hurt. That allowed the Falcons to pick up the ball and run the fumble back for a touchdown. Joe Montana later called the hit on Nehemiah one of "the scariest moments" he'd ever experienced on the football field. Nehemiah himself never quite got his nerve back afterward and would be out of football after another season.

Nonetheless, the Niners seemed to have a victory in hand, 24–21, when Atlanta had the ball with time for only one more play left in the game. The Falcons quarterback then threw a Hail Mary pass toward the end zone, which Niners linebacker Keena Turner seemed to have batted down, but the ball instead caromed into the arms of a Falcons wide receiver, who surged toward the end zone. Walsh would later say the films of the play showed decisively that the Falcons receiver's knee was down before he crossed the goal line, but it was called a touchdown, Falcons 28, Niners 24. "I cannot recall ever being so stunned and sickened by a defeat," Walsh remembered years later. "When we went to the dressing room, there was really nothing I could say. No use pointing fingers, just live through the agony. Ed DeBartolo came in and was terribly distressed and wanted to vent his frustration, but everybody was in such a state of shock, nobody could pay much attention."

After another loss the next week against Chicago, played in freezing sleet, the Forty Niners were only 7-6 and hardly looking like a Super Bowl team, a fact the local press noted every time it got the chance. The Niners, however, weren't prepared to roll over and responded with two wins in a row so that with one game remaining—at home against the Dallas Cowboys on Monday night—they faced a make-or-break situation: win and they were division champions and in the playoffs, lose and their season was over. And the doubters were legion. "The 49ers have not seemed like one of the best teams in the league," one columnist noted. The team "got pushed around whenever it faced tough, physical teams—even mediocre ones. [They] lost the ball on turnovers at the worst possible times and established a reputation as a team that kills itself."

Not this week, however. "By now," Walsh pointed out, "we had the Cowboys' number." In a game marred only by Dwight Clark's season-ending knee injury, the Forty Niners bashed Dallas 42–17. They were now 10-6, division champions, and headed for the playoffs, and this game would turn out to be an extraordinary watershed in NFL history. From here on, it would be fifteen years before any Forty Niners team finished worse than 10-6 and only once in that string would the team miss the playoffs, a record unmatched by any other franchise. Bill would remember the Dallas trouncing that began it as the Niners "announcing we were back."

The press room at Candlestick was overflowing with media after the game. One reporter described Bill's demeanor when he took the podium as like "an emperor gazing upon disloyal subjects," and ran his account of the victorious coach's press conference under the headline WALSH RELISHES HIS HOUR OF REDEMPTION.

"Were you surprised?" someone asked for openers.

Bill denied any surprise at all and seemed a bit offended at the suggestion. He insisted this was a very good Forty Niners team that had played hard all year long.

"I know some of our local people had written us off completely," he said, pointedly referencing the host of reporters who were regulars on the Niners beat, but "we're hoping we can sort of let them down."

The assembled media had been anticipating something far more lighthearted and celebratory from Walsh, so his acidic remark and obvious resentment generated stunned silence in the packed room. And before any of his interrogators could regain their balance to ask another question, Bill walked out, ending the press conference.

As far as Bill Walsh was concerned, only a return to the Super Bowl would count as genuine redemption. "I needed to prove that first one wasn't some kind of fluke," he explained. And Eddie DeBartolo, of course, agreed with him. Their erratic team, however, seemed to be a shaky foundation for such aspirations. The Niners were lucky to survive their first playoff game, against the Detroit Lions, 24–23, when the Lions kicker, with unsteady footing on Candlestick's slippery turf, missed a forty-three-yard field goal that would have won the game. Lucky or not, the Niners flew back to Washington, D.C., the next week for the NFC championship game against the Redskins, just one more win away from the Super Bowl. The Redskins were the defending Super Bowl champions and heavily favored. "The eastern press was already hailing them as one of the greatest teams of all time," Walsh remembered. "They'd been dominating everybody." By the time of his final press conference in the week before the game, Walsh was sick of being asked how his team could possibly cope with the mighty Skins. "Our players have a history of winning too," he bristled. "We've won the Super Bowl. As I recall, we were an underdog there too. We're not just being herded in here to play a game."

The other set of questions that dominated the pregame buildup all had to do with Eddie's conflict with the league. These were answered by the Niners PR man, who insisted the DeBartolos were not involved in any conflict of interest, that Eddie would never sell his team, no one could make him do so, and that everyone ought to drop this subject and concentrate on the upcoming conference championship.

That contest was played on a sloppy field at RFK Stadium in weather just a bit above freezing. Bill had admitted ahead of time that his team would have to be at its best to win and in the first half that seemed anything but the case. The Niners moved the ball, then misfired at critical moments. "It wasn't that we were relaxing or uptight," Joe Montana remembered. "It was simply a matter of missing on a couple of long passes down the field that would have put us ahead." At halftime, the score was Redskins 7, Forty Niners 0.

In the third quarter, however, the roof seemed to fall in on Walsh's team. First Freddy Solomon fumbled on the Niners' thirty-six and Washington quickly drove down the short field. The most significant play in that effort was the first in a series of penalty calls against the Niners' defensive backfield that would end up deciding the game. This time, Ronnie Lott got entangled with a Redskins receiver and ended up being called for pass interference. Lott protested that the foul was actually committed by the man he was guarding, but Washington was given an automatic first down on the six-yard line. Three plays later the score was 14–0. The Niners were forced to punt when they got the ball back and Washington took over at its own thirty. Unfortunately, Bill recalled, "they had figured out our defensive coverages" and immediately struck deep with a seventy-yard pass play for another touchdown, making the score 21–0 with a minute left in the third quarter.

The Niners were now in desperate straits. "With the Redskins' band blasting 'Hail to the Redskins' and the RFK crowd sure they had the 49ers rocking and reeling," Montana recounted, "either you bag it or you search for something that will somehow turn the momentum." What they found was their passing game and they now began, in Montana's words, turning "chickenshit into chicken salad." Using Solomon and Mike Wilson, who was replacing the injured Dwight Clark, the Forty Niners drove seventy-nine yards in nine plays and put their first seven points on the board in the first minute of the fourth quarter. The Redskins tried to answer but, after bogging down at the Niners' twenty-four-yard line, missed a field goal attempt. On the sidelines during that Washington drive, Bill conceived and diagramed a brand-new play for his offense and called it on the first down of their ensuing possession. The result was a seventy-six-yard touchdown from Montana to Freddy Solomon, 21–14. The Redskins failed to move the ball after getting it back and punted it to the Niners' forty-seven. Montana then led another drive, fifty-three yards in four plays, and with 7:18 remaining, the score was tied and it was anybody's ball game.

"When the momentum starts to change in a game, especially that fast and that drastically," Montana explained, "it's really hard for the other team to stop the tidal wave." The Redskins, however, gave it their best shot. Using a grinding ground attack, they moved from their own fourteen to the Niners' forty-five. Then, with Washington facing second and ten with four minutes left on the clock, the decisive play of the game transpired. The Redskins threw deep along the sideline and the pass sailed high over the head of their wide receiver—so high, Bill Walsh noted, that "not even a ten-foot Boston Celtic" could have caught the ball. The NFL rules specified that if a pass was "uncatchable," pass interference penalties did not apply, but nonetheless, a pass interference penalty was called on Eric Wright. "Neither man had a play on the ball," Walsh pointed out. "Possibly Eric had a hand touching the receiver, but you couldn't find anything that might affect him." The result of the call was a twenty-seven-yard gain. Now on the Niners' eighteen, a Redskins field goal was a given. The question was whether the Niners would get the ball back with enough time to respond.

That was answered when the Redskins reached a third and five at the thirteen. Again they passed and again the ball was uncatchable, but this time, on the other side of the field, away from the action, Ronnie Lott was called for a defensive holding penalty that had no effect on the play at all. "We got jobbed," Bill later complained. "There was nothing there to call." Nonetheless, the Redskins received an automatic first down at the Niners' eight with the clock ticking. Three more plays only gained another yard, but with only forty seconds left the Redskins kicked the winning field goal, 24–21. Montana tried to rally one more time, but his first pass was intercepted and the game was over. He later called this "the toughest loss we had ever experienced."

Bill was infuriated and in anguish, but he refused to criticize the officiating to reporters in the locker room afterward. Eddie D., however, was still too hot to follow suit. He was convinced the controversial calls were linked to his own problems with the NFL.

"If the league is out to get me," Eddie declared in a rush of anger, "they did a good job."

Walsh, standing nearby, reached over and patted his owner on the shoulder as if to soothe him.

DeBartolo's anger still hadn't ebbed by the time he returned to Youngstown, and once there, his fury turned in Walsh's direction, though Bill never learned of it until years later. Still in a fit over being denied his second trip to the Super Bowl, Eddie met with his friend and attorney, Carmen Policy, and told Policy that Walsh had failed to deliver and he wasn't going to put up with it anymore. He said he should have fired Bill the year before when he had the chance. Now it was time to get rid of him and he wanted Policy to call Walsh and tell him he was through. Policy put off doing so long enough for Eddie to drop the idea, once he finally cooled off, but it was nowhere near the last time a frustrated Niners' chairman of the board, faced with having to accept less than he wanted, would raise the prospect of showing Walsh the door.

The Forty Niners listen to their owner's rant after the Houston game, 1984

║║║║ ║║║║ ║║║║

23

AS CLOSE TO PERFECT AS YOU CAN GET

onths later, once his pain and anger had receded into memory, Bill Walsh would come to think of that playoff loss at the end of the 1983 season as one of the most significant games in the Forty Niners' history, largely because of its seminal impact on 1984. "It became our biggest motivation," he recalled, "without me even trying to make it so." His players emerged from their landmark disappointment at RFK Stadium and entered the off-season believing that they were the better team and should have won, but rather than whining about it or pointing fingers, they—spontaneously, to a man—dedicated themselves to making sure it didn't happen again. The team's adolescence was over. That much was obvious as soon as training camp opened in July. "I picked up certain indicators that the team meant serious business," Joe Montana remembered. "There was a certain kind of intensity that I spotted immediately, a no-nonsense attitude. Defensive backs were playing in practice as if it were a game. . . . Ordinarily . . .

practice is practice. But in '84, we were going to do everything in our power not to be denied."

As usual, Walsh had spent the off-season tinkering with his roster, but this year, for the first time, he was looking for depth rather than trying to fill holes in his starting lineup. During the draft, that circumstance allowed him to focus on the best players available regardless of position. The result was one of the better drafts of Walsh's career. Five of that year's choices— linebacker Todd Shell, tight end John Frank, offensive guard Guy McIntyre, nose tackle Michael Carter, and safety Jeff Fuller—would eventually become starters after a period of backup apprenticeship. Carter, one of the world's best at throwing the shot put, was another case of Bill's affinity for using track-and-field athletes, though Michael had also been a two-time All-American in football at SMU. Carter reported late to camp because he was competing in that summer's Olympic Games in Los Angeles, where he won a silver medal.

In Walsh's estimation, nose tackle was the closest thing to a hole on the Niners roster. Pete Kugler, who had played the position well during 1983, had signed with the USFL, even though the new league was struggling and would survive for only one more season. To replace Kugler, Bill had gone shopping for veterans, acquiring Manu Tuiasosopo from the Seattle Seahawks for a fourth-round draft pick and then massive Louie Kelcher from San Diego for an eighth-rounder. To further bolster his defensive line, Bill cut another deal with San Diego as the season was beginning, exchanging sixth- and ninth-round picks for Gary "Big Hands" Johnson, a former Pro Bowl tackle who had teamed with Fred Dean in the days when the Chargers had one of the best pass rushes in the NFL. The Chargers had soured on Johnson after a contract dispute. "Picking up Big Hands and Louie was possible because of Eddie and his financial support," Bill pointed out. "They were there and available and we paid them good salaries to come and be backups. There were a lot of teams that wouldn't do that—that wouldn't even think of doing it. For us it was just a question of selling Eddie and deciding it. Eddie wanted to do everything we could to make it back to the Super Bowl and money wouldn't stand in the way."

Most of the franchise's off-season drama surrounded contract negotiations. The combined impact of Eddie D.'s Montana and Clark deals and the advent of the USFL had a lot of Niners looking for new financial arrangements, even if their current contracts still hadn't expired. Two of those renegotiations were particularly critical.

The first was with Ronnie Lott. Lott's contract still had a year left, but he was woefully underpaid by the current standards and Bill and Eddie admitted as much. Ronnie's demands, however, were over the top. He wanted $800,000 a year, equaling the highest-paid defensive player in the NFL—New York Jets defensive end Mark Gastineau. Those numbers would also have made Lott the highest-paid member of the Forty Niners, surpassing even Joe Montana, and that, Bill insisted, was not going to happen. He and Ronnie met to discuss his demands and, at moments, their vehemence could be heard all over the Nevada Street headquarters' second floor. To keep the pressure on the Niners, Ronnie entertained feelers from the USFL's Arizona Wranglers. Then, when July camp opened at Rocklin and no deal was yet done, Ronnie refused to report. "I had to do it," he later explained to the press. "I thought the emotions would run very high if I came into camp [and] there would have been more tension between myself and management. I thought the way it was handled was better for the team. I know I'm a very emotional person and I probably would have made some irrational statements."

A little more than a week after Lott's holdout began, he signed a new contract for $2.3 million over four years and reported for work. Bill was glad to have Ronnie back, but, according to the *Chronicle,* "for the time being, at least, things are a little frosty between the two." The newspaper's evidence was the fact they passed each other in the hallway on Lott's first day back and didn't say a word. "I didn't think anything of it," Ronnie explained. "I didn't think I was supposed to bow or genuflect or anything. I don't know how good our relationship was before [but] I don't think it's hurt it. I don't know if it's helped it. I just have to go out and perform for him."

The other critical renegotiation was with Fred Dean and it was even more contentious. Dean had led the conference the previous season with seventeen and a half sacks and he wanted his old contract—which still had two years left on it—rewritten to pay him at least $800,000 a year. Fred thought he was better than Gastineau and ought to be worth more too. As part of his negotiating strategy, the Niners defensive end also filed suit to have his current contract nullified and make him a free agent, able to negotiate with whomever he wished. Walsh offered a four-year deal for $1.5 million instead, but Dean's agent refused and declared that if Fred's minimum demand wasn't met, he was prepared to sit out the entire year while he waited for his lawsuit to bear fruit. As camp broke, the Niners made a final offer of two years for $1 million to begin in 1985 but Dean's agent dismissed it as "not even worth a counteroffer." Then the agent made one anyway, several days later, saying Fred would play this year for $805,000 and the right to free agency in 1985. Eddie D. in particular was infuriated by this last demand.

After the Niners rejected it, Dean talked to the press for the first time. He noted that Dwight Clark hadn't had any trouble getting his deal rewritten. "I've noticed the difference in treatment," he pointed out to the *Examiner,* and "it hurts. I'd be lying if I said it didn't bother me. I'm willing to sit out this season. I'm willing to go farther than that. I miss football, but I gotta do what I gotta do." In sympathy with him, the defensive line showed up one day at a training camp practice with their jerseys turned inside out, but it made no difference. By the time camp broke, with the season about to begin, Walsh was saying the prospect of signing the Niners' preeminent pass rusher "doesn't look terribly positive." John McVay, who was doing most of the actual negotiating, was even more pessimistic. "I don't expect," he said, "we'll have him back—ever." Dean's holdout continued full steam as the season began, as did the stalemate generating it.

Nonetheless, Walsh was more confident in this team than any he had ever had. After five years, Montana had mastered the full range of the offense; they were at least two deep at every position; the defense was the best it had ever been, with enough quality defensive linemen to come at its opponents in waves. His roster was, in Bill's estimation, "without weaknesses." Ronnie Lott would call it "the most talented team I'd ever been around" and his teammates would agree with him. Much later, after his career was over and this squad had long since made its mark, Bill would even go so far as to describe the 1984 Forty Niners as "one of the two or three best teams in NFL history."

The season opened with a repeat of last year's playoffs—first a game with Detroit, followed by a rematch with Washington.

The Niners always seemed to have trouble with Detroit and this year was no exception. Walsh's squad finally won a back-and-forth contest with a forty-nine-yard drive in the final minutes that yielded the winning field goal with only four seconds left on the clock, Niners 30, Lions 27.

Next came a chance for revenge against the Redskins—the game the Niners had been waiting for all off-season. Walsh didn't have to do anything special to get his team up for this one. "If someone had bottled the adrenaline we had stored inside us since we lost that NFC title game to the Skins," Joe Montana noted, "we could have propelled a rocket back and forth to the moon at least ten times." And they jumped on the Redskins right out of the chute. For the first half, the *Chronicle* observed, "the 49ers played football as close to perfection as the rules allow." Montana moved the team up and down the field dumping short passes to Roger Craig, hitting Solomon and Clark on deeper routes, throwing under the linebackers to Russ Francis, running the ball with Wendell Tyler, and even running himself when the opportunity arose. Over the entire game, Joe would throw for more than 367 yards and in the first half alone, the Niners gained 111 yards on the ground. All the while, the Forty Niners defense was stalwart, holding Washington to six straight possessions of three and out to open the game. In the first half, the Niners made twenty first downs to Washington's four, gained 322 yards to their 65. The Redskins didn't score until they kicked a field goal on the last play of the half and San Francisco went into the locker room leading 27–3.

It was not, however, going to be that easy. The Redskins were among the NFL's elite teams, having been to two straight Super Bowls and winning one of them. On top of that, the Niners had spent themselves. "When we came into the locker room at halftime," Montana remembered, "we were physically and emotionally drained. All our adrenaline was gone. We knew the entire second half would be gut check time." And it certainly was. Walsh would describe that second half as "a little reminiscent of the last game we had with them—but, of course, the tables were turned this time." The Redskins attacked the Niners' seemingly untouchable lead by throwing on almost every down and, minus Fred Dean, the defense had trouble bringing enough pressure to disrupt them. All told, Washington would gain 255 yards through the air in the second half. And the Forty Niners made their task easier. Wendell Tyler fumbled twice in the Niners' territory, both leading to Washington scores. Montana led a drive to answer as the fourth quarter got under way, but sustained a serious rib injury in the process. Nonetheless, he ran the ball in himself to make the score 34–17.

The Niners would pick up another field goal but the Redskins offense did not roll over. Once again they drove for a touchdown. Twice the Niners defense turned the Redskins away with crucial stands, but then gave up a fifteen-second-long, two-play, forty-four-yard drive and the score was 37–31 with 3:44 left to play.

To hold on, the Niners needed to run the clock out, and that was problematic. Their ground game had disappeared in the second half, so they would have to throw the ball to keep the chains moving. "It got dicey," Bill remembered. "We had the ball and we didn't want them to get it. I had to throw passes to hold on and when throwing passes at the end of a game with a six-point lead, you're looking at possible disaster on every down." Montana, however, was up to the challenge, sore ribs notwithstanding. With third and three and the Redskins having just used their last time out at the 2:42 mark, he found Dwight Clark for eleven and kept the clock moving. Finally, after the two-minute warning, one of the Redskins defensive ends was called for roughing the passer, giving the Niners another first down and the margin they needed to maintain possession until time expired.

On the final stat sheet, San Francisco had accumulated thirty first downs and 534 yards, both records for a Walsh team. Even more important, they had vindicated themselves and confirmed their off-season resolve. "It was a big game for us," Bill observed, "a very big game. It lifted us to another level."

And over the next month, the Niners went on a tear. They handled New Orleans by ten points despite losing Montana for half the game when his ribs got worse. Then they beat Philadelphia by a dozen despite not having Montana at all. Joe returned to help dispense with Atlanta by nine and then take the New York Giants apart by three touchdowns. When they returned to San Francisco afterward, they were 6-0 and looking invincible.

The Forty Niners' seventh game was against the Pittsburgh Steelers. Again, it was a Youngstown bragging rights game for Eddie D. Even though the USFL was in its death throes, his dad's attempt to compete with the Steelers on their home turf had upped the emotional ante even further. Eddie would spend the afternoon in his Candlestick box, unable to stay still, standing up and sitting down and standing back up, occasionally screaming at the field below. The Steelers were not quite the powerhouse the Niners had beaten three years earlier on their way to The Miracle, but they were still a playoff team that was well coached and dangerous. San Francisco also went into the game without a couple of key players. Wide receiver Freddie Solomon was out with a hamstring injury and right offensive tackle Keith Fahnhorst, who had started ninety-five straight games, was sidelined with back spasms. Montana was relatively healthy but didn't play particularly well and was admittedly "out of sync" for most of the game.

The result was a cluster of missed opportunities that would haunt the Niners all afternoon long: Montana had Mike Wilson down the sideline behind the last defender, but the wind caught his pass and held it up long enough for the Pittsburgh defender to recover and swat it away. On the same play, Dwight Clark had been all by himself in the middle of the field with no one between him and the end zone, but Joe didn't see him. On a second down at Pittsburgh's thirty-eight, Wilson was again wide open at the fifteen, but Montana overthrew him. The following play, Joe threw a swing pass to Roger Craig, who had a clear path to a first down, but Craig dropped it and the Niners had to punt. When kicker Ray Wersching made a fifty-one-yard field goal, the absolute limit of his range, it was disallowed because a San Francisco blocker had lined up wrong, taking three points off the board, moving the Niners back five yards, and forcing a punt.

Despite those and other miscues, the Niners were nursing a 17–10 lead with 3:32 remaining in the game. And then it was suddenly déjà vu all over again.

The Steelers were at the Niners' six-yard line, fourth and goal, and decided to go for a touchdown. The Steelers quarterback faded back to pass and threw toward one of his wide receivers running a crossing pattern in the end zone, covered by Eric Wright. "Wright," according to the *Chronicle* account, "made a desperate dive in front of [the receiver] and knocked the ball down with his right hand, making what appeared to be a marvelous play. Then [the official] dropped his flag, [ruling] that Wright had prevented [the Steeler] from catching the ball by pushing him with his left hand. If there was contact, it appeared to be incidental [which the rules allow]." Walsh would later describe it as a "phantom call," the Bay Area press was agreed that "the 49ers undoubtedly would have won had it not been for that questionable penalty," and one headline would summarize the play as MILLION DOLLAR GAME, 10 CENT OFFICIATING. In the moment, however, the

Steelers were given the ball at the one-yard line with a fresh set of downs. Two plays later, the game was tied, 17–17.

The Niners offense now set out to retake the lead. Montana hit Craig out of the backfield for fifteen yards, followed by a couple of lesser plays, and then, with 2:03 remaining, attempted another pass to halfback Bill Ring running up the sideline. Mike Wilson was wide open in the middle but Joe tried to hit Ring instead, only to wish he had the ball back as soon as it left his hand. The halfback was double-covered and a Steelers linebacker in front of Ring caught the ball with a leaping one-handed play and ran the interception back forty-three yards to the Niners' three. The defense stuffed Pittsburgh's attempts to move the ball farther, but the Steelers kicked a field goal. And with 1:36 on the clock, the Niners got the ball back with no time-outs remaining, down 20–17.

Montana then seemed to find himself. He completed six of his next seven passes to move the ball from the Niners' twenty-six to the Steelers' twenty with time enough to attempt a field goal to tie the game and send it into overtime. Wersching, who hadn't missed in the previous six games, then missed, and the game was over.

This would be the Forty Niners' only defeat all season long.

During the next week after that loss, while the team prepared to play Houston, one staff member recalled, "Bill was tight, just being an asshole in practice. He was jumping everybody. If you saw him coming down the hall, you'd jump into the broom closet and hold the door shut." Houston was considered to be one of the worst if not the worst team in the league that year, but Walsh was haunted by the possibility of some kind of cataclysmic letdown.

He needn't have been. There was no shortage of sloppy play, but the Niners led throughout, accumulated 517 yards of offense, and won 34–21. Still, there wasn't a lot cheering in the locker room afterward. Everyone knew they should have played far better than they had.

"Bill got the team together and gave a short speech," one staff member remembered. "We'd just finished the postgame prayer and the guys were all on a knee. Bill said, 'We didn't play well in the first half, but got it together in the second half,' and he was proud of the way we came through. He said, 'We are going to have to have a lot better effort the next week. We've got the

Rams in Anaheim and that's going to be a dogfight.' The meeting was about to break up but then Eddie jumped in and said he had something he wanted to say. He'd flown in from Youngstown for the game through a thunderstorm in his Learjet and he looked like he'd been hitting it pretty heavy along the way. He then started this rant: 'You guys played like shit today. If you don't play better next week in Anaheim the Rams are going to walk all over you.' Finally he summed it all up with, 'All I can say is if you wanta get ass, you gotta bring ass.' At that point guys are looking like, 'What the fuck would you know?' Bill was standing off a ways and you could see he was just like, 'How dare you talk to my team like that?' Then Eddie swept away with his posse. Bill was so pissed he just walked into the coaching room. You could see his face was red even in the dark."

Any worries Walsh might have had about his team's intensity, however, were quickly allayed. In Anaheim the following Sunday, the Niners massacred the Rams 33–0, virtually clinching the division championship just nine games into the season. By now, they were back in the "next" mode they had ridden to The Miracle in 1981. "Talk about confidence," Dwight Clark recalled. "It was like, no matter what the other team does, no matter what the refs do, we can win, we can overcome it. That season there was no doubt we would go all the way." And everyone on the roster felt the same. "We knew we were better," Randy Cross agreed, "and whoever we were playing knew we were better too. It was just a matter of how much we were going to win by and who was next in line to lose to us."

"Next" in this instance was the Cincinnati Bengals. Before the season, when Walsh had been assessing the games ahead, this had been the one he thought most likely to give his team troubles. Partly that was because the Bengals were so talented and partly it was because of their new coach. Looking to get back to the Super Bowl himself, Paul Brown had hired Sam Wyche, Bill's protégé, away from Indiana University. Walsh knew Sam would have his team ready to play and that Sam knew the Niners better than any coach they would face all year. And, sure enough, he almost made his mentor pay for that knowledge. The Bengals intercepted Montana four times and the Niners were down 17–7 at halftime. It wasn't until Joe finished off a touchdown drive with 1:36 left that they put the Bengals away, 23–17.

Having cleared that hurdle, the Forty Niners celebrated the following Sunday with a crushing of the Cleveland Browns by thirty-four points.

Halfway through November, they were 10-1, and seemed to be gaining momentum every week. "We were on a roll," Bill remembered. "The team now had the bit in its teeth and wouldn't be stopped."

And then they got even better.

Fred Dean's holdout had now lasted six months and as November began, Dean's agent and John McVay accepted the idea of involving a mediator to see if they couldn't make some progress. The man they settled on was Willie Brown, a San Francisco attorney who was also Speaker of the California State Assembly and one of the most powerful men in California politics. The two parties and Brown gathered on two successive weekends in a Holiday Inn in suburban Cleveland. Brown met first with one side, then with the other, only occasionally allowing them to meet face-to-face. It took a while for the belligerence of the long standoff to fade, but when it did, Brown established that the Niners still wanted Dean to play for them and Dean wanted to keep playing for the Forty Niners. Eventually they reached an understanding that Dean would finish this year under his old contract and then start a four-year, $2 million deal that included a large signing bonus.

As details were being sorted through, McVay remembers searching his mind for some extra element to put the process over the final hump and seal the deal. "I was talking to Fred," he explained, "and I said, 'I'll tell you what. We'll give you a bonus for every sack you get.' This is a common thing today, but back then it wasn't. Fred liked that and asked me how much. I said a hundred dollars. Then Fred wanted to know if we could pay him in cash. He said his wife handled the money and if she knew he got it, she'd want it right away. He wanted to hold onto it for some walking around money. So we arranged for him to come in and get the cash every Monday. With that, we had a deal."

Eddie D. was in the locker room in Cleveland following the thrashing of the Browns when word was sent to him that Fred was finally on board, giving him even more to celebrate than the win. He, like Walsh, was convinced that having Fred back in the pass rush just might be the last weapon they needed to secure another Super Bowl trophy and, once again, money was no object.

True to form, Dean stepped in the next week and began playing just like he'd never left. The Niners won their next four games by a combined margin of one hundred points. The final game of the season was a rematch with the Rams, the division runner-up with a 10-5 record, and the Niners coasted through it, 19–16.

With that, the Forty Niners became the first team in NFL history to win fifteen regular season games. Ten members of the squad were named to the Pro Bowl, including Montana, Tyler, three offensive linemen, and all four of its defensive backs—the first and only time one team's entire defensive backfield had been voted best in their conference. And Bill Walsh, once again acclaimed The Genius, was named Coach of the Year.

Redemption was now just three games away.

Bill Walsh confers with Joe Montana during the NFC championship game against Chicago at the end of 1984 season

24

||||| ||||| |||||

REDEMPTION

The Forty Niners had home field advantage throughout the playoffs and if they survived that, this year's Super Bowl, XIX, was being staged at Stanford Stadium, fifteen minutes south of their Redwood City head-quarters—the only NFL championship game ever played in the Bay Area. The first team to visit Candlestick in this string was the New York Giants, winners of the wild card matchup with the Rams.

Afterward, this game would be almost universally panned as "boring" but it started out looking anything but. The Niners got the ball to open the game and Walsh's first call was a trick play, a hook and ladder in which Montana threw to Clark, who lateraled to Solomon for a thirteen-yard gain. Seven more plays and fifty-eight yards later, Joe found Dwight in the end zone. The Giants' attempt at an answering drive lasted five plays, gaining fif-teen yards, and the fifth play was an interception by Ronnie Lott, starting his first game after more than a month out with a shoulder injury. Lott grabbed the ball after it had caromed off two other Niners and ran the interception down to the Giants' twelve. Two plays later, Montana hit Francis for another touchdown and with some eight minutes remaining in the first quarter, the score was San Francisco 14, New York 0.

Not long thereafter, the game got "boring." Bill could see that the Giants couldn't move the ball well on offense and, while their defense was stout, that wouldn't be enough, so he decided to save most of his game plan and, before the first quarter was over, went to a vanilla approach that was aimed at holding on and keeping the lead while revealing as little as possible to whoever their next week's opponent would be. It was a safe decision. The Giants managed to score only because of two Montana interceptions. The first bounced off Clark and into the hands of a Giants linebacker as the Niners were moving in New York territory. That was followed by a forty-six-yard New York drive that netted a field goal. Five minutes later, Joe threw another interception to the same linebacker at the San Francisco fourteen and he ran it in to make the score 14–10. The Niners offense immediately answered with a five-play, seventy-three-yard drive, ending with a twenty-nine-yard touchdown pass to Solomon, 21–10.

And that was all the scoring for either side. The Forty Niners had several opportunities—a blocked field goal at the Giants' twenty-three, a missed field goal wide left also at the twenty-three, and a third Montana interception after reaching the Giants' fourteen—but none of them was necessary. With two minutes left to play, Eddie D. popped the cork on his champagne up in the owner's box and started celebrating.

Afterward, the Forty Niners' stat sheet was less than impressive. Montana was twenty-five of thirty-nine for 309 yards, but the three interceptions had been critical mistakes. And the running game had been anemic. Wendell Tyler only gained 35 yards on fourteen carries and Roger Craig picked up 34 on fifteen. The Niners' leading rusher was Montana, by virtue of a fifty-three-yard scramble that he then followed with his third turnover. The defense looked better—holding the Giants under 300 yards and collecting six sacks, two by Fred Dean—but most pundits were left unconvinced that this Niners team was going to advance much further than it already had.

The press, having been banned from the Forty Niners' practices in the two weeks leading up to the game, swarmed over the winners' locker room in a feeding frenzy. Almost all their questions were about the team's desultory play. San Francisco hadn't looked anything like invincible. And next week they would have to face the winner of the Washington-Chicago game, which would likely be favored on a trip to Candlestick, despite the Niners' record. Most players agreed with the reporters who cornered them that today's effort wouldn't be enough to beat either. "I would imagine we will play Washington," Eric Wright offered, "but if we don't play better than we did today it won't make much difference. We'll be a forlorn team watching somebody else play in the Super Bowl."

The doubts about them would persist. But so, of course, would the Niners.
Their next opponent turned out to be the Chicago Bears, 10-6 in the regular season and with whom the Forty Niners also had some outstanding issues. The two teams had last played the year before in a sleet storm in Chicago, and the Bears defense had kept the Niners from scoring anything but a field goal in a 13–3 loss. As that game wore down, the Bears players had been jeering at the Niners from the sidelines and Buddy Ryan, their defensive coordinator, afterward derided the vaunted San Francisco offense as "predictable." This year, immediately after their 23–19 playoff victory over the Redskins, several Bears players went on record guaranteeing they would do the same thing at Candlestick the following week and talked on and on about how they were looking forward to hanging around San Francisco afterward while they waited for the Super Bowl, maybe ride a few cable cars. They made no secret that they considered themselves too tough for a "finesse" team like the Niners to handle.

The source of the Bears' swagger was their "46" defense, which had been dismantling opponents all season long. Invented by Ryan, who was being called a "genius" around Chicago for doing so, it was "a funny type front," Joe Montana remembered. "They play eight men on the line of scrimmage and like to mix things up with a lot of stunting, twisting, and constant motion. This confused me because I didn't know which defender would be blitzing and which defender was going to drop back to cover our receivers." In their previous game, the Bears had thwarted the Niners with heavy pressure up the middle from blitzing linebackers, which Walsh's team had not been able to account for. "The Bears had a combination of outstanding personnel functioning in an unfamiliar style of defense," Bill pointed out. "An opposing quarterback just didn't have time to set up and throw his normal patterns."

As his preparations for the Bears began, Walsh again closed practices to the horde of media that had descended on Redwood City and, with no one to talk to and deadlines to meet, reporters began speculating. "Why have the 49ers headquarters turned into a fortress?" one columnist asked. "One theory is that Walsh is scared to death of the Bears. . . . He has yet to prove he can handle Chicago's defense." And that defense was hyped all week long in the media as the best in the league, perhaps the best ever, and very possibly too much for any team to handle. More than a few "experts" predicted the fearsome Bears would run roughshod over Walsh's squad.

For his part, Bill wasn't scared, but he was decidedly nervous. "You couldn't pull a pin out of his asshole with a Mack truck," one player observed during that week. Walsh was anxious enough on the Monday after the Giants game that he even considered changing his practice routine, an almost unheard-of step. "Bill was real nervous," Keith Fahnhorst recalled. "So he came to the team captains. We were supposed to have the day off the next day, and he said that he'd like to have us come in and practice and have a regular day, just because of the importance of the game. Well, the assistant coaches were aware that he was gonna do this. So they came to the captains and asked us to tell Bill that we'd rather not come in. Because they didn't really want us to come in. They wanted to get the game plan prepared and everything. But as good a coach as Bill was, he was pretty demanding. So they thought it would be easier for the players to say, 'let's not come in.' So we were prepared for Bill, and we politely said we didn't think it would a good idea. Bill listened to us. Bill was good that way."

When the team did return to Nevada Street, Walsh had figured out how he was going to handle the "46." First, he wanted to shore up the pass protection. The Bears never blitzed both a middle linebacker and an outside linebacker, so on every pass play, one or the other of the Niners guards, either Randy Cross or John Ayers, would be assigned to check for the middle blitz and, if it didn't materialize, swing wide to get the outside one that was surely on its way. In addition, the running backs would be on full blitz protection on every pass, checking for unaccounted rushers and, if they weren't coming, swinging into the flat for outlet passes. The final and most important part of Walsh's plan was to use only three-step drops by the quarterback, getting the ball out quickly before the pressure had a chance to get to Joe. That meant giving up the long-passing game and focusing almost entirely on four- and five-yard completions. If those worked, Walsh was convinced that would open up the running game and they would be able to run the ball down Chicago's throat.

In addition to being nervous, Bill also had a chip on his shoulder for the Bears and he made a point of sharing it when he presented his plan to the team downstairs in the big meeting room. Players were overflowing into the hall and everybody was hanging on the coach's words. "The Bears think in their own stupid way that they're going to intimidate us," he growled, "then just knock us around the field. That's the way they're going to figure it. Right now, they're struttin'. Like all they have to do is come in here and kick the shit out of us. This game is going to be a goddamn grudge game from our standpoint. With all this tough talk, they're just selling themselves. Anytime a guy thinks he's rough and tough, four out of five of those guys get their asses kicked. Most of those kind of guys are dumb. Three-step drops are going to make the difference. Just throw the ball on time and catch it. Then we can knock their ass off running the ball. We've got the plays to do it. All of these things will shatter these guys. Just take the goddamn ball and run it. Just knock their can right off the field."

On Sunday, once the ball had been teed up, Bill's plan worked just like he'd drawn it up. "We moved the ball at will," Joe Montana remembered, "and the Bears defense couldn't stop us." Only a couple of Montana miscues kept the game close through the first half. At the end of a seventy-three-yard, nine-play opening drive, facing third and goal at Chicago's two, Joe fumbled the snap from center and had to fall on the ball. Wersching then kicked a field goal for 3–0. The Niners' next drive got down to Chicago's two again, with a first and goal, and Joe threw an interception. During the second quarter, they drove sixty-five yards in twelve plays, and reached Chicago's four, but had to settle for a field goal after two runs that went nowhere and a deflected pass, 6–0. While still close on paper at this point, the game in fact was already out of Chicago's reach. All the intensity and momentum was on the Niners' side. "Everyone was playing as if his life depended on this game," Joe remembered.

And the Forty Niners defense was dominating. None of the Bears' first six possessions got past the fifty-yard line and their only chance for a score in the entire game came on a forty-one-yard field goal attempt that sailed wide right. Otherwise, their offense was nonexistent. They only managed to gain 186 yards total and their quarterback was sacked nine times. "After the first drive," the Bears quarterback admitted, "we quit executing. We messed up a lot on first down and we're not very good at throwing on third and long over and over." One of the Bears offensive linemen allowed afterward that the Forty Niners defense "reminded me of ours. They were coming from all different directions."

The Niners started the second half up 6–0 and completely convinced they could put the Bears away. They began doing so after an exchange of punts and an excellent return by the San Francisco special teams let Montana start the next drive on Chicago's thirty-five. Now Bill turned to calling runs. Wendell Tyler for five yards, then Wendell again for eleven yards, a short pass, and a penalty on the Bears defense, and the Niners were first and goal on Chicago's nine. Then Walsh called Tyler's number again and he broke two tackles on his way into the end zone to enlarge the lead to thirteen points. As the fourth quarter opened, the Niners offense set out to drive a final stake through the Bears' heart. Starting on San Francisco's twelve, Joe hit Mike Wilson to move up to the twenty-five, then hit Wendell with a short pass up to midfield. Bill then called a sweep left by Roger Craig and the Bears didn't catch up to Craig until he was at their fourteen. After that, Joe finished it off with a pass to Freddie Solomon in the back corner of the end zone and the score was 20–0.

Wersching would add another field goal later in the quarter, but for all intents and purposes, the game was over with 11:55 still left on the clock. The margin could easily have been thirty or more, rather than 23–0. All told, the Forty Niners offense extracted 387 yards and twenty-five first downs from the touted "46," and afterward no one repeated their suggestion that Bill Walsh was afraid of facing Buddy Ryan's defense. As the fourth quarter wound down, fans on one side of Candlestick began shouting "Super" at the top of their lungs and fans on the other side answered "Bowl," back and forth and back and forth in sheer delirium. At Broadway and Columbus in North Beach—where San Franciscans traditionally gather to celebrate—restaurant staffs ran into the street beating on pots and pans as the intersection began to fill up, two blocks were closed by revelers down in the Mission District, on the Peninsula drivers leaned on their car horns while passengers hung out the windows, and sports bars as far south as Fresno and as far north as the Oregon border erupted with shouts of,

"We're number one, we're number one." When the final gun sounded and the teams headed for the tunnels, hundreds of fans poured onto the field, many tearing up hunks of sod for souvenirs.

The final word was left to Buddy Ryan in the losers' locker room.

"The real Genius prevailed," he said.

It was as simple as that.

There were no cross-country slogs through snow drifts for Eddie D. this Super Bowl. Instead, he staged a black-tie dinner in the de Young Museum in Golden Gate Park at the end of the first of the two weeks leading up to the game. As usual, Eddie was the generous host, making sure everything was "first class" and basking in his stature. Much of San Francisco's high society was there, along with a number of NFL owners and general managers, and a few Hollywood celebrities. The Niners' chairman of the board professed nothing but confidence about the game itself. "In 1981," he mused, "one minute we were losers, the next we were in the Super Bowl. Nobody expected it. This year, it's pretty much gone the way I thought. The season was like Old Man River, it just kept rolling along." The most regaled of Eddie's guests that night at the de Young was his team's president. Handsome, even dashing in his tuxedo, and looking, in the words of the *Chronicle*'s social columnist, "calm, cool, and confident as he sipped champagne," folks lined up to get a chance to talk to Bill. He seemed to enjoy the break from game preparation and apparently resisted the temptation to draw up new plays on Geri's shoulder.

Otherwise, however, he was focused on nothing but the approaching game. His team was once again the underdog, despite their unprecedented record. The Niners' opponent, the Miami Dolphins, had finished 14-2 in the regular season, had manhandled the Seattle Seahawks and the Pittsburgh Steelers in the playoffs, and was the darling of the eastern media. Their offense had averaged thirty-two points a game and was being hyped as the nearest thing to unstoppable. Miami's brilliant second-year quarterback, Dan Marino, had broken just about every single-season NFL passing record in getting the Dolphins this far. Miami's "Killer B's" defense—a swarming, relatively undersized group named for its three best players, all of whose names began with a *B*—also got a lot more ink than San Francisco's. About the only advantage the media conceded to the Niners was playing so close to home, but Bill didn't even buy that. "All the distractions were only multiplied" by playing in their own neighborhood, Walsh insisted. "Family and friends traveled to the Bay Area for the game, so players had to deal with parties, gatherings, reunions, and monumental ticket requests. Though we enjoyed not having to travel and adjust to a different time zone, there was certainly no special advantage for us playing at Stanford."

Even Bill had his own version of that phenomenon: his father, then suffering from Alzheimer's disease and accompanied by one of Bill's old friends from San Jose State, visited the Niners' practice sessions on several days, giving the coach one more distraction himself.

The pregame media scripts largely focused on two "matchups" that the pundits projected would determine the outcome. The first was Dan Marino against Joe Montana. Marino was coming into the Super Bowl on a hot streak, having thrown seven touchdown passes in the playoffs, after a season in which he'd thrown for forty-eight touchdowns and more than five thousand yards. Joe had been good enough to win in the Niners' two playoff games and masterful during the regular season, but not particularly flashy. Most judged the comparison "Advantage Miami" and talked endlessly about Marino. On media day, Montana was forced to answer question after question about the Dolphins quarterback, and while nothing but respectful about Marino and his skills, he bridled inside at being dismissed like that. By game time, Joe was more than ready to show all his doubters just how good he was.

The other matchup on the media's minds was Bill Walsh versus Don Shula. The Dolphins coach was a legend, having gotten the early start as a head coach that Walsh had been denied and made the most of it, going to his first Super Bowl when still in his early thirties. Among other accomplishments, Shula had coached the 1972 Dolphins squad that was the only NFL team ever to go undefeated, in the days when the regular season was only fourteen games long. During the run-up to Super Bowl XIX, many were conceding him the title of best coach in football, even when going head-to-head with The Genius. Bill complimented Shula and his team at every opportunity, but about the latter he had real doubts. "I felt there was still a mystery about how good they really were," he remembered. "They'd won fourteen games and dominated in the playoffs and Don Shula had done a great job coaching them to this level, but there was a mystery to it. I could stack up our personnel over a broad base against theirs and we were certainly better. We just had more talent and more depth of talent than they did. Frankly, I thought that for Miami to have gone 14-2 and won two play-off games was a real tribute to Don."

Walsh made a joke out of the media's crush on the Dolphins when talking with his own team. At the meeting where the game plan was introduced, Russ Francis remembered, "Bill came in and said, 'Well we're the underdogs. We're probably going to get killed. We should probably just send in our respects.' Then he laughed." He didn't need to emphasize how little credit the Niners were getting. "Dan Marino and the Killer B's was all we heard about," Randy Cross recalled. "When the game finally came around, we had the chip on our shoulder honed to a razor's edge." And, Russ Francis added, "Bill had so perfectly constructed the game plan. He said I don't care if you're on offense or on defense or are the water boy, if you get a chance to hit Dan Marino, I want to see blood on his jersey. I want that guy on his back. I want him dazed."

On game day, Walsh's confidence was reinforced when the teams went out onto the field for warm-ups. "When they went ahead of us," Bill observed, "I looked at them from behind and then I knew. We were going to beat these guys. I walked past them when they were doing their stretching and I felt it even more. They weren't as big or as athletic as us and that was obvious to me. I didn't think they could match our speed either." He told his team as much when they returned to the locker room to wait for the game to start. The players were sitting around on benches and Bill was sprawled across some equipment bags with his hands behind his head. He spoke like he was just thinking out loud. "All they can talk about is Miami's offense," he said. "What about our defense? All they can talk about is Marino, Marino, Marino. We've got some guys who can play too."

At first, however, it looked like all the hype about Miami might have been right. The Niners took the opening kickoff but, with Montana a little bit too worked up for his own good, couldn't move the ball and had to punt. In a surprise, the Dolphins came out in a no-huddle offense that moved the ball forty-five yards in seven plays and kicked a field goal to draw first blood. The Niners answered with a seventy-eight-yard, eight-play drive for a touchdown in which Joe found his rhythm and the Niners running game picked up yardage wherever and whenever Bill called its number. Then the

Dolphins answered that with a touchdown drive of their own, again using the no-huddle to perfection. At the end of the first quarter the score was Miami 10, San Francisco 7.

But the Dolphins' dream went no further. Defensive coordinator George Seifert, who usually made extensive use of situational substitutions but was prevented from doing so by the no-huddle, realized that the Dolphins' running game was almost nonexistent, so he simply went with the Niners' nickel defense the rest of the game, playing them for a pass on every down. That slammed the door shut and the Dolphins would manage only two more field goals—one by virtue of the Niners' fumbling a kickoff right before the half—and those points came only after the Niners had seized control of the game. Now every time Marino went back to pass, Peewee Board and Big Hands Johnson and Fred Dean were constantly in his face and the Dolphins quarterback ended most plays picking himself up off the turf. Eventually Marino would be sacked four times, knocked down countless others, and forced into two interceptions. After the game, he would turn to one of his friends and say, "Did we get our butts kicked or what?"

While the defense was slamming its door, the Niners offense was kicking its own door wide open. Montana, operating the Walsh offense flawlessly, engineered three straight touchdown drives using all the team's weapons, including running with the ball himself for almost sixty yards. Bill had pointed out to him right before the game that the Miami linebackers would be running with the Niners backs out of the backfield and that might very well leave no one to watch Montana. When Joe saw such an opening, Bill wanted him to take off. The most memorable example of that was one play where Roger Craig was running a pass pattern down the sideline, a linebacker was running behind him with his back to the line of scrimmage, and Joe was running with the ball almost on the linebacker's heels without the linebacker having a clue what was going on. Eventually a defensive back had to force Joe out of bounds. Every play Walsh called seemed to work, and the Niners would end up averaging 7.1 yards every time they hiked the ball. "We played an almost perfect game," Bill later asserted. "We took control and turned it into a lopsided game by halftime." The score by then was 28–16.

The San Francisco defense opened the second half by sacking Marino three of the first six times he touched the ball and it didn't get any better for him the rest of the game. The Niners added a field goal and another touchdown in the third quarter and were on the verge of adding another touch-down in the fourth but Walsh just ran plays he knew the Dolphins would stop and surrendered the ball on Miami's five-yard line. All told, the Forty Niners gained 537 yards—more than 100 yards beyond the previous Super Bowl record—and accumulated thirty-one first downs to the Dolphins' nineteen. They out-gained Miami on the ground 211 yards to 25 and dominated time of possession thirty-seven minutes to twenty-three. Dan Marino completed twenty-nine of fifty for 318 yards, 100 yards less than the team had averaged in their eighteen games up to that point. Joe Montana was twenty-four of thirty-five for 331 yards, another Super Bowl record. Montana was also named the Super Bowl's Most Valuable Player, just like in 1981. Bill later described this as "the greatest game" Joe ever played. The final score was San Francisco 38, Miami 16.

The other key matchup went San Francisco's way as well. "Walsh proved his is the best mind in football," one *Chronicle* columnist crowed, "and that Shula is just another bright, hard working guy in a sweatsuit. The differ-ence between the two is that Shula is a clever, solid tactician, but Walsh has a vision. . . . Walsh exposed every one of Miami's defensive weaknesses [and] pushed Miami's defense backward all day like a bulldozer moving a pile of dirt. . . . Walsh's greatness is that he made the second-best team in the league look bad. No one else could have done that. He was like a con-ductor who knew how every note in a symphony should be played and he was able to convey his idea to his players. The music they made was nearly perfect, and at one point they reached such wonderful harmony that it was as though they no longer had an opponent. By then Shula had become irrelevant."

Similar accolades were piled on Walsh in the game's aftermath but his fa-vorite took place in the locker room, where the champagne was flying, the Super Bowl trophy was being paraded about, and Eddie was again hugging everyone in sight. Then the squad took the game ball—normally awarded to the player who contributed the most to the win—and presented it to Bill.

Looking back on that day years later, Bill Walsh would claim, "That ball meant far more to me than all the rest."

Shortly after that, Bill phoned one of his friends, his legendary calm long since abandoned and sounding completely incredulous at what had come to pass. "I won the Super Bowl," he gushed over the sounds of champagne

*Bill Walsh and Eddie DeBartolo flank Mayor Dianne Feinstein
in the victory parade following Super Bowl XIX*

corks popping and random shouts of joy. "Can you believe it? I won the Super Bowl."

There was no shortage of celebrations for this victory. The city of San Francisco staged another parade the next day, again drawing hundreds of thousands; the team held a ring ceremony several weeks later; and Eddie D. would host a smaller event back in Youngstown, where he invited twenty players and gave each of them a Rolex watch. Immediately after the game, Eddie also hosted a party in a hospitality tent outside Stanford Stadium. But the celebration closest to Walsh's heart was his own private one back at his home on Valparaiso Avenue in Menlo Park.

Once he'd extricated himself from Eddie's do, Bill and one of his buddies from San Jose State ended up in Bill's backyard, working on a couple of drinks and ruminating deep into the night. Bill talked about the old days and, with almost childlike awe, marveled that he had ended up here with two Super Bowls under his belt. He never anticipated success and was always amazed when it happened. Bill recognized what a special moment this was and, unabashedly joyful, described the season he'd just finished as quite possibly the apex of his professional life. He knew this team and its almost perfect record would be the stuff of legends and he was quietly ecstatic at his achievement. There was no sadness about him that night at all, but rather, his friend remembered, "he appreciated what had happened in ways that were unique and new to him." Bill Walsh's satisfaction was profound, and for the first time in more than two years, all the echoes of 1982 had now vanished inside his head.

IV

ANYTHING BUT EASY

Jerry Rice being introduced as the Forty Niners' first-round draft choice at team headquarters, 1985

25

"WHAT DO YOU THINK OF THAT WEST COAST OFFENSE NOW?"

Even before Super Bowl XIX there was a lot of talk that Bill Walsh might now retire—as there would be every year from here on—but that issue was finally put to rest for the 1985 season when Eddie D. tore up the two years remaining on Walsh's old contract and signed him to a new four-year deal that would pay the Forty Niners' president and head coach almost $1 million a year, twice what he had been earning and more than any other coach in the National Football League. Carmen Policy, the lawyer who negotiated the deal for Eddie, told the *Chronicle* that "Eddie DeBartolo wants Bill Walsh not only running the franchise, but on the field. . . . It was thought that within four years, Bill would be in a position . . . to pretty much have everything stabilized, perhaps have another Super Bowl under our belt and establish the 49ers as a true power within the NFL. [Then] Bill [would] actually be in a position to either move upstairs . . . or retire." As a further demonstration of his appreciation of Bill and a reward for having won his second Super Bowl, Eddie also gave Walsh a vacation home on Lake Tahoe's pricey northwest shore near Tahoe City.

The money meant a lot to Bill. A child of the Depression who'd labored as a schoolboy to help feed his family, Walsh was, according to his son Craig, "a very frugal person" who enjoyed being richer than he'd ever imagined. But the money wasn't everything. In the aftermath of his triumph in Super Bowl XIX, recognizing that his accomplishments were already extraordinary, Bill had found fresh motivation in the vision behind his new contract with Eddie. What remained for him was institutionalizing his success in a dynasty that, like the Packers and Steelers before him, could dominate its time, becoming the one among many, year after year after year, the team of the eighties and maybe even the nineties too, an accomplishment that Bill knew would be his ultimate monument. He now wanted that jump to the next level with much the same compulsion as he had wanted to prove himself with his first Super Bowl, then prove with his second that the first wasn't a fluke. As always, fear of failure and his need for approval would energize his quest and turn it into what felt like a life or death enterprise in which his very existence was at stake.

Walsh's motivation was reinforced by almost everyone around him. Others' expectations of his mastery had been a sometimes painful constant in his life since the 1981 miracle and had now, with the Niners' almost perfect 1984, taken another quantum leap, beyond simple expectation into the ingrained assumption—by the fans, by the media, and, of course, by Eddie—that his team belonged in the Super Bowl every year. Being "good" was no longer good enough. Only being "great" was now acceptable and anything less was without compelling value. For Bill Walsh, the bar had now been raised as high as it could get.

To Bill's thinking, however, that requirement of greatness and its assumptions of endless Super Bowls—though predicated on extraordinary respect for his skills as a team builder—ignored just how difficult and complex reaching the Super Bowl actually was and how a seemingly infinite number of factors had to line up exactly right for that to happen. The perspective Bill put forward as a far more realistic vision was to visualize each season as an expedition to conquer Mt. Everest. Some teams made such assaults from base camps far in the valley below, sometimes rising near the peak but then sliding back down to the place they started, where they would often remain for extended periods before summoning themselves for another assault. The Niners, however, by virtue of their accumulated accomplishments, now had a base camp far up the slope, within striking distance of the summit, from which they would sally forth every year. "Even though we might not reach the summit," Walsh pointed out, "we were always close. We were always in the playoffs and had our shot." That in itself was a unique level of success.

Unfortunately for Bill, however, just having "a shot" didn't measure up under the Niners' new rules of engagement. Henceforth, only Super Bowls counted. And he was the one who would be held accountable when they didn't materialize.

Walsh entered this new stage of his career with two of his most significant relationships in flux, amplifying his sense of the ground shifting under his feet.

The first was with Eddie D. So far in their partnership, Eddie had by and large deferred to Bill, unwilling to quibble with his coach's extraordinary accomplishments in their five years together. But the Niners' second Super Bowl trophy imparted a new level of confidence and assertiveness to the owner. And his meddling and complaints—not to mention demands for championships—became more aggressive than ever.

"The pressure from Eddie grew and grew after that second Super Bowl," a friend of Bill's remembered. "Pretty soon he was calling Bill in the middle of the night with ideas or demands or questions—something he never would have done before. Sometimes he would rag on Bill, sometimes just make suggestions. Usually it would happen when Eddie was out with people, partying or whatever, and they would come up with some brainstorm Eddie decided he had to pass on. Depending on Eddie's mood, that could sometimes become antagonistic. For his part, Bill was not the kind to tell Eddie to stay out of his end of the business. Eddie was the boss and Bill didn't want to lose his job. So if Eddie wanted him to do something, he would try to accommodate. He wanted to keep the owner happy, but that became harder and harder to do."

"Eddie treated him like dirt in certain cases," another of Bill's friends recalled, "but Bill would always be able to get through it. He wasn't the kind to say, 'that's the end of this, I'm not taking this anymore.' He doesn't do that. He has this capacity to just plug through problems that are relational.

He kind of massages the situation, marinates in it, just works his way along, and manages to maintain without confrontation. He was a master at avoiding conflict and getting outcomes that were sometimes negative, but sometimes quite positive. He was able to paddle through some of the worst swamps and come out whole, no matter who bumped him along the way."

Eddie would certainly challenge that capacity. As Bill remembered it, "it was at this point that our relationship became more abusive."

The other relationship undergoing change in the months after that second Super Bowl victory was Bill's marriage. The tensions between him and Geri had finally provoked him to distance himself. There was another woman involved in the separation as well. Kristine Hanson, twenty years younger than Bill, was a television meteorologist in both the Bay Area and Sacramento and a former *Playboy* Playmate who had been shifted to doing human interest sports stories by the Sacramento channel for whom she was working in 1982—the first woman ever on the sports beat for an NBC affiliate. She met Bill on assignment in Rocklin during training camp. Eventually he asked her to dinner and a romance began.

"Bill was not a superstar in his own mind," she remembered. "He was a down-to-earth guy. We would go out to Denny's for dinner. He had a real sense of humor and was very much like a big kid. He was never pompous or full of himself. Instead he was kind of naïve. I could tease him. He was gregarious, but somewhat shy. And fun to be with. He was thoughtful, bringing me gifts, and he was flattering. From a woman's point of view, he was very sexy. He was always loving and respectful when he talked about Geri, but I think I offered him a romance and a love affair that let him be someone different than he could be in the rest of his life."

By 1985, the relationship between Walsh and Hanson was serious enough that the two rented a house together in Foster City, a bayside development several freeway exits further up the Peninsula, which they maintained until early 1986. By that point they would be seriously thinking of getting Bill a divorce and marrying, but when Edward DeBartolo Sr. learned of it, he would object so strongly that Bill, unwilling to buck Senior's disapproval, would retreat from his commitment to Kristine and, for a while, return to his wife.

In the meantime, Walsh commuted from Foster City to Niners headquarters, regularly staying in his second-floor office until midnight during the season, trying to fashion another Super Bowl victory, back-to-back with his second.

Part of Bill's 1985 answer to the challenge of repeating as champions was to make sure the Super Bowl XIX celebrations ended earlier than they had after XVI. He declared the festivities officially over in the second week of April, when the Niners staged the premiere of their 1984 highlight film at San Francisco's Palace of Fine Arts. Eddie D. flew in everyone from the Super Bowl XIX–winning squad at his own expense. It was a black-tie event, players included, and invitations were sent only to a select list of notables. Bill gave the keynote speech. "We hear about dynasties in football," he declared, but "I can't think of any previous team in the National Football League that could beat these Forty Niners. . . . These [1984] Forty Niners may be the best team of all time."

That said, it was on to next year.

For starters, Walsh had no intention of standing pat. He had won his first Super Bowl with one team and won his second with a different team, constructed around a core from the first. Now he set off to make a third around the core from the second. Key to that process was deciding whose time had come to retire. Bill had a gift for anticipating the shelf life of a football player and was intent on making sure that expiration date didn't come up while he was still on Bill's team. Better a year too early than a year too late was his rule. And he already had a reputation for being merciless in his judgments, which made his players both wary and often resentful. "A coach has to be very strong in his player moves," Bill explained. "If he becomes overprotective of a player's feelings or sentimentalizes his history with the team, he can damage the team over the long haul. Nor can he afford to consider how a move looks to the press and public, or to give too much consideration to how a player's teammates will react. His only obligation is to the improvement of the team." Replacing men who had served him well was essential and he didn't shrink from it or look back after he'd pulled the trigger.

Prominent on Walsh's replacement list in the 1985 off-season was Freddie Solomon. Solomon's chronic injuries over the last two seasons were among the signs Bill looked for in determining when a man's time was up, evidence that his body was losing the edge professional football demanded. In the last Super Bowl run, Freddie had been unavailable for play as much as or more than he was fit. Walsh had once thought that Renaldo Nehemiah would replace Solomon, but, still shaken by the ferocious hit he had absorbed in the 1983 Atlanta game, Nehemiah had given up football to return to track, so Bill focused on that year's collegiate draft to find a new wide receiver.

The prospect who captured Bill's imagination was Jerry Rice, a senior at Mississippi Valley State, an obscure Division I-AA school, enrollment 2,500, in Itta Bena, Mississippi. Rice would be the first draft choice since 1980 from the conference in which Mississippi Valley State played. Most of the football public had never heard of him, but he had been setting receiving records against the likes of Southern and Grambling for his entire career. He hailed from Crawford, Mississippi, a hamlet with a block-long downtown anchored by a Shell station and a combination city hall and library housed in a portable trailer. Jerry had worked summers helping his bricklayer father, carrying and catching bricks in the hot sun at rural worksites, and had hardly been recruited out of backwoods B. L. Moor High School.

Rice first caught Walsh's attention during the 1984 season, when the Niners were in Houston to play the Oilers, and Bill returned to his hotel room on Saturday night after the day's last meeting. "I was laying in bed watching the evening's sports news on television," he remembered. "They were showing college football highlights and the commentator said something to the effect of, 'and now we'll show you the phenom from Mississippi.' It was Jerry Rice, from Mississippi Valley State. And he was sensational. People would argue that the level of competition wasn't high because it wasn't Division One, but what I saw was just a sensational player, regardless of the competition. I vividly remember thinking, 'Damn, we're going to have to play against that guy.' I lay there wondering who was going to get him and thinking somebody's going to have a great player."

The next spring, however, Walsh was unwilling to easily cede that opportunity to someone else and took steps to get in position to draft Rice in the first round. He did so against the advice of his scouts—indeed his director of scouting had the Mississippi Valley star rated no better than a fifth-round pick and opposed the choice with great vehemence. Bill pursued Jerry anyway. He was convinced that the Niners' first-round pick, twenty-eighth overall, was too late in the order and should he stay in that position, someone else, probably the Dallas Cowboys picking seventeenth, would get Rice instead. So Walsh and John McVay called around the league looking for a team that would trade picks. Eventually the New England Patriots bit and Bill negotiated an exchange of the Niners' first-, second-, and third-round picks for the Patriots' sixteenth overall pick, as well as their pick in the third round. Walsh didn't finalize the deal until the first round reached number fourteen and Rice was still on the board. Bill had identified a second wide receiver as a fallback option and when the sixteenth pick went on the clock, Bill retreated to a projector and watched film clips of the two in one last comparison. Then he picked Rice.

And the choice couldn't have turned out better. Like Joe Montana and Ronnie Lott, Jerry Rice would emerge as one of Bill's great draft picks. Though not as much of an inspirational leader as the other two, he would still become a living icon of what Forty Niners expected from themselves. One staff member pointed out that Jerry "insisted on perfection. I don't care if it was just the way his pants fit, the way his socks looked, how his numbers were aligned, the way he looked in his uniform before he went out on the field. He refused to accept anything less than absolute perfection. And he refused to believe that he ever approached that standard. Every year he would come in like a rookie trying to make the team and work harder than anybody else. He set a standard that Bill could literally point to for everybody else in the building."

Rice's addition also, like that of Roger Craig two years earlier, brought another dimension to Bill's offense. With opposing defenses increasingly shortening up and using man-to-man pressure coverage to stymie his horizontal passing game, Walsh felt he desperately needed a weapon that could make them pay for that tactic. And Jerry Rice had the speed to stretch the field vertically and the skills to beat man coverage anytime he faced it, giving Bill a whole set of offensive options that he'd never had before—and then some. Before Jerry Rice was done, he would be considered the best wide receiver who ever played the game. Early in 1985's training camp, Bill made him the starter and Freddie Solomon became a backup and then retired at the end of the year.

Hacksaw Reynolds didn't even last that long.

Hacksaw was at the top of Walsh's replacement list. Despite the enormous contribution Reynolds had made in building the franchise, Walsh had started asking the almost-thirty-eight-year-old linebacker—now too slow to play on anything other than first down, when a run was the most likely—to retire the year before, but had relented and kept him as a backup during that Super Bowl season. The next spring, however, Walsh insisted. He told Reynolds his choices were either hit the road or exercise the option in his contract to sign on as a coach. Hacksaw would later complain loudly that Bill had ended his playing career prematurely, but, in the moment, reluctantly accepted a coach's job, then quickly discovered he was completely unsuited for it. The player who watched endless film and took meticulous notes found sitting around in a room with the other coaches making candid assessments of his former teammates completely unsettling and, after twelve days on the job, retired and left the game for good.

The other prominent aspect of Bill's 1985 approach to repeating in the Super Bowl was emphasizing to his team just how hard it would be to accomplish, hoping to both adjust their sights and inspire them. "The theme during training camp was how difficult it is to repeat as champions," Joe Montana recalled. "Maybe all this talk put us in a negative mind-set—who knows?"

In any case, Bill almost always framed the difficulties in store for his team as an internal challenge to his players' performance. But, of course, there was more to it than that. Even coming off an almost undefeated season, the external realities facing his squad were daunting, to say the least. There was no sneaking up on anyone anymore. The rest of the league had been studying everything Walsh did for several years now and had adapted a raft of new defenses to thwart the Niners' vaunted offense, challenging Walsh's capacity to invent new wrinkles to stay ahead of the curve and his players' ability to execute his inventions. On top of that, the league's National Football Conference included a bevy of talented squads, three of which were making their own dynastic runs in hope of being crowned *the* team of their era. All three would eventually make claims to being among the best of all time and all three would have to be beaten in order for the Niners to succeed this year and for the rest of the decade.

The first of those was the Chicago Bears. Coached by Mike Ditka, a Hall of Fame tight end from the Bears' last era of dominance, they had risen from the bottom of the standings during The Miracle season to playoff stature in 1984. Ditka, while colorful and competent, was not nearly the coach Walsh was, but his team was stout, very tough, and its now infamous 46 defense would strike terror in a lot of its opponents for the rest of the decade. "Their defense was a challenge," Walsh acknowledged. "You have to have the nerve to break from your own style of football a little bit to beat it and even that didn't always work." Facing the 1985 season, the Bears seemed on the verge of reaching the next level, and beating the Forty Niners would signal their arrival.

The second rival in the Niners' way was the New York Giants, coached by Bill Parcells, who would eventually establish himself as one of the best coaches of his time. Parcells's Giants hadn't mustered a season better than 9-7 thus far in the decade but had made the playoffs twice, losing to the Niners in the first round both times. Like the Bears, their forte was defense. "I'm a little Neanderthal," Parcells bragged. "I think defense is the key to any sport. That was my intent when I started coaching. That's what I wanted to coach. Not football. Football *defense.* It's not glamorous to those who are into what's aesthetically pleasing. But it's glamorous to *me.* I think defense is the key to the game." His teams took pride in their brute force and had both a generalized disdain for all "finesse" teams and a particular grievance with the Niners for having thwarted them twice before. Parcells typically insisted that his style of football "never had anything to prove. It's the fancy-pants stuff that needs to prove itself." Also like the Bears, the Giants were a team on the come.

The third—and to Walsh's eye the most challenging—roadblock to the San Francisco dynasty was the Washington Redskins, coached by future Hall of Famer Joe Gibbs. Gibbs had joined the Redskins at the beginning of The Miracle season and had already been named NFL Coach of the Year twice, winning Super Bowl XVII and losing XVIII. Bill considered him his principal coaching rival and always evaluated their games against each other as true tests of just how good his own team was. Though not considered the offensive mastermind that Walsh was, Gibbs was no slouch on that side of the ball and always mustered sound defenses as well. His Redskins were consistently formidable and forbidding. And ever since that controversial NFC Championship game after the 1983 season, both the Niners and the Redskins took their matchup personally.

In truth, perhaps no era in NFL history had a collection of contenders that compared in quality to the string of teams the Forty Niners would have to fight their way through to get back to another Super Bowl.

To hone his team's focus going into the 1985 season, Walsh organized his training camp to reduce distractions. He set up fences and ropes and hired a number of local kids outfitted in T-shirts identifying them as "Camp Security" to keep the fans at bay who now swarmed to Rocklin to watch their team get ready, even taking steps to limit the availability of autographs. Walsh himself, however, was his most accessible to the press. "He eats in full view," one reporter noted. "He talks to anyone. He has time. He is so available, in fact, we all know about his bad back, how he wears a brace that looks like a plastic girdle, and how he stops what he's doing from time to time to lean his arms against a table and bend forward and stretch to ease the pain."

Walsh also attempted to keep camp lighthearted. At Bubba Paris's suggestion, Bill organized a fishing contest in which a pond on the Sierra College campus was stocked with catfish and the roster divided into teams to compete, fishing in half-hour sessions. The team that caught the most fish in its half hour received a hundred dollars per man. It was welcome comic relief. Walsh also arranged for a squad outing to take in a Huey Lewis and the News concert in nearby Sacramento and laughed with the beat reporters about the speeding ticket he got in his Porsche on what he claimed was the way back from seeing Geri up at Tahoe. Bill even joked about Bubba Paris's weight.

The point of all of Bill's postures was to get his squad's mind right for the coming challenge, but once the season began, none of them seemed to have worked.

The omen for the Niners' year to come appeared when they flew to Minnesota for the season opener. There, while unloading one of the team's travel bags, the equipment manager discovered a snake inside. When word got around the locker room, the presence of the snake was judged, according to Dwight Clark, "one of the worst-luck things you can ever have." And the ensuing game looked it.

The Forty Niners—eleven-point favorites against an opponent that had finished 3-13 the year before—got on the board first, recovering a Vikings fumble on Minnesota's twenty-four-yard line and then taking just two plays—a fourteen-yard pass to Roger Craig followed by a ten-yard Craig run into the end zone—to make the score 7–0. Then the mistakes began. Deep in Minnesota's territory and driving to make it 14–0, Craig fumbled the ball away. When San Francisco returned to Minnesota's territory on its next possession, Montana threw a pass right into the arms of a Vikings defensive lineman. Even deeper in the Vikings' territory on the following drive, Wendell Tyler lost a fumble inside the ten-yard line. Thanks to that succession of miscues, the score was still 7–0 at halftime.

Nonetheless, San Francisco started the second half seemingly in control, driving fifty-nine yards in ten plays. Unfortunately, the last one was a pass to Freddie Solomon on second and goal, which he fumbled away at the Vikings' eight. After an exchange of punts, the Vikings finally mustered a seventy-eight-yard drive—including a forty-one-yard pass play—to tie the game 7–7, and make a contest of it. The Niners answered with a seventy-yard drive, featuring an acrobatic leaping catch over the middle by Jerry Rice. Already nicknamed "World" by his teammates, that play convinced Montana that the rookie would "go anywhere to catch one of my passes." An eighteen-yard swing pass to Craig then made the score 14–7. The Vikings responded with a forty-four-yard touchdown pass on which Ronnie Lott bit on a fake and was burned. The Niners again answered, scoring on another pass to Craig, making the score 21–14 deep in the fourth quarter.

It looked like the game was in hand at this point, but instead, the wheels fell off. After his team stopped the Vikings and took over the ball, Walsh thought they would now produce a drive to put the game away. Before the offense took the field, he warned Wendell Tyler about fumbling and instructed him to be sure to hang on to the ball. Instead, Tyler broke through the line on his first carry, ran into one of his teammates, and dropped it. The Vikings picked the ball up, returned the fumble to the Niners' one, and scored on the following play to tie the game again. Then, before the ensuing kickoff, Walsh warned his kick returner to protect the ball at all costs, even if he had to kneel down with it at the twenty. Instead, the return man ran the kick back, fumbled, and the Vikings recovered at the Niners' thirty-four. Three plays later, Minnesota was ahead for the first time in the game, 28–21, despite having been dominated all day long in every facet of the game.

The Niners now had 1:30 in which to rally for a tie but again self-destructed. Montana fumbled on the second play of the drive but managed to recover it. Earl Cooper dropped a pass. Montana retreated to throw but fell down, effectively sacking himself. Keith Fahnhorst was called for two penalties. Even so, the Niners clawed their way into Minnesota's territory. Then Clark was called for offensive pass interference, taking them out of scoring range. Joe's final desperation toss came on an attempted hook-and-ladder play that broke down and was intercepted. All told, their 1985 opener was one of the Forty Niners' worst efforts in recent memory. "You have to go back to the Dark Ages, maybe to 1980, to find a game when we played this poorly," Walsh admitted afterward. The Forty Niners had accumulated 489 yards of offense, over 200 more than their opponents, but they had fumbled the ball seven times—losing possession on five of them—thrown two interceptions, and had ten penalties, not counting several the Vikings had refused.

And that pratfall was only the beginning. Walsh's team went on to lose four of their first seven games in similar fashion. "We just tended to play in sort of a reckless, irresponsible way," Bill later explained. "We'd mishandle the ball. We'd fumble. We failed to take advantage of scoring opportunities. We let games get away from us and suddenly we would lose."

Searching for causes, Bill immediately revisited some of the issues that had derailed their attempts to repeat back in 1982. One of those was distractions, and again Walsh focused on Montana. In this case the issue wasn't endorsements and the like, but Joe's family life. The quarterback had married in the off-season and his wife was due to deliver their first child during the opening weeks of the schedule. "Emotionally," the *Chronicle* noted, "Montana obviously has been distracted for much of the early season by the impending birth of his daughter." After talking privately with Joe about getting his head back in the game and feeling Joe wasn't listening to him, Walsh voiced his concerns about the impact of his quarterback's impending parenthood in the press. Any controversy that might have developed out of his remarks was cut short by the actual birth and Bill dropped his public complaints.

Another issue Walsh revisited was drugs and, here, he focused on Ronnie Lott. In their encounter on the subject, according to Lott, Walsh "screwed with my head and tore up my heart." It happened the day after they got back from Minnesota. At the time, Lott was still smarting from the forty-four-yard touchdown he had given up and a missed tackle that had helped set up another Vikings score. "Walsh summoned me to his office," Lott later recounted, "and said, 'Ronnie, we're going to test you for drugs.' I was shocked. 'Why? Because I messed up on two plays? . . . You've got to be kidding me. You know I don't use drugs.' That was the worst moment in my NFL career. To think that anyone would accuse me of playing under the influence of drugs. . . . I would never jeopardize myself or my football career [like that]. I left Walsh's office in tears. I locked myself in my condominium and pulled the plug on my phone. I didn't speak to anybody. I cried all night and barely slept."

The next day, Lott confronted Walsh about it—summoning defensive coordinator George Seifert and defensive backs coach Ray Rhodes to witness the conversation. "I was boiling with emotion," Lott explained. "I was so choked up I had a hard time spitting out the words. . . . 'I want all three of you guys to hear me say this,' I said. 'I have never played a game on drugs. And I never will. If you want to test me every day from now on, go right ahead. But I promise you I'll never test dirty.' . . . I wanted Walsh to understand the type of person I was. If he was going to insinuate that I made mistakes because I was using drugs, I wouldn't stand for it."

Bill dropped his testing request and never brought the subject up with Ronnie again.

In the meantime, Bill's team remained snakebit. And the losses hadn't become any easier for him. The worst of them was a 26–10 thumping at the hands of Mike Ditka's still-undefeated Chicago Bears, who had come of age and were tearing the league up on their way to a 15–1 regular season. The Niners, the *Chronicle* reported, "were flat-out hammered by a better team," proof that they, "champions no longer, [were] ordinary, just a bunch of guys in search of a direction." And Walsh agreed. He called the game as bad a beating as his team had absorbed in a half dozen years. "We had faced that 46 defense the year before and beat it badly," he remembered, "but this year we didn't handle it worth a damn." Ditka's squad already had the look of champions.

Along the Niners' stumbling way, though, even Jerry Rice's promising start evaporated. The rookie was sidelined for a couple of games with a shoulder injury, but both before and after he persisted in dropping passes that were thrown right to him. "He was just anxious catching the ball," Bill pointed out, "wanting to run with it before he caught it. The fans weren't very nice to him when he started dropping balls and that hurt him a lot more than I thought it would, made him anxious. I had to work at keeping his confidence up. I'd talk to him personally. I gave him examples of people who had disappointed themselves and others initially and then became great players. I sort of embellished it a bit but I knew he'd work through it."

Time, however, was getting short. Entering the season's home stretch, the Forty Niners were 5-5 and running out of games in which to salvage their hopes of repeating. They had started the year as favorites to win the Super Bowl but their hopes of even making the playoffs now looked, in the words of one commentator, "dim as a 40 watt bulb." Even Walsh was being chastised as seeming "slow-witted, cautious, lost without his script" as his team floundered.

But, of course, neither the Niners nor Walsh were done yet. One of the trademarks of Bill's teams was that they rallied down the stretch, and this one was no exception. From 5-5, San Francisco won three in a row, including a 35–8 victory over Joe Gibbs's Redskins that would give the Niners a tiebreaker over Washington in the race to the playoffs. Despite the score, Walsh claimed his team had been "dominated" by Gibbs's squad—saved only by its defense, while the offense, according to the *Chronicle,* "wandered around the field like amnesia victims." A loss to the Rams followed, but at least Jerry Rice finally found his comfort zone in it and caught ten passes for 214 yards. The Niners returned to their winning ways the next week and approached the final Sunday of the season 9-6, tied with the Redskins for a wild card berth, and needing only a final win to push past them. That last game was three days before Christmas, at home against Dallas, which, though not quite the powerhouse it had been earlier in the decade, had already clinched their division championship and a spot in the playoffs. The Niners put the contest away with a second half in which their defense held the Cowboys scoreless in seven possessions—ended by two interceptions, two sacks, a fumble, and two fourth-down stands—while Montana went eighteen of twenty-one for 279 yards. When the dust settled, the Niners had triumphed 31–16—their fourth straight victory over their onetime nemesis—and were headed for the playoffs against Bill Parcells's New York Giants the following weekend.

Afterward, Walsh had the perfect opportunity to say "I told you so" to his team's doubters, but held his tongue—likely because he had few illusions about what was going to happen next.

Niners' diehards looking for a positive omen pointed out that their team had opened the playoffs with wins over the Giants in both their Super Bowl years, but they were pissing into the wind. Walsh's squad was now a group of walking wounded: Joe Montana had pulled a chest muscle against Dallas and had to have six painkilling injections in his ribs just to take the field; Wendell Tyler was going to play despite having had knee surgery two weeks earlier; nose tackle Michael Carter could barely walk with an ankle sprain; Randy Cross was hurt badly enough he didn't even suit up; Roger Craig had a hyper-extended knee, would sprain the other early in the game, and was, in Bill's words, "all used up"; Eric Wright's torn abdominal muscle kept him from playing at all; middle linebacker Michael Walter had a dislocated thumb; and Ronnie Lott was playing with a broken hand and a finger so badly smashed that part of it would be amputated in the off-season. The Giants—though 10-6, just like the Forty Niners—were on their home field, looking to make a statement, and while the Niners were game, they were overmatched. And Bill Walsh knew it going in. There would not be a repeat this year either.

New York opened the game with a drive into San Francisco territory for a field goal, then added a touchdown in the second quarter before the Niners finally mustered a drive for a field goal of their own. A third-quarter touchdown by the Giants completed the scoring for the entire game. It was the first time in three years the Niners had been held without a touchdown. The final score was 17–3 and it was obvious to everyone who watched that the better team won.

Afterward, in the home team's locker room, Bill Parcells was beaming. "What do you think of that West Coast offense now?" he chortled. The remark provided the contest with its principal historic footnote, as "West Coast offense" would be the name attached to Walsh's offensive scheme forever after, much to Bill's annoyance—since it was his design, not the West Coast's, and even though he never said as much to the press, he resented not getting the explicit credit.

Over in the Niners' locker room, a glum Eddie D. was shuffling around looking stunned, and the scene felt like a hospital ward. "I resembled a mummy," Montana remembered, "wrapped in a number of ace bandages with ice underneath." When interviewed, Bill ignored his pain and disappointment at what he privately called "my failure," and waxed philosophical about the loss. "Even if we got by the Giants," he pointed out, "I don't know who I would have suited up next week."

The Giants would move on to play the Bears, only to be manhandled, 21–0, as the Chicago juggernaut advanced to its first Super Bowl title. The Niners flew back to San Francisco a couple of hours after the game with the Giants ended. When their plane landed, a crowd of some two hundred diehard fans carrying banners were there to welcome them home as they limped through the terminal.

"We'll be back," Walsh assured the press, not sounding nearly as desperate as he felt. "We will be back."

Bill Walsh's sideline demeanor rarely changed.

||||| ||||| |||||

26

BANGED UP, BEATEN DOWN, THEN SHATTERED

The "we" Walsh referred to would not, of course, be the same "we" as the year before. Once he emerged from his despondency after the failure to repeat, Bill continued to remake his roster. He had added only four new players in 1985, but for 1986 the additions would be on a far larger scale. First, however, came the subtractions—this year featuring two mainstays of the Niners' dynasty to date.

The opener was Fred Dean, who had not had a good year in 1985. Walsh had even called him out on his lack of productivity at a team meeting, but to no avail. "He didn't play worth a damn," one rival general manager noted. "He looked like he was disinterested. He didn't have the same enthusiasm and intensity. Maybe the years are catching up with him." Walsh met with Dean twice in the off-season to deliver the same message in somewhat gentler terms and Dean got the point. Once the Niners negotiated a settlement of his contract that would provide him with enough money to set up a car-repair business down in San Diego, Fred Dean called it a career after eleven years in the NFL.

The other notable subtraction was Dwight Hicks, a three-time Pro Bowler whose contract had expired and was in off-season negotiations with the Niners. During 1985, Bill had moved Ronnie Lott from corner to Hicks's free safety spot—figuring correctly that this was where Lott fit best—and switched Hicks to corner, where he had not played particularly well. When Dwight's agent rejected the team's lowball offer in contract talks, Bill cut him. The move marked the end of Dwight Hicks and the Hot Licks, the standard-bearers for The Miracle that now seemed like a long time ago. Eric Wright, the other corner in that tandem, was still injured from the year before and, while he would stay on the roster for another four years, he would never come back to form. Carlton Williamson, the other safety, had only another year left before being replaced. In the meantime, Hicks looked around for another team but, finding no takers, found himself out of the NFL for good.

Bill's first addition of the new year was on his staff. Quarterbacks coach Paul Hackett had left to take an offensive coordinator position with the Dallas Cowboys and Bill spent part of February interviewing potential replacements. The least experienced of all those he interviewed was Mike Holmgren, who had spent the last four years coaching quarterbacks at BYU, a program Walsh considered "the most sophisticated passing offense in college football." Before BYU, Holmgren had been a high school coach in the Bay Area, where he had grown up. He had just been turned down for the head coaching job at the University of Montana when the Niners called to see if he'd like to interview with Walsh. Mike figured he had no chance of getting the job but that the interview would be a great learning experience and jumped at the opportunity.

His estimate of the odds against him at the beginning of the process was pretty much on the mark. "Mike Holmgren wasn't a real serious candidate for the job," Bill remembered. "I had some really top guys who wanted it, but I wanted to interview him just to see. Then the minute I did I knew he would be the one and dropped the other candidates. Mike and I exchanged openly and he had a better feel for football than anyone I knew. It wasn't difficult to hire him. He was obviously the man." Holmgren reported to 711 Nevada immediately and began spending long hours studying the playbook and piling through the videotapes of Walsh installing his offense. "There was an enormous amount of material," Mike explained. "I was like a kid in a candy store." One of the first people to whom Bill introduced his new offensive alter ego was Joe Montana: "I went outside with Joe by myself to talk and he told me, 'I want you to coach me hard. I want you to watch everything I do.' Joe was the easiest guy to coach and he made my job easier. His personality was such that he had this inner fire but would also have a blast at practice."

After hiring Holmgren, Walsh turned his attention to the draft. And his 1986 effort would become legendary.

Sizing up the incoming group of collegians before draft day, Bill concluded that while there weren't many truly outstanding players, there was a deep field of players who could become serviceable starters. So the strategy he adopted was to go after quantity and to trade down to get as many picks as possible. Since the Niners already had a reputation for making draft-day trades, John McVay had been collecting a long list of options over several weeks when Bill started to make moves, and come draft day, the second floor at Forty Niners headquarters took on the air of a commodities market. McVay often had a phone on each ear and several more callers on hold, all wanting to deal. Most thought Walsh's commitment to going lower in the draft order was a mental aberration and were quick to want to take advantage of him. Eddie D. was back in Youngstown, following the action on a speakerphone, and jokingly asked Bill at one point if he was going to keep trading until he owned every pick in the tenth round. It was a heretofore unheard-of set of maneuvers.

Bill traded the number eighteen pick in the first round to Dallas for its pick at number twenty plus a fifth-rounder. Then he packaged the Dallas pick, plus one of his own in the tenth round, to Buffalo for their second- and third-round selections. Buffalo's second-rounder was traded to Detroit for their second- and third-round picks. He also moved another second-round pick to Washington for their first-rounder in 1987. Along the way, the Philadelphia Eagles called to ask if the apparently crazy Forty Niners president would trade his backup quarterback, Matt Cavanaugh, for a third-rounder now plus a second-round pick next year. Putting that proposal on hold, Mike Holmgren remembered, "Bill hung up the phone and said he had a chance to trade Cavanaugh and asked, 'What do you think?' Cavanaugh was an excellent backup, and to a man, every coach in the room said, 'Don't do it.' Bill listened politely and then said, 'You guys don't know anything,' picked up the phone and says, 'Trade him.'" To cover that sudden vacancy on the roster, Walsh then moved one of his third-rounders from Detroit to the Rams for two fourths and backup quarterback Jeff Kemp.

All told, Bill had made six trades, leaving him with one choice in the second round, three in the third, three in the fourth, one each in the fifth and sixth, and another five between rounds eight and ten. The Niners didn't even make a selection until the draft had been going for more than five hours. Then, declaring, "It's time to get to work," Walsh proceeded to prove that his analysis of what this draft offered had been right on the mark. In round two, he selected Larry Roberts, a defensive end out of Alabama, whom the Niners would have taken with their first-round pick if they had kept it. In round three, Bill chose fullback Tom Rathman of Nebraska, cornerback Tim McKyer from Texas-Arlington, and wide receiver John Taylor from Delaware State. Round four yielded linebacker and pass rush specialist Charles Haley out of James Madison, offensive tackle Steve Wallace from Auburn, and Miami defensive tackle Kevin Fagan. In round six, he picked up cornerback Don Griffin from Middle Tennessee State. All eight would become starters for the Forty Niners—the two corners in their rookie year—and five of them would eventually be selected for the Pro Bowl.

His director of scouting told Bill afterward that their draft had been a disaster, but Bill knew better and paid no attention. In fact, his 1986 performance was easily the most productive draft in anyone's memory and, considering where he had started, Bill called it "maybe the best draft in NFL history." The future backbone of his team's third incarnation was in the fold and his reputation as The Genius had been buttressed yet again.

When his 1986 squad closed up training camp and advanced toward the regular season, they had a feeling that their luck had to have improved from the year before, but they couldn't have been more wrong.

It got worse, much worse, though that wasn't yet obvious in their opener on the road against the Tampa Bay Buccaneers, a team struggling to escape doormat status. Tampa was quarterbacked by the now journeyman Steve DeBerg and the Niners treated their former teammate mercilessly. They intercepted him seven times and, when on offense, the *Chronicle* noted, "everything went as 49er coach Bill Walsh had planned." There had been concerns over Montana's health going into the game—he'd had shoulder surgery in the off-season, suffered from chronic back stiffness, and was nursing a sore ankle—but he completed thirty-two of forty-six for 345 yards on the way to a 31–7 trouncing. Walsh was even able to rest Montana late in the game and give his new backup, Jeff Kemp, a little time at the helm. The Niners' dominance over Tampa was such that one columnist predicted, "In their best years, [the Forty Niners] have been Super Bowl champions, and I expect this will be another Super year."

A development that had gone largely unnoticed anywhere but the Forty Niners' sideline, however, would quickly consign that optimism to football oblivion. Right before Bill sent Kemp in to finish off the game, Montana, forced out of the pocket by the Tampa pass rush, had rolled to his left and thrown across his body. The maneuver tweaked his back and left him sore after the game and even more so when the team reconvened in Redwood City. It wasn't a major concern at first—Joe had played with a sore back off and on for much of the previous season—but it didn't improve over the week and Bill had no choice but to sit Joe for that Sunday's Rams game while the doctors tried to figure out what was wrong with him.

Jeff Kemp started in his stead, but despite Kemp's credible performance, San Francisco lost 16–13 on a Rams field goal with two seconds left. At his press conference afterward, Walsh, with "a strangely passive expression on his red and sweaty face," congratulated the Rams, the defending NFC Western Division champions—and praised Kemp's effort. Then Bill dropped a blockbuster. "Joe Montana will have back surgery tomorrow," he announced. "He'll be out, conceivably for the season" or longer. Stunned silence pervaded the room. "In athletics these things happen," Walsh continued. "Men do not sob in a corner when someone is taken away."

Nonetheless, Bill was clear about how dire the team's circumstance had just become. "There was a strong possibility that Joe wouldn't play again, ever," he remembered. "None of us knew much about backs in those days and back surgery was thought of as totally debilitating. I thought that certainly you couldn't play football after back surgery—it wasn't even in the cards, it wasn't even reasonable to think that was possible. I thought 'this is it.' We had to adapt very quickly to Joe's loss and I concentrated on that, but our prospects going on without him looked bleak."

Montana's injury was described by his doctors as a ruptured disk between the bottom vertebra in his lower back and the bony structure at the base of his spine called the sacrum. The disk, composed of a soft pulpy material surrounded by a hard casing known as the annulus, cushioned the vertebrae from shocks. When running left and throwing across his body in the Tampa Bay game, the pressure of the twisting motion had split the annulus—apparently already damaged from the 1985 season—causing the disk's pulpy insides to leak out and press against Joe's sciatic nerve, generating intense pain and numbness along the lower spine and down his legs. In Joe's case, the injury was complicated by a congenital condition known as spinal stenosis. The openings that housed his nerves in the internal bony structure of his vertebrae were narrower than normal, making his sciatic nerve particularly susceptible to pressure, such as that caused by his damaged disk. In a two-hour procedure at St. Mary's hospital in San Francisco, a surgeon extracted the disk's pulpy insides and left the annulus in place to act as a shock absorber. He also used a drill to enlarge the nerve canals in the quarterback's two lowest vertebrae.

The surgery generated front-page headlines in Bay Area newspapers, including, IT'S 50/50 THAT HE'LL EVER PLAY AGAIN. Walsh announced afterward that "there were less complications than they thought might have existed, and so we're optimistic that he'll be back in football." Nonetheless, fans throughout the nine counties held their breath and no one imagined Joe would return for this season. His doctors said it would be at least twelve to fifteen weeks before that option was theoretically possible and even at that point he might have trouble walking, let alone playing in the NFL. In the meantime, St. Mary's set up a dedicated phone line to handle the hundreds of calls they were receiving to tell Joe that they loved him and to get well soon.

Two days after the surgery, Ronnie Lott and Dwight Clark came by for a visit. "Joe was chattering on, boasting about all the exercise he was getting," Lott recounted. "As we were getting ready to leave, the nurses suggested he accompany us to the elevator to stretch his legs. Montana seemed eager to demonstrate his progress. . . . That's when reality struck. First of all, Montana had trouble getting out of bed. It took a couple of nurses to sit him up and lift him to his feet. Just that little bit of movement seemed to exhaust him. He looked so fragile, I was afraid to touch him. Montana began to walk us down the hall, taking tiny steps, moving inch by inch like a 100 year old man. . . . When we finally reached the elevator, I was quite upset. Montana said happily, 'Thanks for coming. I'll see you guys.' The elevator door closed, and I felt like crying. I thought, my God. This guy's never going to play again."

"The 49ers . . . had arguably been the best team in the NFL," one of the *Chronicle*'s columnists wrote on the day of Montana's surgery, but had now "suddenly become just another good team."

It would require all of Walsh's skills to keep his squad from letting Joe's loss send them sliding backward down the slope they had just begun to ascend. Afterward, the same prognosticators who were lining up in September to announce the Niners' impending doom would, come the end of December, pronounce this "the best coaching job in Walsh's career with the Forty Niners." He showed no external signs of panic at the situation. "We really leaned on the foundation we'd built," he later explained, "on intensity, on communication, focus and the rest. We'd built a really solid foundation for when things would go wrong and we managed to keep things going. As vital as Joe was, the team just continued to play."

And Bill immediately adjusted his system to fit his new quarterback. Kemp was under six feet tall, mobile, and possessed a strong arm, but his height made seeing downfield and getting enough clearance to make his passes in the face of a pass rush problematic. To compensate, "our linemen were asked to engage their pass rushers earlier and stay in front of them," Bill explained. In so doing, "they sacrificed their ability to sustain their blocks, but if they stopped the rushers early, Jeff could get some clearance and his height disadvantage wouldn't be a factor. We also emphasized the play pass because faking the run would take some of the heat off. But, again, anytime you play-fake and offensive linemen drive out much as they do when they're run blocking, they can lose their men quickly. In Jeff's case, he'd get the time he needed to get the ball off, but he'd be hit right after he threw, almost without exception." Bill also put more emphasis on deep pass patterns to make maximum use of Kemp's arm. The results were impressive. Jeff Kemp, who had averaged under 50 percent completions heretofore in his career, began completing almost 60 percent of his throws and, within three weeks, was leading the league in passing.

After losing to the Rams, the Niners formed up behind Kemp and handled the Saints at home, 26–17. The following Sunday they faced the Dolphins down in Miami and, despite Miami's ranking as the second-best offense in the NFL, plus ninety-degree temperatures accompanied by 60 percent humidity, the Niners defense was dominant. "Marino was made to look more like Steve DeBerg than the quarterback who a week ago became the NFL's top rated passer of all time," the *Chronicle* reported. "He finally left the game to a chorus of boos midway through the fourth quarter, after Lott's second interception [which] he lateraled to Tom Holmoe [who] went 66 yards for a touchdown." The final score was 31–16.

After another win and a loss, the Niners' bad quarterback luck reared its head again in a 10–10 tie with the mediocre Atlanta Falcons. Jeff Kemp played the whole game but sustained a hip injury that would sit him down for at least three weeks. Now San Francisco was down to its third-string signal caller, Mike Moroski, a journeyman backup who had been with the team barely two weeks. Nonetheless, Bill coached him up and turned him into a 59 percent passer the next week against the struggling Packers in Green Bay, where the Niners won 31–17. Going into New Orleans in week nine, Walsh's Montana- and Kemp-less squad was nonetheless 5-2-1 and in the thick of the division race. At the same time, the Bears were leading their division on the way to a 14-2 season, the Giants were leading theirs, also headed for 14-2, and the Redskins were only a game back and headed for 12-4 and a wild card berth.

The Saints game was a big one for Eddie D. The DeBartolos had significant business interests in New Orleans, so it was something of a bragging rights contest. The Niners, however, went into the contest missing some significant players. In addition to Montana and Kemp, Lott was out, and so was Eric Wright; Wendell Tyler was fresh off the injured list, Michael Carter would last a quarter before leaving on crutches, and Roger Craig would sustain a hip injury that made him little more than a decoy for the bulk of the game. And the Saints, in the process of extricating themselves from among the league's weak underside, were no easy mark.

Stumbling out of the gate, the Niners gave up two quick touchdowns and fell behind 14–0. It looked like they had gotten one of those touchdowns back when Rice broke open for what would have been a thirty-six-yard scoring pass, but he dropped the ball. The Niners managed a field goal instead and next brought the score to 14–10 after an interception return down to the Saints' one. Then Walsh's offense started screwing up. On a series that had reached New Orleans's nine, Moroski threw a second-down pass outside when his receiver broke inside and gave the ball back to the

Saints. On the following Niners drive, with less than two minutes remaining in the half and the Niners on the Saints' twenty-four, Wendell Tyler coughed up the ball. Then on the first series of the second half, a fifty-two-yard pass from Moroski to Russ Francis put the Niners on New Orleans's five, but the next three plays lost ten yards, and when the Niners settled for a field goal, it was blocked. After that, the game was essentially over. The offense couldn't move and the Saints drove for three straight field goals and won going away, 23–10.

Afterward, Eddie—who had apparently been drinking—was beside himself. He watched the end of the fourth quarter in the Niners' locker room, where he threw a glass at the television monitor, sending shards flying all over. According to one reporter who witnessed the scene, DeBartolo looked as though "his eyes might rocket out of his skull. . . . Eddie D. was seething and he suddenly noticed one of the 49er public relations men. . . . Eddie grabbed the guy from behind and wheeled him around and started yelling at him. You would have thought Eddie D. owned the guy." When one of the team doctors showed up, Eddie gave him similar treatment, but saved his worst for the players as they straggled in, covered with sweat, blood, and rug burns from the Superdome's artificial grass.

The Niners' owner was yelling at them when Bill entered the locker room. Walsh immediately pulled his boss toward the head coach's office, the first room off the corridor that led to the lockers. Bill told Eddie he couldn't talk to the team that way—he wouldn't allow it—and with that, the two went ballistic, yelling at each other at top volume. It was, one witness remembered, "fuck you this and fuck you that." When Mike Holmgren walked in from the press box where he'd been manning the headphones, the two were in the hallway, screaming at each other with Carmen Policy wedged between them. Holmgren squeezed by as quickly as he could. Eddie finally ended the confrontation by telling Bill to have his lawyer call Eddie's lawyer in the morning to talk about terminating his contract. Then he stomped out with his entourage in pursuit.

Decades later, when asked what provoked Eddie to this outburst, Walsh would speculate off the record that it had a lot to do with whatever DeBartolo had been imbibing and he would also suggest that "Eddie had probably done some pretty heavy gambling" on the game. By then, Bill had come to accept DeBartolo's abuse—though hurtful and disturbing—as part of the price he had paid for keeping his job. At the time, however, it was devastating, coming as it did on top of his own postgame trauma. Bill retreated into the coach's room to gather himself and then went out to face the press. To them he spoke bravely about the Niners still being in the division race, just a game back of the Rams. "We're not ready to concede anything," he insisted.

"A few moments later, however," according to a report in the *Chronicle,* "Walsh walked into his private dressing room, which had a glass door. Looking through the door, one could see Walsh become a tired, deflated, white-haired figure slumped in a chair, his eyes on the floor. It was as though, with his speech to the press completed, he had wandered back into that room, sat down, and hit rock bottom."

It was a long flight back to San Francisco that night. And when he was finally holed up in his office at 711 Nevada, Bill called Kristine Hanson and told her he didn't know if he still had a job.

In fact, he did, though no one who saw it—least of all Bill—would ever forget the set-to in New Orleans. "It took another forty-eight hours before we got back together on the phone to smooth things over," Walsh later recounted, "reminding each other how hard we had worked to get where we were, and that we could deal with bad times like these."

By then, the two of them were facing a small miracle that brightened the Niners' prospects enormously. Joe Montana's recovery from his back operation was beyond what anyone had anticipated. His surgeon called it "amazing, simply amazing," and Eddie was shocked. "I thought he was done, or at least facing a long road back," he admitted. Instead, Montana was on his feet after two weeks and throwing footballs by the time he reached four. At the end of his seventh week, his doctors cleared him to play in a game, though admitted they thought he was "crazy" to do so. Joe's only lingering symptoms were a slight atrophy in his left calf muscle and spots of numbness in his left leg and foot that sometimes prevented him from knowing if his foot was flat on the ground or turned over. He would continue therapy for more than a year to deal with those sensations but none of them was debilitating.

"The tough decision was whether to play Joe or not," Walsh explained. "He had been given an okay to play by the doctors but then it was up to me to play him. I had to really search my soul to decide whether to do that or not. I didn't want to be the one responsible for sending him out to get hurt even worse. But after he'd practiced for a week, everything seemed fine. The doctors said he was stronger than he was before the surgery so that relieved my fears, and he played."

Montana's first game back was at Candlestick against the St. Louis Cardinals—on their way to a four-win season—and it was a walkover. Joe was thirteen of nineteen for 270 yards. The game "was a strange one, a tribute to his stature in a very unusual way," one reporter noted. "The St. Louis defensive linemen would get right up in Montana's face but not hit him. Nobody wanted to be the one to apply the hit that might paralyze him." The Niners gained 460 yards and won 43–17.

There was a lot of talk afterward about how the season had been saved now that Joe was back, but next Sunday's game, in Washington against Gibbs's Redskins on Monday night, put the kibosh to that fantasy. Tempted by the Redskins' man-to-man coverage on his receivers, Walsh overused Montana and threw the ball too much. Joe passed sixty times, completing thirty-three, a dozen of those to Jerry Rice, who was leading the league in receiving yardage. But by the fourth quarter, Montana was visibly fatigued, and while the offense rolled up yardage it didn't produce points, thanks in no small part to a team record fourteen penalties and an offensive line that did its best impression of a sieve. The Niners gained 501 yards in the game, but set an NFL record by being the first team ever to gain more than 500 yards and still not score a single touchdown: Washington 14, San Francisco 6.

The Niners, after reaching 7-4-1, were back on Monday night for week thirteen, this time at Candlestick against Parcells's New York Giants. Throughout his career Bill Walsh had a penchant for labeling losses "the worst" he'd ever experienced and this would be the latest of those. The Chronicle would describe it as "a collective failure of imagination and nerve and character." Montana led the Niners to a 17–0 halftime lead, but that was all the offense could do. Parcells's defense boxed them up and threw away the key while the Giants offense answered with three touchdowns in the third quarter. In the fourth quarter, Joe had Jerry Rice open behind the defenders for a sure touchdown and overthrew him. Then on a critical fourth and two deep in the Giants' territory, he threw another incompletion when he had an obvious opening to scramble for a first down. That provoked inevitable surmising that Joe before the surgery would have made the run and a host of questions about whether he was now gun-shy. The final score was 21–17 and Bill was described afterward as "looking ill."

The loss haunted him well into the next week. On Thursday, one of his San Jose State buddies came by 711 Nevada to visit. He found Bill in his office, despondent and preoccupied. "I blew that game," he told his friend, "and I can't get it off my mind. I'm still thinking about it." Bill went on to explain that on the final drive, faced with fourth down, he'd had a play that would have worked but couldn't get it in to Montana, so they'd ended up running the wrong one and it had failed. "It was my fault," Bill declared. Then he continued, as though to snap himself out of obsessing about it and convince himself to move on: "But I can't lament that. I have to go out there with my team now and I have to step forward—be the guy and be the leader."

It apparently worked. After two straight wins against AFC playoff teams, the 9-5-1 Forty Niners faced off against the 10-5 Rams for the Western Division title. Fortunately, according to the *Chronicle*, "the 49ers saved their best for last." Joe jumped the Rams early with a forty-four-yard touchdown throw to Rice. A field goal made the lead 10–0 in the first quarter. The Rams closed the gap to 10–7 after intercepting Montana, and the game seemed for a moment like it would be a dogfight, but the combination of Walsh and Montana thrashed Los Angeles' hopes before the half. The drive that effectively decided the game began with the Niners on their own eight. What followed was a ninety-two-yard juggernaut that consumed fifteen plays and was described in postgame newspaper accounts as "brilliantly conceived" and featuring "a vintage performance from Joe Montana." Bill later called it "our best drive of the year." When the final whistle blew, the Niners had outgained the Rams 408 yards to 229, rolled up twenty-seven first downs to the Rams' twelve, and held the ball for thirteen and a half more minutes. The Rams only crossed the fifty-yard line twice in their first twelve possessions. The final score was 24–14, but the game wasn't nearly that close. "Bill called a great game," Dwight Clark remembered. And everybody else agreed.

Having become Western Division champions against all odds, Walsh's Forty Niners were back in the playoffs once again.

And once again, their first game would be with the New York Giants. This year the Giants were champions of the NFC East, having dominated most of their opposition, and were favored to end up playing the Bears for a trip to the Super Bowl. The San Francisco papers nonetheless put up a brave front. "The New York Giants have the best record in pro football," one columnist noted, and "they'll be at home Sunday. But the 49ers have Bill Walsh. . . . The Giants [admittedly] have many advantages going into the game, but Bill Walsh gives the 49ers a big one [of their own]."

The expectation that he would single-handedly—through his game plan and play calling—provide the margin between victory and defeat was a heavy load, but Bill showed no signs of the pressure he was under in the two weeks leading up to the game. In his rambling speech that opened the final week of practice, he attempted to reinforce his team's confidence and, as usual, played the disrespect card. Bill noted that all the commentators were talking about the Giants-Bears matchup they expected to take place a week after the Niners were eliminated. "We're just the team they allow to play the Giants before that happens," he scoffed. "We're low profile. We have a lot of respect for them but there isn't any reason to think that we can't go back there and take this game. Get yourself ready for a championship effort. All the hype doesn't mean a thing. Many of us remember the experience leaving there a year ago—how humiliating it was. And we don't want to go through that again. Remembering that is the key."

His team appeared confident enough when they reached Giants Stadium, and motivated as well, but it seemed to make little difference. The closest the Niners came to victory was on the fourth play of the game, with their offense at midfield. Montana hit Rice on a slant pattern and once he caught the ball, Rice was wide open and racing toward what looked to be a fifty-yard touchdown play. Then Jerry dropped the ball at the Giants' twenty-seven. Trying desperately to pick up his fumble, Rice booted the ball, which went bouncing out of his reach until the Giants finally recovered it in their own end zone. After that, the roof fell in. "There's no way to put a pretty face on this one," the *Chronicle* noted the next morning. "The 49ers couldn't run, they couldn't pass, they couldn't block, they couldn't defend, they couldn't tackle." In one twenty-two-minute stretch, the Giants scored a touchdown all six times they possessed the ball—five on offense and one on defense.

It was the latter that provided the game's signature play. Trailing 21–3 shortly before halftime, Montana went back to pass and center Fred Quillan lost his block on the Giants nose tackle, who came flying at Joe full steam, hitting him just as he released the ball. The Giant led with his helmet, striking Montana full force under his chin, and the ball fluttered short, right into the arms of a Giants linebacker who ran the interception into the end zone. In the meantime, Montana was on the turf, briefly unconscious. The Niners trainer helped Joe—obviously suffering from a concussion—off the field and into the locker room, where he changed into street clothes and was done for the day. He watched the rest of the massacre from the sidelines, but when he kept getting dizzy and nodding off, Joe was hauled on a stretcher to a hospital for observation.

The final score was Giants 49, Forty Niners 3, a playoff beating second only to Chicago's 73–0 thrashing of Washington in 1940. The loss ranked as the second worst in the Niners' history as well, topped only by a 56–7 debacle in 1958. It also set a record for the fewest first downs the Niners had ever accumulated while Walsh had been coach.

"We were shattered by a great team," he admitted to the press afterward. "They just shattered us."

That same weekend the Redskins upset the Bears, setting up an NFC final in which the Giants would decimate Washington and go on to Parcells's first Super Bowl title.

In the meantime, the Niners boarded the team charter glum and in silence. Montana would stay behind in a New York hospital overnight and, receiving a clean bill of health the next morning, would fly home in one of the DeBartolo Corp.'s private jets. When the team plane landed at San Francisco International without him late that night, 350 fans were waiting to show their loyal support.

Bill gamely talked about next season, but at that moment his heart wasn't in it. As far as he was concerned, he had failed miserably, for the second year in a row.

Dr. Harry Edwards and Ronnie Lott in the Forty Niners' locker room

27

A DIFFERENT DRUMMER

While Bill Walsh knew that he would end up being judged far more by the number of Super Bowls he won than anything else, he also aspired to address issues that were, to his thinking, far more significant than just how the game was played. The result was a groundbreaking effort to reshape some of the ways National Football League franchises operated, transcending the ball with a point on both ends and impacting the social fabric itself.

In Walsh's quest, 1986 had been a pivotal year, beginning with the hiring of Dr. Harry Edwards during training camp. Dr. Edwards was a Ph.D. and tenured associate professor of sociology at the University of California's Berkeley campus, but was far more than just an academic. One of eight children raised in the ghetto of East St. Louis, Illinois, Edwards—six foot eight and close to three hundred pounds—had thrown the discus and played basketball on a scholarship at San Jose State in the 1960s and had become a visible activist on issues of civil rights and black identity. He attempted unsuccessfully to persuade black American athletes to boycott the 1968 Olympics as a statement about the racial inequality rampant in the nation they were about to represent, but did help generate the famous black-gloved, clenched-fist salute by American sprinters John Carlos and Tommie Smith on the victory stand that summer. His application for tenure at Cal became a racial cause célèbre that eventually led the university's chancellor to overrule the faculty and award Edwards his position. By 1986, he was a frequent writer and national lecturer on the subject of sports and racial identity.

Walsh had followed Edwards in the newspapers over the years—with the usual proprietary interest he reserved for fellow San Jose State alumni—occasionally dropping him notes. "He would say things like, 'I saw you on so and so,' " Edwards recalled, " 'I really thought that was a thoughtful appraisal,' or, 'I never thought of it exactly that way but you're right.' Once he sent me a tape of a talk he'd given—'Thought you might be interested in this.' It was stuff like that." Then Walsh pushed to expand their contact. "I'd always wanted to meet him," Bill remembered. "Then I saw another interview with him in the paper and I felt that maybe I could add to the knowledge he had developed in sports. I wrote Harry a letter about that and when he wrote back, I called him. We had a great conversation and I invited him up to Rocklin for our training camp. He spent a few days there; we shared meals and talked. Then I asked him to join us as a mentor-consultant-type person—to oversee and observe, get acquainted with the players."

The situation Walsh wanted "Doc"—as Edwards was quickly nicknamed—to address had been on Bill's mind for weeks. As he explained that summer, there were demographic changes that were taking place in the NFL that, if left unaddressed, might cause "the whole thing to come apart." Over the last two years, the number of blacks in the game had grown dramatically and Bill told Edwards he needed help with the team's adjustment to that and other accompanying changes. He had already approached three other people for help but they were bored by the issue or they didn't understand or they didn't have the time to devote to it. He needed someone who was prepared to make the Forty Niners locker room his office—working not just with black players but with the whole team to secure its footing in what Bill saw as a new era. By the end of the 1986 training camp, Doc had agreed to give it a try. "Harry added a lot of wisdom and working knowledge about people and people working together," Bill later explained. "He had a great sense of people and his presence was noted immediately. Players gravitated towards him and he began to connect. He would discuss the needs of the players and any shortcomings on our part. He became a kind of intermediary and, more importantly, a counsel for players independent of us. It was very, very effective and I was excited about having him." After Bill secured Eddie's approval, Edwards was hired.

Doc's first contact with Eddie D. came early in the 1986 season on a game day after a Niners loss. Edwards was in the locker room—where Bill had told him to be—and Eddie saw him. DeBartolo didn't recognize who Edwards was and, pissed off about the loss, immediately looked at the huge black man and told him to get the fuck out. Harry responded, 'No problem, I'm gone,' and left. As soon as Bill learned, he ran after his new consultant and caught him out in the parking lot. He told Edwards that Eddie was just angry and not to worry about it. That was just him. Harry said it was Eddie's team and if he said go, Harry would go. He didn't have a problem with that.

Then the next morning Edwards received a phone call.

"Hey, Doc," the caller opened.

Edwards asked who it was.

"It's me," the caller said, "Eddie."

Harry immediately called him Mr. DeBartolo but Eddie insisted he call him by his first name. He said he was sorry about the night before—he had just been angry. He wanted to apologize—he'd been so wrong. Then he told Edwards he was doing a great job and wanted to know if there was anything he needed. Could the two of them meet?

Doc said that wasn't necessary but Eddie wouldn't hear of it. No, they had to meet. Was he being treated well? Was he being paid enough?

Edwards said all he needed was to get in the locker room and Eddie answered that he was in the locker room and any other place he wanted to go. Did he need an office?

When Harry saw Bill next, Bill said he'd told Eddie to call and was glad everything had been smoothed out. Now Doc could work however he needed to—which Doc proceeded to do. In short order, he developed an analysis that fleshed out Bill's sense of the situation.

"Two things were happening at that point," Dr. Edwards later observed.

"The number of black athletes in the NFL was increasing phenomenally and at a lot of positions where they hadn't traditionally played, so there was a transition going on in the locker room, just as Bill had grasped. The best athletes and team leaders were increasingly black. That was the first demographic change. The second and related change was that the money was suddenly so much bigger for players coming out of college into the league. The age of the agent had hit full stride and now you had guys coming out of college making more money than guys who had been in the league five, six, or seven years. So the locker room was not only substantially different than it had been in terms of race—in terms of money, it was upside down. Some rookie might have a $2 million contract with a locker next to a veteran who had barely made $800,000 total over seven years. This in turn impacted the authority structure in the locker room. That vet now had a difficult time telling the rookie what it took to be successful in the league. The rookie wasn't going to hear it. And the issue then became how then to tell them the Forty Niners' way to approach their craft and continue to generate the ethos and chemistry the team needed to be successful. That challenge was what made Bill say he needed some help in the locker room."

In addition to just providing a sounding board and a degree of informal mentoring, that "help" soon generated what Bill called the "Life Skills Program," with at least four major thrusts, all aimed at equipping otherwise unprepared players for adult life. The first provided the opportunity to continue their education and finish work on bachelor degrees, holding classes at the 711 Nevada Street headquarters in conjunction with several universities. The second was a confidential system of personal and family counseling, designed, according to Edwards, "to address issues like domestic violence, lifestyles and how these guys were spending their evenings, how to take care of their families, and all that." The third was a drug counseling program—again confidential—for all kinds of substance abuse, both performance and recreational. The fourth thrust was a financial counseling, investment, and tax program, where the Niners brought in bankers and others with expertise to teach these suddenly flush young men the basics of managing their money.

Bill counted all four as major successes and within just a few years, his and Edwards's pioneering effort would be duplicated around the league, effectively turning NFL franchises into social agencies as well as football businesses.

. . .

Another NFL issue Walsh addressed in an organized way before anyone else in the league was the scarcity of black coaches. As yet, the league had never had an African American head coach, nor did it have any process designed to change that or to train African Americans for that role.

Bill himself had always had black assistants, including four on his staff as the 1987 off-season began—two of whom would become head coaches once the color barrier was broken—and had been an advocate for increased opportunities since his first days as a college assistant. While at Cal in the early sixties—when Jim Crow was still the national norm and most black athletes had to go to black schools to play—he had recruited the first significant influx of black players to the UC football program and did the same thing when he moved to Stanford. When Walsh was with the Bengals, the Olympic symbol Tommie Smith—who had been drafted by the Rams before the games but was afterward given the cold shoulder and never signed—had approached him through a San Jose attorney, looking for a chance to play. Bill told Smith to come to Cincinnati and he'd get a fair shake. Smith made the practice squad there before leaving football with an injury. "It's hard to imagine [now] how bitter the animosity was toward Smith," the lawyer who approached Bill remembered, "and how much guts and courage it took to give him a chance." By the time he reached the Niners, Walsh already had a reputation. "I don't know of any black player who played for Walsh who ever thought he was treated unfairly," noted a black player who had been with him both at Stanford and the Bengals.

By 1987, the NFL had an "internship" program for black coaches, but, Bill observed, "they were all drawn from predominantly black schools and were just invited to training camps to observe. Most of the schools they came from were rural and most of the men they recruited to the program were not necessarily men with high ambitions. They weren't looking to become part of the NFL and, quite frankly, weren't very good candidates for the league. Mostly the program was just a kind of good times junket that was meant to look good but had no impact on the league's approach to race. I thought we could do a lot better than that. With Eddie's backing, we decided on an internship at our training camp for men who already had jobs with Division I universities, for which applicants had to fill out an application, write a letter stating their interests, and go through an interview. It was more of a formal thing and they would spend two to three weeks at our training camp acquiring the skills they would need for a future in coaching. We would take two or three candidates every year and the idea was to help get them ready to come into the NFL and rise through the ranks once they got here."

First Bill took the idea to the NFL's Competition Committee. This was the most powerful of the league's operational committees, composed of representatives from various franchises and charged with overseeing all modifications to rules and procedures. Bill had become a member of the group at the end of the 1986 season and this was his first meeting. "I didn't get a very good response to my internship idea," he remembered. "They weren't that interested at that time in doing anything like this. They said the league already had a program. So we just went ahead with ours. We seriously recruited for it—circulated a fancy brochure—and we got some of the top people at top universities. They spent three weeks with us at training camp and were involved with coaching first-year players and were included in all coaching staff meetings. Thus they became familiar with the NFL, were exposed to football as taught at the professional level, and further refined their own coaching skills. In addition to football and organizational skills, they were also taught things like how to interview for a job. Two of our first graduates became head coaches—one at a major university and another eventually with an NFL franchise."

In the end, the Niners' program that Walsh designed was so successful that commissioner Pete Rozelle began pushing it for the rest of the NFL and eventually expanded it leaguewide.

Bill broke a barrier on another societal front as well, though not by initiation or design.

When Walsh had first arrived at the Niners in 1979 and began reconstructing the organization, one of the vacancies he had to fill was for head trainer. One of the applicants, Lindsy McLean, had begun his career at San Jose State in the late sixties and then moved on to the University of Michigan, where he'd been the trainer for its football squads for more than a decade. McLean had been looking to return to the Bay Area and was friends with the orthopedist who had tended to Walsh's teams at Stanford. On paper he was eminently qualified and, after an interview with Walsh, was hired.

There was, however, one facet of McLean that had not been covered in his application or his interview. While back at Michigan, Lindsy had finally admitted to himself that he was a homosexual and had embarked on a seven-year gay relationship with a Detroit bartender, all the while staying firmly in the closet at work and in the rest of his life. The end of his relationship was one of the things that provoked McLean to move west, and he was still closeted when hired by the Niners. "Bill had no idea," Lindsy remembered. "I didn't ever come out on the job. I just lived my life." But after a while that life was a dead giveaway, whether he made an announcement or not. The revelatory moment came at the team's Christmas party in 1982. By then, McLean had begun a new relationship that would last twenty-four years, until the death of his partner, George, from AIDS. That Christmas, throwing caution momentarily to the winds, Lindsy brought George to the party. "Bill figured it out at that point," McLean explained, "but he never said anything to me about it."

Indeed, the only time during his stewardship of the Forty Niners that Walsh ever even indirectly addressed the open secret of his trainer's sexuality was after the loss to Washington in 1983. As a reward for their work over the season, Bill offered the staff a trip to Hawaii for the Pro Bowl. They could either take one first-class ticket or two in coach. When McLean signed up for two, Bill sent John McVay to tell him that if he brought someone along, it should be a woman. "It wasn't meant to condemn me," Lindsy pointed out. "Bill was only concerned with the image of the Forty Niners in the eyes of the rest of the league." Otherwise, "Bill was just accepting of my lifestyle. I never felt judged by him. I don't think it mattered to Bill and he was such a supportive person for me. There was no homophobic bone in his body. He respected my private life and left it at that."

By virtue of that tolerance, however, an extraordinary precedent was set at 711 Nevada. In a sport where *queer* and *faggot* were almost universal derisions and Lindsy McLean would in all likelihood have been fired at that telltale Christmas party by any other franchise, the San Francisco Forty Niners, led by their head coach and president, accepted a gay man as their primary caregiver in the locker room and on the sideline without ever making a point of it one way or another. McLean would stay in that job twenty-four years.

. . .

The vision Walsh brought to all his pioneering efforts and postures was a function of his perception of himself as someone who was far more than a football coach. He cherished his standing and participation in the larger world outside of the NFL and nurtured them at every opportunity.

"Knowing Bill Walsh was kind of like the blind man describing an elephant," one of the sportswriters who covered him observed. "We all knew just one little piece of him. But he had all these other areas we knew nothing about. He dealt with lots of people outside of football, outside of our scope entirely. He was able to deal with politicians, people who were intellects in other areas. They were impressed by him."

"He was a Renaissance man," suggested an artist who dealt with Bill on an almost daily basis. "For someone who spent his life coaching football, which takes an inordinate amount of time, it was amazing that he has so many other interests. He came off as a man of letters and was pretty well-read. He appreciated the arts and loved going to cocktail parties and mixing with the literary people. He really appreciated beauty. Altogether he was an extraordinary person."

Perhaps no one was more struck by Walsh's breadth as a person and social figure than Harry Edwards, the Berkeley professor. "He was a giant," Edwards remembered. "He was among the brightest people I've ever come across. He may have been the greatest football coach of all time but it has not infrequently crossed my mind what a waste of talent that was. He should have been president of the United States. He had absolutely brilliant tactical and management skills. And he had feet in so many different camps and stayed on the topside of all the people in those camps. He made a point of surrounding himself with people of substance.

"Once we went back to play a game in New York and Bill and I were sitting in the lunchroom of the hotel. I listened to him talk for fifteen minutes to a busboy who was clearing the table about the differences in West Coast teams and personnel and East Coast or Midwest teams and personnel. It got down to the level that people from the west rarely wear hats and seldom smoke. And Bill was sitting there, fascinated to be talking with a busboy about regional cultural differences. Then that night, after the team's walkthrough, I went up to his room and there are several people sitting around. One was a guy involved in New York's fashion industry. Another was Admiral Stockdale, the former Vietnam POW. Then there was me, this former sixties radical. And also a California state assemblyman who had flown out on the plane with us. And Bill was leading this discussion about war and peace, about how the inner-city sets fashion trends, and what politically can be done about some of the challenges that face inner-city youth. He had this conversation going and everybody was into it and by the end of the thing, he's got it all integrated. It was a fascinating conversation addressing complex and profound subjects and who's sitting at the center of it? A football coach. Who would've believed it?"

Bill Walsh, Edward DeBartolo Sr. (second from right), and Eddie DeBartolo in the locker room after the miraculous win over Cincinnati, 1987

DIMINISHING RETURNS

There is no way to know exactly when Bill Walsh's football career reached the point of diminishing personal returns, regardless of his on-the-field successes, but the process was certainly under way in the 1987 off-season. By then, his relationship with Geri was again in turmoil and he was spending a lot of his free time at a house in Los Altos Hills he was sharing with Kristine Hanson, who became an eyewitness to what she would later describe as his "descent." Henceforth, the devastation after losses would be so magnified and the elation after wins so minimized that the latter would no longer compensate for the former, steadily dragging Bill into a state of cumulative despair in which he was dependent on his psychic reserves to maintain any forward momentum, until those too would be exhausted and he would start coming apart. "I was a tortured person," Bill would later admit. "I felt the failure so personally and blamed myself for the losses and absorbed a tremendous amount of accumulated frustration until eventually I couldn't get out from under it all. Every loss was a mortifying experience and every year it became tougher to lose, not easier. And you can't live that way very long. You can only attack that part of your nervous system so many times."

Walsh had begun wanting out during the previous season, and according to Kristine, "he entertained the idea of not returning for 1987. By then the losses were already becoming major depressions. Often for days afterward, he wouldn't talk and couldn't eat. And it would eventually get a lot worse. Mostly he was disappointed in himself. He blamed himself for every time his team fell short. And when he kept falling short it shook his confidence. He started saying, 'I know how to build a team but I can't sustain it,' and talking about wanting to take an expansion job where he could start a new team. He talked about how he would do everything different and build a team and do it right. But he couldn't quite bring himself to leave the Niners yet. He didn't want to leave with people thinking he couldn't make it back to the top."

Bill raised none of these issues with Eddie when they met in Youngstown that January for their annual off-season conclave, pointing toward the next year's team and establishing the franchise's operating budget. Walsh was fresh from a week in Palm Springs playing tennis and, tan and rested, looked a lot more rejuvenated than he actually felt.

Bill told his boss there was both good and bad news. The good news was that, once again, they would begin this year's quest close to the summit. The bad news was they would have to rebuild before they could reasonably expect to reach it and this was the year that rebuilding would have to begin. He thought 1988 would be a transition year as well, but—convinced that the 1985 and '86 drafts had provided the backbone for a new and better team—he expected to return to the Super Bowl in 1989.

Eddie D. did not like hearing that but grudgingly accepted Bill's assessment and promised to swallow hard and adjust his expectations accordingly.

That, of course, would be easier said than done.

The central element in Walsh's reconstruction plans was the position of quarterback. Bill had been worried about Joe Montana's ability to stay healthy even before his back surgery and had already unsuccessfully shopped around the league looking for the right player to begin grooming as Joe's successor, then did so again in the weeks after Joe went down to back surgery. Going into this off-season, Bill had even more severe doubts about how much longer Montana would last, despite Joe's extraordinary recovery, and knew he had to find a quality backup at the very least, hopefully someone who could step right in and play if necessary.

One of his prime candidates was Steve Young, a left-handed quarterback who was then the property of the Tampa Bay Buccaneers. By 1987, Young was a legendary prospect who had yet to live up to his advance billing. He had set passing records as a collegian at BYU, compiling a 70 percent completion rate in a sophisticated offense, as well as being his team's best runner whenever he was forced to scramble. Touted as having an unprecedented combination of skills, he was drafted by the Cincinnati Bengals with the first pick in 1984's first round, but Paul Brown's team didn't offer anything close to what Young's agent thought he was worth, so the agent turned to the USFL, then at its brief competitive peak. The rival league's Los Angeles franchise made a record offer to the BYU signal caller—including a $2.5 million signing bonus, some $350,000 a year in salary, plus a $37 million annuity that would begin making payouts to him within six years—and he joined the new league. The team he played on in Los Angeles was extraordinarily bad and he spent the two seasons before the USFL folded running for his life every time he went back to pass.

In the aftermath of the rival league's collapse, the NFL held a supplemental draft to divide up the rights to USFL players and Steve was claimed by the Tampa Bay Buccaneers. The Bucs' owner, Hugh Culverhouse, paid Young a $1.1 million signing bonus to persuade him to come to Tampa and declared, "You're my quarterback and you'll always be my quarterback." As comforting as that might have sounded, Steve was once again consigned to a squad that was largely devoid of talent—winning only four games over the next two years—and he bore the brunt of its failures. His coach at Tampa, Young later explained, "would send me out there and say, 'Make something happen.'" The result was, once again, a lot of time spent scrambling to escape an unblocked pass rush. As a consequence, one Bay Area sportswriter noted, Young, "a swift, elusive runner" was considered, by 1987, "a one dimensional quarterback prone to forsaking the pass and taking off downfield, sometimes desperately, to try to move the ball on his own . . . a hopeless, undisciplined scrambler." The Bucs, holding the first pick in this year's draft, had already made it clear they intended to select

Vinny Testaverde, a quarterback from the University of Miami, abandoning their experiment with Young at the helm.

A lot more teams than just the Bucs had given up on his potential by then, but not Walsh. Bill had a longstanding interest in Young. "Don Klosterman, the USFL general manager who had first signed him, was a very good friend of mine," Walsh explained. "We talked about Steve at the time and he said that this was a great athlete who would be a great quarterback. Then he was in the supplemental draft where his rights went to Tampa Bay. We did everything we could, scrupulous or unscrupulous, to get those rights—but we couldn't do it. We wanted to trade picks with Tampa but the league forbade that as part of the format for the supplemental draft. So he went to Tampa instead. Then we played them with him at quarterback and he didn't do that well. What they were having him do wasn't very good. We beat them, but in the back of my mind was everything Don had said and what I'd seen.

"Everybody acknowledged that he was a really good athlete who didn't perform that well. At the professional level, Steve's lack of fundamentals had betrayed him. He just didn't adjust to the quick, explosive players in the NFL. In college, Steve could take his time and throw off his back foot from anywhere on the field, and if he didn't have a receiver open, he could run. But even in the USFL, pass rushers were getting closer to him, so consequently he flushed from the pocket and started scrambling and running before patterns developed downfield. When he reported to Tampa, the style of football again forced him to run far too often. The patterns simply took too long to develop and he didn't have alternate receivers. His team was continually behind so the pass rush was on him every play. Most coaches and general managers of other organizations thought he was too inconsistent to be a starting quarterback, not realizing that with hard work on mechanics and techniques, you can measurably develop a man's consistency."

The prospects of actually securing Young for the Forty Niners, however, looked relatively bleak. Bill had tried to trade for him during the previous season but Tampa Bay's coach and general manager at the time had refused. Then Tampa Bay fired that coach and the man who replaced him responded to Walsh's renewed inquiries by insisting on a first- and a third-round draft pick in exchange, too high a price in Walsh's estimation for a backup quarterback. This impasse over a possible trade to the Niners was broken by Young himself, shortly before the March league meetings in Maui.

By that point, the Bucs were deep into negotiating a possible deal with either the St. Louis Cardinals or the Green Bay Packers, both of whom were among the league's worst and both of whom were willing to part with a number one pick plus others to get Young. But when Culverhouse had first signed Young, they had agreed informally that if for some reason the relationship didn't work out, Culverhouse would give Young some say in where he went next. Steve now called Culverhouse on that promise. He desperately wanted to avoid trying to rescue another team at its nadir and asked the owner to send him somewhere where he had a chance to play for a championship. Culverhouse agreed to see what they could do. "He had put his trust in me," the owner explained, "and I felt we owed him something." Young had been unsure about the Niners at first—given Montana's stature and the possibility of sitting the bench—but a conversation with former Niner Steve DeBerg had allayed his fears. DeBerg told him Walsh was the best quarterback coach in the league by far, so, when Culverhouse asked where he would like to go, Steve told him San Francisco.

Culverhouse then pursued that possibility at the Maui meetings. Eddie was there and when the Niners' owner raised the subject of Young directly, the Bucs owner gave a positive response, effectively restarting the previously stalled negotiations. "I have a special athlete," he told DeBartolo, and "you can have him if you want him."

As Walsh and McVay began dickering with the Bucs over price, Bill felt he had to eyeball Steve Young up close before the deal went any further. He arranged to work Young out at BYU, close to the quarterback's Utah home. The two hit it off immediately—though, as Young remembered it, the first thing Walsh remarked on was that Steve wasn't really six feet two, the height the Bucs listed him at in their game day program. When Young inquired about the Niners' future plans, Bill said that he didn't think Joe would be able to play much longer, if at all. To disguise what was obviously tampering with a player already under contract, their workout session was billed as Walsh scouting some BYU receivers, but the real point, of course, was to watch Steve throw. "I told Steve what passes to throw so I'd get to see all the passes I wanted," Bill explained. "He threw the ball well. He had a great arm—short, long, and in between. When I came back to the Bay Area I told John McVay that he was a little smaller than I'd thought but we had to go for him." In the meantime, Walsh pestered Mike Holmgren, who had coached Young in college, for information. "Bill came in every day," Mike recalled, "asking 'What do you think? Tell me about him.' He thought a lot about the possible impact on Montana too. A deal like that sends messages to everybody."

The exchange the teams eventually agreed to in negotiations between Walsh and the Tampa Bay general manager was a second- and a fourth-round pick for Young, plus whatever was tacked on by Culverhouse in direct talks with Eddie. The Tampa Bay owner, though willing to settle for less valuable draft picks than he might have had elsewhere, knew Eddie and his dad were flush and pointed out that he had invested a million dollars up front in securing a contract with Young and now wanted the Forty Niners to throw that much cash into the exchange as well. Eddie D. was traveling in Florida for the family corporation and had been calling Bill regularly from pay phones along the way, honing their strategy for securing Young. This time he called and asked Bill point-blank if he really wanted to make the deal. A million dollars was a lot of money. Walsh assured him he really did.

"Okay," Eddie answered. "You've got him."

DeBartolo immediately called Culverhouse and agreed to the million. Young learned he was a Niner when his agent had him paged off a Utah golf course.

It was easily the best trade Bill Walsh ever made. A day after it was announced, two other NFL teams called, each offering two number one picks for him. Bill refused and Steve Young would eventually—after playing a central role in the most prominent coaching controversy of Walsh's career—go on to become perhaps the best left-handed quarterback ever to play the professional game.

The other part of Walsh's reconstruction plan was, of course, the ongoing housecleaning of veterans past their prime. Wendell Tyler retired in January after a visit with Bill. Russ Francis was talked out of retiring by Walsh but by November, hobbled by injuries, would retire anyway. The offensive line lost John Ayers against his will and Fred Quillan was benched before eventually being released, with Randy Cross moving over to center and the vacant guard spots going to Jesse Sapolu from the 1983 draft and Guy McIntyre from '84. The Niners' 1987 draft featured Harris Barton, an offensive tackle from the University of North Carolina, in the first round and Jeff Bregel, a guard from USC, in the second. Barton would replace Keith Fahnhorst in the starting lineup before the year was out. Change was clearly the order of the day.

The biggest retirement drama surrounded Dwight Clark, the tenth-round choice in 1979 who had become an All-Pro and whose catch against Dallas during the Miracle had made him a Forty Niners' saint. Dwight endured his second knee surgery in January—the first having come several years earlier—followed by a third in April to figure out why the second hadn't worked. He was at the Redwood City headquarters rehabbing from the third when he got a message that Bill wanted to see him in his office. Dwight went upstairs with a feeling of dread. He knew this conversation was going to be about his future.

Walsh had his business face on and stared at the wide receiver before finally expressing worry that Dwight's knee was so bad he'd end up crippled if he didn't retire. "I can't recommend you play," Bill said. The coach's tone was all concern about Clark's health and he made no mention of the receiver's diminished productivity.

Despite his anticipation, Dwight admitted, Bill's statement "caught me totally by surprise. When you hear that coming out of the head coach's mouth—it blew me away." Clark told Bill that the doctors had figured out what was needed in his knee and he was going to have a fourth surgery to correct it when he recovered from the third and he'd like to at least have a shot at making the team in training camp.

Bill considered Dwight's request for a moment and then allowed that giving him such a chance was fair enough.

Then there was more silence. "We just looked at each other," Dwight recalled. The quiet ended when they both said, "Oh, well," and Dwight went back downstairs. He would spend the next year "being mad at Bill." Clark later described their conversation as like being told that he was about to die. He was plagued by self-doubt well into the summer.

Dwight persevered nonetheless and by halfway through training camp was able to cut and move and run crisp patterns. And his hands were still as good as any in the league. Bill approached him again during camp. "He told me that if I did make the team, he was going to ask me to take half the salary my contract called for," Dwight explained. "I was making a ton of money but being treated like that bothered me. Then later in camp, I went out to dinner with Eddie and some of his friends. Eddie started asking me if I was going to make the team and how I was feeling. I told him I thought I was okay. But I said the damn coach wanted me to take half pay. Eddie didn't say anything about it but when I did make the team, Bill and I never had a conversation about the pay cut and the pay cut never happened. I figured Eddie must have said something. But I knew I was done at the end of this season and I announced I would retire when it was over." In the meantime, he would play sparingly.

Despite Bill's best efforts to retool, the football pundits seemed far from impressed with his squad on the verge of the season. "The 49ers haven't improved markedly over last year," the *Chronicle* declared. "The only thing that's certain is that either they or the Rams will win the NFC West. . . . From this vantage point, it looks like second place for the 49ers in 1987, probably a 9-7 record. They're good, but they have too many questions to be considered a favorite for the division title." If it came true, 9-7 would be the Niners' worst record since 1982.

And they started off looking like even that might be a stretch.

The Forty Niners opened the season in Pittsburgh—the first time the two teams had met since the Steelers inflicted the lone loss on the Niners in 1984—and Pittsburgh, coming off a 6-10 record in 1986, still seemed to have their number. "Certainly the 49ers didn't look like a legitimate NFL team," one columnist noted. "They fumbled the ball and dropped passes and got in each other's way like a bunch of second rate comedians at a burlesque house." The final score was Pittsburgh 30, San Francisco 17, and the game wasn't that close. At the press conference afterward, Walsh's torment was barely concealed—"staring down at the floor," according to one reporter, "as if he had lost something valuable, or was looking for a trap door for a quick exit."

The next week the Niners were back on the road in Cincinnati and again stumbled out of the blocks. At halftime the Bengals led 20–7. In the third quarter, however, Montana rose to the occasion and directed his team to a 20–20 tie going into the fourth. Then it was Cincinnati's turn again and they went up 26–20 and had the Niners pinned deep in their own territory, fourth and eighteen, with a little more than a minute to play. At that point, Walsh made what was, in the moment, a very controversial decision. Rather than try some kind of Hail Mary play in a desperate attempt at a first down, he elected to punt—thinking that with two time-outs left they just might get the ball back for a last try. The Bengals took possession at their own forty-five. Bill was hoping against hope for a Cincinnati mistake that would put them back in the game, but never imagined he would get the one he did.

Cincinnati coach Sam Wyche was intent on running the clock out and had his quarterback keep the ball on the first two downs, while the Niners used up their time outs. Next, with forty-five seconds left, the Bengals quarterback fell on the ball back at the thirty-five. Then Cincinnati's coach made a far more controversial decision than the one Bill had made. Faced with a fourth down, Wyche took a delay of game penalty after running the game clock down to six seconds. Then, rather than punt the ball into the Niners' territory, he elected to try to run the clock out instead and called a sweep to the left. Before the play could develop, however, Niners tackle Kevin Fagan knifed into the backfield and dropped the ball carrier at the Bengals' twenty-five. The clock stopped on the change of possession with two seconds remaining.

Bill immediately rushed his offense onto the field. The Bengals were in a state of confusion and didn't call time to regroup. The play Walsh had already called—76 Tandem Left All Go—split three receivers left and Jerry Rice to the right. At the line of scrimmage, Montana saw that the Bengals—despite having a defense called in which Rice would be double-teamed—were, because of someone's confusion, defending Rice with a rookie cornerback one-on-one. Joe signaled Jerry to head straight to the end zone rather than angling to the corner. Joe then took the snap and lofted the ball high in Jerry's direction. Rice ran across the goal line, pivoted so the shorter cornerback was pinned behind him, outjumped the defender and caught the desperation pass for a touchdown. The extra point made the game, seemingly a certain loss six seconds earlier, 27–26 in San Francisco's favor.

Walsh was so happy he skipped all the way to the locker room. Eddie D., pissed off at what he thought was his team's second straight failure, had already gone to his limo in the parking lot before the final play and had to be fetched back after initially refusing to believe that the man who told him what happened wasn't pulling his leg. When he got to the locker room, the scene was ecstatic. "That particular dressing room rivaled the one after we beat the Steelers in Pittsburgh in '81," Walsh remembered. "It was absolute mania. Everybody was wild, jumping and screaming. You couldn't believe it. It just went on and on, players screaming and hugging each other, lying on the floor and kicking the lockers."

Having secured a 1-1 record by their fingernails, Bill had no idea what to expect from his team the next week.

But before he could find out, a players strike intervened, just as it had under similar circumstances in 1982.

Walsh had seen the strike coming since joining the Competition Committee at the NFL's Maui conclave that spring. "We worked very hard for two straight weeks," Bill said of those meetings. "We worked every day, all day. These were my first with the committee so I learned about the political hierarchy of the NFL in those sessions. I don't think I was ever totally accepted, but I think I contributed. Tex Schramm, the president of the Dallas Cowboys, was the key member. Tex basically managed the league as far as the owners were concerned. If you took him on it was going to be a battle to the death. He was opinionated and often he was right; occasionally he was wrong." At Maui, Schramm was adamant that if the union struck, the NFL shouldn't close down like it did in 1982, but continue the season using strike breakers to replace their regulars. Walsh was leery of this approach, but Schramm's proposal soon became the NFL's policy.

And, leery or not, Walsh and the Niners excelled at preparations for that eventuality. "Bill knew there was going to be a strike," John McVay explained, "so we decided to sign a whole bunch of guys and if there was a strike, then we'd have them trained. That year we had 128 players in camp, to prepare them for two weeks before we had to cut them at the mandatory cutdown point. So when Tex Schramm decides we're going to play through the strike, we had all these kids we'd trained and we brought them back." As they were released at training camp, the possible replacements signed an agreement to return to the club if needed and were paid a thousand dollars to seal the deal. Their names were then placed on a "ready list," along with others the Niners thought might be available for use. "Our contingency plan gave us a great advantage over the competition," Bill later pointed out.

Certainly most teams weren't nearly as ready as the Niners, having refused to believe that a strike would actually happen or been unwilling to aggravate their regulars by preparing to break their strike. The issue this year was over players' rights to free agency, allowing them to negotiate with any and all teams after their initial contract with the franchise that had drafted them expired. Eddie D. was a vociferous opponent of the idea and was the first owner to come out publicly for playing the season, strike or not. "Let them strike," he railed two weeks before the walkout was called. "Free agency is non-negotiable. Let's get on with the other issues. Come on, these guys are making a lot of money, and they're going to make a lot more." Eddie even went so far as to predict that no more than fifteen or twenty Niners would join a strike if it were called—saying he would be "astonished" if it was any more than that—and claimed his franchise would field "a quality team without recalling any guys." Bill only said he hoped the two sides would continue to negotiate while the players continued to play.

As it turned out, DeBartolo's prediction was far off the mark. A strike vote was held by the Forty Niners players on the Tuesday after their miraculous Cincinnati win and only a dozen of the fifty-four union members present voted against the strike. While the union rep, Keith Fahnhorst, had severe doubts about the wisdom of the NFLPA's strategy—"I was hoping that neither the management or the union side would be stupid enough to get in this position again"—he felt that a Niners refusal to join in would cripple the union's effort and they had no choice but to maintain solidarity with the rest of the teams. "We had to not only make a decision for ourselves," Fahnhorst explained, "but we had to decide on how it would affect the rest of the league. I think we all agreed that Eddie DeBartolo has treated us well here. It's certainly not the Forty Niners going on strike against him. But we're not an isolated entity." None of them had illusions about the financial consequences. Players were paid their annual salaries in weekly checks during the season. Each missed game was a loss of one sixteenth of their total football income.

The NFL gave the teams a bye week to get their new replacement squads together—costing strikers at least one week's salary—and the season, now shortened to fifteen games, was scheduled to continue on the first Sunday in October, twelve days after the strike began. The Niners' first replacement game would be in New York against the Giants on Monday night. In the meantime, defections popped up around the league as union members—including two or three large groups—began crossing picket lines and returning to work. Part of Schramm's plan was to recruit as many defectors as possible so the strike would collapse and the owners—well aware that San Francisco's players were largely lukewarm strikers at best—were expecting the Niners to play a critical role in that process. With the strike less than a week old, a group of eleven Niners—including Joe Montana, Dwight Clark, and Roger Craig—leaked word to the press that they were about to return to work. The move was planned for the Friday before the Giants game, the last day they could report and still be eligible to play that weekend and be paid for the week.

That Friday, a picket line was set up outside 711 Nevada Street and a swarm of press was there to record the return of Montana and the others in what was anticipated to be the biggest national sports story of the day. Unbeknownst to them, however, Walsh had snuck out and was secretly meeting with the defectors at Stanley's Deli in Redwood City, four blocks from team headquarters, having arranged to do so over the phone after a consultation with Eddie. "I felt it wouldn't serve anybody for them to come back this week," he remembered. "I thought the strike would be settled once the first replacement game was played. The NFL expected us to entice our players back, but I didn't want to break the team, to affect the camaraderie and compatibility of our squad. Nor did I want the union broken." After a lengthy discussion, Walsh secured an agreement from the defectors to postpone their return for another week in the interest of team unity. Some of the lesser players among them, however, were under severe financial pressure. Bill promised them a loan of half their weekly salary to tide them over for another week of striking and implied that the "loan" would never have to be repaid to the team.

Afterward, "when I arrived back at our Redwood City facility moments before noon," Walsh recalled, "I was hit from every angle by the mass of reporters. Where were Montana and the others as rumored? I tried to honestly explain without misleading people, but naturally I couldn't tell them everything that had been agreed upon. Then I caught hell from the rest of the league, because everybody had been waiting for a substantial number of Forty Niners to return. We were supposed to break the strike, but we were also supposed to accept our team being divided. Nobody seemed to care about that. They just wanted the Forty Niners to lead the charge. I got on the phone immediately with Eddie and he responded with, 'I don't care what the NFL tells us to do. If this is the way you want to do it, we'll take them on.'"

On Monday night, Walsh took his replacements into Giants Stadium. Their bus was greeted with obscene gestures and catcalls as they passed through the picket line manned by fifty striking Giants and Jets, but otherwise their arrival was uneventful. The game itself was hardly the usual Niners fare. "Under a full moon," the *Chronicle* reported, "the 49ers actually blocked a punt and scored on the play; had a successful onsides kick that traveled about forty yards; and had a scoring bomb out of the wishbone formation." The final score was San Francisco 41, New York 21.

The strike, however, didn't end as Walsh had assumed, and the eleven defectors, led by Montana, returned to work the next Tuesday. That it was only eleven, however, was seen as a major disappointment to the owners, who had been fueling expectations of a far larger collapse. Altogether, fourteen Niners had now broken the strike. Only Dallas and St. Louis had more, with eighteen apiece. Nationally, 145 out of the league's 1,600 players had now crossed the picket lines. The next Sunday, eight of the eleven most recent Niners defectors started against Atlanta on the road. Montana stayed in the game long enough to throw eight passes, completing five, including a touchdown to Clark. It ended San Francisco 25, Atlanta 17. On the sidelines, Bill coached the game without his headset. When asked why by one of his friends afterward, he explained that he didn't want his striking players who were watching to see him looking involved. He let his assistants manage the game.

The following week, the Forty Niners were scheduled to play St. Louis at Candlestick, but before that, the NFLPA recognized it could only lose if it went on like this and instructed all its members to return to work without a contract. The union planned to continue negotiations and to file an antitrust lawsuit in pursuit of its program instead. The strikers reported to their teams all around the league that Thursday, but the NFL prohibited them from playing that weekend or being paid any more than a $700 training camp fee for that week because Wednesday had been the management's deadline for playing that weekend. Walsh's replacement team plus defectors had to take on the Cardinals by themselves. Montana played the whole game, completing thirty-one of thirty-nine, and the Niners squeaked by, 34–28.

The rest of the season would be played by Bill's real team, but thanks to the strike breakers, the squad that only a last-second prayer had saved from being winless would now start over with four wins and only one loss.

What remained to be seen, however, was just how much of a "team" Walsh had left.

The Forty Niner locker room after the loss to Minnesota in the 1987 playoffs

29

FOOL'S GOLD

The Forty Niners' first day back from the strike was explosive. "We weren't really talking to each other," Ronnie Lott explained. "I overheard players issuing threats. 'I'm going to get that guy,' referring to teammates who had crossed the picket line. . . . It was the first time I ever heard such backbiting and bitter animosity [in our locker room]. We were no longer a family [and] I felt the 49ers were in danger of disintegrating."

After their initial practice, Walsh gathered his players in a semicircle out on one of the fields. He insisted they all had to put the strike behind them. "I know there are hard feelings," he said. "There have been many unkind words said. But we should let things go and they'll take care of themselves."

Bill had hoped his talk would suffice to initiate the team's healing, but Lott, a committed striker, was not so easily satisfied. He was angry about the under-the-table payments Walsh had made to the initial group of defectors—"Walsh thought he was keeping the team together but he was breaking us apart"—and wanted some answers before anyone moved on. "Why did those guys get paid?" he demanded.

When no answer was forthcoming, Ronnie went off on the strikebreakers and demanded they apologize to everyone else.

Russ Francis, an early defector, took offense, as did several others, and players began shouting back and forth. Bill tried to defuse things by asking Keith Fahnhorst, the union rep, what he thought. Fahnhorst said something conciliatory but Lott was too angry for that. "We're supposed to be a team," he shouted. "We answer to each other."

That remark then set Bill off. "This is my team," he shouted back, "and I'm going to do this my way."

Another verbal free-for-all ensued with Walsh and Lott screaming back and forth at each other, so loud they could be heard at the other end of the field. At one point Ronnie had to be physically restrained from jumping on his coach.

Finally Bill stopped and announced he was going to leave the players to work it out themselves, but when they left the field he didn't want to hear any more about it. He wanted it resolved and behind them.

With that, Walsh walked over to where Dr. Harry Edwards was standing, some forty yards away.

"We stood there while the team was thrashing it out," Edwards recalled, "and Bill didn't say a thing. He just stood there. Finally he turned to me and said, 'You know why Ronnie Lott and I knock heads so much?' Then he answered his own question: 'Because we're so much alike. That's why I love him. He's so much like me. You watch this. Five minutes after the team breaks up on the field, he'll be over here apologizing.' I asked Bill how he knew that. He said, 'Because that's what I would do.' Not three minutes after they broke up on the field, we could see Ronnie shaking hands and hugging some of the guys that had come back during the strike. Then he walked directly off the field over to where we were standing and said, 'Bill, you just have to understand. I had to get that off my chest. I can't have that just floating around during the whole year. It'll impede what we've got to get done.' Bill told him that he understood and said, 'You were right.' Ronnie answered that he just wanted Bill to know there wasn't any disrespect. Bill said he knew that. When Ronnie walked away, Bill looked at me and laughed. It had happened just like he predicted. He knew his guys that well."

Eddie D. also did his best to smooth the strike's aftermath. Recognizing how contentious the issue of the team's "loans" had become, he decided to widen the financial circle and sent a letter to all his players declaring that in the spirit of Forty Niners unity he would match the bonuses paid to players by the league upon making the playoffs, adding at least six thousand dollars to their paychecks, assuming they qualified for the postseason. The players loved it, but at the end of the season, when the NFL learned of what he'd done, it would fine Eddie fifty thousand dollars—the maximum allowed in the league's bylaws—for violating the policy banning specific financial inducements to win games. Eddie D.'s players would all chip in to pay his fine.

Meanwhile, Walsh found himself in something of a no-man's-land. On the one hand, he remembered, "I was really resented by some of the players. There were some tense moments with some of the leaders of the team about me making those loans and allowing guys to come back. People were very challenging. It was a shaky time."

On the other hand, Bill was also a pariah in management circles once the rest of the league learned about his payments to keep people from returning to work. "The repercussions toward me were something," he remembered. "They caught up with me at the next Competition Committee meeting. Tex Schramm was very vehement about me and what I stood for—that I didn't show commitment and loyalty to the National Football League. He was very upset. So was Don Shula. One night at dinner, when we were socializing, and everybody had a drink or two, Tex attacked me right in front of the wives and everybody. He just released it all on me and he was really pissed off, shouting at me. I tried to calm him. I said there was more to this than we think and a lot of things like that, but he wouldn't hear it. Finally the wives calmed everybody down. It was quite an experience. All in all, though, I think I did the right thing. I really do."

In the immediate moment, however, Bill Walsh went into the first post-strike weekend wondering if his fractured team was about to have a repeat of 1982.

Instead, what happened next felt a lot more like 1981 than the disaster that had followed it.

First the Niners managed a two-point win in New Orleans against the resurgent Saints despite looking decidedly rusty. Then they traveled to Los Angeles to tangle with the Rams, the preseason pick to be their chief competition for the division crown. Dissatisfied with how his offense had looked during the previous game, Walsh decided to make some critical changes for this one, moving Roger Craig to halfback from fullback and inserting Tom Rathman, from the 1986 draft, in the fullback slot. Since Keith Fahnhorst had a neck injury, he also inserted this year's number one pick, Harris Barton, at right tackle. Both moves would quickly become permanent. At left tackle, Bubba Paris had a muscle pull in his calf and was replaced by second-year man Steve Wallace.

And all the changes worked. The Rams game was, in the *Chronicle*'s words, "a butt kicking performance," pure and simple. Roger Craig picked up 104 yards on twenty-three carries behind the reformulated offensive line, and his backfield mates brought the team's total running yardage to 149, averaging 4.1 yards per carry. Montana also had a big day, completing two thirds of his passes and throwing for three touchdowns. The most impressive of those was a deep route to Jerry Rice, who was in single coverage but seemed to be blanketed by the defensive back. Joe nonetheless found him with a laser beam of a throw and Rice took it fifty-one yards to the end zone. The final score was 31–10 and was only that close because the Rams scored a meaningless touchdown in the last two minutes of the game.

Next came the Houston Oilers—who were on their way to the playoffs but nonetheless fell by a touchdown, 27-20. Walsh's team was now 7-1 and at his regular Tuesday press conference the following week, he was in good humor, making a succession of wisecracks at the press's expense. Still, Bill put an occasional edge on his remarks. "I didn't see enough about 'Will they improve?'" he complained about all of the preseason prognostication dismissing his squad's chances. "Instead it was 'This is a sorry, worn-out team.'" He also took the media to task for having been so hard on Jerry Rice during his rookie season when he dropped all those passes. When one reporter asked about the previous press conferences when Walsh had angrily chastised them with pointed remarks about "those who wrote us off early," he made light of it. "I was teasing," he laughed. "I don't get mad. There's no need to. I'm right at the end of my coaching career." As usual, however, he declined to expand on that last remark.

Walsh's good mood took a serious nosedive the day after that press conference. At Wednesday's practice, Montana was holding for the kicker and sprained the index finger on his throwing hand. The next day he couldn't even grip a ball. Walsh then announced that if Joe was unable to go in their upcoming home game with New Orleans—emerging as the Forty Niners' actual chief rival for the division crown this season—he would be giving Steve Young his first start.

When Bill signed Young, he had imagined "a great one-two punch with Steve occasionally alternating with Joe, forcing opponents to account for both a right-handed and a left-handed quarterback," but so far Young had yet to throw a pass in the regular season. "Coming to the Niners had been a smooth transition," Steve recalled. "The playbook was similar to the one at BYU. And I think I was a kind of interesting and intriguing project for Bill. Because I wasn't starting, he wasn't that focused on me and just seemed to enjoy the give-and-take between us. Still, I found the not playing frustrating beyond measure." To compensate for his inactivity, Young spent extra time with Holmgren after practices keeping his footwork in sync and trying to stay ready. When told he would start against the Saints, Steve pronounced himself more than prepared.

And he looked good in the first quarter. With the Niners down 3–0, he led the team into New Orleans' territory, using both his arm and his legs. He averaged more than six yards a carry running that quarter and was five of six as a passer. His first drive ended with a forty-six-yard field goal attempt that Wersching missed, but Young's second drive was more successful. Early in it, he absorbed a vicious hit from a New Orleans linebacker but seemed unaffected. He followed that play by handing the ball off several times and running once himself for nine yards. Then, just over the midfield stripe, Young went back to pass and almost fell flat, ending up down on one knee. Regaining his footing, he spotted Jerry Rice open deep and hit him for a forty-six-yard score. The pass carried almost sixty yards on the fly. When Young got to the sideline afterward, however, it quickly became obvious that the blow he had absorbed early in the drive had rung his bell. Steve was dizzy and unsure of which quarter it was, the sideline doctors quickly diagnosed concussion, and despite Young's pleading to go back in, Bill sat the left-hander for the rest of the game.

That put the offense back in Joe's hands, bum finger or not. Unfortunately, this wasn't one of Montana's better games. On his first series in the second quarter, one of his passes bounced off tight end Ron Heller's hands and into the arms of a Saints defender. That led to a New Orleans field goal, reducing San Francisco's lead to one. The very next series, Joe threw another interception that led to another New Orleans field goal, making the score 9–7 Saints. Late in the third quarter, down 16–14, the Niners lined up for a forty-seven-yard field goal to take the lead, but this time Heller missed his assignment; the kick was blocked, scooped up by the Saints, and run sixty-one yards for a touchdown, leaving the Niners down 23–14. In the fourth quarter, San Francisco narrowed the gap with a field goal and then Joe Montana started looking like himself. After moving the team into New Orleans territory, he hit Heller with a twenty-nine-yard touchdown strike, finally giving the Niners their first lead since the first quarter, 24–23, with 2:54 left on the clock. The game was now in the hands of the defense, but they dropped it, allowing the Saints to pass their way down the field for the winning field goal with 1:06 left. Joe led the Niners back in search of the win but time ran out before they reached field goal range.

In the locker room afterward, Walsh blamed himself. "The responsibility's on my shoulders," he acknowledged, "no one else's." He then holed up in his office for the next two days, speaking to no one.

The judgments in the press were harsh on all concerned. Seven wins or not, the Forty Niners "simply were not good enough," one columnist typically noted. All of the flaws "that showed yesterday point to a team that is clearly not of Super Bowl caliber. . . . Instead of looking at a potential Super Bowl team, we are looking at a team that will have to scramble [just] to win its division."

The Niners, however, didn't seem to be reading the papers. Bill regained his balance and the team rebounded from their second loss with three straight wins. By then nothing much was being heard from the doubters and the Bay Area had already begun anticipating another Super Bowl.

The same was true in Youngstown. Eddie D. had apparently forgotten all Bill's talk about "a rebuilding year" by now and was making space for a third championship in his trophy case. He was also raving about the job Bill had done. And, just as Eddie laid into Walsh when he was unhappy, he also made a point of expressing his appreciation when he was pleased. An example of this showed up on one of the surging Niners' road trips.

It was Saturday afternoon and Walsh was back in his room at the team's hotel. He often brought his old buddies from San Jose State along to games and one of them was with him that afternoon, shooting the shit and watching a college game on TV, when there was a knock on the door. Standing outside was a very attractive woman, dispatched by Eddie, wearing nothing but a T-shirt. She had a sign hung off her neck that said I'M YOURS, BILL.

Walsh politely declined his boss's present and sent her on her way.

Back in the room, he turned to his friend. "I can't," Bill explained, motioning at the closed door. "If I get wrapped up in that, he'll have me."

Despite their detractors, the Forty Niners only seemed to get better as they turned down the home stretch.

Their next game was on Monday night, at Candlestick against Mike Ditka's Chicago Bears. The Niners, with only two losses, were a game in front of New Orleans in the Western Division of the NFC, and the Bears, with only three losses, were headed for the NFC's Central Division title. "The hoopla about the 49ers–Bears game," the *Chronicle* noted, had already taken on "Super Bowl proportions." The two teams had not met since the Bears thrashed the Niners during the 1985 season—holding the San Francisco offense to its lowest totals ever under Walsh—and Bill was doing his usual poor-mouthing leading up to Monday night. Asked what his goals were for the running game against the fearsome Chicago defense, he allowed that "if we had them, they'd be so minimal you wouldn't recognize them as goals." He called the Bears middle linebacker "the best linebacker in football" and their defensive talent "above and beyond that of anyone else in the league." On top of that, "they have great running backs" and "a world championship offensive line." He only hoped the Niners could make a game of it.

The crowd for the contest was the largest ever to watch a football game at Candlestick. The two teams began the first quarter trading punts. On the Niners' second series, Montana led the team to just inside the Bears' twenty-yard line. Then, with a play-action pass called, Joe retreated from center and faked a handoff to Roger Craig, but as he retracted the ball and continued to fade back, he stumbled over Craig's foot and collapsed in a heap. Montana had to be helped off the field and straight into the locker room. He emerged later on crutches, having suffered a hamstring tear that was expected to keep him out at least two weeks. While Montana was being tended to, Steve Young was warming up, and after a brief conclave with Walsh, he took the field. For his first play, Bill called Young's number—a quarterback keeper around left end—hoping to shake loose whatever jitters Steve had with a little contact before he had him attempt a pass. Young gained eighteen yards, running over a Bears tackler before being downed on the

Chicago one. Two plays later, he hit Jerry Rice for his first touchdown and the rout was on.

Young's second touchdown pass was to Dwight Clark, making the score 14–0, and two field goals before the half raised it to 20–0. Things only got worse for Chicago in the second half. The Niners had an eighty-three-yard punt return for a touchdown in the third quarter, plus an exquisite finger-tip catch by Rice for another touchdown spanning sixteen yards, then a more ordinary two-yard catch by Jerry in the fourth quarter for yet another. When the game was over, Rice had tied the NFL records for most touchdown catches in a season and most consecutive games with a touchdown catch. And the Chicago offense had turned the ball over six times. The closest the Bears came to a score was a shanked forty-yard field goal attempt. The final score was San Francisco 41, Chicago 0. The Niners' fans were on Ditka's case so relentlessly as he walked past them on his way off the field that the Chicago coach threw his wad of chewing gum at his hecklers in frustration.

The reviews of Young's performance afterward were raves. "All season long he has been a first string quarterback without a gig," one columnist wrote. "Last night, he got his chance and he did everything a quarterback has to do. . . . He ran out of the pocket and left the Bear defenders stumbling around like confused rookies. He threw long. He threw short. . . . Young doesn't have Montana's ability to read defenses . . . but Young will learn. He is rugged and vital, his arm is accurate and strong. . . . And most important, he is the mobile, quick release quarterback who is ideal for Bill Walsh football—the perfect man to keep the 49ers offense rolling if Montana is too hurt to play during the final drive to the Super Bowl."

That drive to the Super Bowl continued with another win, raising their record to 12-2, by far the best in the NFL. The Niners' final game of the season was a rematch with the Rams on the last weekend of December. By then the Forty Niners had clinched the division and Los Angeles had been eliminated from playoff contention. And the Niners administered yet another drubbing. Young started and played the first half, throwing three touchdown passes. Montana, his hamstring now healed, played the second half to prepare himself for the playoffs, and threw two.

And Walsh, uncharacteristically, piled it on. "We threw play-action passes to destroy their defense," he later explained. "We'd fake the run, so defenders couldn't drop as quickly into their zone, and then throw hooking patterns. Then we went into overkill. My conscience bothered me later because we scored on a fake draw and pass when the game was already lopsided. That was poor judgment and it bothers me to this day. Our philosophy has always been to stick with our plan; when the game is completely under control, run the ball, expend the clock. I found myself trying to prove something on this day, I'm not sure what. I found myself feasting on the carcass, in direct contradiction to what I've represented." The final score was Niners 48, Rams 0. Walsh would later describe the game as "too much, too soon," but it certainly didn't seem that way at the time.

Bill's "rebuilding" team finished the year with the best record in the league, having won its last three games by a cumulative score of 124–7. Joe Montana finished the year with thirty-one touchdown passes, a league best. Jerry Rice had twenty-three touchdowns (one short of the NFL record), led the league in scoring (only the third time in nineteen years someone other than a kicker had done so), and was selected the NFL's Most Valuable Player. Both the Niners offense and their defense were ranked number one in the league—the first time in a decade any team had done that. And San Francisco was headed into the postseason as the odds-on favorite to reach the Super Bowl and beat whoever they met there by at least two touchdowns. Pundits were now calling this the best coaching job Bill Walsh had ever done.

The applause, however, would end a lot sooner than anyone anticipated.

The Forty Niners' first playoff game was at home with the Minnesota Vikings. Minnesota had been only 8-7 in the regular season but had dismantled the Saints in the wild card game the week before. The Niners were ten-point favorites and most expected the margin would actually be far larger. By this point, Bill had begun to believe this team was headed for the Super Bowl as well. "We've had a hell of a football year," he lectured his players. "You guys are to be commended. You've established yourselves as a great football team. We should be proud, but we can't let that affect us. We've finished one chapter and now we're on to the next, and it's a deadly serious one. You can't get distracted and lose your edge. You've got to be hungry. You've got to have desperation in the way you play. You're getting ready to climb Mount Everest and go right to the top of the whole sports world. You can do it, you really can." To break the tension, Walsh also did one of his off-the-wall dress-ups, appearing in the locker room one day wearing tights and looking like an aerobics instructor. The stunt, of course, drew guffaws.

But it also belied Bill's own tension. "The expectations were getting to be too much," Kristine remembered. "He was so imbued with people's perceptions of him and he was becoming petrified of letting people down." That anxiety led him into a critical mistake. His teams had always thrived late in seasons because he avoided working them too hard in practices, leaving them relatively fresh while others were flagging, but over the two weeks leading up to Minnesota, he abandoned that approach. "I had not fully developed our deep passing game and therefore was not satisfied with this dimension of our offense," Bill explained, "so we spent a lot of time practicing it. The first week following the Rams game, we threw deep pass after deep pass to our receivers, trying to refine those patterns. We practiced too long and too hard, so we took too much out of our team physically. I sensed too late that they were becoming fatigued. We hardly did anything the last two days of practice, but the damage was already done." His team agreed with their coach's assessment of his mistake. "My legs were dead and my back was hurting," Jerry Rice pointed out. Ronnie Lott was even more blunt, saying "Walsh ran us into the ground."

Another factor in what was about to happen was overconfidence. Despite Bill's admonitions, he remembered, "we were so sure of ourselves we weren't mentally prepared—for a variety of reasons, many of them originating with me." Convinced they were on their way to a championship, several Niners were heard talking about where they were going to get extra Super Bowl tickets as they made their way down the tunnel and onto the field to play the Vikings.

Yet another factor was all those late-night pizzas delivered to Bubba Paris's house. Bubba, now almost out of shouting distance from the 285 pounds at which he was supposed to play, had regained his starting job from Steve Wallace for the Niners' stretch run and had been playing well, but this day, his heavy feet were quickly exposed as a weak link: The Vikings ran an overshifted defense in which three defensive linemen rushed from Montana's left side. Jesse Sapolu at left guard had trouble all day long with the speed of Keith Millard, the tackle facing him, but the most obvious collapse was Bubba on Jesse's left. He was facing Chris Doleman, the NFL's fastest pass rusher since Lawrence Taylor, and Bubba almost immediately reverted to his Highway 77 days. From the Niners' first offensive series,

Montana was swarmed over whenever he tried to pass. He was sacked four times and had to run for his life on several other occasions. "Bubba got beat," Walsh later pointed out, "and Doleman and Millard just dominated the game."

And, uncharacteristically, their pressure affected Joe. By the end of the first quarter he was sneaking peeks to his left whenever he called a pass, even before he looked downfield. And since the Niners' running game was almost nonexistent, he was passing on almost every down. "Every time I was hitting him I would say something like 'I'm killing Bubba,'" Doleman bragged. "I don't know if it affected his game, but he didn't like getting hit a lot." The effect seemed obvious, at least in retrospect. One of the next day's headlines would read, quite accurately, VIKING PASS RUSH MADE JOE ORDINARY. Perhaps the signature play of that ordinariness came in the second quarter when Bill called a play to free up Jerry Rice on an out pattern to the right side. It worked as planned and Rice found himself wide open. But instead of hitting him Joe tried to force the ball in to Dwight Clark, who was double-covered to his left. "It's just possible that sentiment figured in that play," Walsh later commented. "It was Dwight's last season and Joe threw to Dwight almost blindly. They had worked together so well through the years, but it was not a good decision." To say the least. A Viking defender intercepted the ball and ran forty-five yards with it for a touchdown.

By that point, Minnesota was ahead 17–3 and the Niners' defense hadn't been faring much better than the offense. Anthony Carter, the Vikings' journeyman receiver, was catching everything thrown to him, covered or not, including leaping, twisting grabs in which he changed direction in midair. Carter would accumulate more than two hundred yards receiving before the day was done. "We were victimized by a great athlete," Bill explained, "having the best day of his career." Bill would also later point out that George Seifert kept the Niners defensive backs in a "bump-and-run, man-to-man style of pass coverage, which allowed Minnesota to have a near-perfect day throwing the ball." The Niners went in at the half trailing 20–3.

"As we left the field," Bill remembered, "my mind was racing rapidly. From past experience, I knew all too well that only big plays could pull us out. The Vikings were beating us to the punch and that wasn't likely to change. A coach can sense impending disaster. You have that sick feeling in the pit of your stomach. We had a history of coming back from poor starts but in this case, we were getting knocked all over the field physically. I said to myself, 'We worked them too goddamn hard.' But there was nothing to do about that now."

And nothing much changed as the third quarter started. Montana was sacked twice in their first series and the Niners had to punt. By this point he had completed only twelve out of twenty-six, for less than 150 yards. "Joe had all kinds of problems," Walsh remembered, "the main one being the pressure put on him by the pass rush. We couldn't execute anything. Even the simplest play would blow up in our face. It became obvious something had to be done and the stark reality hit that I would have to go with Steve Young. His spontaneous running might break that Viking pass rush and turn the game around. It killed me to replace Joe. When he came to the sideline, I hugged him but couldn't allow myself to get maudlin. I simply said, 'We're going with Steve.' My job was to win the football game and I had to go with my professional judgment. It was an all-or-nothing situation."

Bill had no illusions about how controversial pulling Joe would become. Joe Montana was a Bay Area icon, beyond perhaps any other sports figure in the region's history, and benching him with a trip to the Super Bowl on the line was opening an issue that would plague Bill for months. In case he needed a reminder of the impending response, he got it on his own sideline. Dwight Clark was standing just a few steps away when the decision was made. "That's bullshit," he shouted at the top of his voice. "That's bullshit." Bill heard but paid no attention.

And his strategy actually worked. Young's first pass was a thirty-one-yard completion deep into Minnesota territory and he soon followed that with a quarterback keeper for a score. His ability to scramble generated another touchdown as well, but the defense—with the exception of an interception return for a touchdown before Montana left the game—just yielded more of the same in the second half. Otherwise, Minnesota matched the Niners every time they scored. As the game wound down with defeat staring them in the face, Bill recalled, "there was absolute suffering" on the Forty Niners' sideline. "We were in a state of shock, still not believing what had happened." The final score was Vikings 36, Niners 24. The following week the Vikings would lose to the Redskins, who would go on to win their second Super Bowl, tying Gibbs with Walsh.

In the meantime, Bill was shattered. He left Candlestick after a brief visit with his players and no one saw him the next day when the team packed up its lockers down at 711 Nevada. He just disappeared, apparently hiding out by himself with only his pain for company. After a brief call from the locker room in which he said, "I lost the game," Kristine Hanson didn't hear from Bill for the next month.

Much later, Bill Walsh—as he had already done with so many other games—described the Minnesota playoff as his "worst loss ever." This one, however, really was what he claimed.

In the wake of it, Bill's descent into permanent despair was rapid, steep, and immediate. "He was never the same after that," Kristine remembered. "It was a pivotal moment, the coup de grâce. From then on his own demons made him feel he couldn't do this anymore. He was despondent and nothing could shake him out of it, for months to come. A lot of the time afterward he was just lost. He didn't know where to be or what to do. He couldn't find peace anywhere. He was just emotionally tortured."

The Minnesota loss was also a pivotal moment in Walsh's relationship with Eddie D. Eddie didn't even bother to come to the locker room afterward, leaving Candlestick beside himself with anger, his lawyer Carmen Policy in tow. He and Walsh would not speak for the next two months. "He went his way and I went mine, trying just to recoup," Bill explained. "That game was a real shocker, less so to me than it was to Eddie. Being a coach for so many years and knowing the dynamics of the game, I understand a frustrating loss—hard as it was to take—whereas Eddie just did not. It was difficult because we had played so well during a very distracting season and Eddie really has a thing about winning. That made it a very difficult time for me."

All winter and into the spring, DeBartolo burned Policy's ears with rants about his coach, again and again insisting at the top of his voice that Walsh had to be fired. This was three straight years this goddamn supposed Genius had lost in the first round of the playoffs. For this he paid $1 million a year? Policy tried to defuse the issue by suggesting that perhaps Bill had too many responsibilities and that things might go better if Eddie narrowed the scope of Walsh's job to just football—cut out the oversight of stadium renovations, supervising the custodial staff, and the like. After much back and forth, Eddie was eventually weaned from his insistence on dismissing Bill and settled instead on taking away his title as president and reclaiming it for himself.

Policy would deliver the news of his demotion to Bill during the spring league meetings at a resort in Phoenix. The two closeted privately in a cabana and Walsh became so furious at one point that he threw a glass across the room, shattering it against the wall, and a flying sliver clipped Policy's ear, drawing blood. Policy tried to mollify Bill by giving him a $100,000 raise as well, though he hadn't cleared it with Eddie ahead of time. The raise would lead to another DeBartolo tantrum before being approved.

Bill would later say that losing the presidency meant nothing to him and he was just glad to have a raise, but he was dissembling. In truth, Walsh had always imagined himself leaving the sideline to spend his later years as president, just running the franchise, and now that fantasy was shattered like the glass he'd heaved against the cabana wall. He and his boss eventually smoothed things out as best they could, but it was years before their relationship recovered.

"From that point on," Bill admitted, "I thought about quitting all the time."

Joe Montana and Steve Young

||||| ||||| |||||

30

BILL v. BILL, JOE v. STEVE

When ruminating out loud to the press about his eventual retirement—once he'd acknowledged how exhausting his job was, how ambivalent he felt about continuing, and how tempting leaving the sideline often seemed—Bill Walsh usually funneled the issue into a more abstract discussion about just when was the right time for a coach to quit. And he always identified a decade as the natural ceiling. After ten years, Bill posited, the task got stale, the players stopped listening, the best of a coach's creative energies were spent, and it might just be time to bow out. He pointed to how few coaches had ever stayed more than a decade with the same team and doubted if he would add to the list. Heretofore, of course, that possibility had been an abstraction, but now it was lost on no one, least of all Bill, that 1988 would complete his first full decade with the Niners. Nonetheless, Walsh remained noncommittal about his plans when reporters raised the subject for yet another time.

In any case, the first monument to the eminence he had fashioned over the last ten years had already been constructed.

During the 1988 off-season, the San Francisco Forty Niners abandoned their minuscule, funky, and antique headquarters at 711 Nevada Street in a Redwood City public park and moved into a brand-new facility in the city of Santa Clara, thirty minutes farther south, an hour's drive from Candlestick. The property, just down the street from the Great America amusement park, had been secured through a fifty-five-year sweetheart lease with the city of Santa Clara, and the Niners' new 52,000-square-foot building with three adjacent football fields—two natural grass and one artificial turf—had been built at a cost close to $10 million by the DeBartolo Corp. Bill had overseen the floor plans and Eddie D. named it the Marie P. DeBartolo Sports Centre after his recently deceased mother. Its address was 4949 Centennial Boulevard. And it was palatial.

The building's downstairs—fronted by a lobby and reception area with marble floors and floor-to-ceiling trophy cases, all guarded by a tight security system—featured a locker room five times the size of the one at 711 Nevada, with sixty permanent lockers arranged along the walls and more than enough space in the center of the room to erect temporary lockers when the team's roster was enlarged for training camp. That core was flanked by a thoroughly modern weight room that dwarfed its antiquated predecessor, five large meeting rooms including one with a foldout stage for use in press conferences, and a 120-seat auditorium for gatherings of the entire team. Computerized video equipment was wired into the ceilings and walls. Next to the locker room was an expansive training area, with an office for the trainer, two examination rooms for the team doctors, and an examination chair for the team's dentist. A players lounge—equipped with a television, a microwave, and five telephones—had room for twenty-five very large men at a time. There was also a sauna, a spa, a steam room, a thirty-by-forty-foot therapeutic indoor swimming pool, and two full-size racquetball courts. Two other locker rooms—one for the coaches and one for the front office staff—had their own sauna and steam rooms as well. The least spectacular facilities included a laundry, an equipment storage area, and a room right off the front lobby adjacent to the parking lot that was reserved for the press.

The building's second floor housed the team offices, both coaching and business. The two most sumptuous of those belonged to Eddie and Bill. The floor and three of the walls in Eddie's office were done in soft leather reminiscent of that used to manufacture footballs. Eddie's other wall was covered with TV and computer monitors displayed behind smoky glass. On top of that, the *Chronicle* architectural critic noted, "silken and linen fabrics, Oriental rugs, chairs of woven leather and of precious woods, including costly branching cuts of trees that are called 'crotch mahogany' create an air of opulence." Those digs were a short hallway from Bill's, which, though lower on the luxury scale, were even more spacious. His oversize mahogany desk was arranged so he could look out the floor-to-ceiling sliding-glass doors and see his players on the three fields on that side of the building. If he wanted a closer look, he could stand on the wide deck outside the doors. His office's interior included "a profusion of mahogany and leather" and his bathroom was so large and fancy the *Chronicle* considered it "almost decadent." That spirit of excess was also replicated in a nearby boardroom that featured "a golden clawed conference table . . . in quasi Empire style . . . whose inlaid centerpiece of rare woods is a helmet symbol of 49ers supremacy."

On the outside, however, "the façade seems grudgingly cheap. Clad in synthetic buff colored stucco, the front of the building bends weakly outward in a post Modern cliché. . . . Fixed metal awnings, in a sort of rusty red, make bad proportions worse. . . . If it were not for the scarlet and gold Super Bowl XVI pennant flying with Old Glory from the flagstaff, the building could be taken for a schlock job in any roadside office park." In the end, the architectural critic summed up 4949 Centennial as "equal parts Fort Knox, MGM's executive suites, and an upscale country club [with] a dash of the Mayo Clinic." On first sight, one player described it as a "Taj Mahal." In any case, it was better than any other in the league and, literally, a coach's dream.

Walsh had designed the layout with his usual attention to detail. He had personally designated a distant and quite separate corner of the building for the press, effectively isolating them in ways that had been impossible on Nevada Street, and actually bragged to several other NFL executives that he had managed to exile the media to "Siberia." In the players' locker room, he divided the dressing arrangements according to his own coach's logic. He had defensive linemen at one end and offensive linemen at the other. Defensive backs were in one corner, diagonally opposite the wide receivers and tight ends. Linebackers and running backs and quarterbacks were similarly

304 IIII THE GENIUS

separated. "When I asked Bill, 'Why do you have it organized like this?' "
Harry Edwards recalled, "he said 'I don't want defensive tackles and offensive tackles sitting next to each other saying, 'Hey, my old lady didn't come
home last night and I'm a little bit under the weather, so if you take it easy
on me I'll take it easy on you.' I want an honest practice.' He didn't even
want John Taylor in a locker next to Jerry Rice. He said, 'I don't want them
comparing notes and becoming alike so they present the same problem to
the defense. I want them presenting different problems.' "

Walsh's biggest worry about the new facility was that its sumptuousness
would spoil his team, an inconceivable issue when they were in Redwood
City.

"I was really concerned that we would become suddenly affluent," he explained, "that our players would lose focus on how challenging the game
was, how fierce the game is, how they had to sacrifice. When the Cowboys
built a new facility like this, I think they lost some of their grit and some of
their focus. But it didn't seem to make any difference for us, so it worked
out okay. Once I was sure of that, I was really glad to be in it. After Redwood
City it was like going to heaven."

Pleasant as the new workplace was, it hardly touched Walsh's inner turmoil. Normally by spring, his wounds from the year before would have
scabbed over and Bill would have found new energy to refresh his drive.
This spring, however, wasn't like that. The now ex-president of the Niners
knew his routines so well that he could construct a deceiving front, but behind it, in the space he allowed few others to see and even fewer to enter, the
pain and confusion were as fresh as the moment the Minnesota game had
ended. And they would stay that way without respite. Inside himself, Bill
Walsh was now almost constantly desperate.

"Even when he was getting ready for the new season," Kristine Hanson
remembered, "he looked terrible, like he was ill. He blamed himself for
every loss and it was eating him up inside. He always hid his pain but he was
in dire straits. He would say 'I can't do this anymore, I have to get out' almost every day. I tried to remind him who he was and that he could do it
but it was always a struggle. He stopped being as productive as he had been
too. He worked harder to get less results, tended to overwork things, and

didn't have the clarity of his early years. He was trying to outthink himself. The man I had known had virtually disappeared. Where before he had been confident and energetic, he was now the flip side of that coin. He looked drawn physically and had lost his sense of humor. He was full of anguish and dourness and always despondent. He became more reclusive and was stuck inside himself. There would be days when his secretary would call and say Bill was holed up in his office and wouldn't talk to anybody and couldn't I call him and pull him out of it. I tried, but it would never work completely. Often the more I tried to talk him out of it, the worse he became. I was worried for his health. I told him that if he kept this up, it would kill him."

Nonetheless, Bill kept it up all year long and that year would be the most difficult of his professional life.

Walsh began 1988 his usual way, tinkering with his lineup. This year, particularly in light of the Minnesota collapse, his focus was on the offensive line. On the left side of it, Bubba Paris had finally eaten his way into a backup role and Steve Wallace was installed to protect Joe Montana's blind side. On the right side, to protect Steve Young's blind side, second-year man Harris Barton took over Keith Fahnhorst's spot for good. Fahnhorst had been injured in the first game back from the strike and spent the rest of the 1987 season on injured reserve. Bill had first talked to Keith about retiring in 1986, but had re-signed him to a short contract instead. Now, however, the end of the tackle's career was unavoidable. In March, during the team's last days at 711 Nevada, Walsh sent word for Fahnhorst to come to his office.

Bill then told the thirteen-year veteran he could either retire or be released. "I knew I was done," Fahnhorst recalled, "but I didn't want to be. And I didn't want to have that conversation with Bill about it. It was difficult for me the way I had to do it, but I've come to accept since that it was time. Still I pretty much scratched the door with my fingernails trying to hold on on my way out."

With Fahnhorst's unwilling departure, the Niners had only five men on their almost fifty-man roster who had played in the franchise's first Super Bowl and only twelve who had been on the field for the second. The makeover Walsh had begun in 1985 was now virtually complete, save for one more possible move—which was, of course, the move everyone was interested in.

And the one which would provide the most intractable of Bill's dilemmas during this, the hardest of his years.

The dilemma had been framed by his decision in the third quarter against Minnesota: "When Bill Walsh pulled Joe Montana out of Saturday's game against the Vikings," one *Chronicle* columnist had suggested on the following Monday, "Joe fell from eminence. Montana is no longer the undisputed leader of the 49ers. . . . Walsh tried to underplay the switch . . . but the fact is that Joe had to be removed from the most important game of the season. He failed. . . . There is no kinder way to put it. . . . It must have galled Montana to loiter on the sideline Saturday when heroics were required on the field. The end of the game was always Joe's time. [On this occasion,] the denouement was taken out of his hands. He watched. His posture slumped. He and Young seemed to avoid each other for long stretches of time. . . . What was once a clear order of supremacy at quarterback—Montana and then Young—is now muddy. Montana probably has the edge [but he] now faces a fight for his job."

Nothing in the cosmology of Bay Area sports could have been more unsettling. Joe Montana was the most beloved icon of the region's most beloved team and the possibility that he might be replaced created a furor every time it surfaced, magnifying everything it touched exponentially. Walsh's initial response was to try downplaying the controversy—"there's always competition at every position"—but his comments almost invariably stirred up more of it rather than less. This wasn't an issue that could be easily finessed and it quickly frustrated Bill.

"Steve's passing had improved so much that, following his first season with us, I was obliged to say that he was in competition with Montana for the quarterback job," Walsh later insisted. "That was consistent with my general philosophy: that any player who had played well should be given a chance to compete for a starting job. But that was clearly not the same as saying that Young would be our starting quarterback. Joe Montana had been the key performer in our previous success and we all believed in him. Undoubtedly, he was one of the truly great players in NFL history. He had mastered our offensive system and directed it brilliantly. Of all my quarterbacks, he had been the most successful at directing my offense. It was ludicrous to think I'd want to bench him if he could play. I regularly said these things to the media about Joe. But whenever anything positive was said about Young, it was considered almost heresy on my part because it might reflect on Joe Montana and his status."

That said, Bill's description after the fact didn't completely reflect his thinking at the time. Actually, one journalist in whom Walsh confided later wrote, "he feared that Montana's physical fragility would bring a quick end to his career. He had brought Young in to be ready [for that eventuality] and he expected that Young would be the starting quarterback no later than the start of the '89 season. This plan was consistent with his philosophy of replacing veteran players with younger players even when it seemed the veteran still had something left. Montana had been a great quarterback . . . but Walsh thought Young would make a great quarterback too and he was preparing to make the switch. By the time Young would be needed as the full time quarterback, Montana's trade value would have dropped precipitously, and so Walsh considered trading Montana a year early."

The trade in question was with the San Diego Chargers and discussions about it had been launched when the Chargers' owner raised the idea with Eddie D. The Niners let the suggestion drop but then revived it in March when someone in the organization, likely Walsh, had second thoughts. The price San Diego had originally offered for Montana was two first-round draft picks plus a linebacker whom Walsh coveted. When the possible deal was revived, though, the Chargers had second thoughts and replaced the linebacker with a running back in whom Walsh had little interest. Still, Bill was intrigued enough to raise the subject at a morning meeting of the coaching staff. Bill asked everyone who thought trading Montana was a good idea to raise their hands. No one did. That afternoon, apparently dissatisfied with the previous response, he reconvened the same meeting, asked the same question again, and got the same answer. At that point, unwilling to swim upstream against his staff's unanimous opposition, he dropped talks with San Diego.

When news of the discussions leaked, however, it caused a veritable shit storm, with reporters swarming to ferret out whatever news they could. At one point in the process, when Bill learned from Al Davis that a particular reporter was asking whether the Niners were "shopping" Montana around the league, Walsh lost his temper. He wagged his finger in the reporter's face and lectured the man in a loud voice. "Let's get one thing straight," he insisted. "We're not shopping Joe Montana. To anyone. At all. Period. Joe is our starting quarterback and will be starting again next season." Before any more questions could be asked, Bill walked away.

When confronted with rumors that Eddie had been pushing the trade over Walsh's objections, DeBartolo backed his former president. "Everything is in Bill Walsh's hands," Eddie responded. "He runs the football team. That's why he makes as much money as he does. And obviously, if there were any discussions concerning Montana or anybody else, he does not feel as though they're serious enough to bring me into them."

To put the whole trade issue to bed, Bill then called Joe into his new office at 4949 Centennial. He told him that other teams had initiated offers but the Niners had no interest. "Bill Walsh said several clubs had inquired about two quarterbacks—me and Steve Young," Montana reported afterward. "It makes me feel better that the 49ers didn't initiate those talks. Bill told me he did not want to trade, but, of course in the right circumstances it could happen."

Despite the disclaimers, the issue of Joe's future wouldn't die—in part, ironically, because Walsh wouldn't let it. Sometimes despite himself, he kept providing quotes that were blood in the water to the media sharks:

"We are not looking to change the quarterback position," he insisted as training camp started, "and don't expect that the starting quarterback position will be changed this year. But we are looking at the alternative of playing Young more than we'd ever consider playing a second quarterback. And I suppose if Young is performing markedly better than Montana, then naturally, like any other position in this competitive game, we would make a change."

Offered a chance to clarify his remarks and unequivocally endorse Montana later in training camp, Bill hedged, thereby adding more fuel to the press's feeding frenzy. "I think it would have to be acknowledged that there will be a controversy related to the quarterbacks this year," he offered. "There is now, I believe. There was toward the end of last season, and certainly after the last game of last season and going into this year, and it will continue."

Perhaps the comment that drew the most attention came at a press conference in London, where the Niners had traveled for a preseason game designed to promote the American sport to a European audience. Asked what worries he had about his team this year, Bill said he was pretty happy, though he thought it might be another year before this squad peaked, then, as a seeming afterthought, he added, "We may have a quarterback controversy."

"The moment I said it I thought, 'Uh-oh, this could be a problem,'" Bill later remembered. "I knew I had opened the door for the media. It was an unfortunate choice of words. But though the original error was mine, the media can be faulted for fabricating a controversy" out of it.

Most of the press covering him didn't buy Walsh's claim of "mistake" as an explanation for his remarks. "He knew exactly what he was doing," one of them observed. "He always knew what he was doing."

Just what that was, however, was subject to dispute.

"He wanted to get the word out because he thought Steve Young was going to take over from Montana that year," one reporter theorized. "He wanted to talk about it at that point because he knew how popular Montana was and if he waited until it happened in midseason then there would have been such an uproar."

Ronnie Lott had a whole different take. "In my mind," he explained, "Walsh manufactured the quarterback controversy to take himself off the hook for our horrendous playoff defeat to the Vikings."

The more common position among the team was articulated by tight end Brent Jones. "I think it was mostly a premature controversy," he observed. "I don't think Steve was really ready and I don't think Bill was really going to make a change. I think it was just Bill motivating Joe. That's the way Bill does it. He didn't want anybody thinking that their job was safe, not even Joe."

And almost everyone in the locker room agreed with Randy Cross. "If Joe's right [physically]," he declared, "then it's an *alleged* controversy" and nothing more.

Whatever Bill's reasoning, he was unable to defuse the issue. Just who would be the team's lead quarterback and how Walsh ought to decide between them would be batted around in the media for months to come and Bill heard all of it as criticism, felt chastised by it, and chafed at all the second-guessing and the disrespect implicit in the process.

And there was no denying all the talk's impact on Montana. For the first time since Steve DeBerg left, he had to compete for his job and that felt hurtful under the best of circumstances. "I just didn't understand it," he later admitted. "I knew Steve was a good quarterback. I knew he was highly touted coming out of college. But to all of a sudden be in a controversy for no good reason? I thought I had a pretty good year. I could understand it if I'd been the shits, but I didn't think I played that way. And for that to happen, I just didn't understand."

Walsh spent the last weeks before the season began trying to smooth the waters surrounding the quarterback position and focus on the games ahead. He told the press that he'd be happy if his team went 10-6 and made the playoffs. He also named Montana the starter—even though he privately thought Young had outplayed him in the preseason—and declared that he expected Joe to have "his best year ever."

Nonetheless, when the Niners broke camp in Rocklin and installed themselves in the brand-new Marie P. DeBartolo Sports Centre, their quarterback was looking over his shoulder, the press corps that covered them was in a feeding frenzy, their owner was already impatient, and their coach was in secret torment.

And it would get worse before it got better.

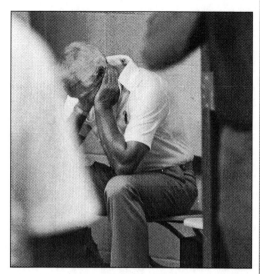

Bill Walsh collapses in the locker room
after a humiliating loss in Phoenix, 1988

31

FALLING APART AND COMING TOGETHER

The Forty Niners' 1988 season began in New Orleans against the Saints, the team everyone figured would give them the most competition within their division and indeed, the pick of more prognosticators than not. The game was back and forth, with the Niners trailing at the half 17–10. Montana had been mediocre during the first two quarters, completing just six of fourteen, including a stretch of five straight incompletions. He was also hurting. Right before halftime, he had picked up six yards on a bootleg and, when tackled, slammed his right elbow on the hard artificial surface of the Superdome. Montana's elbow had been operated on over the summer to remove bone chips and the pounding aggravated his old injury. Worried about being pulled from the game, he did his best to conceal the damage from Walsh, but quarterbacks coach Mike Holmgren noticed. Still, Joe started the second half and put together an extraordinary third quarter—throwing three touchdown passes in the space of eight minutes, covering a total of 126 yards with just fifteen plays to take the lead. By the end of the quarter, however, his elbow was the size of a grapefruit and Steve Young had to come in and finish the game. San Francisco held on for a win, 34–33.

Joe Montana began the next week of practice for their game against the Giants in New York listed as "questionable." Not only had his elbow ballooned but he had contracted dysentery and lost more than five pounds and some of his strength. Joe pronounced himself ready by the end of the week but by then Bill had already decided to use Montana's elbow as an excuse to play his quarterbacks interchangeably as situations dictated, the way he had first imagined when he made the move to sign Young the year before. Walsh figured Steve's running would help against the Giants' fearsome pass rush and on Friday, to almost everyone's surprise, announced that Young would start on Sunday. Bill cited Joe's elbow and his inability to practice as the reasons but, one reporter noted, "Montana practiced on Thursday and Friday and looked fit." At that point, the press corps dusted off their "Controversy" notes and started in on it all again.

The move, however, didn't work out as Bill had planned. Young did not fare well in the first half at Giants Stadium. He was sacked three times, fumbled twice—setting up a Giants score—and, while he was able to move the team, his mistakes were both critical and costly. "Steve was somewhat skittish," Walsh noted. He "had been tentative in his passing and had reverted to his running tactics too often." The score was 10–10 at halftime, but as the Niners headed off the field, Bill found Joe and, to the quarterback's considerable surprise, told him, "Be ready to go in next half."

"I didn't know if he was kidding or not," Montana recalled. Still, he was ready at the start of the third quarter when Walsh sent him in to finish the game.

Joe worked no miracles at first either. The Niners managed a field goal and clung desperately to a 13–10 lead until deep into the final quarter. Then the Giants got a thirty-two-yard punt return just before the two-minute warning and followed it with a fifteen-yard touchdown pass to go ahead.

The ensuing kickoff left the Niners on their own twenty-two with little over a minute in which to move the length of the field against one of the league's premier defenses. On first down, Walsh called Jerry Rice's number. It had been a hard day for Rice—having already dropped a sure touchdown and been called for pass interference in the end zone on another—and he dropped this pass too, a slant pattern over the middle that would have netted at least a first down. On second down, Joe fumbled Randy Cross's center snap but Cross recovered it. That left the Forty Niners with third down and fifty-eight seconds on the clock. Bill now went to the plastic-encased sheet of plays he always carried on the sideline and selected one he thought just might work. "New York had dominated defensively for several years, using a pass coverage that featured two deep safeties," he explained, but "we felt that we could get Rice past the cornerback, before the safety could get to him." In his game plan, Bill had reserved an attack against that apparent vulnerability for just this kind of situation. The play was 76 Two Jet All Go—the same one with which he'd beaten Cincinnati the year before, only out of a different formation. This formation set Rice up one on one with the cornerback, with the safety on that side covering Mike Wilson, the Niners slot receiver lined up inside of Jerry.

At the snap, Rice burned straight down the field and after twenty yards had a step on the corner. Joe faded back and threw a tight spiral some forty yards in the air that Jerry caught in stride on the Giants' forty-six with no one in front of him—a perfect throw. The Giants safety left Wilson and made a desperate run in Rice's direction when he saw where the pass was going, but arrived late and only managed to collide with the cornerback, taking both out of the pursuit. The play covered seventy-eight yards and gave San Francisco an improbable last-second 20–17 win.

"This was a pretty sweet one," Montana noted in the locker room afterward. With it, according to the *Chronicle,* Joe had not only beaten the Giants and given the Niners only their second 2-0 start in the last eight years, but "firmly re-established himself as the 49ers No. 1 quarterback."

That didn't help much the next week at home against Atlanta's sad-sack Falcons. The Niners were favored by two touchdowns but lost by seventeen points to a team that hadn't won before and wouldn't win again until week nine. Bill spent a lot of time in his office with the door shut after that travesty, but just as despair was gaining the upper hand, his team turned around the following week on the road in Seattle—against a team that had been to the playoffs the year before—and produced their best game yet. The Niners whipped the Seahawks 38–7, with the offense accumulating 580 yards. After another win and then a loss, they faced the Rams on the road. Before that contest, Joe received a painkilling injection in his elbow and another in his rib cage, plus was fighting off the flu. He nonetheless played well enough for the Niners to come from behind after blowing a ten-point halftime lead and win, 24–21.

Going into week eight, almost halfway through the season, Walsh's squad had a 5-2 record and trailed New Orleans by a game. And Bill—unable to figure out just how to feel—was both encouraged and apprehensive.

Their next contest was in Chicago on a Monday night and was widely hyped as a preview of a matchup that might very well be repeated in the playoffs. During the week, Bill was worried about Montana's physical condition and about the Bears pass rush and devised a game plan accordingly. In it, he identified several very specific points in the game during which he intended to insert Young. His thought was to give Montana some breaks to conserve his strength while he used Young's legs to slow down the Bears defense. He was also worried that Steve was getting stale—having only played a few minutes of mop-up time since his start against the Giants—and wanted to find a way to put him to use. Those plans, however, had to be scrapped at the last minute. When warming up on Monday night while the crowd was still filing into Soldier Field, Young tweaked his back and began having trouble throwing. At that point, Bill told Joe he was going the whole way.

It turned out to be tough duty. After a quick start, the offense bogged down, largely because of Bill's mistaken strategy. "I miscalculated by worrying too much about their pass rush," Bill later explained. "I had assigned the tight end and both backs as blockers to double every pass rusher they had, to keep them away from Joe. But I had departed from our basic formula on offense, going to unnecessarily restrictive pass protection schemes, and our remaining pass receivers just weren't getting open. We depended too much on Jerry Rice making big plays downfield. And as the game progressed, it was evident the Bears were beating us to the punch. We were doing too much thinking, and they began to sense the kill. Eventually, our pass protection began to break down and Joe took some terrible punishment. He had never recovered his full strength from the dysentery and that began to show. In the fourth quarter, Joe had lost the zip in his arm." Finally, in desperation, Bill inserted Steve for the final four plays of the game, hoping he might somehow carry them close enough for a field goal, but that failed. The final score was Chicago 10, San Francisco 9, and the game ended with taunts coming from the Bears sideline.

Walsh was crushed afterward, convinced he had cost his team the game.

"It was embarrassing and humiliating to have our offense dominated in front of the Chicago crowd," Bill remembered, and no one felt that humiliation more than he.

Eddie D., however, came in a close second. He had flown over from Youngstown for the game and was in a fit at the outcome. And he made it very clear to Bill exactly how he felt. "There were four or five instances out on the road where Eddie was just an awful guy," one of Walsh's close friends explained, "when he treated Bill with tremendous disrespect." And that trip to Chicago was apparently one of them. The venom his boss threw at Bill in the aftermath of that Chicago loss was enough that, once back in California, Walsh called DeBartolo Sr. to complain about how Junior had treated him.

It was a difficult ride home for Bill and an even more difficult night at his office when he got back. The next morning, having hardly slept, Walsh had his usual Tuesday meeting with the press at 4949 Centennial. The principal topics of inquiry were the upcoming game with Minnesota—a rematch of the season-ending disaster of the year before—and Joe Montana. Joe's difficulties against Chicago, including thirteen-for-twenty-nine passing and four sacks, had been apparent and Bill blamed his quarterback's various ailments as well as his own strategy. "His readiness concerns me," Walsh explained. "He's got a great heart and tremendous courage [but] he needs a rest, to be honest with you. He needs a week off." Asked if that meant that Young would be playing more against the Vikings, Walsh said yes. Would he start? Quite possibly. Did that mean Young was now the number one? No, Walsh replied, Joe was the starter no matter how much Steve played against Minnesota next Sunday.

After those remarks, several enterprising reporters went to Montana and twisted what the coach had said to make it sound as if he were replacing Montana and sending him down the depth chart. "Fatigued, frustrated by the loss, embarrassed because Young had replaced him in the waning moments of games," Bill pointed out, "Joe responded emotionally." Angrily, to be exact, and defensively in the face of what he thought was his coach's attack.

When Bill learned, he immediately met with Joe in his office. "It was cordial," Walsh later recalled. "We never had harsh words at any time. I apologized in a sense and reminded him of my feelings about him and what I anticipated for the rest of the year. I reassured him that he was still an outstanding performer and I expected him to continue to be the class of the league. But at the same time, I felt he was not physically up to par, almost exhausted."

Joe did not agree and made it clear he thought he should start on Sunday against Minnesota. When Montana stood up to leave, however, his back went into spasms right there in Walsh's office and the team orthopedist had to be called. Bill told Joe to stay out of practice until further notice and within forty-eight hours, Montana was scratched from the lineup and Steve Young was announced as the starter against the Vikings, who were on their way to an 11-5 season and being described by several observers as the league's best that year.

On Sunday, after a mediocre first half, Young came back in the second half with two long touchdown drives and then, with the game on the line, made a forty-nine-yard run that would be replayed on highlight shows for years to come, weaving through the whole Minnesota team, until he stumbled across the goal line with the winning score: Forty Niners 24, Vikings 21.

Afterward, citing Montana's ongoing exhaustion and Young's stellar second half, Bill named Steve the starter for the next week's game as well.

Joe was upset when he heard and insisted to the press that Bill was "trying to get rid of me."

And with that, one reporter observed, "the quarterback controversy got even more so."

The scuttlebutt rampant among the press that week was that if Young played well and the Forty Niners won the next game, Young would take over the starter's role. Bill denied it several times—with increasing irritation that he, the acknowledged master of the quarterback position, was constantly being second-guessed by a bunch of sportswriters—but the rumor persisted. The game was on Eddie D.'s forty-second birthday, against the Cardinals in Phoenix—where the former St. Louis franchise had moved in the off-season—and the Niners were expected to win handily against a team that hadn't had a winning season in three years. The weather, however, would be difficult. All the college teams in Arizona played their games at night to avoid the heat, but the NFL game was scheduled for an outdoor stadium in the teeth of the hottest part of the day. At game time, temperatures on the field were already over ninety degrees and would reach a hundred before the game was finished.

For the first two and a half quarters, however, the conditions seemed to make no difference to the Niners. "I remember leaving the field at halftime," Bill explained, "thinking this was the best 49ers effort ever. I'd never seen us better." The score at that point was 23–0 and stayed that way until the last minutes of the third quarter. By then the game seemed to be in the bag and Walsh had clearly taken his foot off the offensive accelerator. For the remaining twenty-two minutes of play, the Niners would throw just three passes, only one of those in the final quarter. The San Francisco defense had been dominating as well, not allowing the Cardinals past the Niners' forty-two-yard line on their first eight possessions. For those last twenty-two minutes, however, the defense went into the tank. During that time, the Cardinals had sixteen first downs to the Niners' two, and outgained the visitors 251 yards to 59. The question soon became whether the Niners, now visibly sapped by the heat, could hang on.

They were handicapped in that effort by their own mistakes. Young missed Roger Craig open for a touchdown and John Taylor dropped another pass in the end zone. But even worse were the penalties—eleven altogether, for more than a hundred yards. The offense lost five first downs because of them, including three by Jesse Sapolu alone and two that shut down what looked like scoring drives. In the fourth quarter, Eric Wright was called for a penalty when the Cardinals were punting on fourth and twenty and that gave them a fresh set of downs. Injuries also made holding the lead difficult. The Niners had come into the game short Tim McKyer, one of their starting corners, and then the other, Don Griffin, dislocated a shoulder during the third quarter but had to keep playing. That left a cornerback on one side who couldn't raise one arm and the other cornerback slot manned by Darryl Pollard, a player who had only been on the squad for two weeks, didn't know all the formations, and kept lining up in the wrong spot. Needless to say, the Cardinals began to pick on the Niners secondary with great success.

Bill would later describe that Sunday in Phoenix as "terribly ugly, about as ugly a game as I've ever experienced." And as things started going bad, even he was injured. Walsh was standing on the sideline with his back to the action, talking into his headset to Holmgren up in the press box, trying desperately to figure out a way to stem the bleeding, when two players came flying out of bounds at the end of a play and smashed into him from behind. "They knocked me flat," Bill remembered, "just wiped me out." They also cracked one of his ribs and he spent the rest of the game in intense pain every time he took a deep breath.

With 6:31 remaining in the fourth quarter, ugly or not, the Niners were still up 23–10. With 2:19, it was 23–17—but the Niners had the ball in what would prove to be the critical drive of the game. Walsh's goal was to use up the time remaining, so—since incomplete passes stopped the clock—he called runs exclusively. The Niners picked up one first down quickly with a Young bootleg. Another first down would pretty much put the game away and their first attempt at it gained eight yards. Facing second and two, Bill then made the first of what he would later label as two successive "strategic errors" with the game hanging in the balance. First, "I called a run by Roger Craig that stretched the defense to the outside," he explained. "I had failed to account for the fact that the weak safety was playing close to the line in what was really a short yardage defense. He nailed Roger for a loss." Afterward, the Cardinals spent their last time out and Steve came to the sidelines to confer with Bill. Steve argued for another bootleg to his left, sure that he could beat the Cardinals defensive end to the yardsticks. All he needed was three yards and, he pointed out, he had just picked up a first down with a bootleg for even more yardage than that. Bill finally agreed and sent Young in to run it. As play resumed, though, Bill began wondering if he shouldn't have called the bootleg to the right instead of the left. But by then it was too late to change.

Steve took the snap and spun to his right with the ball. Behind him, both guards pulled out of the line and sprinted to the right, as though to block for the back sweeping that way. Craig moved up as if to accept the handoff on his way toward the right end, but Steve withdrew it while Roger continued right, hunched over as though he had received the ball. Steve then headed left, seemingly out of the play entirely, but with the ball hidden against his hip. The entire Phoenix line took the fake, except the defensive end who stood between Young and the first down. He and Steve raced to the yard markers on the far side of the field and crashed out of bounds together. Bill and Steve both thought he had made it—and the game films later confirmed their judgment—but the official marked the ball six inches short and Bill sent in the punting team.

Bill Walsh would relive that third-down bootleg for the rest of his life. "We should have had him run to the right," he lamented. "We normally liked to have Steve run to his left, because he's a left-hander and the ball would be in his left hand. But in this case, the defensive end to the other side wouldn't have been as alert. Steve had previously run that play to his left for a first down, so the end on that side was ready. All we had to do was run it the other way. The end over there wouldn't have figured out what was happening and Steve would have been around him. I have regretted that call ever since."

In the meantime, however, the clock had been stopped because Steve carried the ball out of bounds, so Phoenix regained possession at their own thirty-four with 1:27 remaining. And the Forty Niners defense couldn't derail their passing game. Finally, with the clock stopped on an incompletion with six seconds left and the ball on the Niners' nine-yard line, the Cardinals had time for one last play. Defensive coordinator George Seifert knew it would be a pass and dialed up a blitz to pressure Phoenix's quarterback, but that left Darryl Pollard one on one with the Cardinals' best receiver. Sure enough, the pass came his way and the two of them went for the ball and fell out of the end zone in a tangle with both men clutching it, but the official signaled touchdown Phoenix. The extra point sealed the loss, 24–23.

Standing on the sideline, beaten, Bill remembered, "I had never been so enraged." He was furious at Seifert for calling a defense that put the inexperienced Pollard trying to cover one of the league's premier wideouts. He was furious with the referee whose call had cost them the first down that would have won the game. He was furious with his team for all those penalties. But mostly he was furious at himself for having called that sweep to Craig with the safety shifted up and for having called that bootleg to the left instead of the right. He blamed himself and he blamed his assistants and he blamed his players and then he blamed himself some more. In physical and mental pain deep enough to make him howl, Bill's fury was unlike anything his players had ever seen from him. "My pride, my self-esteem was really hurt," he explained, "and it was terribly humiliating. It was an utterly embarrassing game."

For once, Bill was even madder than Eddie—but not by much. DeBartolo, his birthday ruined, was the first to reach the locker room and, Randy Cross recalled, "he was smoking." Offended that anyone would talk louder than a whisper after this debacle, he shut everybody up. "When I walked into the locker room," Ronnie Lott wrote, "I found DeBartolo slumped in a chair with his head down. The only sounds were helmets and shoulder pads bouncing on the floor and into duffel bags, and tape being ripped from ankles, wrists, and hands. [Then] Walsh walked in and began yelling. He never, ever, lost it, but this Sunday he screamed so loud and hard that spit flew from his mouth. He didn't yell at anyone in particular. He just rambled on and on. Then he stormed into his office and slammed the door behind him. The door popped open and I saw Walsh with his head in his hands, looking devastated and distraught."

And Bill was only just catching his wind. He soon assembled all his assistants behind closed doors in the coaches locker room and screamed so loud at them he could be heard back up the tunnel. And it was a long time before he was finished.

Afterward, Walsh had trouble getting dressed in his street clothes because of his ribs and by the time he was done, he felt weak and light-headed. He and the rest of the team boarded the bus to the airport, but ended up sitting in it on the airport runway cooking for more than half an hour, while the insides of the bus got more and more oppressive. That was too much for Bill and when it finally came time to board the plane, his knees buckled when he stepped onto the tarmac and he fell on his face. Embarrassed, he quickly regained his feet, but on the plane, Lott recalled, Bill "looked ashen and appeared to be in great discomfort." The flight crew was concerned enough that they radioed ahead for San Francisco International to have an ambulance waiting at the gate for their arrival.

While the Forty Niners' charter was taxiing, the cabin was devoid of sounds until someone in the back let out a nervous laugh. That laugh caused Bill to lose his cool again. He and all the other coaches and staff were sitting in the front of the plane and he called the team's PR man over and told him he wanted him to go to the back of the plane and find whoever was laughing and shut him up. And if there was any more laughter it was going to cost the PR man his job. They had just lost the goddamn game and been humiliated in the process. There was no cause for anyone to laugh. He wanted to know who thought this was so funny and when he found out, that person was never going to fly on the Niners plane again. "He instructed . . . our public relations director to walk through the plane and tell everybody to shut up," Lott recounted. "It was a scene out of the movie *The*

Caine Mutiny. Walsh was our Captain Queeg." For the rest of the flight, the plane sounded like a flying coffin.

"It was at that point," according to Harry Edwards, "that I really sensed that Bill might be maxing out in terms of that stratospheric intensity that this environment at the Niners had become."

Bill refused the ambulance at San Francisco International and drove himself down to Santa Clara for another long night of staring at the wall and coming apart.

The next week, he started Joe Montana at Candlestick against the dismal Los Angeles Raiders—who were coming off a losing season and headed for another one—but his team lost again, 9–3, in a performance he considered "even worse" than against the Cardinals. Bill almost got in a fight when accosted by two fans afterward, but didn't lose it in the locker room again. By the time he got there, Eddie D. had already kicked in the glass face of the soft drink cooler.

With the Niners now 6-5, trailing both the Saints and the Rams in their division, two games back and seemingly about to collapse completely, Bill Walsh halfway expected Eddie D. to fire him on the spot. And he might have been right.

The two of them met that Sunday night after the Raiders debacle back at the Santa Clara headquarters. "Eddie was not happy," Randy Cross remembered from the locker room that afternoon, "very not happy." And he came prepared to tell Bill all about it. "He did not use Policy as his go-between," according to a source close to Walsh, "because he intended to fire him" and "wasn't going to let Policy talk him out of his decision." Bill, on the other hand, was at the end of his rope and "broke down," just came apart before Eddie had an opportunity to upbraid him over the team's failures, much less terminate his employment. The owner was confused by the sight of the normally confident Walsh in such a state and, after listening to Bill's woe for a while, agreed that the two of them would meet again Tuesday to discuss the future of the team.

On Monday night, Bill met with his coaching staff over take-out food at 4949 Centennial. "I told them I was meeting the next day with Eddie," Walsh explained, "and that they shouldn't assume that we had permanent status, that the owner was concerned." All the coaches had already picked up on the import of the moment. Mike Holmgren called it their "Last Supper" meeting. "There was a feeling among everyone that we were going to be let go," he recalled. "There was a lot of anxiety about it. We talked about the team and what it needed and different guys brought up different things." The subject that got the most attention was the quarterback position. Holmgren had been lobbying Bill for weeks to pick one or the other, either Joe or Steve, and stick with him. Everyone weighed in on just who that should be and the vote was unanimous to start Montana for the remainder of the season, a conclusion Walsh would accept and follow. Once that issue was out of the way, Walsh broke out a couple of bottles of wine and the group began to reminisce about the successes and good times they'd had, until the emotion got too much for him and Bill had to leave the room before he collapsed into sobs.

On Tuesday, he and Eddie sat down again in Eddie's leather-carpeted office. Bill was back in control of himself by this point. He pursued the two hours they spent together much as he had their meeting after the 1982 season, giving his boss a list of four options for his and the team's future. One was for Bill to step down immediately; a second involved his staying on until season's end, then retiring as coach and remaining as general manager; the third was for him to retire from both jobs at season's end; and the fourth would keep him on for next season just as he had been. After their two-hour talk on Tuesday, they took another two hours on Wednesday to talk more.

"Eddie was really concerned about the future of the franchise," Bill remembered. "We were 6–5 and we had lost that playoff game the year before. First thing you do in a case like that is look at the head coach. In sports you either win or lose and that's what led us to that point. I realized Eddie was really upset so I had initiated the meeting to put him at ease. Otherwise he may have just been seething right under the surface. I made my proposals to let him off the hook so he could feel at ease as best he could and I could too. I think that conversation cleared the air because he no longer had to worry—he had the destiny of his team firmly in his hands. We talked a lot about each other and what we'd been through together but we didn't decide anything. We just opted to go on while Eddie could mull over his options for the long run." Their Wednesday meeting ended with a hug.

For Bill, of course, all the options he presented to Eddie weren't equal. He now had one foot out the door and felt good about it. On Thursday, he played his weekly tennis game before the afternoon practice session and brought the conversations up with his playing partner.

"I just told Eddie to stuff it," Bill said. "I told him it won't continue anymore, the way he's treated me."

What'd you do? his partner asked.

"I told him this is it," Bill replied. "This is my last year."

While he in fact had not made up his mind about that, certainly Walsh was obviously relieved when his consultations with Eddie were over. "I felt like I had a weight off my back," he explained. "I didn't have to worry about my job anymore. Whatever was going to happen with it would happen. I could just coach."

And his relief showed up around 4949 Centennial right away.

"That day at practice," his tennis partner recalled, "Harry Edwards came up to me and said, 'Something's going on here. Do you notice how light everybody is on their feet all of a sudden?' I said he was right, something was going on. The staff was all walking around with a new spring to their step. It was amazing. That practice was startlingly different from the way things had been just days before. And it was all radiating out of Bill. He was night and day different than he had been on Monday. By lifting the burden off himself, he lifted it off everybody else too."

In the meantime, his players had not been waiting on the coaches to get it together. "Obviously something had to be done to turn the team around," Ronnie Lott noted, "but Walsh was too emotionally wrung out to take the first step. So on the practice field [the first day back after the Raiders game] I lost my temper. 'What the hell is going on?' I screamed to everyone in sight. . . . I was shocked by the lack of enthusiasm. . . . They were strolling in slow motion from drill to drill. 'I can't believe your fucking attitudes,' I shouted. 'You're walking around like you don't give a damn. We've been getting our asses kicked! Look, this is ridiculous! If we're going to lose, then let's go down kicking somebody's ass.' Players stopped dead in their tracks. All eyes were on me. 'We've got to play up to our standard of football,' I continued shouting. 'If we play up to our standard and we lose, so what? But our standard isn't lethargic football. . . .' The tempo picked up from there."

Lott's outburst was followed by a players-only meeting later in the week where a half dozen members of the squad with the most credibility spoke. Lott's remarks were the most memorable. "Nobody said things quite like Ronnie," Brent Jones recalled. "He said screw the press, screw the doubters, screw the coaches—forget everybody, stop making excuses, and do what you're capable of doing. I'd like to bottle up what we had in that meeting that day. From then on there was no looking back."

By the end of the week, Lott remembered, "we were ready to rumble."

And, deep in the hole they'd dug for themselves with only five games remaining, they had a lot of rumbling to do and not much time to do it in.

At least around the nine Bay Area counties, there was always a sense of the supernatural surrounding the Niners during the Walsh era—a feeling that the team had a capital *D* destiny driving it forward—and that sense was confirmed by what happened in the remaining weeks of the 1988 season. It was not quite The Miracle, but it was close.

The Forty Niners' next game was at Candlestick on Monday night against the Washington Redskins, the defending Super Bowl champions. The Redskins were also 6-5 and struggling. As their teams were warming up, Walsh talked a little with Redskins coach Joe Gibbs. "They were having a season like us," Bill remembered, "so I tried to commiserate. I said, 'Well, we may not make it this year, but we'll be back.' Gibbs didn't want to hear it. 'The hell we'll be back,' he said. 'We're going to make it this year.' Gibbs was a very emotional guy and he obviously meant it. And what he said shook me up. Afterward I said to myself, 'What am I doing apologizing about anything?' It was a like a slap in the face to wake me up. It was a very good motivational tool for me."

Bill's team, however, had all the motivation it needed. The locker room was absolutely silent before they took the field. Then, when it was time, Walsh said, "Let's go," the players roared, and ran out the tunnel. "We didn't play with great execution," Bill pointed out, "but we had incredible intensity."

The game turned in the second quarter when the Niners were clinging to a 10–7 lead and forced the Redskins to punt. John Taylor fielded the kick at the Niners' five-yard line—even though punt returners were trained to leave any ball inside the ten alone—then juked an onrushing Redskin, broke an arm tackle, and took off upfield. The last man with a chance to stop him was the Redskins punter, whom Taylor hurdled and kept running. It was the longest punt return in the Forty Niners' history. The Redskins then got the ball back and on their first play from scrimmage threw an interception that Joe and the offense turned into a touchdown shortly thereafter—one of four Washington turnovers, three of which led to Niners scores. Montana also had his best day in a while. Having thrown only one touchdown pass in the previous five games, he threw two that Monday and ran in for a third score. He had to come out of the game briefly with a knee sprain but, after icing it, returned and continued to play what Randy Cross called "the kind of game that was just classic Joe." The final score was San Francisco 37, Washington 21.

"Hold the funeral notices," the *Chronicle* advised. "The 49ers aren't dead yet."

Not by a long shot. The following week, the Niners traveled to San Diego to play the mediocre Chargers and it was a walkover. Montana hit Rice—who was finally recovered from an October ankle sprain—for two touchdowns, one covering forty-one yards, the other ninety-six. And the offense accumulated 475 yards in a 48–10 thrashing. Bill, however, did not seem pleased.

"You expected Bill Walsh to be smiling when he came to the interview room [after the game]," one columnist noted. "Instead, he had a sour expression on his face and he snapped when writers asked routine questions. . . . He gives the impression that something is gnawing at him. . . . He must be appalled by the criticism he's received this year. . . . Maybe he seems so distant because his feelings are hurt. It could be that simple, although with a man as complicated as Walsh, you tend to think nothing is simple or as it appears. Perhaps Walsh really is thinking about stepping down. [If so] a Hollywood scriptwriter couldn't have come up with a better scenario: Beleaguered, veteran head coach weathers a vicious quarterback controversy and a crisis of confidence with the fans and his owner, and leads his demoralized team into the playoffs when they seemed dead only a few weeks before. . . . If he succeeds, it will be the most startling triumph of his career. It will also be a brilliant farewell—if that's what he has in mind."

Walsh's next step toward that scenario was on the road in Atlanta, where the Niners redeemed their early-season collapse with a 13–3 victory. That win improved their record to 9-5 and the situation in the Western Division had now been transformed. While the Forty Niners had been winning three in a row, their next opponent, the Saints, had lost two of three, squandering their two-game lead, and entered the game 9-5 as well. Improbable as it had sounded just three weeks earlier, a win against New Orleans, combined with a loss by the Rams, would make the Forty Niners division champs.

And the game, according to the *Chronicle,* "was never in serious doubt." The Niners offense put the Saints away with a nine-minute stretch in the second quarter when they scored three touchdowns, gaining 194 yards with eighteen plays, an astounding eleven-yard average every time they snapped the ball. Afterward, their locker room received word of a Rams loss, clinching the division and a first-round bye in the playoffs, and turning their matchup with the Rams next week into a meaningless encounter that Walsh would essentially forfeit.

"Four weeks ago," one of Walsh's more frequent critics observed the next morning, when "the 49ers [lost] to the Los Angeles Raiders, [it] was a low point for the franchise. After that, all you heard was how coach Bill Walsh couldn't get along with owner Eddie DeBartolo Jr., how Walsh couldn't communicate with his quarterbacks, and mostly, how the 49ers were about to receive last rites. . . . That low point seems like a century ago. Walsh even seems happy after a month of being a recluse. . . . He came out after yesterday's victory eager to meet the press. . . . His eyes twinkled. 'I know a lot of you picked this team to go all the way,' he said. He meant the Saints. He was entitled to gloat. [All of a sudden] he looked like a guy who knew he was a pretty good coach and was proud of it."

Joe Montana and Bill Walsh after beating Minnesota in the playoffs, 1988

32

DESTINY

I n advance of the Forty Niners' first playoff game, much of the sports media's attention focused largely on two subjects. The first was Walsh's future status and the possibility that he would retire whenever the team's current string came to an end. As usual, Bill refused to say one way or the other, only increasing the already rampant speculation. In fact, he was halfway sure this would be his last game ever at Candlestick Park, though he couldn't yet bring himself to tell anyone.

The second subject was the Niners' opponent, the Minnesota Vikings, victors in the previous week's wild card game. The scenario surrounding these two teams' matchup was virtually the same as it had been in the 1987 playoffs, when the Vikings came into Candlestick off a wild card victory, and now "Déjà vu or not?" was being flogged all over the sports pages. Most stories, of course, included a rehash of that devastating thrashing Minnesota had delivered twelve months earlier. This time, though, Walsh felt little of the anxiety that had led him to run his team's legs off trying to get ready for last year's playoff. Indeed, Bill, who had personally managed every detail of his team for ten years, startled his staff as the playoffs began by letting go of tasks that he had previously reserved for himself. He even told Mike Holmgren to draw up the game plan and then bring it to him for approval, a delegation of offensive responsibility that had never ever happened before. Nor did the déjà vu aspects seem to bother Walsh. "Last year we were on such a big roll," he pointed out, "and the atmosphere was so positive, nobody seemed to be able to stay with us. This time, we're really sober, and that's probably the best state of mind to be in."

Not that the situation was without pressure. Eddie D. had not forgotten last year and made it very clear that a repeat might very well doom any future Walsh might have with the Niners. On the Thursday before the game, Bill played tennis, and afterward, he and his tennis partner were soaking in the coaches' hot tub when Eddie's lawyer, Carmen Policy, walked by. Policy stopped long enough to admonish Bill that he had better win this game. "He said it," the tennis partner recalled, "like, if you don't win you're not worth a shit."

When Policy was gone, Bill shook his head. "Isn't it amazing?" he said. "I'm going to let a guy like that define my career by this game?"

On Sunday, the field at Candlestick was its usual slick surface. There had been rain earlier in the week, but, rather than covered with a tarp, the turf had been left open to the elements and showed it. By then everyone knew that the winner today would play the Chicago Bears, who had won their playoff with the Philadelphia Eagles on Saturday. During warm-ups, Walsh seemed as loose as his team had ever seen him, though he did have a moment of intense déjà vu. "Everything looked the same," he recalled, "their uniforms and ours, the weather, the crowd. It seemed like a continuation. But this time, we owned the psychological edge. We came in with the inspiration, as they had the year before. I went into this one confident that we would beat them, and beat them soundly."

Minnesota nonetheless got on the board first, with a field goal on their opening drive. After that, however, the Niners seized the game by the scruff of the neck. San Francisco's first two possessions ended in punts, but the offense clicked the third time around when a Minnesota punt left them with a short field, taking possession on the Vikings' forty-eight. Montana then ran for one first down, used three more plays to get two more, then hit Rice for a touchdown and it was 7–3. Minnesota started its next possession by throwing a pass right to Ronnie Lott, who returned the interception to their thirty-yard line. Montana immediately gave the ball to Jerry Rice on a reverse and he wasn't stopped until he reached the nine. Roger Craig then ran the ball twice before Joe hit Jerry again in the end zone. It was now 14–3 and Joe Montana had thrown six passes without an incompletion. The second quarter was more of the same. After an exchange of punts, the Niners defense picked up its first two of six sacks in the game, and the offense took possession on its own twenty-nine. Seven plays later, Rice caught yet another Montana touchdown pass and the Niners went in at halftime leading 21–3. Montana had been eleven for fourteen and Rice's three touchdown catches in one half was an NFL record, leading the CBS television analyst John Madden to declare that "the Forty Niners came out here as close to perfect as you can be."

The second half wasn't quite that good, but almost. Minnesota again scored first, a touchdown and missed extra point, but, after that, they were done. The Niners consumed the last five minutes of the third quarter and the first minute of the fourth with a drive that started on their own twenty and ended with a four-yard touchdown run by Roger Craig. After giving the ball up on a fumble on their next possession but stopping the Vikings on downs deep in their own territory, the Niners took the ball back on their own thirteen. Tom Rathman carried up to the twenty on first down and then San Francisco slammed the door and nailed it shut. On second and three, Walsh called Craig's number off the left side behind Steve Wallace and Jesse Sapolu. The two linemen opened a huge gap for Craig, who burst through, juked a defensive back, and was gone—eighty yards to make the score 34–9. The Niners botched the extra point but it didn't matter. "Looks like they're going to Chicago," one of the CBS announcers offered.

Over the remaining nine minutes of the game the television network did its best to fill airtime with lingering shots of Steve Young going into the game to mop up and Joe Montana coming out and being greeted by his coach, all intercut with the backdrop of exultant Niners fans already celebrating. The newspaper writers close by in the press box were already working on their stories for the morning editions and they would be nothing but laudatory of the Niners: The offensive line had been "impregnable"; Seifert's defense had been "bewildering"; Roger Craig had "showed why he was voted NFL Offensive Player of the Year"; Joe Montana had been "undeniably brilliant"; Jerry Rice had "exorcised his playoff demons"; Bill Walsh's play calling had been "brilliant and beautiful"; and the Forty Niners "didn't just even a score—they dominated and humiliated."

Back live, coming out of a commercial break, CBS's John Madden said he didn't expect Walsh to return to coaching next year. "The end is near," he predicted.

When the clock reached 3:00, CBS cut to a live shot of the Niners' locker room. There, a jubilant Eddie DeBartolo was waiting for his team to arrive. And the soft-drink cooler was noticeably intact.

Walsh's players briefly lifted their coach onto their shoulders after the final gun, then they all ran up the tunnel together to meet Eddie.

Bill would later describe the next week's game in Chicago as "one for the ages." But before he got to it, his life intruded on his football.

Walsh's family had been in something of a shambles for months now. His separation from Geri had become public knowledge early in 1988 when the *Chronicle*'s gossip columnist ran an item about his "affair" with Kristine Hanson—only adding to Geri's fury, his own sense of disconnection, and his children's feelings of alienation from him. But, while Bill felt badly for her embarrassment and missed the stabilizing anchor Geri had always provided, he remained apart, living with Hanson in Los Altos Hills and sometimes sleeping in his office at 4949 Centennial Way. That, however, was about to change.

After the Minnesota win, Walsh received the worst family news he could imagine. His eldest son, Steve, thirty-four, had been experiencing mysterious symptoms for weeks, which had led him to undergo a bevy of medical tests. When the results finally came in, they were horrifying. Steve Walsh had been infected with HIV, the dread viral precursor of AIDS. Given the state of medical technology then, it was, in effect, a death sentence.

Bill was stunned and inundated with feelings of guilt. "I felt like I had let my family down," he explained, even though he, of course, had nothing to do with the infection. His response was to try to support his son—though for public consumption he would always refer to Steve's illness as "leukemia"—and to reconstruct his family as best he could.

In a matter of days, Bill shut down his romance with Kristine, reconciled with Geri, and moved back into his home in Menlo Park. "He just didn't know how to go on without his team, with his son ill, and the loss of his marriage," Kristine explained. "It was too much for him to cope with."

In the meantime, Walsh turned back to the football field to immerse himself in his Niners' final magic moments.

On Friday, Bill flew to Chicago in advance of his team's arrival in order to take part in the league-mandated pregame press conference. He thumbed through a pile of papers in his limo on the way from the airport and noticed that all the Chicago media outlets were unanimously convinced the Bears would crush the Forty Niners. Some were even speculating about how many points the Bears would then go on to win the Super Bowl by. Partly that confidence was just a matter of records. Chicago, 12-4 in the regular season, had tied the AFC's Cincinnati Bengals for best record in the NFL and had bludgeoned the Forty Niners on Monday night back in week eight. The other part of what made them so sure was the weather forecast. Despite Friday's balmy fifty degrees, there was a winter storm on its way out of the Yukon that promised to drop temperatures to zero or lower by the next day. This was "Bears weather," which everyone in Chicago agreed would be far fiercer than any California team could ever hope to handle.

"At the press conference," Bill remembered, "I reminded the media that we were a competitive team and warned them not to be too sure of themselves. I was strongly challenged as to how I could be so positive about this team, when the Forty Niners had been 6–5 at one point and had had a season-long quarterback controversy. In their minds it was a matter of getting this game over with so they could go on to Miami for the Super Bowl. They doubted we would even make a game of it. In a television interview following the press conference, a Chicago sportscaster became quite argumentative when I spoke positively about our chances, and concluded by reminding his viewers that the Forty Niners must now face 'the team of destiny.'"

The weather forecast for game day proved right on the mark. On Sunday, the temperature at Soldier Field, counting wind chill, was twenty-six below. And the hours before kickoff were consumed with both teams playing psychological warfare around the freezing conditions. The underdogs went first, with Ronnie Lott, Eric Wright, and Jeff Fuller taking the frozen field to loosen up, wearing just their uniform pants topped with cut-off T-shirts. When Harry Edwards, bundled in a parka, strolled out into the frigid wind, he found three of the Chicago defensive starters watching Lott and the others. The Bears were without pads, but wearing long-sleeve jerseys, ear muffs, turtlenecks, and gloves. "Ronnie, Jeff, and Eric were running up and down the field," Edwards remembered. "They ran about five one hundred's, then back and forth across the field, and all the rest of their usual warmup, backpedaling and the like. Eventually I said to Ronnie, 'How does it feel?' And Ronnie says, 'It's great, Doc. It feels great.' They were all dripping sweat and had soaked through their T-shirts. I stood there for a while and then one of the Chicago players walked past me and says, 'Hey, I want every one of them boys drug tested.' "

The next round was the home team's. When the rest of the Niners emerged to get loose, dressed in their pads and game gear, two of the Bears defensive tackles came out in their jerseys, with their arms bared to the weather, seemingly impervious, hands on hips, and just stared at Walsh's players, thinking to intimidate the California boys. "We began to joke about it," Bill remembered, "how they looked. We were even more exhilarated returning to the dressing room, saying that the Bears were so contemptuous of us that they thought they could intimidate us simply by standing there with their hands on their hips, holding in their stomachs. Word got around the locker room about their staring us down during the pregame warmups and everybody was joking and laughing about it."

As kickoff time approached and his team prepared to leave the locker room and step into the meat-locker conditions of Soldier Field, Bill would later say he had never seen a team "more up for a game" than his was in that moment. Harry Edwards agreed. "There was a crackle in the locker-room air," Doc recalled. "Bill called the guys to gather up and everyone was standing there and he looks at them and says 'Let's go. We know what we've got to do.' They didn't scream or bust the door down. They just walked out like guys going to pick up something that they knew already had their names engraved on it."

Once the game was under way, the first two series went nowhere for each team, but Walsh was confident. The game plan Holmgren had devised reverted to the approach Bill had used to dismantle the 46 defense in 1984 and he was sure it would work. "Short, timed passes were well-suited for such weather," he noted, "and could be thrown and caught before the defense could respond. The Bears wouldn't be able to get close to Joe and their cornerbacks didn't have the quickness to stay with Jerry or John Taylor. And our style of cut blocking was ideally suited to stop their tall, rangy defensive linemen. We were much quicker than they were and just attacked them." That approach began bearing fruit after Chicago's third possession went nowhere and the Niners ended up with the ball at their own thirty-eight.

Their first two plays only picked up a yard between them and it was starting to look as though this was going to be a grind-it-out contest in which even first downs would be hard to come by. Then Walsh called Jerry Rice's number. Rice ran up the right sideline and after fifteen yards was behind the cornerback. The pattern was the same one Mike Wilson had run to bail the Niners out with a critical first down during the second half against Cincinnati in Super Bowl XVI. This time, Montana let fly in Rice's direction but the wind picked the ball up and Jerry had to leap to secure it. The cornerback wasn't close enough to tackle him when he came down, but the safety was charging over with a bead on the Niners receiver. Jerry gave him a hip fake that sent him sprawling, cut toward the middle of the field, and didn't stop until he reached the end zone, sixty-one yards away. San Francisco 7, Chicago 0.

The Bears tried to answer early in the second quarter, but strong safety Jeff Fuller picked off their pass and carried it to the San Francisco forty. Then Montana went to work, finding Rice on a slant pattern for twenty yards. Tom Rathman followed that with a rumble down to Chicago's twenty-seven. Then Walsh called Rice's number again. This time, Jerry went in motion from right to left and the Chicago cornerback shadowed him across the field. When the ball was snapped, the corner moved up to bump Rice and throw him off stride but missed, and Jerry broke across the middle, waving his hand to tell Joe he was wide open. Montana's pass was down at Rice's knees, but he scooped it up and bolted twenty-seven yards to pay dirt. San Francisco 14, Chicago 0.

And by then the game was essentially over. The final score would be 28–3, but the margin could have been even larger. Throwing into the teeth of the famous "Hawk" blowing off Lake Michigan, so cold that just looking into it made his eyes water, Joe Montana was seventeen of twenty-seven for 288 yards. Jerry Rice's five catches accounted for 133 of those yards as well as two touchdowns. This was "one of the greatest games Joe Montana has ever played," Bill proclaimed afterward. But the game itself was devoid of suspense. Bears fans began evacuating Soldier Field in the third quarter. And no one had any more disparaging remarks to make about the Forty Niners. As unlikely as it had once seemed, they had defeated two straight playoff opponents by identical margins of twenty-five points and were headed for their third Super Bowl in eight years.

"The idea that the 49ers had something to prove this season seems ludicrous now," one *Chronicle* columnist crowed the next morning, "a bit of ancient history. They are clearly the best team in football."

Of course, the Niners would have to prove that at Super Bowl XXIII in Miami. In a poetic twist, their opponent would be Paul Brown's Cincinnati Bengals, giving Bill Walsh the chance to finalize his legacy against the man whose shadow had dominated much of his early NFL career and whose rejection had been the most hurtful experience of his professional life.

When the Niners arrived at their Miami hotel, Eddie D. attempted a reprise of Walsh's famous masquerade in advance of Super Bowl XI in Detroit. DeBartolo, wearing a bellhop's uniform, walked up to Walsh and started to take his briefcase. A brief wrestling match ensued until the owner was revealed under the bellman's hat. Afterward, when a reporter asked Bill if he had tipped Eddie, he chuckled and said he didn't, but Eddie'd "had his hand out."

Later in the week, Eddie would also weigh in on Bill's future—a subject about which Bill himself was not commenting. Eddie D. said he didn't know what Walsh was going to do, but his "gut feeling" was that his coach was not coming back. "Bill seems very at peace with himself," Eddie observed. "He's just enjoying what he's doing. That makes me think he's made up his mind. I wouldn't say it's etched in stone that he's not going to coach. I think [it's] 80–20. I can't unequivocally say that, but I don't think he's going to coach. He just wants to wait till after the season's over [to deal with it]. I believe that Monday, probably, or maybe Tuesday at the latest, he'll [make an announcement]."

At the moment, of course, Walsh's concentration was on the Bengals. They were a formidable squad. Their quarterback, Boomer Esiason, was the league's Most Valuable Player; their left tackle, Anthony Munoz, was the league's best at his position, maybe the best ever; and their rookie sensation at running back, Ickey Woods, had been turning heads all season. And they were coached by Sam Wyche, Bill's old friend and protégé, who had a knack for causing the Niners problems whenever he coached against them. Cincinnati had been only 4-11 during 1987, and their 12-4 record this season amounted to the biggest one-year turnaround in NFL history. "We know what they can do," Bill said. "They're explosive on offense and Sam is the most creative coach in football." Walsh told everyone who would listen that the Bengals posed an enormous challenge, but in truth, he thought "we had a much stronger and more experienced team." If the Niners did win, they would do so with the worst regular season record, 10-6, of any NFL champion since 1934.

The game itself would eventually be described by NFL commissioner Pete Rozelle as "the most exciting Super Bowl ever," but Bill called it "one of the most frustrating games I ever coached." The first half was certainly nothing much to write home about. The Niners drove deep into Cincinnati territory in the first quarter but a critical incompletion at the Bengals' two-yard line forced them to settle for a field goal. Cincinnati answered that with a drive and a field goal of their own in the second quarter to make the score 3–3. Before the half, San Francisco mustered another drive that ended up with a fourth down in front of Cincinnati's goal line. Walsh chose to play it safe and went for the field goal, but the attempt was botched by a bad snap and they came away with nothing. Walsh would spend a lot of time in future years wishing he could have taken that decision back. Contrary to everyone's expectations, these two highly touted offenses went into the locker room at halftime tied with one field goal apiece.

The second half was more back and forth. Matching field goals and a Cincinnati touchdown on a kickoff return in the third quarter were followed by an eighty-five-yard Forty Niners touchdown drive early in the fourth, bringing the score to 13–13. San Francisco missed another field goal and its chance to take the lead, and then Cincinnati tipped the balance with its own field goal and went on top 16–13. The Niners then got the ball back with 3:10 remaining, on their own eight-yard line. And it was only at this point that the game got really, really good.

Later, when looking back at the Niners' effort in Super Bowl XXIII, the most obvious attribute of Walsh's team that day was that their great players played great. San Francisco's three superstars, all future Hall of Famers, all came up big.

Jerry Rice would eventually be named the game's Most Valuable Player, and he earned it. He caught eleven passes before it was over, for 215 yards—the first number tying a Super Bowl record and the second breaking another. On the team's first touchdown drive he caught one thirty-one-yard bomb and then, from Cincinnati's fourteen, took a short throw at the five and fought his way into the end zone. For much of the game, he seemed to be single-handedly keeping the Niners in it.

As was his habit, Ronnie Lott's contribution set the tone for everyone else. During the first two quarters, the Bengals rookie back, Ickey Woods, had gained almost sixty yards, and as Walsh's team was headed to the field after halftime, Bill told them they had to stop Woods and if they could shut down the Bengals' running game, they would win. Ronnie'd had his eye on Woods for a while. "I had studied film of him for two weeks," Lott explained, "and I hadn't seen any free safeties make a good straight-on hit. When Woods rambled into the secondary, guys just brought him down from the side. Why hadn't anyone laid any wood on this guy? I felt as though Woods thought he had a big red *S* on his chest. I was determined to hit him full speed. I wanted to make sure he remembered me."

That memory arrived when Ickey broke through the Niners' line on the Bengals' first possession of the third quarter, seemingly headed for a big gain. Then here came Ronnie, head on, full speed. The sound of their collision could be heard from one end of the stadium to the other and Ickey stood straight up, then fell over backward. Harry Edwards was on the sideline just a few yards away, standing next to Forty Niners staffer R. C. Owens. "That boy wasn't the same after that hit," Edwards noted, "not only for the rest of that game—he wasn't the same for the rest of his career. I turned to R.C. right after it and said, 'R.C., I think that boy just decided he don't want to play football no more.' A lot happened after that, but the thing that turned that game around was that hit Ronnie put on Ickey Woods."

The most dramatic role in the legend of Super Bowl XXIII, however, belonged to Joe Montana, starting with the clock stopped at 3:10 for a television timeout, his team down by three, and backed up about as far as it could be. Walsh sent his quarterback out after a brief consultation on the sideline. They had time, Bill said. No reason to panic. They would go with their basic offense. "In that kind of situation," Bill explained, "with the pressure that's on the team, you want to have familiar plays that men are confident they can execute, rather than trying high-risk plays and depending on great individual effort. In this circumstance, we were going to depend heavily on our 'standard of performance.' We put together a series that I felt confident Joe, with his poise and spontaneity, would execute. These were plays selected to attack the basic Bengals defense. They were high-percentage plays that would result in steady gains if properly executed."

When Joe reached the huddle, the tension in the stadium was so thick you could have chopped it with an axe, but "Joe was real calm," Tom Rathman remembered. The quarterback's attention was immediately caught by right tackle Harris Barton. Barton was the team worrier, known for his anxiety about everything that could possibly go wrong. He had also gained a reputation during the previous week for always pointing out celebrities in town for the game. At that moment, Barton had a face full of worry. "Hey, H.," Joe said, trying to break the tackle's reverie and nodding with his head toward the end zone seats behind him, "isn't that John Candy over there?" Joe sounded like he was sitting on the grass after practice, just having fun. Everyone in the huddle looked and sure enough, the comedian was where Joe said he was. The distraction over, Montana got down to business.

What followed would be remembered in Forty Niners' lore as "The Drive."

Just as Walsh had strategized, the Niners began by grabbing off yardage in manageable chunks. Joe hit Craig out of the backfield for eight yards, then tight end John Frank for seven more and a first down. Next he went to Rice in the flat for seven, followed by a Craig run to the right side for one, another Craig run to the right for four, and another first down. By now, the Niners were at their thirty-five with the clock stopped at 1:54. When play resumed, Montana went back to his workhorse Jerry Rice on the left side for seventeen, then found Craig for another thirteen. Now, however, with the stadium so loud it was hard to hear the play being called in the huddle, Montana hit a speed bump. He had another pass play to Rice called but when he started screaming the signals, he remembered, "I felt I was yelling as loud as I could, but no one could hear me." The effort caused Joe to hyperventilate. And as he took the ball and faded back, he almost passed out. He only just managed to throw the ball away for the first incompletion of the drive. Joe signaled over to the sideline for a time-out to let him recover, but Bill, not having any idea what was going on, waved off his request.

With 1:22 to go, the Niners' endgame ran into its first serious setback when Bill called a complex pass play that required faking a screen pass to

Craig on the left side and then having Craig wheel into a pass pattern across the middle instead. To make the fake, Randy Cross had to pull out as though on a screen. "It had been a good play for us in the past in games like this," Bill later explained, "and they were in the right defense for us to utilize it. I wasn't happy with myself even as I called the play, though, because it was too low a percentage play for that situation." Sure enough, Craig was bumped and delayed getting into the pattern and Randy Cross ended up across the line of scrimmage and was called for a ten-yard penalty. That moved them back to Cincinnati's forty-five, facing second down and twenty yards to go. Seemingly up against it, Montana went back to the game's MVP. Rice, who had been running outside routes all day, now broke one over the middle, caught Joe's pass, split two defenders, and wasn't stopped until he had gained twenty-seven yards and another first down. It was the second most important play of the drive.

Now they were well within field goal range and Craig got them even closer with an eight-yard pickup to the Bengals' ten. Montana called a time-out with thirty-nine seconds left and came over to talk with his coach. First, Bill laid out their larger strategy. He wanted to go for the end zone twice now and if those efforts failed, he was going to kick the field goal to tie the game. Then Bill selected the next call, 20 Halfback Curl X Up. "That play was designed specifically for the coverage the Bengals used," he pointed out. "Inside their own fifteen, they locked their linebackers on the tight end and running backs and had their safeties double cover the wide receivers in combination with the cornerbacks. Roger would run the same pattern as he had on the previous play, occupying the linebackers, and John Taylor would break open behind him, after first faking a move to the outside." The last thing Bill told Joe as he headed back onto the field was not to force it. They had another shot after this one.

The play almost turned into a disaster. Craig and Rathman, essentially interchangeable on most plays, often switched positions in the backfield of their own volition and they mistakenly did so again now. Craig realized they were lined up on the wrong sides but decided to carry out the pattern he would have if he had lined up where Bill expected him to. Rathman, thinking he had Craig's responsibilities now, ran the pattern as well, so there was no one left in the backfield to pick up the blitz. The last thing Craig saw on his way into his pass pattern was two blitzers headed straight for Joe. At the same time, the cover linebackers chased Roger. Montana saw the Bengals

Joe Montana, Eddie DeBartolo, and Bill Walsh
in the locker room after Super Bowl XXIII

coming and looked to his left for Taylor, his hot receiver. At the same time, the safety bit on Taylor's fake to the outside, allowing him to clear the cornerback to the inside, and he popped open. Joe delivered a strike to his wideout before any defenders could reach him. Touchdown, Niners 20, Bengals 16, and not enough time left for Cincinnati to do anything about it.

On the other side of the country, San Francisco erupted into the streets when Taylor cradled the ball in the end zone. The celebration there would last all night and lead to more than forty arrests for disorderly conduct. The next day's *Examiner* would be headlined, TEAM OF THE '80S, and by then *Dynasty* would already be in widespread use, right after the words *Forty Niners*. Back at Miami's Joe Robbie Stadium, the Niners' postgame locker room was awash in champagne, with Eddie D. cavorting about, soaked to the skin, hugging anybody and everybody. Eddie's Super Bowl party, in a tent outside the stadium, would last until morning as well. After the commissioner had presented the championship trophy, one of the television announcers caught up with Bill Walsh.

Bill was standing there, drenched in wine and sweat, with one arm around the shoulder of his son Craig, looking both dazed and ecstatic. The announcer asked him if this had been his last game.

Walsh started to answer but broke down crying, fell into his boy's arms, and couldn't go on.

That question didn't really get answered at his press conference the next morning either. Walsh talked around it, listing the reasons to retire and the reasons not to, but repeated that he was not yet ready to choose one or the other. He said he was going to consult with Eddie first, when they both were back in California. Then he'd make up his mind.

Otherwise, Bill Walsh's Monday morning remarks were most memorable for the grudge he demonstrated against the reporters there from San Francisco. The press conference began with an extraordinary show of respect when the assembled media gave Bill an ovation as he took the podium—something reporters just don't normally do for the subjects they write about. But after the applause died down, Bill started things with his first backhand slap at the people who covered him every day. "I see none of our local press were clapping," he sniped. He returned to that theme whenever another opportunity presented itself. "I love my work," he noted at one point when talking about coaching, "even though at times some of these gentlemen don't," motioning at the Bay Area locals. When asked about earlier in the season when there were rumors that Eddie D. might fire him, Bill claimed, "I know there were a lot of people locally in our press that were really rooting for it." One Denver reporter counted up a total of seven such swipes, causing a number of the national reporters to shake their heads as it went on and on.

And the Bay Area media were even more put out. "He was his most ungracious," one of them recalled. "I wondered what is it with this guy that he can't enjoy this moment and has to spend it taking potshots at the press? He's the most revered coach on the planet at his hour of triumph and he has to go after a bunch of sportswriters? I sat there with my mouth open. I thought, 'This guy is really lost.'"

In any case, Bill was back in California by that afternoon, riding in a convertible down Market Street next to Eddie D. as tens of thousands cheered while he tried to sort out in his head what to do next.

It would be hard to locate when exactly Walsh made up his mind to step out of his coaching harness. Bill himself often gave different versions of it, varying from back when his team was 6-5 to the night before he actually

quit. In truth, it was probably all of the above. The burnout that was pushing him out of the NFL had been around for at least a year, perhaps longer.
But he also kept accumulating additional reasons to leave along the way.
The most recent was his decision to try to patch together his family. When
he and Geri discussed reconciliation, she had given him a clear ultimatum.
"She was on him constantly about it," their son Craig explained. "She brow-
beat him through a number of scenarios to get out. Otherwise she threat-
ened to divorce." It was a demand Bill had a hard time resisting in the
depleted state he was in. "I had a choice to quit coaching or to quit being
married," Walsh later recalled. "When it came down to it, it was a decision
of love."

Nonetheless, he would come in retrospect to regret his timing. "I should
have coached a couple more years," he speculated. "I really should have. But
it was hard to see at the time. I didn't have anybody to talk to about it. If I'd
had someone to talk to, it wouldn't have taken much to have me stay and
just take a furlough for thirty days to clear my head. I think I had more
coaching left." That idea, however, may just have been a retired man's pipe
dream. "I don't think he ever really regretted it," Kristine Hanson offered.
"There was no way he could have continued on. Leaving was his only real
option. There was no other way out of the emotional corner he was in."
Certainly his compulsion to step down was apparent. "He just had this 'I've
got to get out of here' attitude," one of his longtime coaching buddies observed. "It was almost like a kind of claustrophobic panic."

Bill told Eddie he was leaving that Wednesday. DeBartolo was staying at
a resort down in Carmel in advance of golfing in the pro-am event of the
AT&T tournament at nearby Pebble Beach, and Bill drove down to discuss
it. Eddie had Carmen Policy with him and their first response was to try to
talk Bill out of hanging it up, even offering a considerable raise in salary if
he would stay on. Bill was adamant, however, and they ended up spending
most of their time deciding that George Seifert would be the man to replace
him. On Thursday, they told the press.

It was a historic moment and everyone there seemed to sense as much.
The ruffled feelings from Monday's press conference were put aside. This
was the end of an era and the departure of a figure who would dominate
Bay Area sports history for the foreseeable future, a man for the ages. The
announcement itself, at a press conference in Monterey, was—by Walsh's
design—anticlimactic. He centered the event on introducing Seifert as the

new head coach and treated his own resignation as a secondary by-product. Bill wanted a seamless transition for the good of the franchise and that meant no lingering on his exit.

Nonetheless, the import was unavoidable. Eddie D. seemed a little stunned and often near tears. When not skirting tears himself, Bill seemed full of light, like a man who had just discovered an open door along the back wall of his life. It would take several months to completely extricate himself from the organization he had built, but, for the first time in thirty-one years, Bill Walsh would not have a team to call his own come next football season. The decade that enshrined him forever after as The Genius was now done.

Stanford Memorial Church,
Stanford University, August 9, 2007

EPILOGUE · THE GENIUS, REST IN PEACE

The loose ends to this story eventually converged in Stanford University's Memorial Church some eighteen years after the story ended and ten days after Bill Walsh's death, late on an August morning at much the same hour as he would have been putting his team through its first daily workout at training camp in the old days.

The *San Francisco Chronicle* had headlined THE GENIUS, 1931–2007 across half of its front page when news of Walsh's July 30 passing was released and, along with an eleven-inch-tall photo of him under the headline, devoted three more pages on the inside of its front section and four in its sports section to a review of his life and contributions, then followed that two days later with a full-page color photo of him inscribed, "You made us believe. You made us proud. You made us champions." *The New York Times* printed Bill's picture on the front page with a jump to the obituaries where he was given four full columns above the fold, citing his reputation as "The Genius" and describing him as "one of professional football's most influential figures." *Time* and *Newsweek* ran obituaries as well, along with virtually every publication in the nation with a sports page. A public memorial was planned for the following day, at which thousands would assemble in Candlestick Park to remember him, but the Memorial Church gathering was the "private" ceremony meant for some eight hundred invited family, friends, colleagues, and teammates. Bill had spent his last months designing the event, making it, in effect, his final game plan.

His choice of Stanford as a venue was an obvious one. Bill had lived just up the road since his Genius decade ended and the university had been a refuge to which he had returned twice in the meantime. The initial return had been his last hurrah as a coach. Bill had first tried working as a television commentator with NBC, broadcasting college games, but he had not enjoyed it. There was too much show business, too much preparation required, too much time on the road, and he dreaded the seemingly incessant hectoring from his producers. After two years Walsh gave up on television and Stanford hired him to reprise his first tour there on the sidelines. That lasted three mostly disappointing years. Genius or not, Bill no longer had the edge and drive required for big-time football coaching and he left the profession for good after two straight losing seasons with the Cardinal. He returned to Stanford again ten years later, as assistant and then interim athletic director, the job he was holding when his cancer emerged and turned him into an almost full-time patient over the last year of his life, though he continued to appear at the athletic department offices whenever he was able. His bond with the university was by then central to who he was. Stanford's current football team, dressed in slacks and game jerseys, served as the memorial's ushers.

The religious portion of the service was eclectic, but more Catholic than anything else. Walsh had been raised a Baptist but had had little to do with any religion for most of his life. Then seven years before his death, he had converted to Catholicism at the urging of Geri, herself a lifetime Roman Catholic. In addition to a welcome from the dean of the chapel and an opening prayer and commentary from Stanford's Catholic chaplain and Bill's personal priest, the program included readings from the apostle Paul and from the Psalms, with religious music supplied by a Protestant choir from Glide Memorial Church in San Francisco. The other music in the program was a stirring tenor solo of the song "Danny Boy." Bill had been searching for someone to perform "Danny Boy" during his last weeks, when he happened to mention his quest to the psychiatrist he had retained to help his family adjust to his coming demise. The psychiatrist, it turned out, was an amateur entertainer known for his tenor renditions of Bill's favorite song, and, at the service, he brought tears to the eyes of most of the crowd.

There was also a welcoming speech by Bill's son Craig, and his daughter, Elizabeth. Bill's eldest son, Steve, had died of "leukemia" in 2002, after spending his last years as a railroad engineer in the southwest. Geri sat in the front row. Her marriage with Bill had endured and by the time of his death had lasted more than fifty years. Geri had suffered a stroke eight years earlier and was partially incapacitated. With nursing assistance, Bill had been her primary caretaker while he was still able, and now that he was gone she would sell their home in Woodside and move into an assisted-living facility in Palo Alto. Seated behind the family among the front pews were a number of Walsh's friends from his San Jose State days. They had remained part of his life to the very end. The group of buddies had played a lot of golf together in his last years and referred to Bill as "The Toe," citing his alleged proclivity for improving his lie with a quick stroke of his foot. They all still considered him as good a friend as anyone could hope to have. "Bill did friendship like no one else," one pointed out.

Aside from Steve's, there were a few other ghosts afoot that morning in Memorial Church as well. Bill's mother, Ruth, and father, William Archibald, were long since dead, but their picture was in the ceremony's glossy eight-page program, standing with their five-year-old son in front of the family's Los Angeles bungalow. Bob Bronzan, the coach at San Jose State who had inspired Walsh to take up coaching and whom Bill had helped support in his old age, had died the previous January. Edward J. DeBartolo Sr., whose fortune had bankrolled the Bill Walsh era at the Forty Niners, had died in 1994, leaving an estate estimated in excess of $1 billion, divided equally between his son, Eddie, and his daughter, Denise DeBartolo York. And Paul Brown, who gave Bill his first big chance in the NFL and then did his best to sabotage his career, had died in 1991. Bill had interviewed his former mentor for NBC before his death, and the two had reached a reconciliation of sorts. "He told me he'd made a big mistake," Bill explained, "but there was no conversation about when I left or anything. The subject was just too fraught with conflict and terrible feelings."

There was no such negativity among those gathered in Memorial Church, however. "This is like a family reunion," Dwight Clark observed.

Bill's reconciliation with Eddie D. had been far more successful than the one with Paul Brown. The wounds from those last years with the Niners had healed relatively quickly. Indeed, DeBartolo had even brought Bill back to the franchise a decade after he left. By then, however, Eddie's status as an NFL owner was in deep trouble. His difficulties began in 1997, when he was implicated in the bribery and conspiracy investigation targeting Louisiana governor Edwin Edwards. The FBI produced wiretaps and a bag full of cash as evidence Eddie had paid $400,000 to Edwards in order to secure a New Orleans casino license for the DeBartolo Corp. Eventually Eddie D. pled guilty and turned state's evidence against Edwards. In the meantime, he voluntarily promised the NFL he would maintain an "inactive" status as an owner until his legal problems were resolved, installing his sister, Denise, as the franchise's temporary CEO. At the same time, Eddie had broken with his former lawyer Carmen Policy, whom he had installed as the team's president after Bill's departure, and the dynasty was starting to come apart. In 1999, he asked Bill to come back and reconstruct his team as general manager.

Bill agreed, but before their reborn partnership could go very far, Eddie ran afoul of his sister and the family corporation. In late 1986, at the end of Bill's second straight year of falling short of a third Super Bowl, Eddie had ignored the league rules prohibiting corporate ownership and transferred official title of the franchise to the DeBartolo Corp.—an arrangement that allowed him to use DeBartolo Corp. funds rather than his own to pay for not only the team but also his trips via corporate jet to see his team play and other indulgences. By 1999, his sister, Denise, fed up with Eddie's high rolling, had the family corporation cut off his jet and join her in a suit to force her brother to reimburse almost $100 million in personal extravagances that he had charged off on the corporation. Eddie countersued, then attempted to buy out his sister's interest in the football franchise, all to no avail. Before 1999 was over, his legal settlement with his sister forced him to cede control of his beloved Forty Niners to Denise and her husband, John York.

Eddie's unanticipated departure left Bill working for the Yorks, and that was not a well-made match. "John York hated Bill," one team employee later observed, "but not as much as Bill hated York." On top of that, Bill Walsh was not the same football presence as he had been. "Walsh can't do it anymore and that now is obvious," the *Chronicle* claimed after he'd been at the GM job for a year. "The problem is that he's not the independent, confident decision maker he once was, a man who acted decisively and didn't give a damn what anybody thought about it. . . . The Walsh of the '80s had a lot more inner fight than Walsh has now." In any case, Bill stepped down as the Niners' GM in 2001 for a job as a team consultant and was gone from the Niners altogether before two more years were out, having by then become a commonly ignored office fixture without a clear or important role.

In 2006, Eddie, now reportedly a billionaire himself, staged a reunion of all his Super Bowl teams—including the ones that had won two more after Bill's last—in Las Vegas for three days, flying everyone from around the country and putting them up on his tab. He dubbed the affair "Five Rings." At the reunion banquet, his former players had presented Eddie with a framed Niners' jersey autographed by everyone, with the name "Mr. D" sewn across the shoulders on its back. When DeBartolo learned not long afterward that Walsh was sick, he flew out to the Bay Area immediately. And at the memorial service, Eddie was one of those Bill selected to give a "reflection" on his life.

Standing in front of the altar with its huge black-and-white photo of Bill in his coaching gear, Eddie read a brief speech. "Not one conversation I ever had with Bill was wasted," he pointed out. The most recent of those had been on his former coach's deathbed. Then Bill had told him, " 'Well, this is it. I'm at a place and in peace with everything.' Bill died the way he lived," Eddie continued, "with sublime grace and with class. He was coaching us, making us stronger and more prepared [for his death]. He told me once that he was in the fourth quarter. Well, the coach was masterful in managing [that] fourth quarter with talent and poise that was better than any of his Super Bowl championships."

In his last years, Eddie closed, Bill "always said 'I love you' " at partings and now Eddie did the same. "Bill, may God bless you. I love you very much."

Another of the "reflections" in the ceremony was offered by the U.S. senator from California Dianne Feinstein, who had just succeeded to San Francisco's mayoralty when Bill was first hired by Eddie D. She recounted how much joy Walsh's teams had brought to the city and remarked at how much happier that first Super Bowl had made everyone, saving the Bay Area from what had been an almost smothering depression. "He gave this city a shot in the arm in some of its darkest hours," she pointed out, "and we owe him a debt of gratitude that can never be repaid."

Feinstein was followed by Roger Goodell, the new NFL commissioner. Noting that Bill had been elected to the league's Hall of Fame in 1993, the first year he was eligible, Goodell offered that "if you gave him a blackboard and a piece of chalk, he would become a whirlwind of wisdom. He taught all of us not only about football but also about life and how it takes teamwork for any of us to succeed as individuals. . . . If there were a Hall of Fame for mentoring, he would be in it too."

In addition to the spoken tributes, there were also eleven short written ones printed in the program, including statements from current secretary of state Condi Rice, former secretary of state George Shultz, and former speaker of the California Assembly Willie Brown. Perhaps the most compelling of the written comments was from Mike Holmgren, Bill's former assistant who had gone on to win one Super Bowl as head coach of the Green Bay Packers and lose two others, one with Green Bay and another as head coach of the Seattle Seahawks. Mike had flown down from the Seahawks training camp to attend the memorial and was seated near the rear, fighting back tears. "Bill was unique in the coaching business," he pointed out. "He was an artist while the rest of us were blacksmiths."

The "reflections" in Bill's plan for his memorial followed a keynote eulogy, delivered by Dr. Harry Edwards. Doc was now a professor emeritus at Cal, but was still doing the same job for the Forty Niners that Bill had hired him for more than twenty years earlier. When Bill had told Edwards that he wanted him to deliver his eulogy, Doc had agreed and asked if Bill would like to read his speech once he had written it.

In response, Walsh had smiled and declined the offer. "Surprise me," he said.

When Edwards delivered his eulogy that morning in Memorial Church, he had to fight back tears. Bill Walsh "was the most gifted teacher I have ever been associated with," he recounted. "Everywhere one turns in this league, one finds the influence and imprint of Bill Walsh. [He] wanted to be remembered as a man who cared about people. He believed that people are at their very best as individuals when they are working with and for each other. . . . He walked with generals, senators, and secretaries of state, but he never lost his common touch. . . . Bill Walsh's life was a portrait of a life well lived. . . . He was a giant. . . . And how truly blessed we have been that someone such as Bill Walsh had passed this way."

Like Eddie and several others, Doc paid homage to the bravery with which Bill Walsh had faced his end.

Bill's illness was first discovered in a 2005 annual exam by his family physician during Walsh's athletic department stint at Stanford. His blood tests indicated he was anemic and his doctor wanted him to see a specialist about it, but, feeling fit and sound, Walsh dragged his feet in following up the recommendation and went on with his life. When he finally saw a specialist almost a year later, the news was bad. Bill was diagnosed with a myelodysplastic syndrome, a leukemia precursor known as MDS, which would eventually become a full-blown cancer of the blood and bone marrow. When Walsh asked what he should do, the doctor responded that there were treatments to help him cope and extend his life a bit, but urged him to get his affairs "in order."

Over the next few months, Bill's symptoms of weakness and exhaustion intensified, sometimes making it difficult just to walk out to the athletic department parking lot to reach his car. And then they got worse. In late October 2006, he had his first crisis and was hospitalized at the Stanford University Medical Center in critical condition. After reaching the edge of death, however, his body fought back and achieved a momentary reprieve, so he was able to spend the first six months of 2007 preparing for his end.

His principal regret remained his decision to retire after Super Bowl XXIII. By then he was convinced he could have won not only a second Super Bowl in a row had he stayed on, but quite possibly a third as well. The team had presented him with a ring for the Super Bowl they had won, finally going back-to-back the year after he left, but the jewelry depressed him so much that he eventually gave it to his son Craig and was glad to be rid of it. Otherwise, as he reflected on his seventy-five years during his rounds of outpatient chemotherapy and transfusions, he found relative peace. "I take solace in my accomplishments," he said. "I've lived a good life. How can I quarrel with it? I'm leaving a legacy and an estate. That probably wouldn't have occurred if Dwight Clark hadn't caught that pass. And I feel very good about that. I'd like to appreciate each day the more I live but I have a hell of a time doing it when I'm in and out of the hospital all the time. I'd like to smell the roses but I can't get outside to smell them. Even so, I've had a good life and I'll be ready to leave when the time comes."

Perhaps Bill's most intense focus in his last months was on trying to remake his relationships with his players. Now capable of showing the feeling he'd had for them all along, he felt compelled to do so.

Jesse Sapolu, an offensive guard during Bill's last two Super Bowls, had experienced his coach's newfound outreach the year before Bill's death. Jesse now lived on the Peninsula and helped out with the coaching of his son's high school football team. "I came home and my wife said, 'Coach called,' " he remembered. "I thought it was one of the coaches from high school and she says, 'No, Coach Walsh called.' I said, 'What did he say?' And she said, 'He called to say that he loves you.' And I sat down and I wept. [Bill] was such an intimidating presence in my life—for him to show the other side was just something else. . . . In the conversation I had with him, when I found out he was ill, we must have spoken a hundred words and fifty of them were, 'I love you.' "

Many others who had played for Bill rallied to his side as he faced death and even more showed up at Memorial Church.

Russ Francis, the tight end who drove Bill crazy with stunts like buzzing the practice field in a World War II fighter plane, had retired to the Islands but flew back to California to honor the man he considered "a close friend." He wore a Hawaiian shirt to the ceremony.

Randy Cross, who had started on the offensive line for every one of Bill's ten seasons, had retired right after Bill's last game and gone into broadcasting, where he was still a regular on CBS's Sunday NFL games. He had flown in from Atlanta, where he now lived. Randy considered Bill the best coach ever, but, like several Niners standouts, Walsh's reputation—credited so widely with the team's success—cast a shadow over Cross's own recognition. Despite being the best offensive lineman on the best offense in the NFL for a decade, Cross had never received serious attention from the Hall of Fame.

Roger Craig, now working with a software company in Silicon Valley, was in a similar position. Despite being the best back Bill Walsh ever coached, an NFL Offensive Player of the Year, and the first back ever to gain a thousand yards rushing and receiving in the same season, he too had been ignored by the Hall. His feelings for Walsh remained intense. "Coach Walsh understood me as a player better than any coach I'd ever had," he explained. "He knew how to utilize my skills to best serve the team. When he retired, part of me died. I wasn't the same running back after he stepped down."

Ronnie Lott had made the Hall of Fame as soon as he was eligible. After leaving the Niners when the league adopted its first tentative version of free agency, he'd played two-year stints with both the Raiders and the Jets before getting out of the game. During the first season after Bill left, Ronnie had angrily insisted that the team play its best to "show Walsh" that they were even better without him and weren't just one of The Genius's constructions. That year gave Ronnie his fourth Super Bowl ring. He retired to the South Bay, where he now pursued media work, community charities, and capital investment. Lott was at Memorial Church, sitting near the front, and contributed one of the written tributes in the program. "What really made Bill special," he wrote, "was that he understood that the game was bigger than him. His genius . . . was centered around his ability to create a platform that made the game inclusive to others. He will forever be cemented with the likes of George Halas, Paul Brown, and Vince Lombardi as the best ever."

Fred Dean, the team's dominant pass rusher in its first two Super Bowls, would make the Hall of Fame as well, but not until after Bill's death. Fred had moved back to his native Ruston, Louisiana, and was rumored to be in ill health and financially pressed. Dean didn't make it to the memorial service, but six months later, when the Hall announced his inclusion, he would say that now that Bill Walsh was dead, he had no idea who he would ask to present him at his induction ceremony.

John Ayers, the offensive guard whose blocks on Lawrence Taylor had helped beat the Giants in the Niners' first playoff game, wasn't at Memorial Church either. John had tried to catch on with the Denver Broncos after Bill let him go, but didn't last a season and had retired to his ranch in Texas, where he'd died of cancer in 1995.

Jack "Hacksaw" Reynolds, the veteran linebacker whose work habits had helped precipitate that first Super Bowl, also wasn't at the church. He was still alive, however, reportedly living on the island in the Bahamas to which he had retired after his short, failed stint as an assistant coach.

Jerry Rice, now universally acclaimed as the greatest wide receiver ever, lived nearby and drove over to Stanford for the memorial. He had finally retired from the NFL just the year before, bowing out in a ceremony at Candlestick Park, where Bill Walsh had been prominent among those paying him tribute. He described Bill as having been "like a father" to him.

Dwight Clark, the tenth-round draft choice who became a mainstay of the Forty Niners' passing game and a Bay Area legend thanks to "The Catch," had flown in from North Carolina and sat in the last pew near the church's doors. He had learned the football business from the ground up in the Forty Niners front office after Bill left, eventually rising to be the team's general manager. As a consequence, he was the only one of his teammates to have rings from all five of the franchise's Super Bowls. He left the Niners along with Carmen Policy and took the general manager job at the Cleveland Browns until finally being let go after limited success. Like most of the men he played with, Dwight still carried the physical leftovers of his playing days. With a bent screw in one shoulder and arthritis in the other, it now hurt when he tried to throw a football and hurt even more when he tried to lift his arms above his head. Done with the NFL, he had "moved back to where I grew up" and was building custom homes in Charlotte. "Even though it's a sad time," he noted after the service, "it's awesome to be around all these people and tell Bill Walsh stories over and over."

Keith Fahnhorst, the anchor on the right side of Bill's offensive line for eight seasons and the team's union rep, had his share of ongoing physical dilemmas as well. His hands often ached from the beating they had taken blocking defensive ends and he couldn't quite reach his six-feet-six height anymore due to the impact of degenerating disks in his back and neck. He'd also undergone a kidney transplant four years earlier. Now a financial counselor and investment advisor, he flew in from Minneapolis, where he'd moved after Bill retired him.

Charle Young, the tight end and locker-room preacher on the Miracle team, had traveled here from Seattle, where he now ran a learning center for "at risk" teenage boys. Charle also provided one of the program's written tributes. "Bill Walsh is the greatest coach to stimulate the minds of his players and those he touched," Young wrote. "What made Bill unique was his ability to bring together different people and unite them for a common goal."

Walsh had picked two from among all the players present to provide verbal "reflections" to the church full of their former comrades. And in a final ironic tweaking of the "quarterback controversy" that had bedeviled his last and most difficult season, Bill's choices for the task were Joe Montana and Steve Young.

Steve, the best trade Bill ever made and second-best quarterback he ever coached, spoke first. Young had taken over the reins of the Niners offense after injuries again caught up with Joe Montana in 1991 and went on to be selected the NFL's Most Valuable Player twice and named to seven Pro Bowls. In 1994, he set a then NFL record for passer ratings with a 112.8 and was named MVP of Super Bowl XXIX, when he threw six touchdown passes to lead San Francisco to a 49–26 pasting of the San Diego Chargers. That win was widely hailed as Young finally getting "the monkey off his back," put there by years of trying to live up to the standards set by Joe. Steve had retired during the 1999 season after a succession of severe concussions and had been voted into the Hall of Fame in 2005. He now lived on the Peninsula and worked as an ESPN football commentator.

That morning in Memorial Church, Steve drew the biggest laughter— some of it a bit nervous—when recounting how Bill used to greet him on the sideline after he'd screwed up, gnashing his teeth and moaning, "Can't you do it like Joe?" He credited Bill with having made him the player he eventually became. "Bill was blessed with one of the greatest gifts you can have," Steve explained, "which is the ability to see the future potential of another human being. . . . He saw in me much more than I ever saw in myself well before I ever had a chance to understand it. That is the ultimate compliment to the word *coach*. There's nothing more a coach should be than to see the full potential of a player unfolded. I am eternally grateful to Bill Walsh."

Joe Montana, identified in the next morning's *Chronicle* as "perhaps the athlete Walsh admired and revered the most," was the event's final speaker before a closing prayer and, by Bill's design, had the last word. Joe had gone on to two more great years for the Niners after Bill left, spurred on by the presence of Steve Young on the bench, just as Walsh had intended. "Before Steve arrived," Keith Fahnhorst pointed out, "Joe was the best in the league. After Steve arrived, Joe was the best ever." Early in the 1991 season, however, Montana's elbow gave out and he spent the rest of that year and all but the last game of the next season on the injured list. Upon his return, the Forty Niners traded him to Kansas City for a first-round draft pick. He played there for a couple of seasons before retiring to a ranch in the Napa Valley, where he pursued advertising endorsements and motivational speaking in his spare time.

Montana had been elected to the Pro Football Hall of Fame in 2000. During his thirteen seasons with the Niners, Joe had compiled a 100-39 record as a starter, was the NFL's Most Valuable Player twice, was selected for the Pro Bowl eight times, and had retired with the highest quarterback rating ever yet compiled. And he paid a significant physical price along the way. "Montana's left knee is essentially shredded," the *Chronicle* had reported earlier that year. "His right eye occasionally sags from nerve damage, [the result of] repeated blows to the head. . . . He [has] had spinal fusion surgery [and] his neck is so stiff, he could not turn his head to look at a reporter asking him questions. . . . Montana turned both shoulders instead."

Joe and Bill had finally put their "creative tension" behind them and became friends after both their careers were over, playing golf together regularly during Bill's last years. The peace and affection that now characterized their relationship was one of Walsh's great joys and touched a deep place in Joe as well. "For me personally," the quarterback explained, "outside of my dad he was probably the most influential person in my life." Montana had to clear his throat several times during his presentation, hoping to overcome the sobs trying to rise out of his chest. Tears were visible on his cheek. He credited Bill with having given him—"a 189-pound, skinny-legged quarterback from western Pennsylvania"—his chance. And with being a guiding light in his life forever after.

Joe too told a story of Bill on the sidelines, admitting that he, like Steve, dreaded coming back to his coach and his pointed stares after screwing up. In one game, though, Joe, having just thrown his second interception, decided not to retreat from Walsh's view but talk back instead.

"What was that?" Bill demanded as Joe ran off the field.

Feeling bold, Joe answered his coach's obviously rhetorical question. "That was an interception," the quarterback declared.

Not expecting a response, Walsh had paused for just a moment and then smiled. "Yes," he said, "and a darn good one. But let's not do it again."

Knowing laughter welled up from the pews.

Joe ended his "reflection" by talking about his last encounter with Bill. By then Walsh was done with the hospital visits and was at home in Woodside under hospice care with just a couple of days left. He had asked Joe to come see him and the two talked at length about their teams and all the men who had played for him and how much he cared for all of them.

"He wanted people to know that he loved you," Montana told his teammates. "So I'm saying that now. And in closing, as I say goodbye to my friend and my coach, I just want to say, 'We love you too.' "

After little more than two hours, the crowd emerged from Memorial Church and onto the surrounding Quadrangle, breaking into small clots of people, greeting one another and talking as they slowly made their way across campus to a catered lunch down by the athletic department. They told Bill Walsh stories for another two hours but none of them referred to him as "The Genius." Most had been the bricks and mortar out of which Walsh's legend had been constructed and found little use in invoking a nickname conferred to capture his attributes and accomplishments for strangers. They knew him too well for that.

To these folks, he was just "Bill." *Complicated* and *special* were the adjectives they used most often about him. They spoke of his humor, his caring, his foibles, his frenzies, and his devotion to people, even when he was arranging and rearranging them, often against their will. Their focus was not so much on how he mattered to the game as how much it had mattered to him. And how much he had mattered to them.

On that sunny day at Stanford, even his actions or behaviors that had disturbed or offended them in real time became episodes to laugh over or shake their heads about. And even those who had knocked sparks off Bill and carried resentments for years spoke of him wistfully. Today, they all agreed there was a magic in his presence and they had been touched by it. They knew full well there would never be anyone like Bill in their lives again and their depiction of him—suffused with the pangs of loss and the fatalism of grief—made it seem as though all the extraordinary things he had accomplished flowed naturally from his extraordinary person in an epic—almost effortless—emergence that was somehow meant to be and could not have happened any other way.

There was more to it than that, however, much more. Bill himself would have been the first to point it out.

"This was no Cinderella story," he had cautioned. "It was full of frustration and disappointment. For different reasons—some self-inflicted, some not—it was a battle for survival. Nothing was given and everything was up in the air. I suffered. Believe me, this was no fairy tale."

And, of course, football had never been the same since.

The informational heart of this book was constructed out of a series of interviews I did with Bill Walsh between April 2006 and June 2007. Those were reinforced by material from Bill's two books, *Building a Champion* with Glenn Dickey and *Finding the Winning Edge* with Brian Billick and James Peterson. I also had access to Bill's private collection of videotapes, including recordings of his game plan installations from most of his seasons and of a number of speeches and workshops he gave after leaving the Forty Niners. With Bill's permission, I have occasionally melded quotes from all these sources together when all the material involved was internally consistent.

I reinforced and amplified Bill's recollections with several dozen interviews of his players, fellow coaches, colleagues, relatives, friends, and acquaintances. Among this group, two memoirs were of enormous use to me: Ronnie Lott's *Total Impact* with Jill Lieber and Joe Montana's *Audibles* with Bob Raissman.

Finally, I made use of extensive public-record reportage, particularly that of the *San Francisco Chronicle.* On that account, I am indebted to the generous assistance of Richard Geiger, the *Chronicle*'s librarian. I also owe particular mention to the contemporaneous reporting of Glenn Dickey, Ira Miller, and Art Spander, all of which was invaluable. As was Dickey's book *Glenn Dickey's 49ers*.

A number of people helped me make this project into a reality and I am indebted to all of them: my old friend Michael Murphy, who first introduced me to Bill Walsh and shared his arcane reservoir of Forty Niners knowledge; my friend and neighbor Mike Shumann, who pointed me in the right direction on a number of occasions when I needed it; my research assistant, Linda Richards, without whose patient work I would have been lost; my buddy John Sullivan, who read what I wrote and gave me advice; my teacher Richard Rapson, and his wife and my dear friend, Elaine Hatfield, who acted as both my sounding board and my cheering section; my friend and computing advisor, Will Kirkland of Computers in Plain English, who rescued me from digital purgatory time in and time out without complaint; and my sweetheart, Cheri Forrester, who read what I wrote, listened to my worries, bolstered me when I needed it, and gave me someone to come home to at the end of the day.

I am particularly grateful to my editors at Random House, Bob Loomis and Mark Tavani, for their encouragement, observations, guidance, and steadfast support. And to my dear friend and agent, Kathy Robbins, who has never failed to be there for me in my times of need, has kept me working all these years, and always helped me feel good about myself and my craft.

1 | "A LITTLE BIT OF DIGNITY AND CLASS"

INTERVIEWS
Albaugh, Glen; Nov. 22, 2006.
Barr, Ron; Apr. 17, 2007.
Cross, Randy; Apr. 17, 2007.
Dickey, Glenn; Apr. 12, 2007.
Durslag, Melvin; Oct. 1, 1984.
Klein, Gene; Sept. 14, 1984.
McVay, John; Jan. 23, 2007.
Rozelle, Pete; Sept. 25, 1983.
Shumann, Mike; Jun. 8, 2006.
Valley, Wayne; Sept. 25, 1984.
White, Mike; May 23, 2007.
Wyche, Sam; May 3, 2007.
Zagaris, Mike; Apr. 19, 2007.

DOCUMENTS
Davis, Al, deposition, *LAMCC v NFL,* Nov. 25, 1980.
Rozelle, Pete, letter to Edward J. DeBartolo Sr. and Edward J. DeBartolo Jr., Mar. 11, 1977.
Rozelle, Pete, testimony, *NASL v NFL,* Apr. 21, 1980.

NEWSPAPERS AND MAGAZINES
Forbes: Oct. 1, 1984.
Los Angeles Times: Apr. 2, 1977.
San Francisco Chronicle: Mar. 15, 16, 1977; Apr. 4 ,6, 25, 1977; Dec. 23, 1981; Jan. 10, 19, 1982; May 6, 1983; Jan. 8, 1984; Mar. 20, 1984; Dec. 28, 1984; Jan. 4, 1988.
San Francisco Examiner: Apr. 2, 5, 22, 1977; Mar. 20, 1984.
Sports Illustrated: Apr. 18, 1977.

BOOKS
Barber, Phil, *We Were Champions: The 49ers' Dynasty in Their Own Words,* Triumph Books, Chicago, 2002.
Dickey, Glenn, *Glenn Dickey's 49ers:The Rise, Fall, and Rebirth of the NFL's Greatest Dynasty,* Prima, Roseville, Calif., 2000.
Georgatos, Dennis, *Stadium Stories: San Francisco 49ers,* Insiders' Guide, Guilford, Conn., 2005.

Tuckman, Micheal W., and Jeff Schultz, *The San Francisco 49ers: Team of the Decade,* Prima, Rocklin, Calif., 1989.

Walsh, Bill, with Glenn Dickey, *Building a Champion: On Football and the Making of the 49ers,* St. Martin's, New York, 1990.

2 | YOU CAN ONLY KISS A GUY'S ASS SO FAR

INTERVIEWS

Benjamin, Guy; Nov. 9, 2006.
Clark, Dwight; Apr. 19, 2007.
Cross, Randy; Oct. 26, 2006; Apr. 17, 2007.
Dickey, Glenn; Apr. 12, 2007.
Fahnhorst, Keith; Mar. 8, 2007.
Jones, Brent; May 2, 2007.
McVay, John; Jan. 23, 2007.
Miller, Ira; May 28, 2007.
Rooney, Dan; Oct. 4, 1984.
Shumann, Mike; Jun. 8, 2006.
White, Mike; May 14, 2007.
Zagaris, Mike; Apr. 19. 2007.

NEWSPAPERS AND MAGAZINES

San Francisco Chronicle: Apr. 7, 8, 20, 21, 27, 1977; May 7, 1977; Oct. 8, 14, 1977; Feb. 24, 1978; Mar. 25, 27, 1978; Apr. 19, 1978; Sept. 4, 6, 7, 1978; Oct. 17, 20, 31, 1978; Nov. 1, 2, 7, 11, 13, 14, 28, 29, 1978; Dec. 6, 19, 1978; Jan. 10, 1979; Nov. 16, 1985; Jan. 17, 1989.
San Francisco Examiner: Jun, 23, 1974; Mar. 6, 30, 31, 1977; Apr. 1, 2, 10, 24, 1977; Aug. 4, 1977; Sept. 9, 1977; Apr. 16, 1978; Sept. 28, 1978; Nov. 7, 1978; Dec. 31, 1978; Feb. 13, 1983.
Sports Illustrated: Apr. 18, 1977; Oct. 31, 1977.

BOOKS

Barber, *We Were Champions.*
Dickey, *Glenn Dickey's 49ers.*
Georgatos, *Stadium Stories.*
Hession, Joseph, *Forty Niners: 49th Anniversary Collector's Edition,* Foghorn Press, San Francisco, 1995.
Lott, Ronnie, with Jill Lieber, *Total Impact: Straight Talk from Football's Hardest Hitter,* Doubleday, New York, 1991.
Tuckman and Schultz, *Team of the Decade.*

3 | THE RIGHT FIT

INTERVIEWS

Albaugh, Glen; Nov. 22, 2006.
Barr, Ron; Apr. 17, 2007; Jul. 11, 2007.
Benjamin, Guy; Nov. 4, 2006.
Dickey, Glenn; Apr. 12, 2007.
Walsh, Bill; Apr. 5, 2006; Dec. 9, 2006; Jan. 8, 2007.
White, Mike; May 23, 2007.

DOCUMENTS

Walsh, Bill, speech, "Playing the Game to Win," Sierra College, Mar. 3, 1990.

NEWSPAPERS AND MAGAZINES

San Francisco Chronicle: Nov. 24, 1976; Dec. 10, 13, 14, 1976; Apr. 28, 29, 1977; Oct. 24, 1977; Dec. 2, 23, 1977; Jan. 13, 1978; Dec. 5, 13, 1978; Feb. 13, 1979.
San Francisco Examiner: Nov. 22, 1981; Dec. 27, 1981.

BOOKS

Barber, *We Were Champions.*
Dickey, *Glenn Dickey's 49ers.*
Georgatos, *Stadium Stories.*
Lewis, Michael, *The Blind Side: Evolution of a Game,* W. W. Norton, New York, 2006.
Tuckman and Schultz, *Team of the Decade.*
Walsh, *Building a Champion.*
Walsh, Bill, with Brian Billick and James A. Peterson, *Finding the Winning Edge,* Sports Publishing, Champaign, Ill., 1998.

4 | GROWING INTO THE GAME

INTERVIEWS

Albaugh, Glen; Nov. 22, 2006.
Benjamin, Guy; Nov. 9, 2006.
Hanson, Kristine; Dec. 19, 2007.

Matthews, Al; Jun. 22, 2007.
Mayer, Ed; Jun. 15, 2007.
Vermeil, Dick; Jun. 14, 2007.
Walsh, Bill; Apr. 5, 2006; Dec. 9, 2006;
    Mar. 14, 2007; Jun. 21, 2007.
White, Mike; May 14, 2007.

DOCUMENTS
Walsh, Bill, "Playing the Game to Win."

NEWSPAPERS AND MAGAZINES
San Francisco Chronicle: Jan. 21, 1982;
    Dec. 12, 1984; Aug. 10, 2007.
San Francisco Examiner: Dec. 27, 1981.

BOOKS
Walsh, *Finding the Winning Edge.*

5 | CLIMBING THE LADDER

INTERVIEWS
Albaugh, Glen; Nov. 22, 2006.
Shumann, Mike; Jun. 8, 2006.
Vermeil, Dick; Jun. 14, 2007.
Walsh, Bill; Dec. 9, 2006; Feb. 1, 2007;
    Mar. 14, 2007.
White, Mike; May 14, 2007.

DOCUMENTS
Walsh, Bill, speech, PEMCO, Northwest
    All Sports Clinic, Seattle, Wash., 1995.
Walsh, Bill, "Playing the Game to Win."
Walsh, Bill, "Flank Formation Football
    Stress: Defense," Jan. 1958.

NEWSPAPERS AND MAGAZINES
San Francisco Chronicle: Jun. 6, 1979; Jan.
    25, 1982; Jun. 29, 1982; Dec. 12, 1984;
    Feb. 14, 1984; Dec. 19, 1984; Jan. 17,
    1985; Oct. 31, 2002.
San Francisco Examiner: Oct. 25, 1979;
    Dec. 27, 1981.

BOOKS
Georgatos, *Stadium Stories.*
Lewis, *The Blind Side.*
Tuckman and Schultz, *Team of the
    Decade.*

Walsh, *Building a Champion.*
Walsh, *Finding the Winning Edge.*

6 | THE GREATEST DISAPPOINTMENT

INTERVIEWS
Albaugh, Glen; Nov. 22, 2006.
Barr, Ron; Apr. 17, 2007.
Ralston, John; Jun. 8, 2007.
Shumann, Mike; Jun. 8, 2006.
Walsh, Bill; Apr. 5, 2006; Dec. 9, 2006;
    Jan. 8, 2007; Feb. 1, 2007.
Walsh, Craig; Sept. 20, 2007.
White, Mike; May 14, 2007.
Wyche, Sam; May 3, 2007.
Zagaris, Mike; Nov. 19, 2007.

DOCUMENTS
Walsh, Bill, lecture, Coaches Career
    Development Symposium, 1998.
Walsh, Bill, "Playing the Game to Win."
Walsh, Bill, speech, Northwest All Sports
    Clinic.

NEWSPAPERS AND MAGAZINES
San Francisco Chronicle: July 28, 1980;
    Dec. 5, 1981; Jan. 22, 1982; Feb. 8,
    1982.
Sports Illustrated: Sept. 10, 1962; Aug. 12,
    1968; Sept. 15, 1969.

BOOKS
Dickey, *Glenn Dickey's 49ers.*
Georgatos, *Stadium Stories.*
Lewis, *The Blind Side.*
Walsh, *Building a Champion.*
Walsh, *Finding the Winning Edge.*

7 | OPPORTUNITY KNOCKS

INTERVIEWS
Barr, Ron; Apr. 17, 2007.
Dickey, Glenn; Apr. 12, 2007.
Murphy, Michael; Aug. 27, 2007.
Walsh, Bill; Apr. 5, 2006; Jan. 8, 24,
    2007.
White, Mike; May 14, 23, 2007.

NEWSPAPERS AND MAGAZINES
San Francisco Chronicle: Jan. 2, 6, 8, 9, 10, 1979.
San Francisco Examiner: Jan. 7, 1979.

BOOKS
Barber, *We Were Champions.*
Tuckman and Schultz, *Team of the Decade.*
Walsh, *Building a Champion.*
Walsh, *Finding the Winning Edge.*

8 | MARCHING ORDERS

INTERVIEWS
Albaugh, Glen; Nov. 22, 2006.
Barr, Ron; Apr. 17, 2007.
Benjamin, Guy; Oct. 27, 2006.
Clark, Dwight; Apr. 19, 2007.
Cross, Randy; Oct. 26, 2006; Apr. 17, 2007.
Edwards, Harry; Feb. 9, 2007.
Fahnhorst, Keith; Mar. 8, 2007.
Jones, Brent; May 2, 2007.
McLean, Lindsy; May 24, 2007.
McVay, John; Jan. 23, 2007.
Miller, Ira; May 28, 2007.
Shumann, Mike; Jun. 8, 2006.
Turner, Keena; Mar. 13, 2007.
Walsh, Bill; Apr. 5, 2006; Jan. 8, 11, 24, 2007; Mar. 14, 2007.
White, Mike; May 23, 2007.
Wright, Eric; Mar. 13, 2007.
Wyche, Sam; May 3, 2007.

DOCUMENTS
Walsh, Bill, "Playing the Game to Win."
Walsh, Bill, lecture, Coaches Career Development Symposium.

NEWSPAPERS AND MAGAZINES
San Francisco Chronicle: Jan, 10, 1979; Dec. 18, 1981; Jul. 28, 1993.
Sports Illustrated: Jul, 26, 1982.

BOOKS
Barber, *We Were Champions.*
Dickey, *Glenn Dickey's 49ers.*
Walsh, *Building a Champion.*
Walsh, *Finding the Winning Edge.*

9 | AN EYE FOR TALENT

INTERVIEWS
Benjamin, Guy; Nov. 27, 2006.
Clark, Dwight; Apr. 17, 19, 2007.
Dickey, Glenn; Apr. 12, 2007.
McVay, John; Jan. 23, 2007.
Shumann, Mike; Jun. 8, 2006.
Walsh, Bill; Jan. 8, 11, 24, 2007; Feb. 1, 2007.
White, Mike; May 23, 2007.
Wyche, Sam; May 3, 2007; Aug. 22, 2007.

NEWSPAPERS AND MAGAZINES
San Francisco Chronicle: Jan. 19, 1982; Apr. 25, 1983; Dec. 7, 1984; Jan. 11, 1989; Apr. 22, 1995.
Time: Jan. 25, 1982.

BOOKS
Craig, Roger, with Matt Maiocco, *Roger Craig's Tales from the San Francisco 49ers Sideline,* Sports Publishing, Champaign, Ill., 2004.
Dickey, *Glenn Dickey's 49ers.*
Georgatos, *Stadium Stories.*
Harris, David, *The League: The Rise and Decline of the NFL,* Bantam, New York, 1986.
Montana, Joe, and Bob Raissman, *Audibles: My Life in Football,* Morrow, New York, 1986.
Tuckman and Schultz, *Team of the Decade.*
Walsh, *Building a Champion.*
Walsh, *Finding the Winning Edge.*

10 | HOW TO COACH

INTERVIEWS
Albaugh, Glen; Nov. 22, 2006.
Barr, Ron; Apr. 13, 2007.
Benjamin, Guy; Nov. 4, 27, 2006.
Clark, Dwight; Apr. 19, 2007.

Cross, Randy; Oct. 26, 2006; Apr. 17, 2007.
Edwards, Harry; Feb. 9, 2007.
Fahnhorst, Keith; Mar. 8, 2007.
Holmgren, Mike; Apr. 19, 2007.
Jones, Brent; May 2, 2007.
McLean, Lindsy; May 24, 2007.
McVay, John; Jan. 23, 2007.
Shumann, Mike; Jun. 8, 2006.
Turner, Keena; Mar. 13, 2007.
Walsh, Bill; Apr. 5, 2006; Jan. 8, 11, 16, 24, 2007; Mar. 14, 2007.
White, Mike; May 14, 23, 2007.
Wright, Eric; Mar. 13, 2007.
Wyche, Sam; May 3, 2007.
Young, Charle; Apr. 16, 2007.
Zagaris, Mike; Apr. 19, 2007.

DOCUMENTS
Albaugh, Glen, "Developing a Coaching Style: The Bill Walsh Story," Department of Sports Sciences, UOP.
Walsh, Bill, lecture, Achieving Coaching Excellence, "Theory of Passing Offense," Mar. 3, 1994.
Walsh, Bill, lecture, Forty Niners training camp, 1987.
Walsh, speech, Northwest All Sports Clinic.
Walsh, lecture, Coaches Career Development Symposium.

NEWSPAPERS AND MAGAZINES
Sports Illustrated: Jul. 26, 2002.

BOOKS
Craig, *San Francisco 49ers Sideline.*
Dickey, *Glenn Dickey's 49ers.*
Montana, *Audibles.*
Walsh, *Building a Champion.*
Walsh, *Finding the Winning Edge.*

11 | FORTY NINERS FOOTBALL

INTERVIEWS
Albaugh, Glen; Nov. 22, 2006.
Benjamin, Guy; Oct. 27, 2006; Nov. 4, 27, 2006.
Cross, Randy; Oct. 26, 2006.
Edwards, Harry; Feb. 9, 2007.
McVay, John; Jan. 23, 2007.
Shumann, Mike; Jun. 8, 2006.
Turner, Keena; Mar. 13, 2007.
Walsh, Bill; Apr. 5, 2006; Jan 11, 24, 2007; Feb. 1, 2007.
White, Mike; May 23, 2007.
Wyche, Sam; May 3, 2007.

DOCUMENTS
Walsh, Bill, lecture, team meeting, Sept. 1, 2000.
Walsh, "Playing The Game to Win."
Walsh, Bill, lecture, training camp, 1987.
Walsh, Bill, coaching video, Chicago Bears, Jan. 6, 1985.
Walsh, speech, Coaches Career Development Symposium.
Walsh, Bill, speech, Achieving Coaching Excellence, Mar. 3, 1984.
Walsh, Bill speech, Northwest All Sports Clinic.

BOOKS
Barber, *We Were Champions.*
Walsh, *Building a Champion.*
Walsh, *Finding the Winning Edge.*

12 | THAT KIND OF SEASON

INTERVIEWS
Benjamin, Guy; Oct. 27, 2006; Nov. 4, 9, 2006.
Clark, Dwight; Apr. 19, 2007.
Cross, Randy; Oct. 26, 2006.
Dickey, Glenn; Apr. 12, 2007.
Fahnhorst, Keith; Mar. 8, 2007.
Holmgren, Mike; Apr. 19, 2007.
Jones, Brent; May 2, 2007.
McLean, Lindsy; May 24, 2007.
McVay, John; Jan. 23, 2007.
Miller, Ira; May 28, 2007.
Shumann, Mike; Jun. 8, 2006.
Walsh, Bill; Apr. 5, 2006; Jan. 8, 11, 16, 2007; Feb. 1, 2007; Mar. 14, 2007.
White, Mike; May 14, 23, 2007.
Wright, Eric; Mar. 13, 2007.

Wyche, Sam; May 3, 2007.
Young, Charle; Apr. 16, 2007.

DOCUMENTS
Five Rings: A Celebration, video, Mar. 23–25, 2006.
Walsh, speech, Northwest All Sports Clinic.
Walsh, Bill, lecture, Achieving Coaching Excellence, "Game Day Prep," Mar. 3, 1994.
Walsh, Bill lecture, Achieving Coaching Excellence, "More Passing Theory," Mar. 3, 1994.
Walsh, Bill, "Theory of Passing Offense."
Walsh, Bill, lecture, Achieving Coaching Excellence, "Game Management," Mar. 3, 1994.
Walsh, Bill, lecture, All Sports Coaching Clinics, Super Football Clinic III, "The Quarterback."
Walsh, lecture, San Francisco 49ers Training Camp, 1987.

NEWSPAPERS AND MAGAZINES
San Francisco Chronicle: Aug. 14, 20, 1979; Sept. 10, 25, 30, 1979; Oct. 9, 23, 1979; Nov. 26, 29, 1979; Dec. 10, 1979; Sept. 7, 1982; Jan. 12, 1985; July 31, 1987; Dec. 30, 1988.
San Francisco Examiner: Sept. 2, 1979.

BOOKS
Barber, *We Were Champions.*
Dickey, *Glenn Dickey's 49ers.*
Georgatos, *Stadium Stories.*
Hession, *Forty Niners.*
Lewis, *The Blind Side.*
Montana, *Audibles.*
Tuckman and Schultz, *Team of the Decade.*
Walsh, *Building a Champion.*
Walsh, *Finding the Winning Edge.*

13 | BUILDING A TEAM

INTERVIEWS
Albaugh, Glen; Nov. 22, 2006.
Benjamin, Guy; Oct. 27, 2006; Nov. 4, 9, 2006.

Clark, Dwight; Apr. 19, 2007.
Cross, Randy; Oct. 26, 2006.
Dickey, Glenn; Apr. 12, 2007.
Fahnhorst, Keith; Mar. 8, 2007.
Holmgren, Mike; Apr. 19, 2007.
McVay, John; Jan. 23, 2007.
Miller, Ira; May 28, 2007.
Shumann, Mike; Jun. 8, 2006.
Turner, Keena; Mar. 13, 2007.
Walsh, Bill; Jan. 8, 11, 24, 2007; Mar. 14, 2007.
White, Mike; May 14, 23, 2007.
Wright, Eric; Mar. 13, 2007.
Wyche, Sam; May 3, 2007; Sept. 18, 2007.
Young, Charle; Apr. 16, 2007.
Young, Steve; Aug. 17, 2007.
Zagaris, Mike; Apr. 19, 2007.

DOCUMENTS
Walsh, "Theory of Passing Offense."
Walsh, "Quarterback Fundamentals."
Walsh, "Game Day Prep."
Walsh, Bill, lecture, All Sports Coaching Clinics, Super Football Clinic III, "The Quarterback Part 2."
Walsh, speech, Northwest All Sports Clinic.

NEWSPAPER AND MAGAZINES
San Francisco Chronicle: Mar. 31, 1973; Mar. 6, 1976; Oct. 21, 1979; Nov. 16, 1979; Apr. 30, 1980; Jul. 28, 1980; Aug. 4, 14, 18, 19, 23, 1980; Sept. 2, 20, 21, 22, 1980; Jul. 31, 1981; Dec. 23, 27, 1981; Jan. 17, 19, 1982; Jul. 31, 1987.
Time: Jan. 25, 1982.

BOOKS
Barber, *We Were Champions.*
Georgatos, *Stadium Stories.*
Lewis, *Blind Side.*
Montana, *Audibles.*
Tuckman and Schultz, *Team of the Decade.*
Walsh, *Building a Champion.*

14 | THE LEAST LIKELY MOMENT TO SAY THINGS LOOK GOOD

INTERVIEWS

Albaugh, Glen; Nov. 22, 2006.
Clark, Dwight; Apr. 19, 2007.
Cross, Randy; Oct. 26, 2006.
McLean, Lindsy; May 24, 2007.
McVay, John; Jan. 23, 2007.
Shumann, Mike; Jun. 8, 2006.
Turner, Keena; Mar. 13, 2007.
Walsh, Bill; Apr. 5, 2006; Jan. 8, 24, 2007;
    Feb. 1, 2007; Mar. 14, 2007.
White, Mike; May 14, 23, 2007.
Wyche, Sam; May 3, 2007; Sept. 18, 2007.

DOCUMENTS

Walsh, "Playing the Game to Win."

NEWSPAPERS AND MAGAZINES

San Francisco Chronicle: Jul. 2, 24, 1980;
    Sept. 8, 22, 1980; Oct. 14, 1980; Nov.
    4, 14, 17, 18, 1980; Dec. 1, 8, 22, 1980;
    Sept. 7, 1985; Jul. 31, 1987.
San Francisco Examiner: Jul. 28, 1980.

BOOKS

Dickey, *Glenn Dickey's 49ers.*
Georgatos, *Stadium Stories.*
Hession, *Forty Niners.*
Lott, *Total Impact.*
Montana, *Audibles.*
Tuckman and Schultz, *Team of the Decade.*
Walsh, *Building a Champion.*
Walsh, *Finding the Winning Edge.*

15 | "OUR TIME WILL COME"

INTERVIEWS

Barr, Ron; Apr. 17, 2007.
Benjamin, Guy; Nov. 27, 2006.
Cross, Randy; Oct. 26, 2006; Apr. 17,
    2007.
Dickey, Glenn; Apr. 12, 2007.
Fahnhorst, Keith; Mar. 8, 2007.
McVay, John; Jan. 23, 2007.
Shumann, Mike; Jun. 8, 2006.

Turner, Keena; Mar. 13, 2007.
Walsh, Bill; Jan. 8, 11, 2007; Mar. 14,
    2007.
White, Mike; May 23, 2007.
Wright, Eric; Mar. 13, 2007.
Wyche, Sam; May 3, 2007.
Young, Charle; Apr. 16, 2007.

DOCUMENTS

Walsh, lecture, Coaches Career
    Development Symposium, 1998.

NEWSPAPERS AND MAGAZINES

San Francisco Chronicle: Jul. 10, 15, 19,
    20, 21, 22, 24, 1981; Aug. 5, 1981; Nov.
    5, 1981; Dec. 4, 10, 1981; Jan. 8, 10, 14,
    18, 1982; Nov. 22, 1985; Aug. 28, 1993.
San Francisco Examiner: Sept. 16, 1979;
    Feb. 2, 1982; Apr. 18, 1982.
Sports Illustrated: Dec. 21, 1981.
Time: Jan. 25, 1982.

BOOKS

Dickey, *Glenn Dickey's 49ers.*
Hession, *Forty Niners.*
Lewis, *The Blind Side.*
Lott, *Total Impact.*
Montana, *Audibles.*
Tuckman and Schultz, *Team of the Decade.*
Walsh, *Building a Champion.*
Walsh, *Finding the Winning Edge.*

16 | WHO'S NEXT?

INTERVIEWS

Albaugh, Glen; Nov. 22, 2006.
Benjamin, Guy; Oct. 27, 2006; Nov. 4, 27,
    2006.
Cross, Randy; Oct. 26, 2006.
Dickey, Glenn; Apr. 12, 2007.
Fahnhorst, Keith; Mar. 8, 2007.
Holmgren, Mike; Apr. 19, 2007.
McVay, John; Jan. 23, 2007.
Shumann, Mike; Jun. 8, 2006.
Turner, Keena; Mar. 13, 2007.
Walsh, Bill; Dec. 9, 2006; Jan. 8, 11, 16, 24,
    2007; Feb. 1, 2007; Mar. 14, 2007.

Wright, Eric; Mar. 13, 2007.
Wyche, Sam; May 3, 2007.
Young, Charle; Apr. 16, 2007.

NEWSPAPERS AND MAGAZINES
San Francisco Chronicle: Aug. 28, 1981;
    Oct. 1, 3, 8, 12, 22, 1981; Nov. 2, 12,
    1981; Dec. 3, 7, 1981; Jan. 26, 1982;
    Jan. 5, 1984; Jan. 21, 2007.
San Francisco Examiner: Dec. 2, 6, 1981;
    Jan. 3, 28, 1982.
Sports Illustrated: Dec. 21, 1981; Jul. 26,
    1982.

BOOKS
Barber, *We Were Champions.*
Craig, *San Francisco 49ers Sideline.*
Dickey, *Glenn Dickey's 49ers.*
Georgatos, *Stadium Stories.*
Hession, *Forty Niners.*
Lewis, *The Blind Side.*
Lott, *Total Impact.*
Montana, *Audibles.*
Tuckman and Schultz, *Team of the Decade.*
Walsh, *Building a Champion.*
Walsh, *Finding the Winning Edge.*

17 | WORST TO FIRST

INTERVIEWS
Benjamin, Guy; Nov. 4, 2006.
Clark, Dwight; Apr. 19, 2007.
Cross, Randy; Oct. 26, 2006.
Edwards, Harry; Feb. 9, 2007.
Fahnhorst, Keith; Mar. 8, 2007.
McVay, John; Jan. 23, 2007.
Shumann, Mike; Jun. 8, 2006.
Turner, Keena; Mar. 13, 2007.
Walsh, Bill; Jan. 16, 24, 2007; Feb. 1, 2007.
Walsh, Craig; Sept. 20, 2007.
Wright, Eric; Mar. 13, 2007.
Wyche, Sam; May 3, 2007.
Young, Charle; Apr. 16, 2007.

NEWSPAPERS AND MAGAZINES
San Francisco Chronicle: Dec. 13, 23, 29,
    1981; Jan. 5, 6, 11, 12, 18, 25, 26, 28,
    1982; Feb. 26, 1982.

San Francisco Examiner: Jan. 11, 1982;
    Jan. 6, 1985.
Sports Illustrated: Jul. 26, 1982.

BOOKS
Barber, *We Were Champions.*
Dickey, *Glenn Dickey's 49ers.*
Georgatos, *Stadium Stories.*
Lewis, *The Blind Side.*
Lott, *Total Impact.*
Montana, *Audibles.*
Tuckman and Schultz, *Team of the Decade.*
Walsh, *Building a Champion.*

18 | LIFE IN A FISHBOWL

INTERVIEWS
Benjamin, Guy; Nov. 9, 2006.
Clark, Dwight; Apr. 19, 2007.
Cross, Randy; Oct. 26, 2006; Apr. 16, 17,
    2007.
Dickey, Glenn; Apr. 12, 2007.
Fahnhorst, Keith; Mar. 8, 2007.
McVay, John; Jan. 23, 2007.
Miller, Ira; May 28, 2007.
Ryan, Joan; Aug. 24, 2007.
Shumann, Mike; Jun. 8, 2006.
Walsh, Bill; Jan. 11, 16, 24, 2007; Mar. 14,
    2007.
Walsh, Craig; Sept. 20, 2007.

NEWSPAPERS AND MAGAZINES
San Francisco Chronicle: Feb. 22, 1982;
    Jan. 8, 1984.
San Francisco Examiner: Jul. 29, 1984.

BOOKS
Dickey, *Glenn Dickey's 49ers.*
Tuckman and Schultz, *Team of the Decade.*
Walsh, *Building a Champion.*

19 | BACK-TO-BACK?

INTERVIEWS
Benjamin, Guy; Nov. 9, 2006.
Cross, Randy; Oct. 26, 2006; Apr. 17,
    2007.

Fahnhorst, Keith; Dec. 6, 1984; Mar. 8, 2007.
Francis, Russ, to KNBR; Aug. 1, 2007.
McVay, John; Jan. 23, 2007.
Shumann, Mike; Jun. 8, 2006.
Turner, Keena; Mar. 13, 2007.
Vermeil, Dick; Jun. 14, 2007.
Walsh, Bill; Jan. 8, 11, 16, 2007; Feb. 1, 2007.
Wright, Eric; Mar. 13, 2007.
Young, Charle; Apr. 16, 2007.
Zagaris, Mike; Apr. 19, 2007.

DOCUMENTS
NFLPA, *Because We Are the Game.*

NEWSPAPERS AND MAGAZINES
San Francisco Chronicle: Mar. 1, 4, 1982; Apr. 26, 28, 1982; May 3, 5, 20, 22, 1982; Jul. 24, 1982; Aug. 6, 13, 20, 23, 27, 1982; Sept. 4, 20, 21, 22, 1982; Oct. 8, 1982; Nov. 3, 11, 12, 1982; Aug. 19, 1983; Jul. 18, 1984; Jul. 31, 1987; Sept. 12, 1987.
San Francisco Examiner: Aug. 1, 29, 1982; Sept. 19, 1982; Oct. 8, 1982.

BOOKS
Harris, *The League.*
Hession, *Forty Niners.*
Lewis, *The Blind Side.*
Montana, *Audibles.*
Tuckman and Schultz, *Team of the Decade.*
Walsh, *Building a Champion.*
Walsh, *Finding the Winning Edge.*

20 | THE COLLAPSE

INTERVIEWS
Barr, Ron; Apr. 17, 2007.
Benjamin, Guy; Nov. 9, 2006.
Clark, Dwight; Apr. 19, 2007.
Cross, Randy; Oct. 26, 2006; Apr. 17, 2007.
Dickey, Glenn; Apr. 12, 2007.
Fahnhorst, Keith; Mar. 8, 2007.
McVay, John; Jan. 23, 2007.

Miller, Ira; May 28, 2007.
Shumann, Mike; Jun. 8, 2006.
Turner, Keena; Mar. 13, 2007.
Vermeil, Dick; Jun. 14, 2007.
Walsh, Bill; Jan. 8, 11, 16, 2007; Feb. 1. 2007; Mar. 14, 2007.
Walsh, Craig; Sept. 20, 2007.
White, Mike; May 14, 23, 2007.
Wright, Eric; Mar. 13, 2007.
Wyche, Sam; May 3, 2007.
Young, Charle; Apr. 16, 2007.

NEWSPAPERS AND MAGAZINES
San Francisco Chronicle: Dec. 4, 13, 21, 1982; Jan. 4, 6, 7, 13, 18, 25, 26, 1983; Sept. 12, 1983; Feb. 15, 1985.
San Francisco Examiner: Jan. 26, 1982; Dec. 5, 26, 1982; Jan. 4, 9, 16, 23, 1983; Sept. 15, 1983.

BOOKS
Dickey, *Glenn Dickey's 49ers.*
Hession, *Forty Niners.*
Lott, *Total Impact.*
Montana, *Audibles.*
Tuckman and Schultz, *Team of the Decade.*
Walsh, *Building a Champion.*

21 | PAIN AROUND THE EDGES

INTERVIEWS
Albaugh, Glen; Nov. 22, 2006.
Barr, Ron; Apr. 17, 2007.
Benjamin, Guy; Nov. 4, 9, 2006.
Clark, Dwight; Apr. 19, 2007.
Cross, Randy; Apr. 17, 2007.
Dickey, Glenn; Apr. 12, 2007.
Edwards, Harry; Feb. 9, 2007.
Fahnhorst, Keith; Mar. 8, 2007.
Hanson, Kristine; Dec. 19, 2007.
Holmgren, Mike; Apr. 19, 2007.
McLean, Lindsy; May 24, 2007.
Miller, Ira; May 28, 2007.
Ralston, John; Jun. 8, 2007.
Ryan, Joan; Aug. 24, 2007.
Shumann, Mike; Jun. 8, 2006.
Vermeil, Dick; Jun. 14, 2007.

Walsh, Bill; Apr. 5, 2006; Jan. 8, 11, 24, 2007; Mar. 14, 2007.
Walsh, Craig; Sept. 20, 2007.
White, Mike; May 23, 2007.
Zagaris, Mike; Apr. 19, 2007.

DOCUMENTS
Walsh, Bill, speech, Coaches Career Development Symposium, 1998.
Walsh, Bill, coaching video, Phoenix Cardinals, Nov. 6, 1988.
Walsh, Bill, speech, Northwest All Sports Clinic.

NEWSPAPERS AND MAGAZINES
San Francisco Chronicle: Oct. 25, 1979; Jan. 1, 1982; Jan. 26, 28, 29, 1983; Dec. 14, 1984; Jan. 17, 1985; Sept. 6, 1985.
San Francisco Examiner: Jan. 7, 1983.
Sports Illustrated: Jul. 26, 1982.

BOOKS
Dickey, *Glenn Dickey's 49ers.*
Lott, *Total Impact.*
Montana, *Audibles.*
Tuckman and Shultz, *Team of the Decade.*
Walsh, *Building a Champion.*

22 | SERIOUS BUSINESS

INTERVIEWS
Barr, Ron; Apr. 17, 2007.
Benjamin, Guy; Nov. 9, 2006.
Cross, Randy; Oct. 26, 2006; Apr. 17, 2007.
Dickey, Glenn; Apr. 12, 2007.
Edwards, Harry; Feb. 9, 2007.
Ellison, Riki, to KNBR; Jul. 31, 2007.
Fahnhorst, Keith; Mar. 8, 2007.
Francis, Russ, to KNBR; Aug. 1, 2007.
Klein, Gene; Sept. 14, 1984.
McVay, John; Jan. 23, 2007.
Modell, Art; Oct. 4, 1983.
Rozelle, Pete; Sept. 25, 1983; Jun. 11, 1984.
Schramm, Tex; Sept. 18, 1984.
Shumann, Mike; Jun. 8, 2006.
Turner, Keena; Mar. 13, 2007.

Walsh, Bill; Apr. 5, 2006; Jan. 8, 11, 24, 2006; Feb. 1, 2007; Mar. 14, 2007.
Wright, Eric; Mar. 13, 2007.
Young, Charle; Apr. 16, 2007.

NEWSPAPERS AND MAGAZINES
New York Times: Mar. 23, 1983; May 25, 1983.
Peninsula Times Tribune: Jan. 9, 1984.
San Francisco Chronicle: Dec. 11, 1976; Jan. 28, 1983; Feb. 3, 1983; Mar. 21, 23, 24, 1983; Apr. 7, 23, 27, 1983; May 12, 18, 24, 1983; Jun. 7, 1983; Jul. 14, 18, 19, 21, 22, 26, 27, 30, 1983; Aug. 24, 27, 1983; Sept. 1, 7, 26, 1983; Oct. 5, 6, 7, 13, 21, 24, 25, 1983; Nov. 7, 1983; Dec. 12, 19, 20, 21, 30, 1983; Jan. 7, 9, 10, 1984; Aug. 17, 1984.
San Francisco Examiner: Apr. 10, 1983; Aug. 7, 1983; Nov. 3, 1983; Dec. 20, 1983; Jan. 8, 9, 1984.
San Jose Mercury: Jan. 9, 1984.

BOOKS
Barber, *We Were Champions.*
Craig, *Tales from the San Francisco 49ers Sideline.*
Dickey, *Glenn Dickey's 49ers.*
Georgatos, *Stadium Stories.*
Harris, *The League.*
Hession, *Forty Niners.*
Lewis, *The Blind Side.*
Lott, *Total Impact.*
Montana, *Audibles.*
Tuckman and Shultz, *Team of the Decade.*
Walsh, *Building a Champion.*

23 | AS CLOSE TO PERFECT AS YOU CAN GET

INTERVIEWS
Benjamin, Guy; Nov. 9, 2006.
Clark, Dwight; Apr. 19, 2007.
Cross, Randy; Oct. 26, 2006.
Dickey, Glenn; Apr. 12, 2007.
Fahnhorst, Keith; Mar. 8, 2007.
McLean, Lindsy; May 24, 2007.
McVay, John; Jan. 23, 2007.
Miller, Ira; May 28, 2007.

Turner, Keena; Mar. 13, 2007.
Vermeil, Dick; Jun. 14, 2007.
Walsh, Bill; Jan. 11, 16, 2007; Feb. 1, 2007;
    Mar. 14, 2007.
Wright, Eric; Mar. 13, 2007.

DOCUMENTS
5 Rings: A Celebration.

NEWSPAPERS AND MAGAZINES
San Francisco Chronicle: Jan. 13, 1984;
    Feb. 28, 1984; Mar. 22, 1984; Apr. 30,
    1984; May 19, 26, 1984; Jul. 16, 17, 26,
    31, 1984; Aug. 8, 29, 31, 1984; Sept. 11,
    24, 29, 1984; Oct. 12, 15, 25, 29, 1984;
    Nov. 6, 12, 15, 23, 1984; Dec. 21, 31,
    1984; Jan. 3, 15, 17, 1985.
San Francisco Examiner: Jul. 29, 1984;
    Aug. 30, 1984; Sept. 15, 1984; Nov. 18,
    1984; Dec. 30, 1984.

BOOKS
Barber, *We Were Champions.*
Dickey, *Glenn Dickey's 49ers.*
Georgatos, *Stadium Stories.*
Hession, *Forty Niners.*
Lott, *Total Impact.*
Montana, *Audibles.*
Tuckman and Schultz, *Team of the Decade.*
Walsh, *Building a Champion.*

24 | REDEMPTION

INTERVIEWS
Clark, Dwight; Apr. 19, 2007.
Cross, Randy; Oct. 26, 2006.
Francis, Russ, to KNBR; Aug. 1, 2007.
Hanson, Kristine; Dec. 19, 2007.
Mayer, Ed; Jun. 15, 2007.
Walsh, Bill; Jan. 11, 2007; Mar. 14, 2007.

DOCUMENTS
Walsh, Bill, coaching video, Chicago
    Bears, Jan. 6, 1985.

NEWSPAPERS AND MAGAZINES
San Francisco Chronicle: Dec. 31, 1984;
    Jan. 3, 4, 7, 10, 14, 16, 18, 22, 1985.
San Francisco Examiner: Dec. 30, 1984.

BOOKS
Barber, *We Were Champions.*
Craig, *Tales from the San Francisco 49ers
    Sideline.*
Dickey, *Glenn Dickey's 49ers.*
Georgatos, *Stadium Stories.*
Hession, *Forty Niners.*
Lott, *Total Impact.*
Montana, *Audibles.*
Tuckman and Schultz, *Team of the Decade.*
Walsh, *Building a Champion.*

25 | "WHAT DO YOU THINK OF THAT WEST COAST OFFENSE NOW?"

INTERVIEWS
Albaugh, Glen; Nov. 22, 2006.
Benjamin, Guy; Oct. 27, 2006.
Cross, Randy; Oct. 26, 2006.
Dickey, Glenn; Apr. 12, 2007.
Edwards, Harry; Feb. 9, 2007.
Fahnhorst, Keith; Mar. 8, 2007.
Hanson, Kristine; Dec. 19, 2007.
McLean, Lindsy; May 24, 2007.
McVay, John; Jan. 23, 2007.
Walsh, Bill; Jan. 8, 11, 16, 24, 2007; Feb. 1,
    2007; Mar. 14, 2007.
Walsh, Craig; Sept. 20, 2007.
White, Mike; May 23, 2007.
Wright, Eric; Mar. 13, 2007.
Young, Steve; Aug. 14, 2007.

NEWSPAPERS AND MAGAZINES
San Francisco Chronicle: Apr. 26, 1984;
    Aug. 17, 1984; Mar. 11, 1985; Apr. 12,
    1985; May 1, 8, 15, 23, 1985; Jun. 11,
    1985; Jul. 25, 31, 1985; Aug. 9, 12,
    1985; Sept. 9, 13, 16, 30, 1985; Oct. 1,
    2, 7, 9, 10, 14, 18, 21, 25, 28, 31, 1985;
    Nov. 11, 18, 19, 20, 1985; Dec. 2, 11,
    13, 16, 20, 23, 24, 30, 31, 1985; Aug.
    30, 1986; Jul. 31, 1987; Sept. 12, 1987;
    Dec. 28, 1987.

BOOKS
Barber, *We Were Champions.*
Craig, *Tales from the San Francisco 49ers
    Sideline.*

Dickey, *Glenn Dickey's 49ers.*
Hession, *Forty Niners.*
Lewis, *The Blind Side.*
Lott, *Total Impact.*
Montana, *Audibles.*
Tuckman and Schultz, *Team of the Decade.*
Walsh, *Building a Champion.*

26 | BANGED UP, BEATEN DOWN, THEN SHATTERED

INTERVIEWS
Albaugh, Glen; Nov. 22, 2006.
Clark, Dwight; Apr. 19, 2007.
Edwards, Harry; Apr. 6, 2007.
Fahnhorst, Keith; Mar. 8, 2007.
Hanson, Kristine; Dec. 19, 2007.
Holmgren, Mike; Apr. 19, 2007.
McLean, Lindsy; May 24, 2007.
McVay, John; Jan. 23, 2007.
Miller, Ira; May 28, 2007.
Turner, Keena; Mar. 13, 2007.
Walsh, Bill; Jan. 16, 24, 2007; Feb. 1, 2007;
    Mar. 14, 2007.
Wright, Eric; Mar. 13, 2007.
Zagaris, Mike; Apr. 19, 2007.

DOCUMENTS
Walsh, Bill, coaching video, Miami
    Dolphins, Sept. 28, 1986.
Walsh, Bill, coaching video, New Orleans
    Saints, Nov. 2, 1986.
Walsh, Bill, coaching video, New England
    Patriots, Dec. 14, 1986.
Walsh, Bill, coaching video, Los Angeles
    Rams, Dec. 19, 1986.
Walsh, Bill, coaching video, New York
    Giants, Jan. 4, 1987.

NEWSPAPERS AND MAGAZINES
San Francisco Chronicle: Aug. 22, 1985;
    Mar. 21, 26, 1986; Apr. 17, 30, 1986;
    May 2, 1986; Jun. 13, 1986; Jul. 23,
    1986; Aug. 23, 1986, Sept. 8, 15, 16, 17,
    18, 19, 22, 29, 30, 1986; Oct. 6, 13, 22,
    27, 1986; Nov. 3, 4, 5, 8, 10, 20, 21,
    1986; Dec. 2, 5, 8, 15, 17, 20, 22, 25,
    1986; Jan. 1, 2, 5, 6, 1987; Aug. 26,
    1987; Mar. 25, 1988; Apr. 15, 1996.

BOOKS
Barber, *We Were Champions.*
Craig, *Tales from the San Francisco 49ers
    Sideline.*
Dickey, *Glenn Dickey's 49ers.*
Hession, *Forty Niners.*
Lewis, *The Blind Side.*
Livsey, Laury, *The Steve Young Story,* Prima
    Publishing, Rocklin, Calif., 1996.
Lott, *Total Impact.*
Montana, *Audibles.*
Tuckman and Schultz, *Team of the Decade.*
Walsh, *Building a Champion.*

27. | A DIFFERENT DRUMMER

INTERVIEWS
Albaugh, Glen; Nov. 22, 2006.
Clark, Dwight; Apr. 19, 2007.
Dickey, Glenn; Apr. 12, 2007.
Edwards, Harry; Feb. 9, 2007.
McLean, Lindsy; May 24, 2007.
Walsh, Bill; Mar. 14, 2007.
Zagaris, Mike; Apr. 19, 2007.

NEWSPAPERS AND MAGAZINES
ESPN The Magazine: Feb. 2, 2004.
New York Times: Jun. 21, 1987.
San Francisco Chronicle: Oct. 27, 1978;
    Feb. 16, 1983; May 22, 1987; Mar. 24,
    1997.

BOOKS
Craig, *Tales from the San Francisco 49ers
    Sideline.*
Dickey, *Glenn Dickey's 49ers.*
Walsh, *Building a Champion.*

28 | DIMINISHING RETURNS

INTERVIEWS
Barr, Ron; Apr. 17, 2007.
Clark, Dwight; Apr. 19, 2007.
Cross, Randy; Apr. 17, 2007.
Hanson, Kristine; Dec. 19, 2007.
Holmgren, Mike; Apr. 19, 2007.
Jones, Brent; May 2, 2007.

McVay, Jon; Jan. 23, 2007.
Miller, Ira; May 28, 2007.
Shumann, Mike; Jun. 8, 2006.
Turner, Keena; Mar. 13, 2007.
Walsh, Bill; Apr. 5, 2006; Jan. 11, 16, 24, 2007; Feb. 1, 2007.
Young, Steve; Aug. 14, 2007.

DOCUMENTS

Walsh, speech, Northwest All Sports Clinic.
Walsh, Bill, coaching video, Cincinnati Bengals, Sept. 20, 1987.

NEWSPAPERS AND MAGAZINES

San Francisco Chronicle: Mar. 13, 1986; Jan. 6, 1987; Jul. 25, 28, 1987; Aug. 5, 19, 1987; Sept. 2, 10, 11, 14, 15, 16, 17, 18, 19, 21, 22, 23, 24, 25, 26, 28, 29, 1987; Oct. 1, 2, 5, 6, 7, 8, 9, 10, 12, 13, 14, 15, 16, 20, 1987; Dec. 31, 1987; Aug. 26, 2005.

BOOKS

Craig, *Tales from the San Francisco 49ers Sideline.*
Dickey, *Glenn Dickey's 49ers.*
Georgatos, *Stadium Stories.*
Hession, *Forty Niners.*
Livsey, *The Steve Young Story.*
Tuckman and Schultz, *Team of the Decade.*
Walsh, *Building a Champion.*

29 | FOOL'S GOLD

INTERVIEWS

Albaugh, Glen; Nov. 22, 2006.
Clark, Dwight; Apr. 19, 2007.
Dickey, Glenn; Apr. 12, 2007.
Edwards, Harry; Feb. 9, 2007.
Hanson, Kristine; Dec. 19, 2007; Jan. 11, 2008.
Holmgren, Mike; Apr. 19, 2007.
Jones, Brent; May 2, 2007.
McVay, John; Jan. 23, 2007.
Miller, Ira; May 28, 2007.
Shumann, Mike; Jun. 8, 2006.
Turner, Keena; Mar. 13, 2007.

Walsh, Bill; Apr. 5, 2006; Jan. 16, 24, 2007; Feb. 1, 2007; Mar. 14, 2007.
Walsh, Craig; Sept. 22, 2007.
Young, Steve; Aug. 14, 2007.

DOCUMENTS

Walsh, Bill, coaching video, Minnesota Vikings, Jan. 9, 1988.
Walsh, Bill, coaching video, Los Angeles Rams, Dec. 27, 1987.

NEWSPAPERS AND MAGAZINES

San Francisco Chronicle: Oct. 22, 24, 28, 29, 1987; Nov. 2, 3, 10, 11, 13, 16, 23, 1987; Dec. 1, 7, 9, 15, 16, 28, 29, 1987; Jan. 11, 12, 1988; Mar. 19, 23, 25, 1988.

BOOKS

Craig, *Tales from the San Francisco 49ers Sideline.*
Dickey, *Glenn Dickey's 49ers.*
Georgatos, *Stadium Stories.*
Hession, *Forty Niners.*
Lewis, *The Blind Side.*
Livsey, *The Steve Young Story.*
Lott, *Total Impact.*
Tuckman and Schultz, *Team of the Decade.*
Walsh, *Building a Champion.*
Walsh, *Finding the Winning Edge.*

30 | BILL V. BILL, JOE V. STEVE

INTERVIEWS

Barr, Ron; Apr. 17, 2007.
Cross, Randy; Oct. 26, 2006; Apr. 17, 2007.
Dickey, Glenn; Apr. 12, 2007.
Edwards, Harry; Feb. 9, 2007.
Fahnhorst, Keith; Mar. 8, 2007.
Hanson, Kristine; Dec. 19, 2007; Jan. 11, 2008.
Holmgren, Mike; Apr. 19, 2007.
Jones, Brent; May 2, 2007.
McLean, Lindsy; May 24, 2007.
McVay, John; Jan. 23, 2007.
Miller, Ira; May 28, 2007.
Turner, Keena; Mar. 13, 2007.

Vermeil, Dick; Jun. 14, 2007.
Walsh, Bill; Jan. 8, 16, 24, 2007.

NEWSPAPERS AND MAGAZINES
San Francisco Chronicle: Nov. 28, 1987;
 Mar. 17, 18, 21, 1988; May 6, 1988; Jul.
 14, 19, 22, 1988; Aug. 3, 25, 30, 1988;
 Sept. 2, 1988; Dec. 19, 1988; Jan. 3,
 1989.

BOOKS
Dickey, *Glenn Dickey's 49ers.*
Livsey, *The Steve Young Story.*
Lott, *Total Impact.*
Tuckman and Schultz, *Team of the Decade.*
Walsh, *Building a Champion.*

31 | FALLING APART AND COMING TOGETHER

INTERVIEWS
Albaugh, Glen; Nov. 22, 2006.
Barr, Ron; Apr. 17, 2007.
Cross, Randy; Oct. 26, 2006.
Dickey, Glenn; Apr. 12, 2007.
Edwards, Harry; Feb. 9, 2007.
Holmgren, Mike; Apr. 19, 2007.
Jones, Brent; May 2, 2007.
McLean, Lindsy; May 24, 2007.
McVay, John; Jan. 23, 2007.
Miller, Ira; May 28, 2007.
Walsh, Bill; Jan. 11, 16, 24, 2007; Mar. 14,
 2007.
Wright, Eric; Mar. 13, 2007.
Young, Steve; Aug. 14, 2007.

DOCUMENTS
Five Rings: A Celebration.
Walsh, Bill, coaching video, Minnesota
 Vikings, Oct. 30, 1988.
Walsh, Bill, coaching video, Phoenix
 Cardinals, Nov. 6, 1988.
Walsh, Bill, coaching video, Los Angeles
 Raiders, Nov. 13, 1988.
Walsh, Bill, coaching video, Washington
 Redskins, Nov. 21, 1988.

NEWSPAPERS AND MAGAZINES
San Francisco Chronicle: Sept. 5, 6, 12, 13,
 19, 26, 27, 28, 1988; Oct. 3, 10, 12, 17,

18, 25, 26, 29, 31, 1988; Nov. 4, 7, 8,
 14, 15, 18, 21, 22, 23, 28, 29, 1988;
 Dec. 5, 12, 13, 14, 19, 1988.

BOOKS
Barber, *We Were Champions.*
Dickey, *Glenn Dickey's 49ers.*
Georgatos, *Stadium Stories.*
Livsey, *The Steve Young Story.*
Lott, *Total Impact.*
Tuckman and Schultz, *Team of the Decade.*
Walsh, *Building a Champion.*

32 | DESTINY

INTERVIEWS
Albaugh, Glen; Nov. 22, 2006.
Barr, Ron; Apr. 17, 2007.
Dickey, Glenn; Apr. 12, 2007.
Edwards, Harry; Feb. 9, 2007.
Hanson, Kristine; Dec. 19, 2007.
Holmgren, Mike; Apr. 19, 2007.
Jones, Brent; May 2, 2007.
Mayer, Ed; Jun. 15, 2007.
McVay, John; Jan. 23, 2007.
Miller, Ira; May 28, 2007.
Ryan, Joan; Aug. 24, 2007.
Turner, Keena; Mar. 13, 2007.
Walsh, Bill; Apr. 5, 2006; Jan. 11, 16, 24,
 2007; Jun. 21, 2007.
Walsh, Craig; Sept. 22, 2007.
White, Mike; May 23, 2007.
Young, Steve; Aug. 14, 2007.

DOCUMENTS
CBS, telecast, Minnesota Vikings v. San
 Francisco 49ers, Jan. 1, 1989.
Five Rings: A Celebration.
Walsh, speech, Northwest All Sports Clinic.

NEWSPAPERS AND MAGAZINES
San Francisco Chronicle: Jan. 2, 3, 9, 10,
 13, 16, 17, 18, 23, 24, 25, 26, 27, 1989.

BOOKS
Craig, *Tales from the San Francisco 49ers
 Sideline.*
Dickey, *Glenn Dickey's 49ers.*

Lott, *Total Impact.*
Tuckman and Schultz, *Team of the Decade.*
Walsh, *Building a Champion.*

EPILOGUE: | THE GENIUS, REST IN PEACE

INTERVIEWS
Barr, Ron; Apr. 17, 2007.
Clark, Dwight; Apr. 19, 2007.
Fahnhorst, Keith; Mar. 8, 2007.
Walsh, Bill; Apr. 5, 2006; Dec. 9, 2006; Feb. 1, 2007; Jun. 21, 2007.
Walsh, Craig; Sept. 22, 2007.
Young, Charle; Apr. 16, 2007.

DOCUMENTS
Five Rings: A Celebration.

NEWSPAPERS AND MAGAZINES
Marin Independent Journal: Aug. 10, 2007.
San Francisco Chronicle: Feb. 13, 14, 1981; Jan 22, 1983; Feb. 12, 1983; Nov. 4, 1983; Aug. 6, 1992; Aug. 2, 1993; Aug. 9, 1995, Apr. 9, 1996; Jan. 6, 1997; Dec. 3, 10, 1997; Jan. 24, 1998; Mar. 27, 1998; Apr. 2, 1998; Jul. 3, 1998; Jan. 14, 21, 1999; Feb. 25, 1999; Jul. 31, 1999; Sept. 9, 1999; Jan. 11, 2000; Mar. 15, 28, 2000; Apr. 20, 2000; Aug. 10, 2000; Mar. 21, 2001; May 2, 2001; May 30, 2002; Mar. 16, 2004; Nov. 2, 2005; Jan. 21, 2007; Aug. 10, 2007.

BOOKS
Craig, *Tales from the San Francisco 49ers Sideline.*
Dickey, *Glenn Dickey's 49ers.*
Hession, *Forty Niners.*

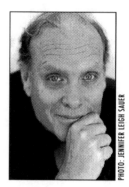

A longtime resident of the San Francisco Bay Area, DAVID HARRIS is a former contributing editor at *The New York Times Magazine* and *Rolling Stone* who has been reporting and writing about a wide variety of national and international subjects for the past thirty-five years. His 1986 book on the struggle for power inside the professional football business, *The League,* was named one of that year's ten best nonfiction books by *Publishers Weekly.* Raised in Fresno, California, where he was a varsity football letterman at Fresno High School, Harris was student body president, an honors student, and winner of the poetry prize at Stanford University while Bill Walsh was an assistant football coach there. This is Harris's tenth book.

Printed in the United States
by Baker & Taylor Publisher Services